Understanding SOCIAL ENTERPRISE

Understanding SOCIAL ENTERPRISE

Theory and Practice

Rory Ridley-Duff and Mike Bull

Second Edition

Los Angeles | London | New Delhi
Singapore | Washington DC

Los Angeles | London | New Delhi
Singapore | Washington DC

SAGE Publications Ltd
1 Oliver's Yard
55 City Road
London EC1Y 1SP

SAGE Publications Inc.
2455 Teller Road
Thousand Oaks, California 91320

SAGE Publications India Pvt Ltd
B 1/I 1 Mohan Cooperative Industrial Area
Mathura Road
New Delhi 110 044

SAGE Publications Asia-Pacific Pte Ltd
3 Church Street
#10-04 Samsung Hub
Singapore 049483

Editor: Matthew Waters
Editorial assistant: Molly Farrell
Production editor: Sarah Cooke
Copyeditor: Gemma Marren
Proofreader: Lynda Watson
Indexer: Martin Hargreaves
Marketing manager: Catherine Slinn
Cover design: Francis Kenney
Typeset by: C&M Digitals (P) Ltd, Chennai, India
Printed and bound in Great Britain by
CPI Group (UK) Ltd, Croydon, CR0 4YY

This book may contain links to both internal and external websites. All
links included were active at the time the book was published. SAGE
does not operate these external websites and does not necessarily
endorse the views expressed within them. SAGE cannot take
responsibility for the changing content or nature of linked sites, as these
sites are outside of our control and subject to change without our
knowledge. If you do find an inactive link to an external website, please
try to locate that website by using a search engine. SAGE will endeavour
to update inactive or broken links when possible.

Library of Congress Control Number: 2015937197

British Library Cataloguing in Publication data

A catalogue record for this book is available from
the British Library

ISBN 978-1-44629-552-6
ISBN 978-1-44629-553-3 (pbk)

At SAGE we take sustainability seriously. Most of our products are printed in the UK using FSC papers and boards.
When we print overseas we ensure sustainable papers are used as measured by the Egmont grading system.
We undertake an annual audit to monitor our sustainability.

Brief Contents

Detailed Contents

List of Figures

List of Tables

List of Case Studies

About the Authors

Dr Rory Ridley-Duff worked for 12 years as a director of the workers co-operative Computercraft Ltd, and has built his academic career through a PhD study of School Trends Ltd during its conversion to a social enterprise. His primary research interest is the process by which democratic relations develop in both informal and formal organisations and affect governing processes. He has now authored 35 scholarly papers, four books and two novels. In addition to this book, he has published 'The Case for FairShares' to articulate findings from a decade of action research at Sheffield Business School, that explores social enterprise as a route to solidarity between social entrepreneurs, producers, consumers and small investors (see **www.fairshares. coop**). His research has been published in *Human Relations*, *Corporate Governance: An International Review*, the *Industrial Relations Journal*, *International Journal of Entrepreneurial Behaviour and Research*, the *Social Enterprise Journal* and *Journal of Cooperative Studies* with best paper awards from Emerald Publishing and the Institute of Small Business and Entrepreneurship. He remains connected to practice through directorships with Social Enterprise Europe and the FairShares Association. His academic leadership roles include Chair of the PRME Group at Sheffield Business School and Acting Chair of the International Cooperative Business Education Consortium (ICBEC).

Dr Mike Bull is a Senior Lecturer and Research Fellow at Manchester Metropolitan University Business School, recently completing his PhD by publication, entitled 'The Development of Social Enterprise in the UK: Some Operational and Theoretical Contributions to Knowledge'. Mike has a decade of experience and knowledge of social enterprise, having led several UK and European funded research projects. He also developed one of the first undergraduate modules on social enterprise in 2005. Mike has held two Directorships in social enterprises during the past decade, as well as gaining industrial expertise, having previously worked for 16 years in the printing industry for private, public and third sector organisations. Mike is an editorial board member of the *Social Enterprise Journal*. He is Track Chair of Social Environmental and Ethical Enterprise of the International Small Business and Entrepreneurship Conference (ISBE). Mike is also on the Programme Board of '*Social Economy*' published by Cracow University of Economics.

Companion Website

Understanding Social Enterprise (Second Edition) is supported by a wealth of online resources for both students and lecturers to aid study and support teaching, which are available at https://study.sagepub.com/ridley-duff2e

Lecturer resources

- Instructor's Manual (Undergraduate/Postgraduate)
- Learning Activities
  - Classroom Exercises
  - Short Case Studies
  - FairShares Materials
- PowerPoint Slides (Undergraduate/Postgraduate)
- Reading Lists

Student resources

- Reading Lists
- Links to Relevant Websites
- Short Case Studies

Acknowledgements

We are grateful to the following companies that granted permission for the reproduction of their copyright material in this book.

Figure 1.1: By permission of Calouste Gulbenkian Foundation. Pearce, J. (2003), *Social Enterprise in Anytown*, London: Calouste Gulbenkian Foundation.

Figure 1.2: Reproduced with permission of NCVO, 'The UK Civil Society Almanac' (2014). http://data.ncvo.org.uk/a/almanac14/civil-society/what-is-civil-society-2/.

Figure 1.3: Reprinted with permission from the Taylor and Francis Group. Defourny, J. (2001) 'Introduction: from third sector to social enterprise', in C. Borzaga and J. Defourny (eds), *The Emergence of Social Enterprise*. London: Routledge, Figure 1, p. 22.

Figure 1.5: With permission from the author. Westall, A. (2001) *Value-led, Market-driven: Social Enterprise Solutions to Public Policy Goals*. London: IPPR, Figure 1.1.

Figure 2.3: With permission from the author. Alter, K. (2007) *Social Enterprise Typology*, www.virtueventures.com/typology (version 1.5, published 27 November 2007).

Figure 2.5: Reproduced with permission of Demos (www.demos.co.uk). Leadbeater, C. (1997) *The Rise of the Social Entrepreneur*, London: Demos.

Figure 4.1: With permission from the author. Spreckley, F. (2008) *The Social Audit Toolkit* (4th edn). Herefordshire: Local Livelihoods.

Figure 5.2: Charity Commission (2005: 11), 'Accounting and reporting by charities: statement of recommended practice', Figure 1, reproduced under the terms of Crown Copyright Policy Guidance issued by HMSO. © Crown Copyright 2005.

Figure 5.4: With permission from SAGE Publications Inc. Wei-Skillern, J., Austin, J., Leonard, H. and Stevenson, H. (2007) *Entrepreneurship in the Social Sector*. Thousand Oaks, CA: Sage. Figure 4.1 and Table 4.1.

Figure 6.3: With permission from the author. Lehner, O. (2013), 'Crowdfunding social ventures: a model and research agenda', *Venture Capital: An International Journal of Entrepreneurial Finance*, 15(4): 289–311, Figure 1.

Figure 9.1: With permission from the authors. Ridley-Duff, R.J. and Bennett, A. (2011) 'Towards mediation: developing a theoretical framework to understand alternative dispute resolution', *Industrial Relations Journal*, 42(2): 106–23, Figure 1.

Figure 9.2: Reprinted with permission of Wiley Blackwell. Purcell, J. (1987) 'Mapping management styles', *Journal of Management Studies*, 24(5): 541, Figure 2.

Acknowledgements

Figure 9.3: With permission from the author. Coule, T. (2008) 'Sustainability in voluntary organisations: exploring the dynamics of organisational strategy', unpublished PhD thesis, Sheffield Hallam University.

Figure 12.1: With permission from the author. Coule, T. (2008) 'Sustainability in voluntary organisations: exploring the dynamics of organisational strategy', unpublished PhD thesis, Sheffield Hallam University.

Table 1.2: Avila, R.C. and Campos, R.J.M. (2006) *The Social Economy in the European Union*. CIRIEC, No. CESE/COMM/05/2005 (The European and Social Committee) p. 45, Table 6.1 © European Communities, 1995-2006.

Table 2.1: This article was published in *Accounting, Organisation and Society*, Vol. 20, Hood, C., 'The "New Public Management" in the 1980s: variations on a theme', p. 93–109, Table 1 © Elsevier (1995).

Case 1.6: With permission from Traidcraft PLC.

Praise for *Understanding Social Enterprise*

Social enterprises are 'stakeholder owned' rather than 'shareholder owned'. With the champion of the 'shareholder value' movement, Jack Welch, describing it as 'the dumbest idea in the world' following the credit crunch, the time for stakeholder value has arrived, and this book sets out exactly what that will mean in practice.

Professor Jonathan Michie, President, Kellogg College, University of Oxford

This book has proved to be an important contribution to social enterprise scholarship that is also of considerable interest to practitioners and policy makers. Its integration of management frameworks, social theory and public policy approaches provides a fresh set of perspectives and insights on this increasingly influential sector.

Professor Alex Nicholls, Professor of Social Entrepreneurship, Said Business School, University of Oxford

The authors have raised the bar. This book is well written, necessary, comprehensive, intellectually stimulating and informed by practical experience. This will aid student understanding of the key debates and issues relating to social enterprises, explores the likely challenges facing social enterprises and offers insights to the evolution of the sector. Packed with examples, case studies and student revision tasks, this is a fine addition to the existing literature and is sure to be a core text.

Declan Jones, Head of Student Enterprise, Caledonian Business School, Glasgow Caledonian University

Combining a thorough study of the current state of literature and a deep understanding of working with social enterprise, the authors present an excellent overview of the state of thinking that will be of use to those studying and those working with social enterprises. It presents the key challenges and different views found within the practice, research and policy community and sets out the debates for future years. This is a valuable contribution to our understanding of this rapidly changing sector.

Praise for *Understanding Social Enterprise*

Professor Fergus Lyon, Director of ESRC/OCS Social Enterprise Research Cluster, Middlesex University

A good thorough analysis of social enterprise and its context, drawing on a range of relevant theory and evidence. It should become an essential text on the field.

Roger Spear, Senior Lecturer and Chair of the Co-Operatives Research Unit, the Open University

This is a well written, well researched, and above all, critical investigation into the notion of social entrepreneurship. It is essential reading to any student or practitioner who wishes to understand how social entrepreneurship has developed, its intellectual antecedents, and why it is so important to contemporary society.

Tim Curtis, Senior Lecturer, Unltd & HEFCE Ambassador for Social Entrepreneurship in Higher Education, University of Northampton

A valuable and timely book which is relevant to academics and practitioners alike. There is a welcome emphasis on providing practical learning activities grounded in a discussion of both historical and contemporary concepts of social enterprise.

Dr Linda Shaw, Head of Research, The Co-operative College

This book is important reading for students of social enterprise, both inside and outside the academy. It illuminates the social and political impulses underpinning current trends in this field, and provides nuanced comparative insights into how practice has developed in different world regions. The book is a rare combination; theoretically informed and practically applicable to the establishment and management of businesses that trade for a social purpose.

Dr Jo Barraket, Associate Professor of Social Enterprise and Entrepreneurship, Queensland University of Technology

Part I

Theoretical Perspectives on Social Enterprise

Exemplar Case: Innovation, Entrepreneurship and Enterprise

In 1941, Father Arizmendi – a Catholic priest – arrived in the civil war-torn town of Mondragon, in the Basque region of Spain. When Union Cerrajera, the largest local employer, refused to open its schools to all children in the community, Father Arizmendi chartered a parents' association and organised door-to-door collections to fund a new technical school.

In 1955, five of Arizmendi's graduate engineers began an industrial enterprise. In 1959 it adopted a co-operative constitution that formalised its commitment to democratic ownership and member-control. Each worker-member contributed capital and arrangements were put in place to hold this capital in a credit union account so that profits and losses from trading could be managed at the end of each year. Members of the community who wished to provide support could open their own credit union account, and 300,000 did so by 1980. Unlike most banks, its workforce received bonuses in proportion to the wealth created for its customers, rather than itself, and shared its own profits with them to spread wealth throughout the entire community. These social innovations enabled the community of Mondragon to eliminate poverty and become a wealthy region in Spain while raising a steady supply of capital for new co-operative ventures.

By 1980, over 80 ventures had been created, providing employment for 17,000 people, with additional support institutions for primary and secondary schooling, higher education, research, housing and social insurance (BBC, 1980). This success attracted interest from researchers at the London School of Economics. They concluded in 1982 that the Mondragon network not only had a 'co-operative advantage' derived from its operational model, but also enjoyed benefits from wage **solidarity** between managers and workforce members created by setting a 3:1 ratio between the highest and lowest paid. When workforce members were asked why the co-operatives were performing so well, the response was the quality of the managers. When the managers were asked the same, they responded that it was due to the quality and commitment of the workforce.

By the turn of the century, 24,000 of the town's 28,000 inhabitants had a stake in one or more co-operative venture, and benefited from profit-sharing arrangements (Long Island University, 2000). The network continued to expand to over 100 member co-operatives with a growing number of overseas partnerships and holdings. Unlike the US, where wage differentials between CEOs and workforce members have grown to 419:1, the members of Mondragon co-operatives continue to limit wage differentials to a maximum of 9:1. To increase the initial wage ratio of 3:1 all account holders have to approve it on a one-member, one-vote basis. In the last 60 years, no workforce has approved a differential of more than 9:1, and the average is steady at 5:1 (Ridley-Duff, 2012).

Growth has slowed during periods of recession, but the trend has been continuous growth for nearly six decades. By the end of 2012, there were over 80,000 employees (of which 85 per cent were member-owners). In addition, 11,382 students were studying in Mondragon's co-operative schools, colleges and university. While the recession has resulted in manufacturing job losses at Fagor (domestic appliances), there is still growth in Eroski, a chain of retail outlets that extends ownership and profit sharing to both staff and customers (MCC, 2014). Those affected by the contraction of Fagor have been redeployed, re-engaged in study or supported by Lagun-Aro, a social insurance mutual that provides better benefits than the state (MAPA Group, 2013; Lezamiz, 2014).

Mondragon is the outcome of visionary social entrepreneurship and collective action. Father Arizmendi, who died in 1976, was lauded for the democratic design of Mondragon's banking and **governance** systems (Bradley and Gelb, 1980; Whyte and Whyte, 1991). His individual vision was buttressed by the collective commitment of a community of people who wished to build an economic democracy based on social solidarity and co-operative business principles. The result has been to eradicate poverty and create a workforce achieving the best productivity, profitability and corporate social responsibility (**CSR**) outcomes in Spain.

Introduction

Those who opt to make history and change the course of events themselves have an advantage over those who decide to wait passively for the results of the change. (Arizmendiarrieta, n.d., Co-Founder of Mondragon Co-operative Corporation)

The Mondragon Co-operative Corporation (**MCC**) which integrates innovation, entrepreneurship and enterprise is an excellent starting point for a book about social enterprise. Social entrepreneurship, and its connection to social enterprise creation, is continually the subject of definitional debates (Brouard and Larivet, 2010). In this introduction, we will start by problematising three 'schools' of social entrepreneurial thought that have come to dominate the academic literature. We set the scene for an exploration of their socio-economic origins to identify the challenges that arise for those engaging directly in social entrepreneurship.

The first school, linked closely to the field of social entrepreneurship, focuses on **social innovation** (Austin, et al., 2006; Perrini, 2006). At Mondragon, the system of entrepreneurship was quickly recognised as an innovation that improves community well-being (Ellerman, 1982). As Turnbull later stated:

None of the existing theories of the firm were used to provide the criteria for designing the structure of the Mondragon co-operatives in the mid-1950s. These co-operatives introduced a number of 'social inventions' (Ellerman, 1982) which have proved to be outstandingly successful (Bradley and Gelb, 1980; Thomas and Logan, 1982). One of the design criteria for developing the Mondragon inventions was based on Catholic social doctrine, which believed in the 'priority of labor over capital' (Ellerman, 1982: 8). People, rather than money, became the fundamental unit of concern. This approach ... is at variance with the Coasian/Williamson theory of the firm, which is based on transactions ... (Turnbull, 1994: 321)

In the social innovation school, entrepreneurs are presented as heroes. In the case of Mondragon, Father Arizmendi – despite his best efforts at modesty – has been identified as the person most responsible for the 'social inventions' behind Mondragon's success. He is now revered as a teacher and founder even though he never held a formal position. His book of sayings is given out to visitors. A museum has been created to tell the story of his role guiding young *coopérateurs*. A statue sits in the heart of the Mondragon University campus.

The second school of social entrepreneurship is linked to the first in its emphasis on understanding and developing social entrepreneurs. However, here the emphasis is on their value propositions and *social missions* (Nicholls, 2006; Martin and Osberg, 2007). Value propositions are translated into *social purposes*, and the definition of purpose becomes the basis for agreeing *social objects*. The Eden Project, in the South West of England, is a good example of how social innovation and social purpose can be integrated (see Part 3, Introduction). In this world, the fulfilment and achievement of social objects is the basis for a new system of measurement aimed at gauging the entrepreneur's (and their enterprise's) social and environmental impact.

Mondragon's corporate management model does have a clear social mission: the achievement of *social transformation* through the education of its members (both politically and technically) so that they can subordinate the interests of capital to those of labour. This is one of ten principles that make up its corporate management model, which also includes open membership, democratic organisation, participatory management, wage solidarity, co-operation between co-operatives and support for social movements committed to economic democracy (Whyte and Whyte, 1991).

The third school of social entrepreneurship emphasises the creation of social enterprises that have *socialised ownership and control*. This is seen as crucial to meet the commitment to democratic principles of organisation and participation in decision-making (Borzaga and Defourny, 2001; Defourny, 2010). In the case of Mondragon, this is achieved through the deployment of a co-operative model that ensures that the bigger the decision, the more likely it will be taken in a general assembly of worker and/or consumer members. In contrast to the unitary boards of multinational corporations (**MNCs**) with appointed **directors**, Mondragon is controlled by over 1000 local boards made up of elected audit committees, governing council and social council members who interact with each other to co-ordinate a complex network of productive activity (Turnbull, 2002; Forcadell, 2005).

This 'socialisation' school is strongly influenced by the concept of a European social economy and sees a clear distinction between the *reciprocal interdependence* that underpins mutual aid and the **philanthropy** that underpins charity (Ridley-Duff and

Southcombe, 2012). **Mutuality** implies a bi-directional or network relationship in which parties help, support and supervise each other. This is qualitatively different from the uni-directional relationship between owner-manager and employee in a private enterprise, or the chain of control (philanthropist to trustee (unpaid), trustee to manager, manager to worker, and worker to beneficiary) in a **charity**. While charity can be present in mutual relations, it is normally framed in law and practice as a financial and **managerial** one-way relationship in which **trustees** give and direct while beneficiaries accept and obey. This asymmetry in obligations (i.e. the lack of reciprocal interdependence) clearly distinguishes mutuality from charity. Social enterprises pursuing a mission tend to structure themselves as philanthropic ventures (e.g. charities and/or foundations). Social enterprises focused on developing mutual relationships between members and the wider community tend to prefer associative forms, such as co-operatives and mutuals.

In Part 1, we stress the need to grapple with the distinction between a *socialisation perspective* that emphasises collective action and mutual principles to develop an alternative economy (Borzaga and Defourny, 2001; Sahakian and Dunand, 2014) and a *social innovation/purpose perspective* that focuses on the missions and innovations of individual social entrepreneurs (Dees, 1998; Martin and Osberg, 2007). The social innovation/purpose perspective emphasises the philanthropic impulse of the social entrepreneur and the social goals of their enterprise (Scofield, 2011) whereas the socialisation perspective emphasises organisation design and stakeholder governance to educate members for participation in the social economy (Moreau and Mertens, 2013). As the Mondragon case shows, these schools are not necessarily in opposition to each other because each of the following are apparent:

- social innovation
- social mission (purpose and impact)
- socialisation of ownership and control.

However, not all advocates and practitioners of social entrepreneurship emphasise all three schools of thought. For example, Betapharm in Germany provides an example of social innovation, purpose and impact, but retains a private sector model of ownership and control (Laasch and Conway, 2015). Organisations in the social economy, particularly Italian **worker co-operatives** and **employee-owned** businesses in the field of engineering, have innovative approaches to ownership and control but do not necessarily specify social missions beyond meeting their members' needs (Arthur et al., 2003; Restakis, 2010). Charities and non-profit corporations may develop trading strategies to support their social mission, but this does not imply a commitment to democratising ownership and control (Low, 2006; Ridley-Duff and Southcombe, 2012).

It is, therefore, worth starting Part 1 by problematising these three schools of social entrepreneurial thought. While each is useful for highlighting single strands of social enterprise development, over-zealous commitment to any one of them will encourage psychological resistance to the transformative model practised at Mondragon. To complete this introduction, therefore, we identify systems of exchange that influence these schools of thought, and argue that it is the ability to combine them in pursuit of a social and solidarity economy (**SSE**) that is most likely to change the socio-economic **paradigm** to one that produces sustainable development (Sahakian and Dunand, 2014).

Socio-economic systems

The Great Transformation (Polanyi, 2001 [1944]) examined the rise and fall of market economies from the beginnings of capitalism to the period after World War II. With the collapse of the Berlin Wall and successive financial crises in different parts of the world, Polanyi's views on the causes of failure in market systems have become important again (Holmes, 2014). His account of socio-economic systems has been of particular interest to European social enterprise researchers (Nyssens, 2006).

Polanyi offers a critique of each form of economic exchange. Firstly, he outlines communal systems that operate on a large scale, based entirely on principles of mutuality and **reciprocity**. In this system, there is little need to record financial transactions because people and institutions create reciprocal relationships and regulate exchanges through a commitment to mutual aid. Next, Polanyi identifies systems for *redistribution*, rooted in the practice of pooling resources so they can be exchanged with other communities. They might be retained for public events or to protect a community against economic uncertainty. Where there is redistribution, some written records are helpful to track contributions to (and drawings from) commonly held funds.

Lastly, Polanyi identifies the idea of *production for markets*, for which notions of gain, profit and loss are needed. Production for markets needs a record of transactions to calculate market prices. Within this system, price changes and the calculation of profit define which opportunities are pursued thereby usurping the logic of reciprocal support or obligation to contribute to common funds. The logic is different. There is no profit in mutual obligation as it encourages symmetrical relationships. The market, on the other hand, is presented as an opportunity to 'profit' from other parties (i.e. engage in asymmetrical trading relationships). From a market perspective, there is no profit in contributing to common funds (public reserves) unless such contributions are invested in activities that increase the profits of contributing businesses. It is this paradox that limits the value of CSR in addressing difficult intractable social and environmental issues (Hawken, 2010).

Polanyi concluded that it is the combination of all three and not the dominance of one that increases general prosperity and leads to sustainable development. Interestingly, Piketty (2014) argues that it is only during the initial post-World War II period (1945–75) that modern economies started to successfully combine modes of exchange and established the foundations for sustainable development. Just as social democracy was finding its feet, financial crises in the late 1970s triggered a swing to the political right and neo-liberalism established dominance through the twin agencies of the International Monetary Fund (**IMF**) and World Bank (Klein, 2007). During this period, a new development pattern emerged: wealth creation for the richest, ever widening wealth inequalities reducing the size of the middle class, and even more extreme poverty for the least well off (Wilkinson and Pickett, 2010; Norton and Ariely, 2011).

Social entrepreneurship research (and social entrepreneurs themselves) are divided on the question of which forms of economic exchange should be prioritised (Kerlin, 2006, 2010). For this reason, it is a worthwhile endeavour to highlight Polanyi's view that societies *dominated* by market logics are recent – not historical – phenomena. In pointing this out, he argues in a similar way to Maitland (1997) that people, money and land should not be treated as commodities as it is the commodification of people, money and land that preceded early capitalist crises. He introduced the concepts of *fictitious* and *real goods* to distinguish destructive forms of trade from trading that meets human need, adds value to society and protects natural resources.

An acceptance of market logic as natural leads to a view that reciprocity and redistribution are less important. The *social innovation* and *social purpose* schools of thought tend to favour the market and institutional support for entrepreneurial individuals. They pay less attention to institutional arrangements that sustain and encourage collective action (Kerlin, 2010; Ridley-Duff and Southcombe, 2012). The consequence of this is a resistance (or lack of attention) to the values of mutuality, reciprocity and **participatory democracy** in achieving **triple bottom line** impacts (Ostrom et al., 1999). In contrast, a view that markets are unnatural (or more peripheral) and likely to produce harm leads to a hostility towards the logic of the market. There is a predisposition to be more favourably disposed towards mutuality, reciprocity and participatory democracy. This perspective prompts arguments for the elimination of money, the eradication of private property and the creation of an intellectual commons where all decisions are made collectively within commonly owned enterprises (Dewar, 2007). The consequence may be to understate the importance of individuals and personal agency in the search for socio-ecological progress.

As authors, we are particularly interested in a third group who seek to establish an equilibrium between market exchange, reciprocity and redistribution in a given scenario, and who are open to maximising well-being across multiple stakeholder groups. This orientation equates to a desire for economic pluralism and a democratic settlement in which multiple stakeholders can participate in the ownership, governance and management of organisations (Novkovic and Webb, 2014). In this case, the power of individuals to challenge groups and the power of groups to challenge individuals are bound together through dialectical relationships in which co-operation is the optimum strategy for both survival and future sustainability (Nyssens, 2006; Restakis, 2010; Erdal, 2011).

In Part 1 of the book, therefore, we will not assume there is a single entrepreneurial pathway or planning system that leads to something called 'social enterprise'. We will assume that there are many pathways with many desired end points, and that the pathways that individuals choose (for themselves and as part of a group) depend both on the socio-economic contexts in which they find themselves and their personal ethics. We will assume that they will be faced with many choices, and will have to make ethical judgements about the relative importance of reciprocity, redistribution and market exchange to the development of their social enterprises.

The structure of Part I

In Part I we present three chapters that explore theoretical perspectives on social enterprise. In Chapter 1 (Social Economy and Big Society) we outline the development of a sector with two distinct heritages that remain distinct from the private and public sectors. The first heritage is rooted in arrangements for pursuing social (rather than commercial) goals. In this case, management systems are geared towards reassuring donors (funders) that their money is being spent in the way they intended. The second approach is rooted in the use of member ownership to promote democratic control over the management and capital to ensure it is invested in meeting the needs of members. Chapter 1 is important for setting the scene and ensuring that students have a nuanced understanding of **civil society**, mutuality, co-operatives, charity, philanthropy and the concept of **Big Society**.

From this base, we present Chapter 2 (Defining Social Enterprise). This chapter engages students in the processes and dilemmas that surround the definition of social enterprise. We examine practitioner, policy-maker and academic perspectives to show that there is limited consensus and significant areas of dissensus. Definitions depend not only on sectoral origins but also political and historical antecedents. We advance the argument that a fourth sector is emerging based on the Franco-Spanish-Portuguese tradition of the SSE. This depends less on established institutions in third, public and private sector institutions, and more on the emergence of a more radical expression of social economy. As Sahakian and Dunand state:

> Today's SSE theories and practices differentiate themselves from the social economy in that they aim towards the systemic transformation of the economy or are part of a 'counter-hegemonic political economy' … While the SSE includes activities traditionally grouped under the third sector or social economy, such as social entrepreneurship, it distinguishes itself by making explicit a set of values that include solidarity and mutual support towards a new economic paradigm. (2014: 2)

In Chapter 3 (The Politics of Social Enterprise) we further explore areas of political dissensus and tension that exist in the field of social enterprise development. We navigate the terrain by making explicit the neo-liberal and communitarian commitments that underpin different approaches to social enterprise. We start by outlining how an era of public administration gradually gave way to new public management (**NPM**) in the final decades of the twentieth century. More recently, economic crises in Asia (1997), Latin America (2001) and **OECD** countries (2008) have led to the emergence of new public governance (**NPG**). This shift has resulted in a call for more pluralist systems of governance and active citizenship. Given this echoes the ideas advanced by Big Society, it closes off the first section of the book and completes our investigation of theoretical perspectives.

The Social Economy and Big Society

1

Learning objectives

In this chapter, we outline the concepts of the social economy and Big Society, and we compare and contrast the types of organisations within them. By the end of this chapter you will be able to:

- explain social economy and Big Society concepts and terms
- critically evaluate the size and scope of the social economy in different countries
- articulate ideological and historical differences between organisations within the social economy
- discuss the political contexts that affect the definition of social enterprise
- identify an emergent social movement that emphasises member ownership and social solidarity.

The key arguments that will be developed in this chapter are: ★

- Social economy organisations vary in their organisational forms, values and beliefs.
- There are third (and fourth) systems that develop alternatives to the state and market systems.

- The 'social economy' is politically branded and rebranded by social groups according to their ideology.
- Social enterprise can be framed both as a neo-liberal agenda to advance public sector reform and as a radical response to neo-liberalism that stimulates social solidarity.

Introduction

In the short history of the social enterprise movement, writers have – not surprisingly – been keen to ask the question, 'What is a social enterprise?' Normally, by the end of the first chapter of a textbook, whether through historical analysis, advocating alternative values and practices, or painting a vivid picture of community life, the reader encounters a definition, or gains a sense of social enterprise as a concept. In this book, we resist the attempt to set out a definition of social enterprise too early in order to consider the historical developments that have led to its emergence. We do this deliberately so we can make the argument (in Chapter 2) that there are three distinct strands in social enterprise development, each with their own histories and trajectories: charitable trading activities (**CTAs**), co-operative and mutual enterprises (**CMEs**), and socially responsible businesses (**SRBs**).

In the last decade or so, organisations labelled as part of the social economy have been drawn more deeply into political agendas to reform public and private sector institutions. In order to take the reader on a journey towards a critical understanding, it is necessary to draw on political, social and historical accounts. For our purposes, the social economy can (initially) be thought of as an umbrella term for initiatives and institutionalised approaches for the creation of **social value**. Every organisation and institution arises out of a combination of socio-political commitments that shape the way it produces and consumes resources. It is the nature of these social-political commitments (and their implications for business practices) that are at the core of this chapter.

We set out our understanding of the context for social enterprise by identifying attempts within civil society, the state and the market to create social value. We link our discussion to three influential ideas: firstly, the identification of *a third system* by Pearce (2003); secondly, policy work by Westall (2001) to illuminate a fourth space in which a *social solidarity economy* is developing; lastly, to the political goals of the *Big Society* (Evans, 2011). Taken together, these provide us with a grounding in political currents, cultural identities and social contexts that feed into debates about the definition of social enterprise (see Chapter 2).

From experience, we are aware that motives for defining economic sectors can be contentious; the definition process is necessarily connected to political and sectional interests (Teasdale, et al., 2013). In the first edition of this book, we observed that historically an argument has been propagated that there is a narrow, but misleading, conceptualisation that the third sector is wholeheartedly a non-profit sector (Ridley-Duff and Bull, 2011). For those new to studying non-profits, the term can mislead by implying that these organisations do not seek to generate a surplus/profit. It is more accurate to say they are 'non-profit distributing' (see Chapter 11 for a full discussion). We continue to deal with this misrepresentation at length by rooting our argument in Ostrom et al.'s (1999) contention that there can be *four* property systems at play within an economy. There are not just two (public, private) or three (public, private, third), but four based on the following types of ownership and control:

- open access (no regulated control)
- local group property (group rights, can exclude others)
- individual property (individual or firm rights, can exclude others)
- government property (state regulation and/or subsidy).

Forty years ago, political and economic **discourses** focused on only the public and private sectors. The rise of the third sector (as a concept) was helpful in elucidating that much of an economy is under the control of trustees rather than property owners. However, even this helpful advance did not distinguish property that has no identifiable owner (and is part of an indivisible commons) from property that is co-operatively owned and managed by *groups* of owners. Ostrom (1990) received a Nobel Prize for her work on the evolution of collective action to manage the **commons**. Her findings identify important limitations in Hardin's (1968) contention that there is a 'tragedy of the commons'. Hardin argued that *common pool resources* had to be owned and managed by either private or state institutions to be sustainable. This orthodoxy reigned for a number of decades and created a public–private dichotomy that obscured the other two property types.

Ostrom rejects this thesis on the basis of findings that *group ownership* (largely ignored in Hardin's argument) is the form of property most strongly correlated with sustainable development (Bruntland, 1987; Ostrom et al., 1999). We now believe that this view underpinned a number of early arguments for social enterprise in the 1970s (Ridley-Duff and Bull, 2014). This was later captured in Westall's (2001) discussion of a 'fourth space' for social value creation. Westall contributes to our understanding of Ostrom's argument by clarifying that member ownership and control is distinct and different from 'no ownership' (trusteeship), 'private ownership' (by individuals and firms) and 'public ownership' (by state authorities). It sets up a critique of three-sector models of the economy and makes it possible to discuss not-for-*private* profit, *more-than*-profit and *for-purpose* enterprises that drive both 'new co-operativism' and the creation of a 'social and solidarity economy' (Monzon and Chaves, 2008; Ridley-Duff, 2008b; Vieta, 2010; Sahakian and Dunand, 2014).

So, to provide the reader with an introduction to the social economy we begin by outlining the concept of civil society. To help this, we present Pearce's (2003) conceptualisation of three *systems* in the economy. He demarcates the differences between state agencies, private businesses and alternatives that embrace a social mission enabling us to identify the characteristics and contexts of social economy organisations. Lastly, we introduce Big Society as a further instance of a market-informed response to a perceived crisis in state institutions.

To conclude, we consider the implications for developing a theory of social enterprise. We initiate our argument that social enterprise (as a field) is more easily understood as a paradigm which is fundamentally different from the dominant (neo-liberal) discourses on the state, market and third sector. This helps to explain why it cuts across (and appears within) the public, private, third sector. This presents such a significant challenge for policy **actors** unfamiliar with the social economy that we devote three chapters to re-orientating students. Over the next three chapters, we present social enterprise as part of, but also able to operate independently of, the third sector. In doing so, we set out the basis for arguing that there is a nexus of social economy activity that seeks to transcend the norms developed by private, public and third sector institutions that is linked to Ostrom's concept of *group property* and which is driven by a philosophy of actively managing common pool resources for individual, community and public benefit (Ostrom et al., 1999; Westall, 2001).

Civil society and the social economy

The UK's National Council for Voluntary Organisations (**NCVO**) decided in 2008 to adopt the term *civil society* to describe the organisations in its flagship publication on the **voluntary sector**.[1] This reflects its CEO's interest in three strands of the debate on civil society (Edwards, 2004; Etherington, 2008). Firstly, 'civil society' describes informal and formal associations that people establish outside the public and private sectors. In this sense, civil society is the coming together of people independently, free from state or commercial intervention, and has roots in the democratic right to 'freedom of association'. Secondly, it captures the concern of these voluntary associations to advance the quality of public debate. Here, civil society is about creating arenas where people can debate social and economic issues, discover their common interests and negotiate their differences. An integral part of the 'quality of public debate' strand is how to provide a check on the power of the state and large-scale corporations. The third strand engages a moral question: what would it be like to live in a 'good society'? In this case, the concern is how society *should be*, rather than how it is, and whether the norms propagated by different institutional and societal processes should be sanctioned or opposed. The *Civil Society Almanac*, therefore, advances these perspectives through acknowledgement of the contribution of voluntary organisations, charities and co-operatives as well as universities, trade unions and housing associations. This perspective theorises an alternative group of organisations that are non-state, non-capitalist in their orientation, and are committed to advancing one or more aspect of civil society.

This framework raises some provocative questions. Firstly, it moves well beyond the views expressed in a paper presented by Murdock at the Social Enterprise Research Conference in 2007 in which 'civil society' is limited to the informal interactions between families, friends and citizens. Paton (2003) also describes civil society as a combination of informal and self-help groups, and leisure networks, that contribute to the development of *social capital*. In contrast, Schwabenland (2006) adopts a critical tone, regarding civil society as a new rhetoric emanating from the *state*, part of a modernisation agenda to restore civic responsibility through involvement in organisations that rebuild community life. She draws a boundary between organisations supporting the state's narrative on civic responsibility (which, presumably, includes NCVO) and other social organisations that continue to challenge it. One aspect of this is the surge of interest in the concept of a Big Society, which centres on the state's relationships to non-governmental organisations (Evans, 2011).

Civil society – while its meaning is not agreed – captures a perspective that is motivated neither by the pursuit of political power using the apparatus of the state, nor by the goal of capital accumulation through market trading for its own sake (Mertens, 1999; Lindsay and Hems, 2004). Monzon and Chaves (2008) set out a definition that now informs thinking on the social economy within the European Union. It integrates social democratic traditions with social purpose goals to create a social economy comprising:

> private, formally organized enterprises, with autonomy of decision and freedom of membership, created to meet their members' needs through the market by producing goods and services, insurance and finance, where decision-making and any distribution of profits or surpluses among the members are not directly linked to the capital or fees contributed by each member, each of whom has one vote. The Social Economy also includes private, formally organized organizations with autonomy of decision-making and freedom of membership that produce non-market services for households and whose surplus, if any, cannot be appropriated by the economic agents that create, control or finance them. (Monzon and Chaves, 2008: 557)

While this definition is helpful, it can also mislead by implying that member-owned (social) organisations are a sub-set of the 'private' sector. In cases where social economy organisations are collectively owned (as group property) and not privately owned (as a firm's or individual's property), labelling them 'private' misleads policy-makers into assuming their needs can be met by private sector institutions. As we will discover, applying private sector norms can undermine the basis on which they have organised successfully and prevent them from making their own distinct contribution to social value creation.

Types of organisations in a social economy

Having introduced civil society and the social economy, we turn our attention to the types of organisation that fall within the boundaries proposed by Monzon and Chaves, and which sit within the umbrella of Pearce's third system (see Figure 1.1). The commonality between these types of organisations is that they are all driven by community development goals, deploying a different logic to the market economy (private sector) and the planned economy (public sector), yet capable of sharing and blending elements of each to create hybrid forms of organisation. Outside the UK, there are other names for the types of organisations we are referring to: North Americans more readily refer to the 'non-profit sector'; in Africa and Asia, the term 'non-governmental organisations' (**NGOs**) is in common use; in South America, there is increasing talk of a 'solidarity economy'.

At EU level, the social economy is believed to include trading organisations as well as non-trading organisations. By considering the history of the sector, we can trace debates back several centuries that clarify the rationale for their inclusion. As Coule points out:

> Voluntary action preceded the development of both state and market welfare provision in the UK, surviving the emergence of a statutory 'welfare state' and continuing to function alongside providers from a number of different service sectors [...]. Indeed, in the late 1800s, the majority of welfare services were provided through private charity or through mutual aid organisations, with state support limited to filling gaps in this provision [...]. By the time of the Wolfenden Committee Report ... published in 1978 there had been a dramatic turnaround, with the report suggesting it is the voluntary sector that exists to fill gaps in state provision. (2008: 1)

An influential attempt to identify alternatives to the public and private sectors appears in Pearce (2003), shown in Figure 1.1. The appeal of Pearce's diagram lies in features that are omitted from other economic models. Firstly, it recognises entities at neighbourhood, district, national/regional and international levels. Most importantly, it differentiates between types of organisations in the third system based on their income mix. For example, Pearce places non-trading charities outside of the social economy, in the planned half of the economy, closer to the state, in lieu of their reliance on grant income from state institutions. This is separated from trading organisations labelled as part of the social economy. Pearce also suggests that co-operatives exist inside and outside the social economy, based on whether their primary purpose is to achieve a social purpose or not (a point we will critique in Chapter 3 discussing the politics of social enterprise). He differentiates between a 'community economy' that may be formally organised and a 'self-help' economy that is grounded in family life. Pearce's model locates informal and formal voluntary groups with non-trading charities, and differentiates these from trading charities, community enterprises and **social firms**. He adds into the model social businesses (that engage in philanthropic trading activities), mutual societies (that use reciprocity as an underlying trading principle), **fair trade** companies (that pay a *social premium* to producers), and co-operatives (designed to promote social and economic participation in production and consumption).

In the following sections, we start by examining trusts and charities to understand the role of trustees and beneficiaries. We then examine the early development of

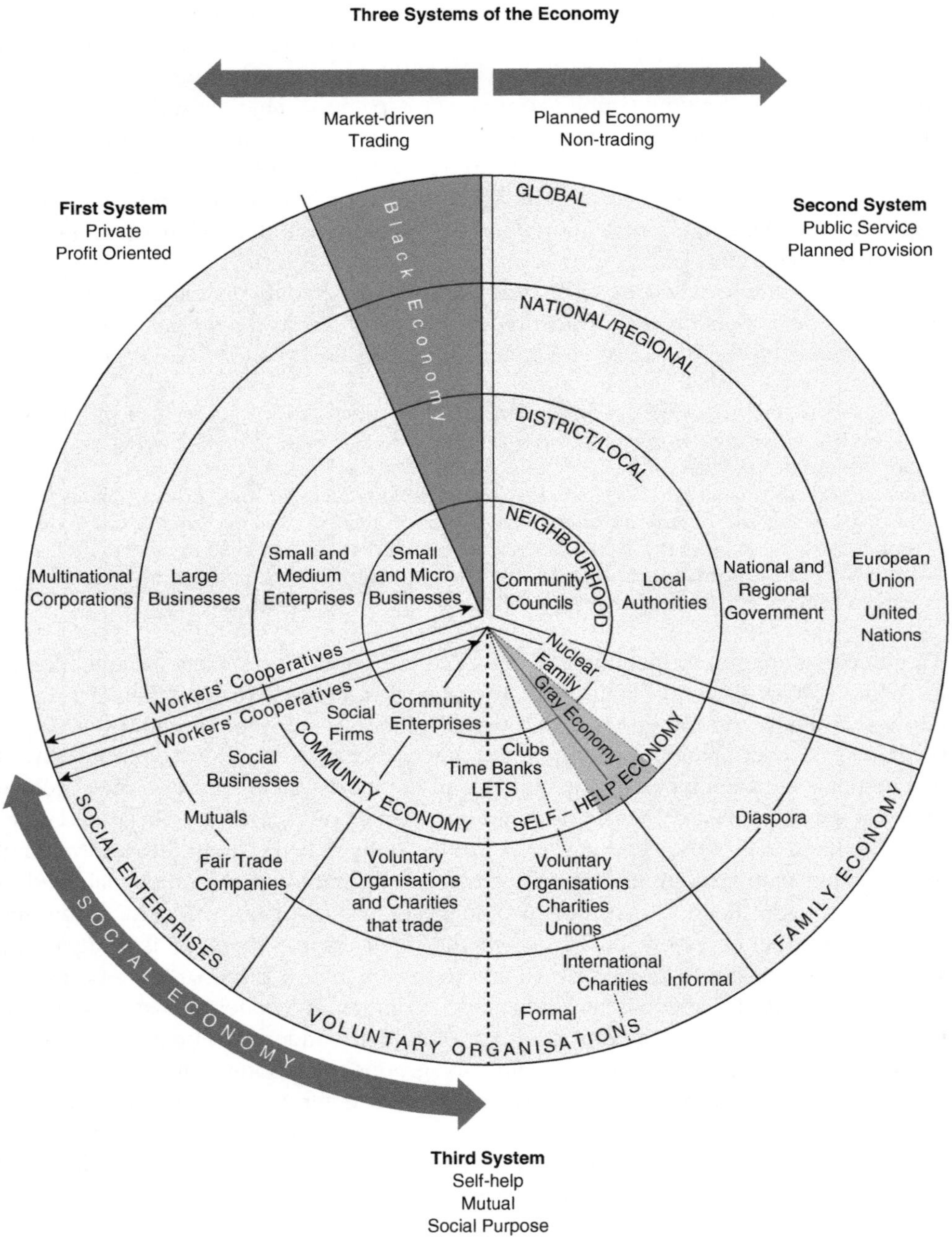

Three Systems of the Economy

Figure 1.1   The first, second and third systems of an economy

Source: Pearce (2003), by permission of Calouste Gulbenkian Foundation

democratic associations through a short exploration of the history of co-operative and mutual societies. Lastly, we examine links between voluntary associations, secular society and the membership principle.

A word of caution is necessary before embarking on the discussion that follows. While charities have a largely religious heritage and co-operatives became associated with more secular traditions, successive generations have been attracted to their legal forms without appreciating their social heritage. Many organisations choose their legal form pragmatically to enhance their perceived legitimacy, and may not conform to the norms depicted in the next section (see Case 1.1 The Scott Bader Group and The Scott Bader Commonwealth).

Case 1.1

The Scott Bader Group and the Scott Bader Commonwealth

Scott Bader Group provides an example of ambiguity in the definition of organisational form. Scott Bader, established in 1921, is a chemicals company that makes and exports polymers around the world. In 1951 the company established an employee trust, and then transferred ownership to a charitable trust in 1963. Employees, upon completing their probation, can become members of the trust. In 2007 there were 630 employees, of whom 77 per cent were members of the Scott Bader Commonwealth. Six of the nine board members of the Commonwealth are elected from the workforce. Four of the ten Scott Bader Group board are elected from the workforce. Each year, any profit-sharing payment must be matched by a payment to the charitable trust. Trust members nominate and vote each year on which two charities will receive £25,000 (source: EOA, 2013).

The Scott Bader Commonwealth is a registered charity and has been structured so that the Scott Bader Group and Commonwealth assets would pass to the UK **Charity Commission** if dissolved. As a company limited by guarantee (**CLG**), owned by a charitable trust, Paton (2003) discusses it as a charity. However, as it is effectively member-controlled with trustees elected from among the employees, Paton also refers to it as employee-owned. Similarly, Oakeshott (1990) claims Scott Bader is an example of a worker co-operative.

Historical underpinnings and the characteristics of charities

In tracing the roots of non-profit organisations, Hudson (2002: 1) points to charitable and philanthropic acts in Egyptian times, using the example of the Pharaoh himself who provided clothing, shelter and bread to the poor. Indeed, Hudson claims the word 'charity' originates from the Greek word *charis*, meaning favour, kindness or goodwill. Morgan (2008: 3) traces the concept of charity not to the Greeks but to early Christian writings on 'love' in the sense of an 'absolute willingness to give everything for the sake of another'. He distinguishes between charity as a mode of human behaviour and the institutional forms that started to develop from around AD 600.[2] As an institutional form, charity involves the organisation of financial giving (donations) to a group of people who are regarded as sufficiently responsible to administer funds and ensure they are used for charitable purposes (trustees).

For well over a millennium, charitable giving was organised under the auspices of the religious institutions. As Luxton (2001) notes, elaborate relationships developed between wealthy people and religious authorities as people started to believe that their charitable donations would guarantee them entry into heaven. As charities grew, however, it became harder to ensure that the funds donated were used for the purposes intended. Although many adopted the form of a charitable trust, **trust law** came to be seen as inadequate. In 1597, a precursor of the Statute of Charitable Uses Act was passed by the UK Parliament, but it was in 1601 that two far-reaching welfare reforms took place. Firstly, there was a revision of the Charitable Uses Act, regulating the use of trust funds by religious institutions in the provision of education and welfare. Secondly, the Poor Law was introduced to enable local councils to raise money from ratepayers to provide welfare benefits to those in need. As Morgan comments:

> From the outset, one of the key planks of charity law has been the principle of voluntary trusteeship – that is, that those who are entrusted with charitable funds should apply them to advance the charity's objects without seeking personal benefit ... (2008: 5)

Even though much of the 1601 Act was later repealed, two principles have remained to this day: there must be a *charitable purpose* (as defined in the original and subsequent Acts), and this must be in the *public interest* (Morgan, 2008). Both of these concepts have been subject to evolution and refinement. For example, the early statutes specified that charities were for the advancement of religion, education, the relief of poverty or anything else that provided a clear community benefit. In the Charities Act 2006 (UK), there was concurrently a broadening of activities that were recognised as charitable (for example amateur sports) and a tightening of the public interest principle (see box).

Charities Act 2006, Section 1, Clause 2(2)

Definition of 'Charitable Purposes':

(a) the prevention or relief of poverty;
(b) the advancement of education;

(c) the advancement of religion;

(d) the advancement of health or the saving of lives;

(e) the advancement of citizenship or community development;

(f) the advancement of the arts, culture, heritage or science;

(g) the advancement of amateur sport;

(h) the advancement of human rights, conflict resolution or reconciliation or the promotion of religious or racial harmony or equality and diversity;

(i) the advancement of environmental protection or improvement;

(j) the relief of those in need by reason of youth, age, ill-health, disability, financial hardship or other disadvantage;

(k) the advancement of animal welfare;

(l) the promotion of the efficiency of the armed forces of the Crown, or of the efficiency of the police, fire and rescue services or ambulance services.

In tracing the influence of charities, a notable date in the UK was 1834 when the Poor Law Amendment Act was passed to save the state money (Harrison, 1969). The Act encouraged a cultural separation between two types of poor – the 'deserving' and the 'undeserving'. The deserving poor could qualify for charity or philanthropic help; the undeserving were sent to workhouses. The government's aim was to halve the welfare budget. The increasingly hostile attitude of both state and charitable organisations towards the 'undeserving poor' led to the growth of new societies that discouraged working people from relying on charity (MacDonald, 2008). Between the amendment of the Poor Law (1834) and the introduction of National Insurance in 1910, membership of friendly societies in the UK rose from under 1 million to 9.5 million. This uptake was not confined to the UK and spread throughout the **British Empire**. In Australia, for example, it is estimated that over 80 per cent of working age men joined a friendly society (Weinbren and James, 2005). Even so, charities continued to grow in influence (Coule, 2008) until nation states took on responsibility for social insurance.

There are a number of value propositions in charities that potentially match or clash with the values advocated by other social economy organisations. Firstly, the act of giving and self-sacrifice (either financially or in the form of labour) is a *core value* built into culture and the legislative framework. In charities, this is expressed both through the requirements that trustees act in a voluntary capacity (unpaid) and through a positive attitude to developing volunteer labour forces. The requirement to act as a voluntary trustee, however, means that positions of power – generally – are taken up by people with the wealth to devote leisure time to charitable work. This tradition survives today in the form of a reliance on celebrities to give credibility to fundraising initiatives, and the inclusion of the 'great and good' on boards, irrespective of their professional or specialist skills (Kelly et al., 2014). There is also an inevitable bias in favour of educated people with social standing who come forward with causes to support, and who public authorities are inclined to trust to manage and account for charitable funds.

As charities have grown and adapted to operating in cultures with employment laws, so the treatment of *employees*, *volunteers* and *trustees* has become more complex. Firstly, by accepting payment for their labour, employees are automatically deemed to have a conflict of interest that compromises their capacity to act as trustees (Frail and Pedwell, 2003). Secondly, there is both a legal and a cultural divide between 'responsible persons' who act as *trustees* and those who are *beneficiaries* (i.e. in receipt of the benefits defined in an organisation's charitable objectives). Culturally, this separation of beneficiaries and trustees demarcated both a class and a religious divide (MacDonald, 2008). It took until the 1990s for the Charity Commission to clarify that there was no legal barrier to members of the beneficiary group becoming trustees, providing they avoided a conflict of interest.

Case 1.2

The Ragged Trousered Philanthropists by Robert Tressell

The Ragged Trousered Philanthropists was published posthumously in 1914, and was based on the author's own experiences after emigrating from South Africa to England. It describes, in fictional form, Tressell's desire for a co-operative commonwealth to end his poverty and exploitation at work, and provide for his daughter Kathleen whom he feared would be sent to the workhouse should he become ill (Hunt, 2004). The book is a powerful analysis of the influence of ideology among working people who view their own employment as the 'philanthropy' of their 'betters'. Tressell highlighted how, and why, people defend an economic system that exploits them when they lack the education to consider an alternative. In one passage, he describes the experiences of those applying for charity:

Another specious fraud was the 'Distress Committee'. This body, or corpse, for there was not much vitality in it, was supposed to exist for the purposes of providing employment for 'deserving cases'. One might be excused for thinking that any man, no matter what his past may have been, who is willing to work for his living, is a 'deserving case': but this was evidently not the opinion of the persons who devised the regulations for the working of this committee. Every applicant for work was immediately given a long job, and presented with a double sheet of foolscap paper ... it was called a 'Record Paper', three pages of which were covered with insulting, inquisitive, irrelevant questions concerning the private affairs and past life of the 'case' who wished to be permitted to work for his living, and

> which had to be answered to the satisfaction of ... the members of the committee before the case stood any chance of getting employment. However, notwithstanding the offensive nature of the questions on the application form, during the five months that this precious committee was in session, no fewer than 1237 broken spirited and humbled 'lion's whelps' filled up the forms and answered the questions as meekly as if they had been sheep. (Tressell, 2004 [1914]: 435)

The extract in Case 1.2 is not historically factual, but it is indicative of the discourse that developed among both liberals and socialists regarding the way poverty is entrenched and reproduced by philanthropic ventures.[3] It fuelled arguments for national systems of mutual insurance schemes and legal rights for workers to protect their employment. Those arguments rested on the need not simply to provide welfare payments to the unemployed, but also to end gaps in welfare provision that some friendly societies regarded as 'too risky', or which failed to cover members' relatives (Weinbren, 2007). Increasingly, a debate developed regarding the role of 'charity' (as institutionalised in law and economic thought) as a site for the reproduction of dependency that prevented (long-term) relief from poverty. Interestingly, it is precisely this argument that David Cameron used in 2010 to argue for a Big Society – that the state (as philanthropist) has acted to reproduce dependency and make it harder to relieve poverty.

Debates among co-operative thinkers have reflected this paradox. There is concurrently a hostility to institutional forms of charity and a desire to keep a distance from the state (Ellerman, 2005). Even though there is a defensible argument that charity and philanthropy contribute to poverty relief and community development (Fulda, 1999; Glasby, 1999), concerned liberals and trade unionists started to experiment with new ways of organising business activity. In Tressell's novel, the seemingly impossible task of persuading low-skilled workers to organise in a different way is articulated through a character called Owen. This was a tribute to Robert Owen, a self-made philanthropist whose 'new view of society' became synonymous with co-operative experiments at New Lanark in the UK and at Harmony in the USA (Owen, 2014 [1816]). Owen – both the fictional and the historical figures – believed that relief from poverty would not occur until we better understand how productive work influences the development of the human mind, and how co-operative principles contribute to forging self-reliance by cultivating a mind-set that is positive about mutuality. For Owen, mutual principles extended to labour: that everyone contributing labour to an enterprise should share equitably in the 'common fund' that it creates.

This brings us back to the distinction between charity as a form of a human behaviour and charity as a particular institutional form. While one interpretation of 'charity' (now embedded in charity law) led to the development of a trustee–beneficiary model that reproduces and reinforces class differences, 'charity' as a commitment to mutual care and reciprocity followed a different development path. In the mid-nineteenth century a new body of law permitted the establishment of fully self-governing institutions called friendly societies. In the next section, we consider their development and their relationship to the idea of a Big Society.

Historical underpinnings of co-operative and mutual societies

Robert Owen is often incorrectly credited as the founder of the co-operative movement. Co-operative storekeepers who pioneered new trading relationships were found in Scotland from 1769 onward (Harrison, 1969), while Rothschild and Allen-Whitt (1986) report that co-operatives appeared in the United States from 1790. Robert Owen is rightly credited, however, with a convincing critique of capitalist production. He presented a report to the House of Commons in 1817, and subsequently expressed his abhorrence at the 'atomisation' that developed in his factories as well as church-led education that reproduced social inequality (Owen, 1849; Harrison, 1969). He also criticised changes brought about by industrialisation that separated women and men in daily life. Owen argued for a co-operative ethic based on community ownership of property. The inherent ambiguity in this statement created disagreement among Owen's followers over the boundary of the 'community' and these debates are still played out today between advocates of 'common ownership', 'joint ownership' and 'co-ownership' (Ridley-Duff, 2012).

Although his experiments did not work as expected, Owen continued as a social reformer, writing and lecturing for the rest of his life. In 1824, the London Co-operative Society was founded and established a journal. By 1844, a group including 'Owenites' constituted the Rochdale Pioneers using a set of principles that have survived to the present day (see Case 1.3). Today, the International Co-operative Alliance (**ICA**) recognises the Rochdale Pioneers as the founders of co-operativism rather than Robert Owen. Nevertheless, the success of worker co-operatives in Italy and Spain shows that Owen's vision of producer co-operation was not unrealistic, but required a longer gestation to become viable.

Two aspects of co-operative thought stand in sharp contrast to the trustee–beneficiary model of charity. Firstly, the 'member economic participation' statement by the ICA in 1995 embeds the idea that members should contribute to, and then share in the economic surpluses generated by, their enterprise. This 'local group property' approach is operationalised through the distribution of benefits in proportion to a member's participation in a co-operative venture. In co-operative stores, members receive a **dividend** (often confused with the loyalty schemes of modern supermarkets) based on their participation in trading. In producer co-operatives (manufacturing goods or delivering services), workers receive a dividend or bonus based on their participation in production (Ridley-Duff, 2007). Volunteering in producer co-operatives – in the sense of working for the organisation without fair pay – is discouraged by international agreements (ICA, 2005).

Case 1.3

The Rochdale Pioneers

The Rochdale Pioneers were a group of weavers and artisans who were inspired by the work of Robert Owen. They opened co-operative stores and pooled their resources to buy and sell items they could not afford individually. They set out principles that have been adapted over the last 150 years, but which are still recognisable today as an aspirational form of organisation that combines economic and social responsibility. These principles are now embedded in codes of governance that inform the development of modern-day co-operative practices.

The 1844 Rochdale Principles

Open membership.

Democratic control (one person, one vote).

Distribution of surplus in proportion to trade.

Payment of limited interest on capital.

Political and religious neutrality.

Cash trading (no credit extended).

Promotion of education.

The Revisions of the International Co-operative Alliance (ICA) in 1966

Open, voluntary membership.

Democratic governance.

Limited return on equity.

Surplus belongs to members.

Education of members and public in co-operative principles.

Co-operation between co-operatives.

1995 ICA Statement of Co-operative Identity

Voluntary and open membership.

Democratic member control.

(Continued)

(Continued)

Member economic participation.

Autonomy and independence.

Education, training and information.

Co-operation among co-operatives.

Concern for community.

For further details see: http://ica.coop/en/whats-co-op/co-operative-identity-values-principles.

The second principle that stands in contrast is the commitment to democratic member control, which can become incompatible with the charity system based on *trustees* and *beneficiaries* (as beneficiaries cannot be trustees, i.e. board members). A co-operative elects beneficiaries (i.e. members) to govern its affairs (thus beneficiaries must be board members). The corporate structure prevents non-members from acquiring power over resource allocation without the consent of the members (i.e. staff, customers or society beneficiaries). For example, a person who opens an account at a credit union becomes a member. They acquire the right to attend annual general meetings and elect members to the credit union's board of directors. Staff in worker co-operatives acquire rights to govern themselves and to elect or dismiss board members and executive directors (Cornforth, et al., 1988; Ridley-Duff, 2009).

These rights are not granted to workforce members in private sector corporations, or to account holders in private banks. Nor can staff in charities play a role in removing their board of trustees (unless the charity is constituted as an association that allows staff members). Instead, such organisations rely on 'whistle-blower' legislation (e.g. Public Interest Disclosure Act 1998) or statutory rules that permit complaints to government appointed regulators. The democratic principles advocated for (and by) social economy businesses, therefore, represent a challenge to political and business systems that seek to divide people into social classes (based on one group's automatic and unquestioned 'right' to govern and manage the affairs of people in 'other' social groups). In co-operatives, the goal is the democratic control of the organisation's (economic, social, human and intellectual) capital by its consumer and/or producer members.

These ideas were advanced by John Spedan Lewis through two books and the evident and enduring success of the John Lewis Partnership (Lewis, 1948, 1954). This example of 'employee ownership' spread to other parts of the world (Gates, 1998). Where a majority of employees directly or indirectly control more than 50 per cent of voting shares, support agencies accept them as (ICA-compliant worker) co-operatives.

The Employee Ownership Association (in the UK) adds a further category of *co-owned* companies where the workforce owns a 'substantial' minority holding (Reeves, 2007). With 25 per cent or more of voting stock, this minority can block any decision that must be taken by **special resolution** (such as rule changes). Therefore to summarise:

- charities have 0 per cent employee ownership
- co-owned companies have 25 per cent or more employee ownership
- employee mutuals have 50 per cent or more ownership held for the benefit of employees
- worker co-operatives have a majority of worker-members holding a majority of shares.

The *quality* of life generated by the social economy is captured in the film *It's a Wonderful Life* (Case 1.4). The political dimension of the film is strongest in the final scenes where the viewers have a chance to consider what life would have been like if George Bailey had never been born.

Case 1.4

It's a Wonderful Life (Frank Capra)

In developing an appreciation of the impacts of 'individual' and 'group' property, popular culture is helpful. In the film *It's a Wonderful Life* (1948), George Bailey runs a credit union called the Bailey Building and Loan that provides a refuge from the profit-maximising activities of Henry Potter. The Bailey Building and Loan is portrayed as having few cash reserves while the Potter business empire is awash with money. A stark contrast is drawn between the economically wealthy Henry Potter and the relatively poor George Bailey. After mislaying $6,000, and facing bankruptcy, George Bailey contemplates suicide. An angel is sent from heaven to dissuade George from killing himself. When George says he 'wished he had never been born', the angel shows George Bailey what the town would have been like if he had not existed. The town is a desolate place, with casinos and bars transforming its landscape and character. The houses and communities built by the Bailey Building and Loan (a credit union established by George Bailey's father) no longer exist because George was not alive to oppose a takeover by Potter. While the town has plenty of *economic capital*, it has little *social capital*. These final scenes offer a proxy for what life would be like without people committed to the mutuality that sustains a social economy.

A longer teaching case with student questions can be found on the companion website at: www.sagepub.co.uk/ridleyduff.

It's a Wonderful Life is a useful example for introducing the social economy concept of *mutuality* as an organising principle, and the way mutuality is linked to the development of *social capital*. The Bailey Building and Loan is cash poor (its capital is invested in house building). During a financial crisis, therefore, it depends on social capital, rather than economic capital, to survive.

Mutual societies share some of the characteristics of co-operatives (e.g. member ownership, community orientation), but – according to Weishaupt, the former President of the Euclid Network[4] – mutuals are formed so that a large group of people can share a financial risk, rather than to join together to engage directly in production activities. Whereas co-operatives have the goal of increasing the incomes of members by enabling them to produce for the market, mutuals have the goal of reducing social risks by collectively sharing the costs of welfare protection.

This view is shared by tax authorities in the UK. They cite the case of *Municipal Mutual Insurance Ltd* v. *Hills* in which the mutual principle was clarified:

> the cardinal requirement is that all the contributors to the common fund must be entitled to participate in the surplus and that all the participators in the surplus must be contributors to the common fund. (HMRC, n.d.: 448)

Mutuals, therefore, are formed when a common fund is created for a given shared purpose, and its fund managers restrict benefits to those contributing to the fund. Case Law in 1972 (*Fletcher* v. *Income Tax Commissioners*) established that this relationship need only be 'reasonable' rather than absolute, enabling new members to share in past contributions, and clarifying that the benefits received are not restricted or limited to a member's contributions. As such, mutuals are a good vehicle for insurance schemes where pay-outs can be more or less than the contributions made by a member. Despite waves of demutualisations in the 1980s and 1990s, the success of mutuals continues to grow, particularly in the wake of the financial crisis that started in OECD countries during 2007 (their market share rose from 22.6 per cent to 28.1 in Europe, from 28.7 per cent to 33.1 per cent in North America, and from 8.6 per cent to 10.9 per cent in Latin America after the collapse of Lehman Brothers in 2008).

Historical underpinnings of secular associations and a voluntary sector

The religious roots of charities and the secular origins of co-operatives have been substantially eroded as successive generations have been attracted to their legal forms without appreciating their social history. Today, secular organisations may adopt charitable status for pragmatic rather than religious reasons. Successful networks of co-operatives have been established in faith communities, particularly where Catholic liberation theology has taken root. In the celebrated case of Mondragon (Whyte and Whyte, 1991), it was a Catholic priest who helped to found both the co-operative schools and the engineering enterprises.

Nevertheless, a distinction can also be made between secular and religious organisations in the *non-profit* (non-market) sector of the social economy. Nowhere is this more acute than in France where *associations* were founded on explicit secular values. As Lindsay and Hems comment:

> The French non-profit sector … did not emerge from a desire to address problems of social need. Neither was it created as a consequence of a number of private organizations addressing social problems, nor as a hinterland between public and private sectors … delivering social welfare provision … Rather, the French non-profit sector emerged as a result of the ideological struggle between republicanism and the Catholic Church over the rights of the individual. Until 1901, the legal right of individuals to associate in groups was heavily restricted and only allowed by specific permission of the government. The creation of associations … was therefore seen as the final victory of the Republic over the Catholic Church in France. (2004: 266)

Similar issues were present elsewhere. There were attempts to shut down friendly societies on the basis that meetings took place in public houses, and therefore breached rules regarding religious norms of temperance (Harrison, 1969). This was, however, primarily a rhetorical strategy that expressed the fears of ruling elites that trade unionism – spread through friendly societies – would trigger a revolution similar to the one in France (Weinbren and James, 2005). In the USA, similar issues arose 100 years later during the early McCarthy era when elites in business and the church expressed concern at the possibility of communism spreading via co-operative societies. Congressional hearings in 1948 were convened to consider how to curb their popularity (Dahlgren, 2007). However, as Fox (1974) notes, it proved hard to attack associations in political cultures that defended liberal values because the right to freedom of association was a priority. Working people were able to use laws established for commerce to defend their right to organise the labour movement.

The success of **secular associations** in maintaining autonomy from churches, states and private companies has given rise to the concept of a voluntary sector. This term broadens the scope of the 'non-market' social economy beyond charity (or charity-like) organisations to include many sports and social clubs as well as performing arts organisations. It also provides a natural home for civil society organisations that, on account of their political lobbying, cannot register as charities.

For many of these organisations the non-profit association structure provides a simple way to incorporate their organisation with the sole purpose of creating a structure that benefits their association. The benefits include attracting funding, philanthropic capital and acquiring property (as well as establishing procedures for managing such funds). For example, amateur sports clubs in the UK have their own status: there are currently 6,200 Community Amateur Sports Clubs (CASCs) (for a table comparing **unincorporated**, charitable and CASC statuses see CASC (2011)).

As Bridge et al. (2009) comment, the association form has spread even further into trade unions, independent schools, housing associations, employer and staff associations, and even political parties. Lindsay and Hems (2004) draw out the restrictions that often apply to associations (particularly in France) where income must be derived primarily from membership fees to prevent competition with private companies in open markets.

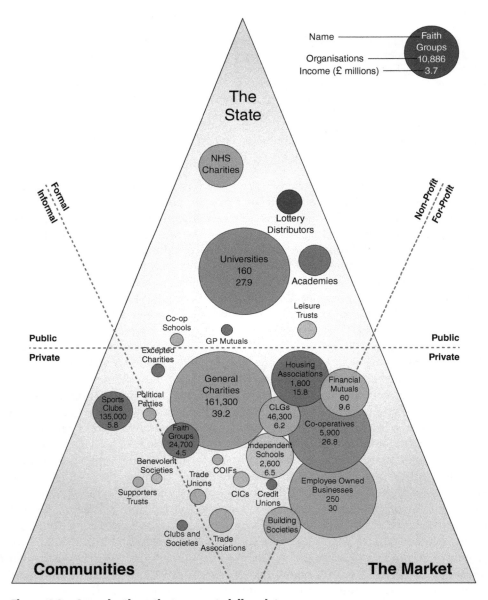

Figure 1.2   Organisations that support civil society

Source: NCVO, http://data.ncvo.org.uk/a/almanac14/civil-society/what-is-civil-society-2/

In the UK, while trading restrictions are not as tight, it is useful to theoretically distinguish associations (who generate income from and act for members) from charities (who generate income from donors and charitable trading to support beneficiaries) and co-operatives (who intervene into the market to advance the interests of producer- and consumer-members). Figure 1.2 sets out the many sub-groups of civil society organisations identified by NCVO and assesses the value of their economic transactions to indicate their scope and influence.

What *unites* members across subsectors is the ability to mobilise collective responses to social issues, engage moral and social reasoning to support business activities, and to generate surpluses that support social value creation. Moreover, they typically share hostility to decision-making power based on capital ownership, and favour member ownership rooted in commitments to balancing social and economic value creation.

Class exercise: Identifying the sectors

Materials to support this exercise can be found on the companion website at: www.sagepub.co.uk/ridleyduff.

On your own, sort the following organisations into three groups:

- group 1: first system, private sector
- group 2: second system, public sector
- group 3: third system, civil society.

Student Union

Oxfam

National Society for the Prevention of Cruelty to Children

British Telecom (BT)

E.ON

The Crown Prosecution Service

The Co-operative Group

Body Shop

Shell

St Thomas' Hospital

(Continued)

(Continued)

Comic Relief

London University

Pair up with another person. Are your groupings the same? If any organisations are placed in different groups, discuss the differences of opinion.

Suggestion: why not include organisations from your own area, region or country? You can include well-known regional services, companies, associations, charities and co-operatives.

Assessing size, scope and contribution of the social economy in the UK

When they start to operate, social economy organisations need both a social and legal identity. Social (business) identities can include: charitable enterprises and associations, foundations, worker co-operatives, **consumer co-operatives**, financial mutuals, **development trusts**, voluntary and community organisations, community businesses and employee-owned businesses (see Figure 1.2). Each identity is supported by a legal structure. Using the UK as an example, Table 1.1 illustrates that there is not a simple one-to-one relationship between social identity and legal structure. A number of different legal structures can be used to advance a particular social identity.

Table 1.1   Legal forms and organisation types in the social economy

Business Identities and Legal Structures	Charities and Associations	Co-operatives and Mutuals	Community Enterprises	Employee-Owned Businesses
Company limited by shares (CLS)		✓		✓
Company limited by guarantee (CLG)	✓	✓	✓	✓
Community interest company (CIC)		✓	✓	✓
Charitable incorporated organisation (CIO)	✓			
Co-operative society		✓	✓	✓
Community benefit society (BENCOM)	(✓)	✓	✓	
Limited Liability Partnerships (LLP)		✓		✓

In addition to incorporated organisations, there are additional third sector organisations (**TSOs**) that choose not to incorporate. This might be due to size, income or desire. These unincorporated forms tend to fall under the radar for statistics about the size, scope and impact of the sector as they do not report or record their existence to any central body. There can be a political advantage to this. If a group disagrees with activities that are legal, yet unethical (e.g. anti-fracking campaign groups; Occupy movement groups) it can assist with protest activities if no legal entity can be sued. Frack Off, Extreme Energy Action Network is an organisation of this type: it informs on the destruction created by fracking and campaigns against this becoming commonplace (see http://frack-off.org.uk/). In Sweden, Planka Nu has had some success lobbying for free public transport in Tronheim through a social enterprise that insures people who engage in civil disobedience (see https://planka.nu/eng/). In each case, over formalising the enterprise can weaken its capacity to achieve social goals (Southcombe, 2014).

There are a number of ways to assess the contribution of the social economy to society. Below, we consider three traditional perspectives (employment, organisation numbers, scale of trading) to illustrate how the frame of reference can radically alter perceptions of size and influence. The US and EU both have legal definitions for civil society organisations. In the US, non-profit organisations fall under Section 501 of the Internal Revenue Code, and include more than two dozen categories of organisation that are tax exempt. These are permitted to provide employment, but cannot pay dividends to shareholders. In the EU, the concept of the social economy embraces a similar, but slightly different, range of organisations. In the mid-1990s it was recognised that classifications based only on investor-led (private) enterprises and intervention-led (public) organisations were inadequate. The EU's national accounting system now includes Sections 11 and 12 (social economy 'business subsector') and 14 and 15 (social economy 'non-market producers'). This makes these organisations more visible (as a sector) and more amenable to government support and intervention (Monzon and Chaves, 2008).

The business subsector comprises co-operatives, mutual organisations and social firms that satisfy democratic criteria set out in the CEP-CMAR *Charter of Principles of the Social Economy*. Unlike the US, dividends are payable to members but must reflect 'activities or transactions with the organisation' rather than capital contributions (Monzon and Chaves, 2008: 558). In addition, there is a 'non-market-producer subsector' that includes associations and foundations producing (or funding) non-market goods and services for household consumption. Whereas the US definition is broadly defined to include philanthropic and political organisations, the EU definition leans strongly towards democratic criteria and the production of goods and services; 'non-democratic' voluntary organisations are only included if they 'conduct an activity with the main purpose of meeting the needs of persons rather than remunerating capitalist investors' (Monzon and Chaves, 2008: 558).

Avila and Campos (2006) published a report for the European Commission on employment in the social economy. In some EU countries, employment is dominated by associations (Belgium, Netherlands and the United Kingdom) while in others co-operatives and mutuals dominate (Italy, Spain and Poland). Across the EU as a whole,

36 per cent of social economy employment (3.7 million jobs) was provided by co-operatives and mutuals, while the remaining 64 per cent (7.4 million) was provided by associations (and charities). Their report highlighted that employment in the social economy was growing faster than in the private and public sectors (at 5–9 per cent a year) but that overall employment remained under 10 per cent of the whole economy (Avila and Campos, 2006: 109).

Table 1.2 suggests that this growth forecast for social economy employment has not only been sustained but could be accelerating. In CICOPA's global report on co-operative employment, the much larger figure of 16 million jobs is estimated (Roelants et al., 2014).

Table 1.2   Co-operative employment worldwide by continent and category

Region	Employees	Worker-Members	Producer-Members	Total
Europe	4,627,953	1,231,102	10,132,252	15,991,207
Africa	1,467,914	237	5,715,212	7,183,363
Asia	7,734,113	8,200,505	204,749,940	220,684,558
Americas	1,762,797	1,409,608	3,048,249	6,220,654
Oceania	26,038	No data	34,592	60,630
	15,618,715	10,841,452	223,680,245	250,140,412

Source: B. Roelants, presentation to International Co-operative Summit, Quebec, 6 October 2014.

N.B. The above figures *exclude* associations and social enterprises that are not owned by a co-op or mutual.

This suggests a four-fold increase in co-operative employment in Europe between 2003 and 2012. Globally, the 2010 estimate of 100 million jobs has been revised upwards to 250 million (with 160 million in China). Four OECD countries with high GDP growth (China, India, South Korea and Turkey) now have more than 10 per cent of their populations working 'within the scope of' co-operatives. Only Italy among developed OECD nations has a similar rate of social economy employment (Italy – 10.9 per cent, Germany – 6.5 per cent, France – 5.9 per cent, UK – 1.4 per cent, US – 1.3 per cent) (Roelants et al., 2014: 31).

The UK situation is complicated by the existence of charity law. While other national classification systems – such as the US or France – include types of associations and non-profits that receive recognition for charity-like activities, UK organisations can apply for charity status where the bulk of their activities or services meet a specified public interest (Morgan, 2008). As charities are approved on the basis of their activities, and not their legal form, it makes it harder to draw distinctions between different parts of the social economy. Nevertheless, a number of mapping exercises have been conducted.

By late 2013, UK data sources estimated that its third sector included 164,000 charities (Charity Commission, 2014), 161,000 voluntary and community groups (NCVO, 2014) and 70,000 social enterprises (Cabinet Office, 2013). Co-operatives UK (2014) claimed there were 6,323 co-operatives. There continue to be issues related to the identification and contribution of micro providers (those organisations with less than five employees) estimated at 2 to 5 million people (MacGillivray et al., 2001). Table 1.3 summarises these findings and highlights the significant number of organisations that make up the third (and fourth sectors) – over 394,000 organisations across the UK.

A significant proportion are charities and voluntary/community organisations (approximately 80 per cent of the number), with social enterprises and co-operatives making up the remaining 20 per cent. The table also shows the significant contribution the sector makes to the UK economy, with £163 billion in total income.

Table 1.3   Approximate number and proportions of UK social economy organisations, 2014

Organisational type	Number of organisations	Percentage of the total number of organisations	Income (£)	Income distribution per organisation (mean)
Voluntary/community organisations (NCVO Almanac, 2014)	161,000	Approx. 40% of the sector	£39.2 billion	Approx. £243,500 per organisation
Charities (Charity Commission, 2014)	164,000	Approx. 40% of the sector	£62.746 billion	Approx. £382,600 per organisation
Social enterprises (Cabinet Office, 2013)[5] (9% cross-over with above, no cross-over with co-ops)	70,000 (63,000 additional)	Approx. 18% of the sector	£24 billion (£21.6 billion)	Approx. £342,860 per organisation
Co-operative Economy (Co-operatives UK, 2014)	6,323	Approx. 2% of the sector	£37 billion	Approx. £5,851,652 per organisation
Total	Just over 394,000	100%	Approx. £163 billion	Mean value £406,000 per organisation

Source: data sourced from NCVO (2014), Charity Commission (2014), Co-operatives UK (2014) and UK Government (2015)

The table highlights that the average income per co-operative is nearly £6 million, nearly 20 times greater than the mean for other types of enterprise (approx. £350,000). This imbalance is a measure of the size of well-established co-operatives in the UK, with the three largest (the Co-operative Group Limited, John Lewis Partnership plc and the Midcounties Co-operative Limited) generating over £24 billion between them in trading activity (Co-operatives UK, 2014). Moreover, the *co-ownership sector*, which excludes consumer co-operatives but includes wholly or partially owned employee-controlled organisations, is estimated to contribute £30 billion to the UK economy, while the broader mutual sector contributes £116 billion (Mutuo, 2012: 10).

Obtaining composite figures is made more difficult by inconsistencies in the way co-operatives are included or excluded from social enterprise surveys. Woodin (2007) points out that smaller (start-up) co-operatives get included, while larger co-operatives and mutuals tend to get excluded. Nevertheless, taking account of the methodologies used to map the sector can help with the preparation of composite figures (Teasdale et al., 2013). The way the Small Business Survey frames 'social enterprise' results in the inclusion of many businesses that pursue a social purpose, but which do not have the **asset lock** characteristic of a voluntary and charitable organisation. Only 9 per cent of the 2012 Small Business Survey sample (UK Government, 2015) reported a lock on assets to ensure they are retained for use by similar organisations. Furthermore, there were no co-operatives and only two friendly societies in the sample. This means that it is reasonably safe to combine figures for voluntary groups, charities, co-operatives and social enterprises to give a composite picture of the number of organisations in the UK that seek to create social value.

The key learning point, however, is that the boundaries chosen, and the lens adopted, dramatically alters perceptions of the size, contribution and potential of the social economy.

The Third Way and New Labour

The scale of activity across civil society today is the product of an updated political philosophy. The concept of the third sector gained recognition after Anthony Giddens (1998) adopted the phrase 'the Third Way' to describe Tony Blair's political philosophy (Labour Prime Minister in the UK between 1997–2007). During the UK Labour government (1997–2010) political ideology shifted towards a new type of state intervention. The collapse of the European communist states led to a new wave of thinking in Europe, the Americas and other Anglo-American cultures. While the Third Way is not synonymous with the third sector, it implied a major shift in the attitude of the public sector towards it. In the UK, the term 'third sector' predates 'Third Way' by nearly a decade (evidenced by the emergence of a trade magazine). Nevertheless, the acceptance of the term in the UK was rapid (Haugh and Kitson, 2007). Commenting on Tony Blair's approach, Dickson argues that:

> there is no ideological commitment to public sector provision – there is a willingness to contemplate private and not for profit alternatives, something manifestly different from more traditional Labour policy which at times was indifferent to the voluntary sector and often hostile to private involvement in welfare … Indeed it is the social services white paper that is the most explicit on this, stating quite clearly that 'who provides' is not important. (Dickson, 1999)

Third Way discourse combined social democratic language with values of mutual support and civic responsibility (Giddens, 1998). As Haugh and Kitson comment:

> The Third Way was a political philosophy that sought to resolve the ideological differences between liberalism and socialism; it combined neoliberalism with the renewal of civil society and viewed the state as an enabler, promoted civic activism and endorsed engagement with the voluntary and community sector to address society's needs. (2007: 983)

While Edwards (2004) is somewhat dismissive of this view, it represents an alternative that rejects both Weber's ideal of bureaucracy (based on logic and rationality) and a market capitalism that is concerned only with higher standards of living (Gates, 1998). Mertens (1999) notes that the term 'third sector' is linked to the idea of a third estate – neither the aristocracy nor the clergy, neither capitalist nor socialist, but a collection of organisations outside the scope of the state and market that fulfil unmet needs. She portrays a sector that grows and shrinks as the fortunes of the private and public sectors change, with boundaries drawn not so much in terms of what the third sector is, but more in terms of what the public and private sectors are not.

There are problems with this view. Historically, as Coule (2008) points out, social economy organisations predate both capitalist production and state welfare provision. As Prochaska (1990: 358) writes, at the turn of the twentieth century 'the average middle class family was spending more on charity than on any other single item except food' and the income of London charities alone was 'greater than that of several nation states'. Weinbren (2007) provides some insights into this by revealing the amounts paid in Bristol (South West England) for sickness and death benefit in 1870: friendly societies and charities (third sector) paid out 73 per cent of all welfare benefits, with the Bristol Corporation (public sector) meeting only 27 per cent of the total.

Another consideration is the role that social economy organisations played in developing institutions that later transferred to the public and private sectors. Hudson (2002: 4) lists well-known hospitals established in the twelfth and thirteenth centuries (St Bartholomew's and St Thomas') that are now part of the NHS. Other trusts and associations now shape modern approaches to welfare and legal rights (e.g. Red Cross and Barnardo's) and are largely state funded (Murdock, 2007). To this, we can add the friendly societies that built a membership of 9.5 million by 1910, an achievement that demonstrated the viability of social insurance covering the whole population (Weinbren and James, 2005). Indeed, 'approved' friendly societies managed the state system until 1942 when services were finally taken over by state employees. Lastly, co-operative stores dominated grocery retailing before World War II and pioneered the concept of a retail supermarket. While price deregulation affected the UK market after the war, in Italy and Spain, retail co-operatives grew and now dominate many areas of retailing (Kalmi, 2007). As Chandler (2008) has successfully argued, many public and private enterprises start life as municipal or third sector initiatives. When their viability is demonstrated, larger organisations use their political or economic muscle to acquire them, not because this is necessarily more efficient, but because they operate on a scale that can be used to advance the interests of the state or private capital.

A useful way to define the third (and fourth) sectors is that they comprise organisations where 'shares' (of social wealth) are allocated to people in proportion to their needs and activities rather than property ownership or political power. Takeovers by state or private sector organisations, therefore, may have motives other than the delivery of greater 'efficiency'. In some cases, takeovers may be motivated by a desire to replace the social economy's approach to resource allocation with an alternative that is less threatening to state or corporate interests; thus power is a factor that always needs to be considered in evaluating the relative contribution of each sector.

The Big Society

Following the collapse of Lehman Brothers in 2008, a global recession hit many of the countries of the OECD (see Case 1.5). This is likely to have affected your life as well as the lives of your friends and families. States are being reorganised amid massive reductions in funding for health, education and welfare services. In the midst of this, there are fresh attempts to advance market mechanisms in the state sector and civil society. Given the scale of the changes – the largest since 1834 – it is worth reminding ourselves concretely of the effects of the financial crisis before we examine the concept of the Big Society as a response.

In January 2009, *The Guardian* newspaper ran a headline, 'Recession Britain: it's official' (Kollewe, 2009). This was the first recession in the UK for nearly 30 years. *The Times* headlined with 'British slump will be worst in developed world, says IMF' (Duncan, 2009a). Whichever government held power, public spending cuts were seen as 'inevitable' and only the speed at which they would occur was under debate. In 2010, the Conservative and Liberal Democrat coalition government came to power and the severity of the cutbacks became apparent. *The Guardian* reported in 2011 that 'more than 200 areas of public spending faced real-terms cuts in the first year of coalition government, with departments having to find £10 billion in savings such as GP care, prisons and the rail network' (Ball and Rodgers, 2011). The relevance of this to the social economy is visible once the concept of the Big Society is outlined.

Case 1.5

Preparing for austerity around the globe

While we focus on the UK, policies to support 'austerity' (the withdrawal of the state from welfare provision) has taken place in nearly all OECD economies. In Japan, the expectation that government spending will have to fall coincides with laws to encourage 'social purpose' enterprises. Laratta et al. (2011) outline pressures on the Japanese state. Starting with responses to a large earthquake in 1995, new laws were passed to allow organisations to incorporate as 'specified' and 'certified' non-profits. In the next ten years, 35,000 organisations did so. Unlike Europe, where public support for philanthropic organisations secures tax advantages, Japanese non-profits have (until recently) been taxed at the same rate as private companies (at 30 per cent). Cultural norms remain supportive of co-operatives and mutuals, but are hostile to philanthropic giving. For this reason, Japan has the world's largest food and agricultural co-operatives within a co-operative economy that is four times larger than the UK (Euricse, 2013). Japanese non-profits, however, are following the worldwide trend by increasing the income they derive from trading. A major aspect of this is the Long Term Care Insurance (LTCI) system which now permits private and non-profit organisations to take over service provision from the state. In many areas (hospices, nursing homes, mental hospitals and elderly care services) the state commissions services, but no longer provides them. In 2011, new laws were proposed to permit the incorporation of worker co-operatives, create new social co-operatives, and offer tax relief on donations to 'certified' non-profits. As in the UK, Japan is restructuring the state and changing its relationship to the social economy.

In 2009, prior to coming into power, the Conservative party leader David Cameron outlined the concept of the Big Society. His key speech is helpful for understanding the political context:

> I want to extend and deepen the argument ... that the size, scope and role of government in Britain has reached a point where it is now inhibiting, not advancing the progressive aims of reducing poverty, fighting inequality, and increasing general well-being. Indeed there is a worrying paradox that because of its effect on personal and social responsibility, the recent growth of the state has promoted not social solidarity, but selfishness and individualism. (Cameron, 2009)

These are bold words. Is it the growth of governments, or the rise of **neo-liberalism**, that inhibits the development of solutions to poverty, inequality, health and well-being? Is it a culture of feeling an entitlement (created by the welfare state) or the rise of consumer culture that leads to selfishness and individualism? Cameron claims that it is the state (under previous Labour governments) that eroded citizens' sense of social responsibility. In short, his argument is that the 'nanny state' has taken decision-making power away from individuals, ostensibly for the good of society, but created a destructive individualism based on avoidance of social responsibility and self-centred behaviour.

So what is his 'Big Society' response? The UK Coalition Government (2010) explains:

> We want to give citizens, communities and local government the power and information they need to come together, solve the problems they face and build the Britain they want. We want society – the families, networks, neighbourhoods and communities that form the fabric of so much of our everyday lives – to be bigger and stronger than ever before. Only when people and communities are given more power and take more responsibility can we achieve fairness and opportunity for all.

To this end, the coalition government set out a policy based on:

- devolving power from central to local government (giving local autonomy and accountability, by abolishing the regions in favour of a district strategy)
- giving more power to communities to take over local state-run services (parks and playing fields, libraries and community centres)
- stimulating volunteering (by building citizenship skills and community engagement among young people)
- creating a right to data so that the public can hold authorities to account for local performance
- supporting the creation of co-operatives, mutuals, charities and social enterprises to run public services, including employee-owned co-operatives to run public services they previously delivered.

According to Evans (2011), Big Society aims to mend 'societally broken' communities by nurturing peoples' sense of altruism, their giving, and their generosity to engage in their community. It also aims to mend 'financially broken' communities through public sector reform. Finally, it aims to address 'politically broken' communities by giving more control of local assets to local governments. The key feature, in a political ideology sense, is that devolution to the lowest possible tier of the governance of the country will return responsibility for it to society. She refers to Big Society as a *political narrative*, too big and varied to be referred to as a coherent policy. For our purposes, it is the inclusion of a commitment to give greater power to 'co-operatives, mutuals, charities and social enterprises' that ties the narrative of Big Society to the subject of this book. Interestingly, Evans (2011: 165) outlines Cameron's views that:

> we will want to do everything we can to help what used to be called, rather condescendingly, the third sector, but should be called the first sector in my view: the excellent charities, voluntary organisations and social enterprises that do so much for our country ... so often these first sector organisations have the right answers to the social problems in our country ...

It is this particular element of the Big Society that interests us, the attempt by a prime minister to reinvent and reframe the notion of civil society by elevating it to the position of a first, rather than a third, sector and jettisoning all trace of condescension. Is this a deep political commitment or political rhetoric to appeal to 'voters' now working in and for the social economy in greater numbers?

Critiquing the concept of the Big Society

On one level, the concept of the Big Society appears to be a continuation of Third Way policies by ostensibly favouring a social economy approach to social and economic reform. However, Piketty's (2014) work calls into question whether the withdrawal of the state from welfare will achieve the stated policy goals. His analysis shows that the only period of modern history in which these policy goals have been achieved took place in the post-World War II period 1945–76 when communist and social democratic governments ran most European states. For this reason, we need to carefully consider the views expressed in Corbett and Walker's (2012) article, 'Big Society: back to the future'. They draw attention to similarities between the politics of Big Society and Margaret Thatcher's contention that there is 'no society'. They argue that:

> On close inspection, the two policy approaches are remarkably similar even though the main thrust of their rhetoric is not, lending credence to the claim of Big Society rhetoric as a political fig-leaf for neo-liberal policy. (Corbett and Walker, 2012: 452)

They unpack the issue a little more by outlining that:

> two strands run through the philosophy of the big society: conservative communitarianism – in its current political guise of Red Toryism (Blond, 2010) and libertarian paternalism – derived from behavioural economics (Thaler and Sunstein, 2008). (Corbett and Walker, 2012: 454)

Within the concept of conservative **communitarianism** is the notion that the power of the state and 'rampant individualism' is constrained by the family, social groups and communities in a property owning democracy. The goal of Red Toryism is still to shrink the power of the state by limiting its power to intervene in economic, social and moral affairs. This ultimately advances a market ideology that in its most extreme form (under Thatcherism) triggered the very individualism that Cameron claims is a product of a 'big' state. In both cases, there is a narrative of self-responsibility combined with rhetoric about care for others, society and the environment (Coote, 2010).

Morality in conservative communitarianism is maintained by the promotion of family values, the church, volunteering and philanthropy while libertarian paternalism encourages the deployment of 'nudge theory' to trigger our moral sensitivities (Corbett and Walker, 2012: 458). Corbett and Walker frame the use of nudge theory as a form of compassionate economics in which actors in the market economy encourage each other to buy and sell goods that improve societal well-being rather than maximise profit.

They give an example of a school canteen where unhealthy food is positioned in such a way that it is less accessible than healthy food. The moral sentiments of the seller give the consumer a 'nudge' towards the healthier option.

While Thatcher's denial of society seems to be ideologically different from Big Society, Corbett and Walker suggest that the policy goal still favours entrepreneurial spirit and enterprise over the power of the state. As Big Society does not mask its preference for market forces, we need to draw on Maitland's (1997: 18) critique that market relations increase the following risks: (a) the erosion of social ties other than purely economic ones and/or conversion of social relationships into instrumental ones ('commodification'); (b) the encouragement of materialistic and hedonistic values; (c) competition as more virtuous than co-operation, and lastly; (d) the promotion of a preoccupation with narrow individual advantage at the expense of social responsibility.

Big Society, therefore, can be regarded as a thinly disguised project to marketise the state even more: public sector workers are being actively 'nudged' to deliver public services through employee mutuals (notionally a form of solidarity co-operative) under the philosophy of compassionate economics. Reminiscent of Willmott's (1993) paper that neo-liberal discourse seeks to convince 'slaves' that they are 'free', Big Society presents its policy as the 'freedom' to take responsibility for public service provision through state-sponsored social enterprises (Curtis, 2008). The 'choice' between market and non-market provision is removed. The new 'choice' is between privatised or socialised (mutual) market economies.

In conclusion, Corbett and Walker make the case that the politics behind Big Society make it similar to Thatcher's policy of funding cuts in the public sector to create the space for conservative communitarianism in public services and liberal paternalism in the private economy. The danger is the further commodification of the social, the creation of power hierarchies based on market forces, a deepening failure to tackle inequality and further atomisation of individuals.

Implications for social enterprise

There are varying, but increasingly clear, views of the relationship between social enterprise and the third sector. Firstly, Defourny (2001) argues that social enterprises are embedded *within* a third sector at the boundary of co-operatives and non-profits (see Figure 1.3). A similar argument is found in Pearce's (2003) *third system* (see Figure 1.1), where social enterprise is depicted as a subsector sitting *between* voluntary and charity organisations and the private sector (which co-operatives also border).

In contrast to both these views, however, comes a perspective influenced in turn by US thinking on social entrepreneurship and a more profound commitment to

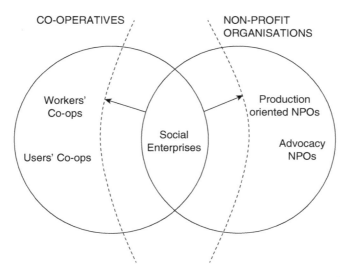

Figure 1.3   Social enterprise at the 'crossroads' of non-profit and co-operative economies

Source: Defourny (2001: 22), Figure 1, reprinted with permission from the Taylor & Francis Group

solidarity among producers and consumers (Leadbeater, 1997; Westall, 2001). In this case, the areas *between* the third and the public sectors, and *between* the public and the private sectors, are the environments in which social entrepreneurship flourishes (Figure 1.4). In this body of theory, the institutional forms created by social entrepreneurs are *de facto* social enterprises (Spear, 2006). *This view, however, places social enterprise at the margins of the public, private and third sectors rather than embedded in their heart.*

In Chapter 2 we will examine these perspectives more closely. For now, it is worth problematising Defourny's view that social enterprises lie *within* the third sector (civil society). Each of the examples in Figure 1.4 represents an organisation that formed, or operates, by drawing together thinking and organisational practices from more than one economic sector. For example, Peattie and Morley (2008) point out how the UK **National Lottery** is an initiative with a clear social purpose, organised through collaborations between the state and private businesses, delivering funds to TSOs. Another example of ambiguity is offered by Jones (2000). Traidcraft (see Case 1.6) achieves its social mission through altering the trading relationships between producers in disadvantaged communities and advanced market economies. Notwithstanding commitments to social activism in the Christian tradition, and a sustainability agenda drawn from environmental awareness, Traidcraft adopted the form of a public limited company (plc), more readily associated with private sector companies.

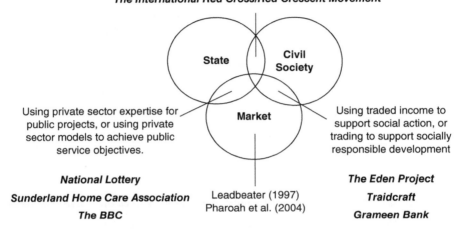

Third sector expertise running public services, or securing public sector partnerships to achieve social outcomes

Royal National Institute for Deaf People
Citizens Advice Bureaux (CAB Service)
The International Red Cross/Red Crescent Movement

Using private sector expertise for public projects, or using private sector models to achieve public service objectives.

National Lottery
Sunderland Home Care Association
The BBC

Using traded income to support social action, or trading to support socially responsible development

The Eden Project
Traidcraft
Grameen Bank

Leadbeater (1997)
Pharoah et al. (2004)

Figure 1.4   Hybrid organisations

Case 1.6

Traidcraft

Traidcraft, founded in 1979, established trading links and market opportunities for handicrafts, cards, books, tea, coffee, paper products and food from overseas co-operative and community businesses. Its business ethics are based on Christian values. It products are sourced from 26 different countries sold through a volunteer network of 5,000 sellers. In 1983 the company took the decision to float on the stock market, to deliberately increase participation, but offered no dividend on the £1 share. Despite this, the offer of 300,000 shares was over-subscribed by 60 per cent. In 1993 Traidcraft plc became the first plc to publish a social audit (undertaken by the New Economics Foundation) and sent it to the stock exchange's top 100 chief executives as part of the campaign to promote social accounting. Traidcraft also established the Traidcraft Exchange, a charity that organises educational projects around the globe.

As a *fair trade network*, Traidcraft plc brings together co-operative and community businesses, then sells their products through a public limited company, albeit with a third sector ethic and a social ownership ethos. The addition of a charity to the group broadens its capacity to undertake educational and social projects.

Traidcraft provides an example of an organisation that is hard to locate in any existing sector.

Source: with permission from Traidcraft plc.

We find that we are increasingly drawn to the arguments of Westall (2001) who positions social enterprise in its own space, with an independent capacity to that of public, private and voluntary sector organisations (see Figure 1.5). In Westall's conceptualisation, social enterprise is defined by governance and ownership arrangements that bring more producers and consumers into membership and which organise governance on a multi-stakeholder basis. We see traction in Westall's model as it provides a framework to understand social enterprises created out of efforts to transform voluntary, private and public sector organisations (at the overlaps), but also a new generation of social enterprises innovating beyond the confines of 'old' public, private and third sector institutions. For Westall, this captures both the organic nature of the

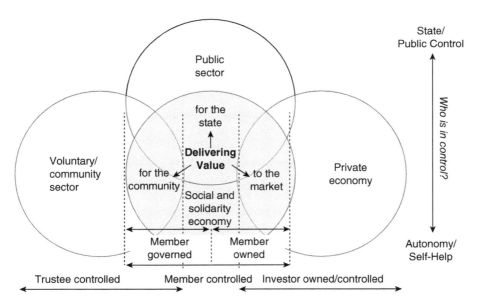

Figure 1.5   Social enterprise as autonomous multi-stakeholder/multiple owner enterprises

Source: adapted from Westall (2001), Figure 1.1

social and solidarity economy, and also its capacity to transcend the limitations of other sectors through a distinctive approach. We will expand our thoughts on this when we discuss the social and solidarity economy further in Chapters 2 and 3.

In a manner reminiscent to Pearce, Westall labels the combination of the voluntary/ community and the social enterprise 'space' as the *third sector*. And yet, given that both Pearce and Westall carefully distinguish trading, member-controlled enterprises (social economy) from non-trading, trustee-controlled enterprises (voluntary sector), it is worth acknowledging the link of each to the 'group ownership' and 'no owner' property types advanced by Ostrom et al. (1999). If policies are developed for the third sector that fail to understand differences between these two property types, the policies are as likely to fail as those designed for the private sector but applied to the public sector (or vice versa).

Different theorisations of the relationship between a third sector and social enterprise lead to different understandings of social enterprise itself. Nevertheless, the third sector has become an important concept in understanding the fabric of society outside the private and public sectors. Crucially, TSOs differ from mainstream business in that they aim to follow a mission that serves a community or public good, with activities not constrained or prioritised on the basis of their profit potential, but on the basis of the impact they have and the well-being they create. For this reason McCulloch (2013) describes them as 'for-purpose' enterprises, rejecting the label 'non-profit' for two key reasons: firstly, the social and solidarity economy includes a *mix* of non-profit and profit-making enterprises; secondly, it is better to frame social enterprises by what they are 'for' rather than what they are 'not'.

Defourny and Nyssens (2006) shed light on two key tensions. Firstly, they acknowledge subtle differences in the ideologies that underpin associations, mutuals and co-operatives. At one end of the continuum is the 'non-profit school' comprising charitable and voluntary organisations. At the other end is a 'more-than-profit' school comprising co-operative and mutual organisations. While the 'non-profit school' ideology has been based on a *non-market* mind-set, the co-operative school accepts *market trading* with altered assumptions regarding the management of capital. The non-profit mind-set is grounded in philanthropy and giving. The co-operative mind-set is grounded in mutual trading activities in markets or with members.

The second tension is the organisation's democratic commitments. The co-operative school is committed to democratic member control, placing control of the organisation's mission into the hands of its wider membership, and (in the case of producer and worker co-operatives) seeking to replace 'employment' with 'member ownership' (ICA, 2005; Birchall, 2009). As a result, they typically have an *internal orientation*, seeking to benefit members and the community. In non-profit associations, the mission is based on and for the good of society, or a particular segment of society. While opposed to the employment of trustees, many charities are comfortable employing staff to professionalise their operations. In this case, there is an *external orientation* with regard to beneficiaries. These, in turn, have impacts on the organisation of labour,

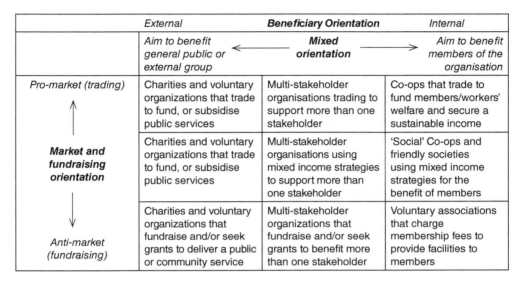

	External	Beneficiary Orientation	Internal
	Aim to benefit general public or external group	Mixed orientation	Aim to benefit members of the organisation
Pro-market (trading) ↑ Market and fundraising orientation ↓ Anti-market (fundraising)	Charities and voluntary organizations that trade to fund, or subsidise public services	Multi-stakeholder organisations trading to support more than one stakeholder	Co-ops that trade to fund members/workers' welfare and secure a sustainable income
	Charities and voluntary organizations that trade to fund, or subsidise public services	Multi-stakeholder organisations using mixed income strategies to support more than one stakeholder	'Social' Co-ops and friendly societies using mixed income strategies for the benefit of members
	Charities and voluntary organizations that fundraise and/or seek grants to deliver a public or community service	Multi-stakeholder organizations that fundraise and/or seek grants to benefit more than one stakeholder	Voluntary associations that charge membership fees to provide facilities to members

Figure 1.6   Theorising orientations within the social economy

human resource practices, and attitudes to management and capital ownership. Theorising these differences helps to understand the variability of TSOs. Figure 1.6 provides a framework to further clarify this diversity.

Our research experiences suggest that there is a good rationale for caution. Social enterprise is used in an increasing number of contexts, cultures and national settings. Social enterprise may be characterised as a sub-group of organisations in the third sector/system (Pearce, 2003) or a new economic engine (Harding and Cowling, 2006). Disarmingly simple and inclusive definitions include organisations 'where people have to be business-like, but are not in it for the money' (Paton, 2003). If social enterprise means different things to different people, it is necessary to build theory that accounts for these variations and which connects them to their philosophical underpinnings.

Conclusions

There are a few points worth summarising that relate to forthcoming discussions about the definition of social enterprise. Firstly, many social economy organisations (trading charities, co-operatives and social businesses) have a claim to the term 'social enterprise' that varies in its beneficiary and market orientation. The more market oriented they are, and the more they are oriented towards public and community benefit, the more they have been accepted as part of the social enterprise mainstream in Anglo-American cultures (Lyon and Sepulveda, 2009). However, in populous parts of Europe and Asia, co-operative working is more commonplace and this means that there is much more receptivity to social enterprise theory that *fully* integrates the co-operative economy (Laratta et al., 2011; Roelants et al., 2014).

Secondly, the social economy and third sector are not the same thing. At EU level, TSOs that do not produce any goods or services for household or business use are not considered part of the social economy (as seen in Pearce's model – Figure 1.1). Moreover, definitions of social economy are more explicit about the social value of democratic governance. While TSOs may have a social purpose, social economy organisations value 'social' rather than 'private' ownership and control based on the participation of those affected by decisions. This being the case, the relationship between the social economy and social enterprise appears to be more direct than the link between the third sector and social enterprise. As will become clearer in Chapter 2, it is easier to draw a direct line between social enterprise and the social economy than between social enterprise and the third sector. This being the case, social economy is a more useful term (and concept) in the forthcoming debate.

Class exercise: Theorising social economy organisations

Materials to support this exercise can be found on the companion website at: www.sagepub.co.uk/ridleyduff.

The purpose of this exercise is to critically review the market and membership orientations of social economy organisations and decide which are part of the social economy.

- Obtain descriptions of the charity status, social aims and ownership structure of some social economy organisations.
- Form students into groups of three.
- Give three descriptions to each student.
- Give the students 10 minutes to read and reflect on the examples.
- Ask each student to summarise their organisations for the other members of their group.
- Ask the group members to locate them on Figures 1.5 and 1.6.
- Ask the students to discuss which (parts) of these organisations are in the 'social economy'.

Why not get students to research the websites of local third sector and social economy organisations and use these instead of the materials provided with the book?

Summary of learning

In this chapter we raise a number of issues that impact understanding of the social economy and Big Society.

Civil society organisations attempt to promote voluntary (rather than coercive) forms of association outside the state and private sectors to advance participatory democracy and ethical action.

A three sector model of the economy (private, public, third) recognises three competing ideologies: (1) market supply and demand; (2) public interest; (3) social purpose.

Third sector language ('non-profit sector', 'charity sector', 'voluntary sector', 'Big Society' and 'social economy') will impact on perceptions of what is/is not a social enterprise.

Big Society continues a 'Third Way' narrative by making rhetorical statements about the value of self-management, but also masks outcomes likely to occur from the marketisation of public services.

A fourth space exists in which group control/member ownership is the preferred norm giving rise to a social and solidarity economy characterised by co-ownership and multi-stakeholder governance.

The organisations of the social economy include co-operatives, mutual societies and charitable and/or voluntary associations that focus on the production of goods and services that improve well-being.

Different perspectives on a social economy's size and scope can be derived from assessing the number of organisations, employment levels and the value of trading activities.

Understanding the history of charities, trusts, co-operatives, mutuals and voluntary associations helps to appreciate variations in value commitments and preferred management practices.

Diversity in the social economy can be theorised by considering the orientation towards beneficiaries (internal and/or external) and income generation (market and/or grants and fundraising).

There are different views about the relationship of social enterprises to a third sector: the first locates social enterprises within the third sector; the second locates social enterprises at its margins.

There is a growing argument that social enterprises occupy a fourth space that is distinctive, and which influences the formation of joint ventures with voluntary, public and private sector organisations.

The definition of a 'social economy' is more directly related to social enterprise than the 'third sector'.

Questions and possible essay assignments

1. 'Big Society is the latest expression of Gidden's "Third Way".' Critically discuss the accuracy and implications of this statement.
2. 'The "non-profit sector", the "third sector" and the "NGO sector" are three ways of describing the same thing – the social economy.' Critically discuss the meaning of these terms and, using case examples, assess whether this claim can be substantiated.
3. Can a co-operative be charitable? Using theory and examples, explore the grey area between charities and co-operatives by examining the operations and impacts of community benefit societies and social co-operatives.

Further reading

To understand the trajectory and mind-set of social economy, we recommend three works. Firstly, the book edited by Amin, Cameron and Hudson titled *Placing the Social Economy* (2002) provides an accessible introduction to the concept of 'international solidarity' and explores why there is growing interest in social economy from both political and business communities. Highly accessible companion material (from the same publisher) is available in the book edited by Novkovic and Webb titled *Co-operatives in a Post-Growth Era: Creating Co-operative Economics* (2014). This book has two parts: part 1 has chapters from people outside the co-operative sector who are committed to sustainable development. Part 2 includes co-operative responses to the challenges raised.

For a full theoretical discussion of the challenges of managing the 'commons', see Ostrom's *Governing the Commons: The Evolution of Institutions for Collective Action* (1990) and Hirst's *Associative Democracy: New Forms of Economics and Social Governance* (1994). If you can get your hands on a copy (by no means easy or inexpensive), it is interesting to compare the arguments made with John Spedan Lewis's book *Fairer Shares* (1954) which explores how the John Lewis Partnership institutionalised approaches to sharing wealth, power and information.

We also provide four articles related directly to the chapter contents. Firstly, there is Williams's article on 'De-linking enterprise culture from capitalism' in *Public Policy and Administration* (2007) which examines the policy implications of research findings that one third of entrepreneurial start-ups are 'social' in orientation. Secondly, there is Monzon and Chaves article 'The European Social Economy' in the *Annals of Public and Cooperative Economics* (2008). This work examines how the social economy is being integrated into frameworks for accounting in Europe and deals directly with the challenge of operationalising definitions. Thirdly, there is Sahakian and Dunand's article 'The social and solidarity economy towards greater "sustainability": learning across contexts and cultures, from Geneva to Manilla' in the *Community Development Journal* (2014). Lastly, we recommend Corbett and Walkers article 'Big Society: back to the future' in *Critical Social Policy* (2012). This article sets out the concept of Big Society and then subjects it to critical scrutiny to unpack its neo-liberal underpinning and link to 'Red Toryism'.

Finally, we still find value in Westall's 2001 think piece for governments titled *Value-led, Market-driven*. This accessible text provides good linkages between the historical development of the social economy and contemporary innovations to hybridise and transcend limitations imposed by previous models of enterprise. It is also the source of the 'fourth space' argument that we have introduced in this chapter and will develop in the next.

Further reading material is available on the companion website at: www.sagepub. co.uk/ridleyduff.

Useful resources

Center on Philanthropy and Civil Society: www.philanthropy.org/

Charity Commission: www.charitycommission.gov.uk/

Co-operative Monitor: http://monitor.coop/

Co-operatives UK: www.uk.coop

EMES European Research Network: www.emes.net

Euclid Network: www.euclidnetwork.eu/

International Society for Third Sector Research: www.istr.org/

National Council for Voluntary Organisations (NCVO): www.ncvo-vol.org.uk/

The Social Economy Alliance: www.socialenterprise.org.uk/social-economy-alliance

The Social Economy Network: www.socialeconomynetwork.org/

The Stockholm Center for Civil Society Studies: www.economicresearch.se/sccss/

Notes

1 The Voluntary Sector Almanac was renamed the Civil Society Almanac in 2008.
2 The oldest active charity on the UK Charity Commission register was established in 597.
3 This is not, however, meant to imply that it is historically inaccurate.
4 Thierry Weishaupt expressed these views in a meeting between MGEN (a French mutual serving 3.3 million teachers) and Social Enterprise Europe Ltd in Paris on 20 June 2011. He is the leader of the Education and Solidarity Network.
5 This is the government's estimate for 'very good fit definition' social enterprises based on research by BMG Research (Social Enterprise: Market Trends, Cabinet Office, May 2013) which, in turn, is based on earlier work in the BIS Small Business Survey 2012.

Defining Social Enterprise

2

Learning objectives

In this chapter we debate the concept of social enterprise, drawing on tensions and perspectives from a number of sources. By the end of this chapter you will be able to:

- explain the practical relevance of debates about social enterprise definition
- explain early social enterprise history
- compare examples of social enterprise based on different approaches to social value creation
- clarify the potential of social enterprise in different enterprise development contexts.

The key arguments that will be developed in this chapter are:

- There are different ways of understanding social enterprise.
- Social enterprise can be defined in terms of:
  - o double/triple bottom lines
  - o developing social and economic capital through community action

(Continued)

(Continued)

- o hybridisation of systems of exchange to increase well-being
- o solidarity between producers, consumers and supporters.

- Social enterprise is developing concurrently in different sectoral contexts.

Introduction

Every organisation that self-defines (or is defined by others) as a social enterprise continually engages in a debate about definition that feeds into policies and practices (both internally and externally). Social enterprise advisers in consultancies and infrastructure bodies will be faced regularly with questions as to whether an individual or organisation will qualify for social enterprise support. Every law to regulate social enterprise, every **kitemark** developed to promote it, every strategy devised to support it, also requires engagement with criteria that will influence the **legitimacy** accorded to individuals and organisations. The definition of a social enterprise, therefore, is not an abstract intellectual exercise: it is a dynamic process unfolding on a daily basis as people decide how to develop their identity, work out the criteria for economic support and which criterion are flexible and fixed.

In Chapter 1 we explored the social economy and its relationship to the state, private and voluntary sectors. This historical account made explicit the political interests and power struggles that shaped their emergence. Internationally, the meaning of social enterprise can differ (Kerlin, 2006). This can give rise to differences not only in regional development, but also in the bodies of knowledge that receive recognition and institutional legitimacy (Dart, 2004). Peattie and Morley (2008) also warn that the nature, role and traditions informing the development of social enterprise are different in the United States and UK.

We seek to go further by highlighting four locations where social enterprise thinking was initiated and then spread successfully to other regions (Bangladesh, Northern England, Northern Italy and Washington DC). We use well-publicised descriptions of social enterprise to illustrate differences in approach and then critique these using three approaches to social enterprise theory. Firstly, we deploy social enterprise theory based on a spectrum of options that give varying emphasis to social mission and enterprise activity. The idea of a spectrum, however, is limited by the way it obscures not only public sector involvement in social enterprise creation but also the concept of sustainable development.

To address this, we turn to cross-sector models that frame social enterprises as capacity building organisations which partner (or integrate) state, private or voluntary sector partners to benefit society. In this case, theory emphasises the ability to build social capital and bridge ideological differences between the operational models of public, private and third sector organisations. However, we also critique this 'three-sector' model on the basis that it confuses *transitioning* activities (the adoption of social enterprise narratives and practices by public, private and voluntary sector organisations to meet their needs) with *emergent* activities that transform mutual and co-operative principles into more local, integrated, sustainable models of production and consumption (Westall, 2001; Connelly, 2007; Ehnert et al., 2013; Baudhardt, 2014).

Lastly, we briefly discuss the view that social enterprise is an activity rather than an organisation. In this guise, social enterprises are reconceptualised as the products of social entrepreneurship. The chapter closes by contextualising these different perspectives and examining whether there are any *defining* characteristics.

The origins of the language of social enterprise

The terms *social enterprise* and *social entrepreneurship* have various historical points of reference. Banks (1972) applied the term 'social entrepreneur' to Robert Owen, widely credited as the philanthropist who pioneered co-operative communities in the 1820s. In the US, Etzioni (1973) described the space for social entrepreneurship as a 'third alternative' between state and marketplace with the power to reform society. Etzioni focuses on the US and Soviet economies, suggesting a movement in public and private management towards a third system that blends both state and private management concepts. He describes a reduced state economy and the rise of alternative business models working in sectors servicing what he calls '*domestic missions*'. These are not as attractive to the private entrepreneur, as the profit motive is not as great as in the market (Etzioni, 1973: 315). Therefore, he argues that an alternative business model draws more on entrepreneurship than a public sector ethos.

We found the term 'social enterprise' first used in Dholakia and Dholakia (1975) to distinguish marketing activities in state and co-operative enterprises from private sector approaches. Westall (2001) claims that another influence was the community business movement who established a magazine called *New Sector* in 1979 to advance social democracy as the preferred alternative to the neo-liberal doctrine adopted by Margaret Thatcher (in the UK) and Ronald Reagan (in the USA).

The two terms gained salience in the UK via different international routes. *Social entrepreneurship* was popularised at **Ashoka** in the USA by Bill Drayton. Throughout the 1980s and 1990s it became associated with international development and fair trade (Grenier, 2006) before appearing, in a 1995 article published by *The Independent*, to describe individuals who founded the UK social entrepreneurial movement (Mawson, 2008). Although Harvard University in the USA used the term 'social enterprise' for its Social Enterprise Initiative after 1993, its approach followed the philanthropic model of commerce rather than the democratic orientation of co-operatives and non-profits highlighted in the **EMES** study (Defourny, 2001). In 1997 the School for Social

Entrepreneurs was established, followed quickly by the Community Action Network in 1998 and UnLtd in 2000. UK scholarship received a boost in 2004 when the Skoll Foundation invested in the Skoll Centre for Social Entrepreneurship at Oxford University.

The terms *social enterprise* and *social business*, on the other hand, started outside the US in three distinct places. Firstly, in the UK, the term social enterprise was used from 1978 onwards at Beechwood College (Leeds, Yorkshire) to describe worker co-operatives that were learning social auditing (Ridley-Duff and Southcombe, 2012). Spreckley (1981) published a definition of social enterprise in *Social Audit: A Management Tool for Co-operative Working* and worked to build education programmes with Jim Brown (1981 to 1984). At around the same time in 1979, co-operative movement activists in the Bologna region of Italy persuaded their local authority to support 'social co-operatives' (Restakis, 2010). Such was their success that national legislation was passed in 1991 and they came to be regarded as social enterprises (Savio and Righetti, 1993). According to Spear (2008) this influenced the formation of the EMES Research Network – the group that partnered **CECOP** (a European federation of 'worker co-operatives, and social and participative enterprises') to produce one of the earliest volumes of scholarly works on social enterprise (Borzaga and Defourny, 2001). Thirdly, between 1976 and 1979, Muhammad Yunus piloted a mutual micro-finance organisation to fund small-scale production in Bangladesh. The initial project was incubated at Jobra then extended to the Tangail district, before becoming an independent bank in 1983 (Grameen Research Inc., 2012). Yunus (2007) defined two types of *social business* and went on to earn a Nobel Prize jointly with the Grameen Foundation.

Within the UK, the term 'social enterprise' initially gained its strongest foothold within the co-operative movement and community regeneration sector (Teasdale, 2012; Ridley-Duff and Southcombe, 2012). By late 1997, a coalition of co-operatives and co-operative development agencies had formed Social Enterprise London (see Case 2.1). As regional links developed, a national body – the **Social Enterprise Coalition** (**SEC**) – was created to lobby for co-operatives, social firms, trading charities, community and employee-owned enterprises. Academically, the earliest UK research study embracing social enterprise is Amin et al. (1999). They studied regeneration, neighbourhood renewal and the rebuilding of marginalised communities through government initiatives such as the Phoenix Fund and National Strategy for Neighbourhood Renewal.

Case 2.1

Social Enterprise London: a founder's story

In 1997, discussions started among London co-operatives and their development agencies (CDAs) on creating a new London-wide support agency. We had several discussions in general meetings at Computercraft Ltd, then Phil Cole and I attended the meetings that established the new agency in early 1998. All but one of the founding subscribers had direct links to the co-operative movement. My recollection was that we discussed this as a rebranding exercise. It was by no means clear that we would use the term 'social enterprise' and we discussed various alternatives. I recollect Malcolm Corbett (from the worker co-operative Poptel) acting as chair. He was aware of developments in Europe through his discussions with Pauline Green, an MEP involved in international co-operative development. Malcolm had sway, so we were persuaded. In 2002, the Social Enterprise Coalition was formed by Helen Barber (of Co-operatives UK) and John Goodman (a consultant with links to Employee Ownership Solutions Ltd). The registered office was the Co-operative Union in Manchester. Jonathan Bland, CEO at Social Enterprise London, moved to the Social Enterprise Coalition, but not before establishing a degree programme at the University of East London, and securing funding for an academic journal.

Source: based on correspondence with Rory Ridley-Duff.

At the end of the 1990s, the Social Exclusion Unit was formed by Tony Blair's **New Labour** government. This body produced a strategy for 'neighbourhood renewal' in which 'social enterprise' was used to describe community businesses and trading charities oriented towards the needs of socially excluded groups (Westall, 2001). As time passed, and particularly after a UK government consultation involving charities and voluntary groups, the co-operative origins of the social enterprise movement in the UK became obscured by a strengthening (US-dominated) discourse on 'earned income' and 'innovation' in charities and public services (Ridley-Duff and Southcombe, 2012; Teasdale, 2012).

In summary, the origins of the language, and the meanings assigned by its advocates, are influenced by experiences in different parts of the third sector as well as

Table 2.1   Framing the boundaries of the social enterprise debate

EU-style social enterprise 'socialised enterprise'	US-style social entrepreneurship 'social purpose enterprise'
• Collective action	• Individual action
• Labour movement or government responses to social issues	• Entrepreneurial (market) responses to social issues
• Incremental building of social capital and assets	• Fast effective achievement of social outcomes
• Solidarity and mutuality	• Champions and change agents
• Accommodation of stakeholders	• Adherence to a 'vision'
• Democracy (bottom-up governance)	• Philanthropy (top-down governance)
• Social economy	• Any sector

public and private sector initiatives to develop approaches to social enterprise. One way of drawing boundaries around the definitional debate is to outline the foci of EU and US traditions. While cautioning against stereotypes, Table 2.1 summarises the dominant narratives at the boundaries of the definitional debate and links them to concepts developed by Ridley-Duff and Southcombe (2012) that distinguish 'socialised enterprises' and 'social purpose enterprises'.

US-style 'social purpose enterprises' have strong links with philanthropy, whereby money raised from wealthy individuals (and increasingly market institutions) or government-backed finance supports non-profit organisations that act in the *public interest* (Dees, 1998). Its individual and philanthropic character is evident in definitional work at Stanford Institute:

> The social entrepreneur's value proposition targets an underserved, neglected, or highly disadvantaged population that lacks the financial means or political clout to achieve the transformative benefit on its own. (Martin and Osberg, 2007: 35)

The emphasis is on solutions *brought to* the poor by an individual or enterprise designed to fulfil a *social purpose*. There is a departure from philanthropy, however, in attempts to design systems that enable philanthropists to recycle their social investments again and again. This requires **social investment** institutions that enable investors to recover any loans/equity invested, and which can provide metrics to decide on which proposals will create the most social impact.

EU-style 'socialised enterprises' draw more on traditions of collective voluntary action, self-help and co-operative principles derived from secular and Christian socialist traditions (Amin et al., 2002). The EU model emphasises solidarity between stakeholders and governance systems that enable workforce members and service users to participate in decisions about the design and delivery of goods and services (Moreau and Mertens, 2013). This 'socialised enterprise' approach is linked more directly to the long-term goal of building a solidarity economy and departs in significant ways from arguments for US-style entrepreneurial action (Lund, 2011).

Westall captures the two dominant approaches when she comments:

> This history of 'third sector' organisations … is in some ways the history of two alternative strands – that of self-help (mutuals and cooperatives) and of charities where the paradigm, at least historically, is more related to helping others unable to help themselves. (Westall, 2001: 24)

This dual history persists but we will argue that a simple dualism is no longer adequate. Westall proceeds to argue that social entrepreneurs seek to 'break free of historical baggage' so a distinction based on third sector traditions is 'no longer tenable'. Having set out where boundaries have been drawn, we now explore different definitions of social enterprise. We start with descriptions that have attracted attention in policy debates to make explicit how they seek to reconcile 'social purpose' and 'socialised' approaches to organising.

Descriptions of social enterprise

The four examples in this section have been selected to illustrate different perspectives. In all cases, social enterprises are seen as socially driven organisations with social and/or environmental objectives combined with a strategy for economic sustainability. By comparing the four definitions, different emphases become apparent. We discuss definitions that have appeared in key publications:

The Social Audit Toolkit – for worker and community co-operatives (Freer Spreckley)

The Emergence of Social Enterprise (Borzaga and Defourny, EMES European Research Network)

A Social Enterprise Typology (Kim Alter, for the Inter-American Bank)

Creating a World Without Poverty (Muhammad Yunus, at the Grameen Foundation)

The first definition appears in the 1981 edition of Spreckley's *Social Audit Toolkit*. It is interesting for its adoption of language familiar to both the co-operative movement and the field of sustainable development (Definition 1), a reflection of Spreckley's own participation in the development of fair trade networks. Spreckley's definition embraces a triple bottom line (personal, environmental and social benefits). These are organised through a worker or community co-operative that subverts the dominant power relationship between capital and labour. The practical issue here is whether the representatives of capital (investors and funders) or those working and benefiting from the enterprise (labour and beneficiaries) have the final say in running the organisation and deciding what to do with financial surpluses and losses. This arrangement is unproblematic if individual members have committed their own money. Issues arise as soon as members go outside the organisation to raise money. In Spreckley's definition, there is a preference that capital, rather than labour, is paid a fixed return. This is, theoretically speaking, the reverse of the employer paying fixed wages to employees then acquiring all residual profits. Instead, capital is hired at a fixed rate of interest (or fixed dividend) and any residual profits go to the workforce or community.

Definition 1: Social enterprise as a co-operative (published 1981)

An enterprise that is owned by those who work in it and/or reside in a given locality, is governed by registered social as well as commercial aims and objectives and run cooperatively may be termed a social enterprise. Traditionally, 'capital hires labour' with the overriding emphasis on making a 'profit' over and above any benefit either to the business itself or the workforce. Contrasted to this is the social enterprise where 'labour hires capital' with the emphasis on personal, environmental and social benefit. (Spreckley, 1981: 8)

This definition gives no recognition to social enterprises that are registered as charities and follow the trustee–beneficiary model, but it does embrace membership associations that use a mix of paid and unpaid labour to pursue social goals. The definition also takes 'community' to mean people in a local area as opposed to a community of interest. While a local focus can be a characteristic of social enterprise, social enterprise does not have to be locally based or small in scale. Lastly, Spreckley's definition gives no recognition to partnerships and multi-stakeholder enterprises involving state and private organisations.

In 1996, a study by the EMES European Research Network set out a series of social and economic characteristics used to select organisations for a pan-European study of social enterprise (Definition 2). The EMES definition has some of the hallmarks of Spreckley's definition, but is less prescriptive about employee ownership and control. Autonomy and entrepreneurial risk-taking, combined with social and economic participation, are hallmarks of the EMES definition, but the door is left open for different stakeholders (users, customers, funders, suppliers and employees) to participate in the enterprise. Compared to Definitions 3 and 4, more emphasis is placed on democratic control over production and delivery of goods and services. There is no intrinsic assumption that the organisations be 'businesses' or that they should adopt 'business practices'. As a definition, the EMES project researchers and participants found that it was useful, but also that it represented an *ideal*. In practice, organisations fulfilled some of these criteria, but rarely all.

Definition 2: EMES (first published 2001)

Social dimensions

> An explicit aim to benefit the community.
>
> An initiative launched by a group of citizens.
>
> Decision-making power not based on capital ownership.
>
> A participatory nature, which involves the persons affected by the activity.
>
> Limited profit distribution.

Economic dimensions

> A continuous activity producing goods and/or selling services.
>
> A high degree of autonomy.
>
> A significant level of economic risk.
>
> A minimum amount of paid work (i.e. at least some labour is compensated).

Source: Defourny, 2001: 16–18.

While the EMES definition remains influential in Europe (where it was adopted for a period by the EU Commission in 2011–12), it did not influence the UK government's consultation (DTI, 2002) on **community interest companies (CICs)**. This consultation marked a departure in the UK from the co-operative/social economy traditions that Spreckley had used as the basis for social enterprise education, and marked a shift that gave social *entrepreneurs* much greater freedom to determine organisation structures and levels of participation. The report setting out the intentions of the UK government (DTI, 2003) established government (rather than the enterprise's own stakeholders) as the authority with the strongest rights of intervention. The claimed 'looser' approach to definition drew a great many people and organisations into the debate. Social entrepreneurs, even those operating on a self-employed basis, could gain credibility for their social ventures. Similarly, trading charities and voluntary organisations (whether formally democratic or not in their decision-making and appointment processes) as well as a broad range of co-operatives (whether commonly owned or owned by their staff) could be accommodated in a national strategy. After this broadening of the definitional debate, it is unsurprising that Peattie and Morley (2008) had difficulty establishing social enterprise's distinguishing characteristics, and eventually had to settle for a theory based on *trading organisations* that prioritise *social aims*.

With hindsight, it is easier to see this as a discursive shift away from 'socialised enterprises' in favour of 'social purpose enterprises' (Figure 2.1).

Teasdale (2012) tracks changes in social enterprise discourse over the period 1999 to 2011, and frames the period 2002–6 as one in which there was a transition away from a co-operative and community enterprise heritage towards one based on social business and earned income for non-profits. This change can be explained by the

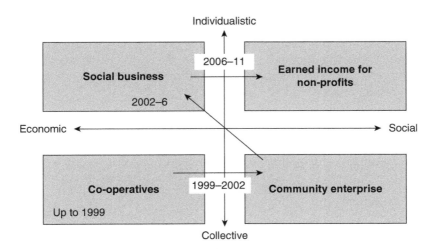

Figure 2.1 An interpretation of S. Teasdale (2012) 'What's in a name? Making sense of social enterprise discourse'

growing influence of US-led social entrepreneurship. A good example of this changing discourse appears in Birch and Whittam's (2008) paper through the advancement of the view that social enterprise policy should seek to align itself with US conceptions of social entrepreneurship.

> This conceptualization makes social enterprise distinct from the common definition used by the Department of Trade and Industry (DTI), which covers an array of different organizations with distinct and sometimes disparate objectives (e.g. charity and workers cooperative) … Therefore, it is more useful to argue that social enterprise concerns the pursuit of particular activities rather than representing certain social forms (e.g. cooperatives, democratically run organizations) with the aim of producing collective benefits … (Birch and Whittam, 2008: 439–44)

The switch to 'activities' is useful for the purposes of public administration: social enterprises can be started to meet public policy goals (and shut down if they do not). A possible incentive for framing social enterprise *as an activity* is that it suits those who want to use social enterprises for 'project management'. This *instrumental* view (that social enterprise trading entities can be set up to achieve public, charitable and CSR objectives) requires an *anti*-democratic argument regarding ownership and control. If social enterprises are constituted as democratic enterprises, their 'parent' organisations will not be able to dissolve them if they achieve social and economic viability and (democratically) change their social or economic priorities. To be controllable, social enterprises must *not* be democratically constituted or be able to make decisions autonomously. This brings back into focus how the 'social' is theorised in definitions of social enterprise.

Nevertheless, this view of social enterprise as a policy instrument under the control of visionary social entrepreneurs continued to gain momentum as a policy option for governments (Somers, 2013). Alter (2007) reviewed a wide range of definitions in the preparation of her *Social Enterprise Typology*. While her definition (Definition 3) is not necessarily representative of all US thinking (see www.se-alliance.org), it does reflect two key aspects of strengthening US influence. Firstly, it reflects the more business-like rhetoric adopted for the US non-profit sector through direct reference to the private sector's 'discipline, innovation and determination'.

Definition 3: Virtue Ventures (first published 2003)

> A social enterprise is any business venture created for a social purpose – mitigating/ reducing a social problem or a market failure – and to generate social value while operating with the financial discipline, innovation and determination of a private sector business. (Alter, 2007: 18)

In common with the **DTI**'s definition in the UK, there is no reference to ownership or democratic control as defining characteristics. As a result, there is scope for the inclusion of US-style entrepreneurial solutions as well as the preference for collective solutions in the EMES approach. One aspect of this definition, absent from all others, is the *direct* focus on solving or mitigating a social problem or a market failure (although this is often taken to be implicit). Alter's definition serves well for ventures like Toms Shoes, a US for-profit social enterprise that was set up by Blake Mycoskie to sell shoes across the developed world to fund shoes for children in the developing world, largely driven by seeing them expelled from school as many had no shoes. This started in Latin America and now serves communities across the world. To find out more watch: http://vimeo.com/2567675.

Alter's model could also describe entrepreneurial 'non-profits' in the USA and elsewhere that run hospitals, schools, colleges, universities and social services. For example, in developing economies (where the state is weak) this definition serves to cover those organisations that act as a proxy for the state by providing services that would attract public funding in the EU. Nevertheless, Alter's definition gives less explicit recognition to employee-owned businesses and co-operatives whose social goal is the creation of a solidarity economy through shared ownership of supply chains to distribute wealth and power more fairly. Instead, her definition highlights rapid responses to social exclusion that is attuned to the rhetoric of 'market solutions' rather than 'mutual relations'.

However, there is something else interesting about Alter's definition. It is the only one that explicitly mentions *innovation*. As Perrini argues:

> Social enterprise entails innovations designed to explicitly improve societal well-being, housed within entrepreneurial organizations, which initiate, guide or combine change in society. (2006: 24)

The focus on innovation is strongest in the US literature where the value propositions of social entrepreneurs are taken as the drivers of social change (Light, 2008; Friedman and Desivilya, 2010). This focus on innovation – particularly in the use of private sector financial instruments within organisations that deploy philanthropic or co-operative characteristics – is also a feature of writings on *social business* (Yunus, 2007).

Yunus sets out two 'types' that have the same goal – the elimination of poverty – but do so using different constitutional arrangements. In a tangible sense, Yunus's first type adopts the characteristics of a 'social purpose business' in which there are locks on both assets and profits. While this follows *some* of the norms of charitable/non-profit enterprises, Yunus argues vigorously for equity instruments and arrangements that enable investors to recover their investment. To this end, he sees a need for a social investment industry to make capital available and establish the metrics that social investors need to make judgements about which investments produce the greatest social returns (Nicholls, 2010).

Definition 4: Two types of social business (published 2007)

[The first type] of social business has owners who are entitled to recoup their investments ... owned by one or more individuals, either as a sole proprietorship or a partnership, or by one or more investors who pool their money ... [or] by government or a charity ... any profit it earns does not go to those who invest in it. Thus [the first type of] social business might be defined as a non-loss, non-dividend business ... the surplus generated is reinvested in the business. [The second type] operates in a rather different fashion: profit-maximising businesses that are owned by the poor or disadvantaged [where] the social benefit is derived from the fact that the dividends and equity growth [will] reduce their poverty or even escape it altogether. With the second type ... goods or services might or might not create a social benefit. The social benefit created ... comes from its ownership. Because the ownership of shares [belongs to] the disadvantaged ... any financial benefit generated ... will go to help those in need. (Yunus, 2007: 26)

Yunus discussed the example of the Rochdale Pioneers in relation to the 'second type' of social business. This clearly adopts the characteristics of 'socialised enterprise' by adopting member ownership principles and mutuality as an organising principle. But while drawn to co-operative principles, Yunus argues that membership should be contingent on a low income so that private sector investment instruments gradually lift people on low incomes out of poverty. Yunus's two types, therefore, differ in subtle ways from both Definition 1 and 3 (by retaining an option for capital to hire labour within an enterprise that operates for a social purpose) and from Definition 2 by countenancing a profit-maximising co-operative model that lifts low income groups out of poverty.

To explore this further with the goal of producing something more fine grained in its analysis than 'trading for a social purpose' (Peattie and Morley, 2008), we crafted a

Table 2.2   Distinguishing characteristics of socialised, socially responsible and social purpose enterprises

Socialised Enterprises (CMEs)

Legal forms: co-operative, mutual, employee-owned business, other social/solidarity economy legal forms

Distinguishing Characteristics	Socialisation Score	Social Purpose Score
• Is (co-)owned by one or more of its primary stakeholders (workforce, customers and/or service users)	129	38
• Offers membership to primary stakeholders (workforce, customers, service users)	117	43
• Ensures that most (or all) of its assets are used for member, community and public benefit	139	70
• Governed by one or more of its primary stakeholders (workforce, customers, service users)	121	56
• Continuously encourages co-operative working/networking	112	76

Distinguishing Characteristics	Socialisation Score	Social Purpose Score
• Allows members to equitably contribute to, and receive distributions of, capital/surpluses	82	53
• Provides technical and political education/training to its members (staff, users and elected representatives)	95	69

Social/Responsible Businesses (SRBs)

Social welfare corporations (Asia), social purpose/community enterprises (EU), B-corporations/low-profit corporations (US)

Distinguishing Characteristics	Socialisation Score	Social Purpose Score
• Is not owned or controlled by a private company or public authority	87	78
• States (and reviews) its ethical values and principles	76	70
• Provides at least some paid employment	60	67
• Provides evidence that it makes a positive social impact and/or runs for community benefit	69	83
• Educates the public about the benefits of its business model	83	106
• Receives most of its income from trading activities, not grants or donations	71	95

Social Purpose Enterprises (CTAs)

Foundations, trading charities, NGOs, non-profit associations/companies

Distinguishing Characteristics	Socialisation Score	Social Purpose Score
• Continuously produces and/or sells goods and services to improve social/environmental well-being	67	98
• Reinvests most of its surplus/profit back into its social/environmental purpose	71	104
• Makes clear statements about its social and/or environmental purposes/objectives	59	97
• Balances member (stakeholder) needs with sustainable development goals	44	88
• Discourages a 'for-profit' mind-set by limiting the distribution of surpluses/profits for private benefit	52	114
• Based on the actions of citizens voluntarily working together to meet a need	51	115
• Has members/founders who bear a significant level of economic risk during venture/project creation.	56	121

Key: Socialised enterprises = socialisation score at least 25 more than social purpose score

Social/responsible businesses = socialisation score within 25 points of social purpose score

Social purpose enterprises = social purpose score at least 25 points more than socialisation score

composite list of characteristics from five 'theories in use' and sent it to 550 social enterprise lecturers, researchers and post-graduate students. We provided them with working definitions of 'socialisation' and 'social purpose' based on previous work

(Ridley-Duff and Southcombe, 2012) and asked for them to be ranked for their contribution to each. If a characteristic contributed to both, we suggested placing it between those that supported 'socialisation' over 'social purpose' (or vice versa).

We received 136 responses (24.7 per cent) and evaluated the results by awarding a score of +2 or +1 based on the strength of the ranking, or awarded 0 if the ranking indicated a contribution to both. From this, we came to a conclusion that there are three broad approaches to social enterprise, each linked to different forms of incorporation, each supporting a cluster of social enterprise characteristics (see Table 2.2).

Class exercise: Social enterprise characteristics

Do you want to input into the next edition of this book? The links to a Social Enterprise Definition survey below (in partnership with the FairShares Association and Social Enterprise Europe) are based on the same statements as our previous survey. For the next edition, we are asking respondents to rank characteristics in *order of importance*. Results are updated in real time and can be accessed in a classroom using the following links:

The survey: www.quicksurveys.com/s/Co28D (you can get students to fill it out in class).

The results: http://tolu.na/1wlOLAh (you can explore the results in real time).

1 Which characteristics do you rank as most important?
2 Which characteristics generate the highest level of consensus?

These results lead us to question the 'lowest common denominator' approach to social enterprise definition (Peattie and Morley, 2008; Doherty et al., 2014) in favour of approaches that deepen our understanding of the cluster of characteristics that define each approach. For example, a co-operative enterprise can concurrently adopt the characteristics of a socially responsible business (e.g. the John Lewis Partnership), or a social purpose enterprise can concurrently adopt the characteristics of a mutual (e.g. a credit union, community benefit society or social co-operative).

In summary, we believe it is fruitful to distinguish (and judge) social enterprises based on the scope and depth of their achievements in three areas: a) *democratic ownership and governance*; b) *ethical and sustainable trading practices*; c) *social purpose and impact*. All achievements are worthy of recognition as contributions to social value creation, even if confined to just one of these areas. However, it is achievements across all three domains that are likely to galvanise the most interest and which activists are most likely to want to replicate.

In the rest of this text, we will frame our discussion in terms of the three broad approaches identified by Social Enterprise Europe Ltd as important to the advancement of social enterprise globally (Ridley-Duff and Southcombe, 2014):

1. *Co-operative and mutual enterprises* (CMEs) which are defined by their commitment to (or innovative systems for advancing) democratic/inclusive ownership and governance. Some examples: John Lewis (UK), Fonterra Dairy Co-op (New Zealand), Barcelona FC (Spain), Desjardin Group (Canada), Co-op Kobe (Japan), WinCo (USA).
2. *Socially responsible businesses* (SRBs) which are defined by their commitment to (or innovative technologies for) ethical trading and sustainable development. Some examples: Ben and Jerry's (USA), Grameen Bank (Bangladesh), Agua (Kenya), SEMCO (Argentina), The Big Issue (UK).
3. *Charitable trading activities* (CTAs) which are defined by their commitment to specified social purposes that positively impact on human or environmental well-being. Some examples: Oxfam (International), UNICEF (International), Barnardo's (UK, Ireland, Australia, New Zealand), World Wild Life Fund (International), the Eden Project (UK).

Class exercise: Defining social enterprise

Materials to support this exercise can be found on the companion website at: www.sagepub.co.uk/ridleyduff. Divide the class into groups of four and give one social enterprise definition to each person in each group. Members should not show their definitions to other group members.

Scenario

You are attending a directors' development meeting to define your approach to social enterprise. Next week, you will brief a network of company owners and local government officers on the potential of social enterprise in economic regeneration and public service delivery. A consultant has researched four definitions but has not been invited to the meeting. Following the consultant's advice, each director has been given one definition to present at this meeting.

- In groups (no more than four people per group):

  Take 5–10 minutes to read the definition and prepare for a 30 minute meeting.

(Continued)

(Continued)

Each group member has up to 5 minutes to read their definition and outline a critique.

After hearing all four definitions, agree *your own* definition for this network (10 minutes).

- As a class:

Ask each group to read out/write on a whiteboard its final definition.

Critically debate issues that may arise if you propose this social enterprise approach to:

(a) a panel of venture philanthropists (investing in charities and non-profit organisations)
(b) a panel of business angels (e.g. similar to *Dragons' Den*) wishing to make ethical investments.

Suggestion: you might adapt this exercise by using definitions from local social enterprise support agencies, or national or international bodies that support local development in your area.

Approaches to researching social enterprise

Each of the four definitions we have discussed draw out a different aspect of what it is to be 'social' and also to be an 'enterprise'. As Bull (2006) found, social enterprises position themselves at all points along a continuum (see Figure 2.2). They adopt a variety of arguments to justify their emphasis, and they show varying levels of conviction to particular positions (the larger crosses and the smiley faces indicate greater conviction regarding their position on the spectrum).

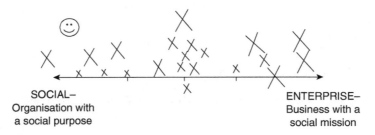

SOCIAL–
Organisation with
a social purpose

ENTERPRISE–
Business with a
social mission

Figure 2.2   Participants positioning themselves on a continuum

'Social purpose' can be *external* (in terms of the products and services offered) or *internal* (transforming social relationships to distribute power and wealth more equitably). 'Economic purpose' is similarly complex, spanning debates about competitiveness in markets, **social inclusion**, individual empowerment and modernisation of the state (Westall, 2001). In the rest of this chapter, we examine three perspectives that researchers adopt when they investigate the contexts and practices of social enterprises: firstly, we consider social enterprise as a spectrum of options; then, we examine the argument that social enterprise involves complex choices about how to combine systems of exchange to maximise social value creation, and; lastly, we further explore Westall's view that there is a 'fourth space' in which social entrepreneurs seek to transcend the limitations of 'old' philanthropy and mutuality by forging solidarity enterprises with multiple owners and/or multi-stakeholder governance.

Social enterprise as a spectrum of options

Social enterprises are often described as *double bottom line* organisations that practise both altruism and commercial discipline. Nyssens (2006) describes this as a process of *hybridisation* that challenges traditional models of organising and produces a cross-fertilisation of ideas. A model by Dees (1998) has been influential in promoting understanding of social enterprise in the non-profit sectors of the USA and the UK where organisations have experienced falls in charitable giving and government grants. Useful as this theory is for stimulating new conversations in charity, voluntary and community organisations, it does not address changes taking place in co-operative, fair trade and private business practices. For example, organisations like Divine Chocolate, Traidcraft, Ben and Jerry's (US), the Mondragon Co-operative Corporation (Spain) and Co-operative Group (UK) have operated in commercial markets from the outset, and routinely made *triple* bottom line commitments that combine commercial success with the protection of people and the environment.

Kim Alter (2007) built on Dees' model to propose a *sustainability spectrum* that describes six gradations between 'traditional non-profit' and 'traditional for-profit' enterprises. She places social enterprise on the 'social sustainability' side, more aligned with traditional non-profit than for-profit enterprises. But given alternative heritages based on co-operation and fair trade (see Chapter 1), we think it is more useful to adapt Alter's model (see Figure 2.3).

Non-profit CTAs as well as commonly owned CMEs often take the form of a CLG that does not issue share capital. The assumption is that this will help to retain surpluses for reinvestment and be attractive to philanthropic capital (see Case 2.2). 'More-than-profit' forms of social enterprise (Ridley-Duff, 2008b) tend to be constituted as a **CLS** (company limited by shares), partnership or co-operative society because social value creation is linked to the enterprise's capacity to distribute surpluses equitably among a large number of stakeholders. Worker and consumer co-operatives as well as employee-owned

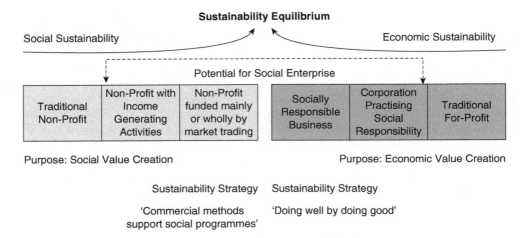

Figure 2.3   The social enterprise sustainability equilibrium (Spectrum 1)

Source: Alter, K. (2007) "Social Enterprise Typology", http://virtueventures.com/setypology/index.php?id=HYBRID_
SPECTRUM&lm=1 accessed 1/9/2008. Kim Alter acknowledges the prior influence of Nicola Etchart and Lee Davis,
Profits for Nonprofits, NESst, 1999.

enterprises may issue share capital to members of staff and consumers (see Case 2.3).
In international fair trade companies, such as Divine Chocolate and Twin Trading, the
form is adapted to distribute surpluses and control rights to enterprise members to benefit each contributor to a **supply chain** (Doherty, 2011).

In practice, we find it counter-productive to debate whether CTAs, CMEs or SRBs have
a greater claim to social enterprise (see Cases 2.2 and 2.3) because the more important
question is the extent to which each advances democracy, ethics and social impact in
enterprise activity. All create social value in different ways. Nevertheless, the granularity
of Alter's model makes explicit some of the tension points between advocates of different
models. For example, both academic studies and practitioner accreditation schemes have
used a threshold of 50 per cent income from *trading* as a benchmark for distinguishing
between charities that use trading to supplement income and enterprises that trade to
pursue a social purpose (Ridley-Duff and Southcombe, 2012; Teasdale et al., 2013).

Case 2.2

Charitable trading or responsible business?

Furniture Resource Centre Group is made up of three organisations. The Furniture
Resource Centre (FRC) was founded in 1988 as a CLG to enable people on low
income to buy furniture. They 'design, manufacture, recycle, refurbish, sell and
deliver furniture to people in need and so create work for the jobless and offer

long-term unemployed people salaried training'. In six years, the FRC switched from being a small local charity (£300,000 turnover with 15 staff) to a company generating £5 million with over 120 employees. Ninety per cent of income is generated through sales of products and services. Grants are only used for particular pieces of work such as building refurbishment. Liam Black, then CEO, stated that 'our financial independence from statutory and charitable trust funding has liberated us. We are masters of our own destiny and we choose where we go and how we do it. Free of funders' handcuffs and the risk averse conservatism of regeneration quangos, we are free to experiment and innovate.'

Liam Black won the 'Social Entrepreneur of the Year' award in 2003. He left FRC in 2004 to manage Fifteen, Jamie Oliver's chain of restaurants. In 2008, after successfully establishing franchises in Holland and Australia, he left to pursue new projects.

This case illustrates the blurred line between CTAs and SRBs.

Source: based on Westall (2001) and subsequent press reports.

Smallbone and Lyon (2005) have criticised restrictive definitions. They argue that early stage social enterprises, or charities increasing their trading activities, often have less than 50 per cent trading income. Should this be used to exclude them from being defined as social enterprises in sector surveys? Should they be refused social enterprise support? However, such an argument ignores that *trading* activity alone does not define a social enterprise (as many community and voluntary organisations are trading organisations, yet fail to exhibit other characteristics linked to social enterprise). Liam Black (see Case 2.2) underlines the *mind-set* that trading is a *means* of achieving autonomy, so that an organisation can choose its own destiny, become more entrepreneurial, and increase its social innovation and impact. This constitutes a counter-argument to Smallbone and Lyon (2005) on the basis that social enterprises use trading relationships to transform (social) power and change patterns of (economic) wealth distribution. If an organisation trades in such a way that it reproduces dependency, or reinforces existing (market) power relations, it has a more tenuous claim to being a social enterprise (Meyer, 2013).

Case 2.3

Socially responsible business or co-operative enterprise?

Sunderland Care Home Associates (SCHA) was formed as a successor to the Little Women co-operative in 1994 and was initially constituted as a CLG (common ownership rules) with a £1 share for each of its 20 members. In 1998, 'for both tax and

(Continued)

(Continued)

philosophical reasons', the organisation voted to change to an employee-owned model based on a CLS. Initially, just over 50 per cent of shares were held in trust, with the remainder held by the original co-operative. After six share allocations, reflecting business performance and the availability of shares through an internal market, the employee trust held 56.7 per cent of the shares, 16.8 per cent were in employees' own names, and 26.5 per cent remained in the founding co-operative. By 2007, the organisation had a turnover in excess of £2 million and employed 223 staff, of which 85 per cent were women.

Margaret Elliot, the founder, felt that this arrangement would give employees a real, growing stake rather than just a £1 share and that this would 'increase their commitment and help to raise staff retention and the quality of the service we provide'. Staff turnover has been reduced to 3.5 per cent, a full 10 per cent below the industry average. The board consists of five elected employees, the founder and a tax/legal expert. General meetings are held bimonthly, and working parties are created to consider specific issues.

SCHA was rated 'Top Social Enterprise' at the 2006 Enterprising Solutions Awards and has now established Care and Share Associates (CASA) to oversee the replication of its business model to other regions. Margaret Elliot was awarded an OBE in the 2008 UK New Year Honours List.

Sources: Companies House; Fame company database; case study published by the Employee Ownership Association (www.employeeownership.co.uk); press reports

See the companion website at: www.sagepub.co.uk/ridleyduff for alternative North American, European and Asian cases in the field of social care.

Both Alter (2007) and Dees (1998) locate social enterprise as sitting on a spectrum between traditional for-profit and non-profit organisations without explicating their relationship to co-operatives and mutuals, or public sector reform. These omissions can be explained in part by Kerlin's (2006) analysis of the United States and Europe. She notes that the term 'social enterprise' means different things stemming from the national context and the influences driving development. She points out that *social economy* has been slow to gain recognition in the US, nor is there a strong public sector tradition in welfare provision and market intervention. The effect is to understate the influence of local and central government in creating an 'enabling environment' which influences the direction and nature of social enterprise development (Somers, 2013). Somers argues that people in the public sector can use social entrepreneurship to act as a *modernising agent* (Spectrum 2), giving rise to a spectrum of options based on the role that the state plays in initiating, supporting and withdrawing from the development of industry sectors in a market economy.

By way of example, the state is actively involved in creating an environment in which welfare services can be delivered through quasi-markets in social and health care (Case 2.4). This is a shift away from the *command and control model* of public service delivery towards a *network model* involving a range of public and third sector organisations, including infrastructure bodies stimulating regional development. Ironically, she argues that this constitutes an expansion, not a contraction, of the state, and constitutes a route to 'Third Way' socialism. Curtis (2008) characterises this as *state-sponsored social enterprise* and cautions that it may undermine the entrepreneurial spirit and know-how needed to ensure the sustainability of the social economy. Is this autonomy from the state? Is this innovation? Nevertheless, both Somers and Curtis recognise that social enterprise cannot be fully theorised without including state and public sector activity. Case 2.4 illustrates how this can concretely affect the mind-set of former public servants.

Case 2.4

Entreprenurses CIC

Established by David Dawes, a former CEO and commissioner in the NHS, and public servant at the Department of Health, Entreprenurses uses the new community interest company legislation in the United Kingdom as a vehicle for the 'right to request' a social enterprise.

> Entreprenurses is a community interest company which is a type of social enterprise. What that means is we want to change the world and we want to do it in a business-like and entrepreneurial way. Specifically we:

- support the growth and development of entrepreneurs (particularly social entrepreneurs and nurse entrepreneurs)
- develop the art and science of nurse entrepreneurship
- encourage the development of social enterprises in health and social care
- improve the delivery of healthcare.

What we want to do is help make the world a better place by improving some of it ourselves but mainly by helping other people improve their bit of the world themselves.

Source: based on www.entreprenurses.net/about/about_us.php (accessed 27 April 2015).
    See the companion website at: www.sagepub.co.uk/ridleyduff for alternative international cases from South America and Europe.

Finally, can there be hybridisation at the boundary of the public and private sectors? As Defourny (2001: 23) acknowledges, 'the [non-profit] literature is not able to embrace the whole reality of the social enterprise'. The realisation that some social enterprises are not ideologically hostile to declaring profits or sharing surpluses has prompted high-profile figures to challenge the sector to adopt a 'more-than-profit' orientation (Ridley-Duff, 2008b). Organisation structures and culture can play a significant role in the re-distribution of power and wealth, and can change stakeholders' engagement in decision-making (Grey, 2005). Secondly, there is the issue of how profits are used. CMEs have a track record of transforming patterns of ownership, power and wealth. Their products and services may be indistinguishable from those produced by others, and may be sold at market rates. This is, however, to miss the point. Trading is the *means* by which a different social mission is achieved (Gates, 1998; Brown, 2006). As Gates argues, a combination of investor, worker and consumer ownership can alter management practices:

> 'Inside' ownership improves performance both directly (by encouraging insider challenges to poorly conceived management decisions) and indirectly – by influencing managers who know that the firm's owners are now working amongst them. Similarly, by including a component of consumer ownership, the utility's managers (and their families) would live among shareholders who are also neighbors, schoolmates and teammates. Such a community-focused ownership stake could change the quality of business relationships. (1998: 13)

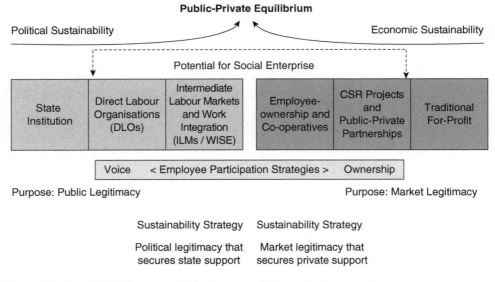

Figure 2.4   Public legitimacy and private support (Spectrum 3)

Large mainstream businesses, and not just those currently identified as part of the social enterprise sector, can lay some claim to effective stakeholder involvement, commitment to diversity, and practices that address social exclusion (see Case 2.5). How then should we theorise their contribution to social enterprise? Does this further compromise the concept of 'social enterprise'? Our view is that it does not. Rather, it invites a fuller consideration of a third axis that spans the public and private sector. As we discussed in Case 2.3 (Sunderland Care Home Associates), social enterprises can switch away from (rather than embrace) common ownership to pursue a social purpose and increase their social impact. For this reason, a third axis is needed that theorises how public and private sector support creates further opportunities for social enterprise (see Figure 2.4).

Case 2.5

Socially responsible business – Merck and the Mectizan drug project

Merck elected to develop and give away Mectizan, a drug to cure 'river blindness', a disease that infected over a million people in the Third World with parasitic worms that swarmed through body tissue and eventually into the eyes, causing painful blindness. A million customers is a good-sized market, except that these were customers who could not afford the product. Knowing that the project would not produce a large return on investment – if it produced one at all – the company nonetheless went forward with the hope that some government agencies or other third parties would purchase and distribute the product once available. No such luck, so Merck elected to establish a trust to give the drug away free to all who needed it ... at its own expense. When asked why the company had pursued the project despite the possibility of making a financial loss, senior executives said that they saw it as important to maintain the morale of their scientists.

Source: adapted from Collins and Porras (2000).

A three-dimensional, rather than two-dimensional, theory of social enterprise leads us into theories that frame social enterprise as a cross-sector phenomenon in which systems of economic exchange are combined to increase opportunities for social value creation.

Cross-sector models of social enterprise

In 1997, Leadbeater used a cross-sectoral model to theorise how social entrepreneurs acquire their skills and outlook (see Figure 2.5). Initially, when social enterprise theory was focused on a continuum between the voluntary and the private sector, Leadbeater's view of social entrepreneurship stood in contradiction to social enterprise theory. By acknowledging the potential for social enterprise in the public and private sectors, cross-sector models offer a way to reconcile social entrepreneurship and social enterprise theory.

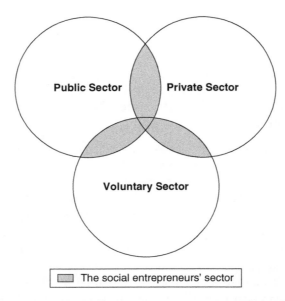

The social entrepreneurs' sector

Figure 2.5   Cross-sector social entrepreneurship that creates social capital

Source: Leadbeater (1997: 10), reproduced with permission of Demos (www.demos.co.uk)

In cross-sector models, social enterprise is seen as a way of bridging sectors by integrating the skills and abilities of statutory providers, private businesses and voluntary organisations. In short, social enterprise creates bridging *social capital* between economic sectors by encouraging dialogue about the mix of economic exchanges that will optimise the bottom lines sought (see the discussion of Polanyi in Part 1 – Introduction).

As Birch and Whittam argue, social entrepreneurship is a process that catalyses co-operation between parties who would normally avoid each other:

> Thus, in relation to social capital, the activity of social enterprise has two major functions in regional development. First is the binding of different groups together in a network,

both within specific places such as local communities and, more broadly, at the regional and national scale. Second is the linking of diverse and often disparate normative frameworks (e.g. mutualism and profit-seeking) and structures (e.g. social firms and private companies), which produces new insights and resources through inter-group learning. (2008: 443)

Seanor and Meaton (2008) argue that social enterprises can benefit from this ambiguity by managing the uncertainties in their identity and tapping into more streams of support and funding. Moreover, they can develop hybrid organisations that serve multiple interests. They also suggest that social enterprises (and not just social entrepreneurs) can be located at the crossover points between the three worlds of the state, private and voluntary/community sectors.

Cross-sector theories take a different position from Defourny (2001) and Pearce (2003). Instead of social enterprises occupying a space in the social economy between non-profit and for-profit businesses, they are regarded as types developing in all sectors and which may take many forms: charity trading, social firms, social responsibility projects, public–private partnerships, multi-stakeholder co-operatives, mutual societies and employee-owned businesses. Cross-sector theories, therefore, are better able to explain the wide variety of CMEs, SRBs and CTAs that can be observed empirically in the field of social enterprise. Figure 2.6 combines the three social enterprise spectra of Figures 2.3, 2.4 and 2.5 to clarify a triangle of activity within which social enterprises can expect to thrive.

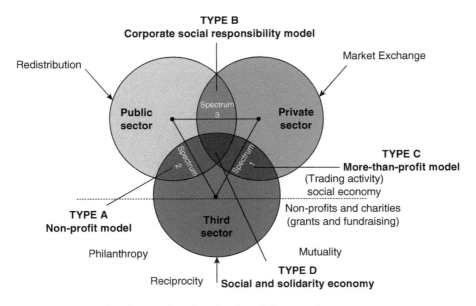

Figure 2.6 A composite theory: the triangle of social enterprise

The advantage of viewing social enterprise as a cross-sector phenomenon is that it helps with understanding the ambiguity, origins and ethos of social enterprise activity (Spear et al., 2007). It provides a mechanism for understanding diversity based on alliances and hybrid organisations that vary in the extent they embrace the values of other sectors. This theoretical perspective was used by us to map out the very different experiences, concerns and approaches to 'responsible management' that new entrants into the social enterprise sector will face (Ridley-Duff and Bull, 2015). A person engaging from the starting point of public service management will adopt different strategies from someone transforming an NGO, converting a private business to a co-operative enterprise, or a co-operative enterprise into an employee-owned business. The result is an updated typology (Table 2.3) that recognises the distinguishing characteristics listed in Table 2.2, but also an *ideal type* based on the multi-stakeholder governance and/or member ownership that seeks to transcend the limitations of single-stakeholder enterprises that deploy one mode of exchange.

Table 2.3   A social enterprise typology

Type A: Non-profit model	Responsible Management Assumptions
Emphasis on reciprocity and redistribution facilitated by voluntary and political action; in the boundary areas of the public and third sectors; shares a 'public interest' outlook and hostility to market logic based on private ownership and equity finance.	Social entrepreneurship as the creation of non-profit organisations that pursue CTAs using grants, donations and contracts with public authorities; structures to prevent profit and asset transfers to the private sector.
Type B: Corporate social responsibility model	
Emphasis on redistribution through new types of market exchange; in the overlap between the public and private sectors; often dismissive of voluntary sector approaches to economic development.	Social entrepreneurship as corporate social responsibility; support for fair trade; social firms and social businesses in private ownership; public–private partnerships.
Type C: More-than-profit model	
Emphasis on market exchanges that encourage reciprocity; in the boundary area between the third and private sectors; sceptical of government interventions that prevent reciprocity and market exchange; conscious of the state's role in oppressing minorities and opposition interests.	Social entrepreneurship as the creation of more-than-profit social firms and businesses, private–third sector partnerships; philanthropy through primary purpose trading; societies and associations that reinvest profits in social objectives and share benefits with members.
Type D: Social and solidarity economy (ideal type)	
Emphasis on the hybridisation of reciprocity, redistribution and market to maximise human and environmental well-being; replaces competitive public, private and third sector models with multi-stakeholder (multi-constituency) co-operatives and mutuals; democratic governance; social auditing to support participative management; solidarity among private stakeholders.	Social entrepreneurship as the creation of multi-stakeholder enterprises: solidarity co-operatives, associations of charities, networks of voluntary organisations, clusters of co-owned businesses, and fair trade networks; democratic control over the distribution of social and economic benefits.

Source: Ridley-Duff and Bull (2015), Checklist for Social Entrepreneurial Management

Nyssens captures the essence of the ideal type when she comments:

> We argue that social enterprises mix the economic principles of market, redistribution and reciprocity, and hybridize their three types of economic exchange so that they work together rather than in isolation from each other. (2006: 318)

Even though cross-sector models address the theoretical weaknesses of two-dimensional spectra, they do not, on their own, provide the same level of detail or insight into practice. Both spectra and cross-sector models are needed to capture the micro and macro aspects of social enterprise theory.

Class exercise: Analysing the nature of social enterprise

Materials to support this exercise can be found on the companion website at: www.sagepub.co.uk/ridleyduff.

On your own, choose five organisations that you believe 'break the mould' in terms of contributing to environmental, social or economic sustainability. Using a cross-sectoral model of the economy, write the names of the organisations you have listed onto the appropriate part of the diagram. Add notes to explain your choices.

Pair up with another person. Compare your diagrams. If any organisations are unknown to the other person, explain why you selected them and how they 'break the mould'. Debate with each other your reasons for selecting these organisations, and discuss whether they are, or are not, social enterprises.

Find another partner, compare diagrams, and have another discussion.

In the next section, we consider the view that social enterprise is an activity that promotes solidarity between stakeholders to create a complete paradigm shift in the nature of business, society and economic thinking.

Social enterprise as a solidarity enterprise

So far, we have covered the framing of social enterprise as a spectrum of options, and as a hybridised form of business that combines the economic logics of redistribution (through states, charities and foundations), reciprocity (through co-operatives, mutuals and associations) and market (through private businesses and general commerce). However, over the last five years, we have become more convinced that it is insufficient to frame social enterprise *only* from the perspective of people who have engaged Ashoka-style CTAs, or built SRBs in which social enterprise language aids the transformation of non-profits, public services and private businesses. For those inspired by the examples from Mondragon (Spain), social auditing (UK), Bologna's social co-operatives (Italy) or the Grameen Foundation's 'second type' social business (Bangladesh) – the question arises as to what innovations in CMEs have been taking place?

Our desire is to avoid the trap of thinking that all social enterprise aims to 'heal' an existing system that is failing, rather than a way to further the development of an alternative economic system that is stable, healthy and committed to furthering human and environmental well-being. From a critical perspective (Alvesson and Deetz, 2000), the 'activity' debate sounds like a rhetorical ploy aimed at obfuscating and neutralising the threat of social enterprise by characterising it as a helpful, even benign development of neo-liberalism, rather than a concerted attempt at pattern-breaking that catalyses radical social change. Dey and Steyaert (2012) agree. They suggest that there is a tendency developing that reduces radical, left-inspired paradigm shifting approaches to social enterprise to one based on a de-politicised, economic engine for public benefit.

Two examples (and Case 2.6) should suffice to illustrate this. Firstly, there is Creative Commons (www.creativecommons.org), a global movement to licence intellectual property (**IP**) in a way that gives, rather than denies, public access. Its 2014 *State of the Commons* report (Creative Commons Foundation, 2014) indicates that there are now *at least* 880 million items of IP licensed using its property system, and that the number of new requests exceeds 24 million a day. All of these items can be shared freely, and many (about 36 per cent) exploited commercially, by following the license terms. The world's most popular encyclopaedia – Wikipedia – uses Creative Commons to license its articles. Its own annual report (Wikimedia Foundation, 2014) claims it was funded in 2012–13 by 2 million people, and that its editors added 5 million new articles and made 160 million edits to existing articles.

Case 2.6

Growing international co-operation

At the International Co-operative Summit in Quebec (October 2014), global reports were submitted by EURICSE, CICOPA and the United Nations (UN) claiming that:

- Estimates for employment in CMEs have been revised upward from 100 million jobs (in 2012) to 250 million jobs (in 2014) following new research in 75 countries by CICOPA.

- Estimates of the value of goods and services traded by CMEs has been revised up from 'over $1 trillion dollars' (in 2012) to '$2.6 trillion' (in 2014) following improvements in data collection by EURICSE for the World Co-operative Monitor. Over a quarter of financial services in Europe are provided by mutual financial institutions.
- The United Nations has found statistically significant links between reported levels of co-operative development and its index of social progress indicators, a finding 'cautiously welcomed' by the International Co-operative Alliance.

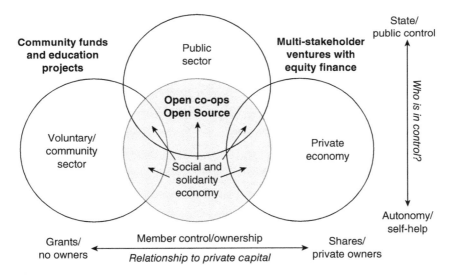

Figure 2.7   The emergence of new member-control/multi-stakeholder enterprises and institutions

Source: Ridley-Duff and Hurst (2014b)

If we think of the framework we introduced in Chapter 1 (Westall, 2001) in which there was a 'fourth space' in which social enterprises proactively build a social and solidarity economy, we can more easily theorise developments in multi-stakeholder approaches to governance and 'solidarity co-operatives' based on member-owned business models (Birchall, 2009, 2012; Ridley-Duff, 2012). These provide a framework for understanding that co-operative schools, **crowdfunding/investing**, open systems for supporting co-operation (like Creative Commons and Loomio) and open source software products (like Linux, Apache, Wordpress and Wikimedia) are not just attempts to 'mitigate failures in the state or market' (Alter, 2007). They are contemporary developments that advance a 'new co-operativism' (Vieta, 2010) that builds on, but is not a slave to, past traditions in co-operation and mutuality (Figure 2.7).

Westall's model *also* makes it easier to theorise efforts at *transformation* that use mutual principles in combination with other legal forms to forge new CTAs and SRBs. This includes: **CIO** (charitable incorporated organisation) associations and co-operative CICs (UK); social co-operatives (EU); solidarity enterprises (US/Latin America); B-Corporations (US); social responsibility corporations (Japan); and all manner of approaches to 'spinning outs' mutualised public services. All of these activities enrich and diversity the fourth space (Figure 2.8).

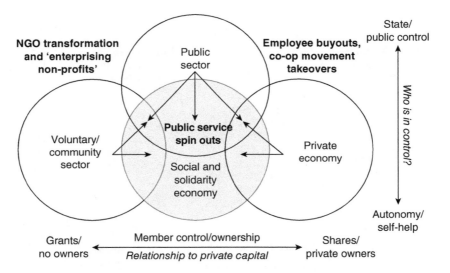

Figure 2.8   Transforming public, private and voluntary community sectors into a social/ solidarity economy

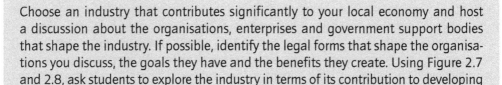

Class exercise: Social enterprise as social and solidarity economics

Choose an industry that contributes significantly to your local economy and host a discussion about the organisations, enterprises and government support bodies that shape the industry. If possible, identify the legal forms that shape the organisa-tions you discuss, the goals they have and the benefits they create. Using Figure 2.7 and 2.8, ask students to explore the industry in terms of its contribution to developing entrepreneurial practices based on the norms of the private, voluntary, public or social and solidarity economics.

- Ask students (in groups) to present their conclusions.
- Play the students the following video to conclude the session: www.youtube. com/watch?v=-RwYZXUQaEw.

Conclusions

Some time ago, Dees (1998) suggested that because of the complex structure of social enterprises, and variance in their definition, any generalisations are problematic. There is no single, agreed set of words that clearly defines social enterprise. Such debate is inevitable, not only because many parties are competing to influence the definitions that are used on the ground, but also because it takes time for a social movement to learn which forms and activities work sufficiently well in practice to warrant institutional support.

Over time, there has been some convergence regarding the 'lowest common denominator' of *trading* to support *social aims* (Peattie and Morley, 2008) even if the social aims themselves vary so greatly that no broader consensus is possible. In our own survey (on 'socialised' and 'social purpose' enterprises) we asked if each characteristic should apply to 'none', 'some', 'most' or 'all' social enterprises. The results showed a very high level of consensus around four of the twenty characteristics:

- stating (and reviewing) ethical values and principles
- making clear statements about social and/or environmental purposes/objectives
- providing evidence of a positive social impact and/or intention to run for community benefit
- reinvesting most surpluses/profits back into social/environmental purposes.

However, we found substantive differences between UK, EU and Asian respondents, with Asian respondents showing a much stronger commitment to the characteristics of 'socialised enterprises' and 'production', and less to 'social purpose' and 'welfare'. This is worth further investigation because it may indicate that social enterprise is perceived as welfare delivery in developed countries, but as a mode of production in others. Moreover, the surprising finding that 'stating (and reviewing) ethical values and principles' generated the strongest consensus suggests to us that we need to explore alignments between the UN Global Compact (2007) regarding 'responsible business' and the social enterprise movement. Ethical capital (Bull et al., 2010) is a more salient concept than we previously thought so we will return to it in Chapter 7.

Going forward, we wish to explore the nascent ideology of 'new co-operativism' to establish what is distinct and different, and whether it is consistent with the centre of the three-sector/four-sector conceptualisations of social enterprise presented in this chapter. Certainly, we see evidence that there is a positive ideology, proactively generating the institutions needed for the growth of the social and solidarity economy. This is rooted not simply in a desire to 'solve problems' but also to proactively create a more open, shared, democratically organised economy because of its intrinsic stability and potential to productively employ more and more people. In this space, the 'defining cluster' of characteristics are those identified by Social Enterprise Europe Ltd for its FairShares Model of social enterprise (Ridley-Duff and Bull, 2013; Ridley-Duff and Southcombe, 2014):

- specifying purpose(s) and evaluating the impact(s) of trading activities (CTAs)
- conducting ethical reviews of product/service choices and production/consumption practices (SRBs)
- promoting socialised and democratic ownership, governance and management (CMEs).

Source: Social Enterprise Europe Ltd, www.socialenterpriseeurope.co.uk/what-is-social-enterprise/.

This definition frames the three approaches we have discussed in Table 2.2 (CTAs, SRBs and CMEs) as a set of foundational commitments – each with a cluster of characteristics and emerging legal forms – that researchers can investigate empirically. The level of innovation in each of these domains will be important so we will keep returning to this in later chapters.

Over the longer term, social enterprise will be determined not by theorists but by social practices and institutions that are associated with, and labelled as, social enterprises. The role of the theorist is to provide frameworks that are adequate for the purposes of making practices and organisational forms intelligible and accessible for discussion. While this chapter provides a number of lenses through which to understand social enterprise, the choices that matter will be made by those who self-consciously pursue sustainable ways of creating social, environmental and economic value.

Summary of learning

Different meanings are attached to social enterprise in the American non-profit sector, UK third sector, European, Asian and Latin American social and solidarity economy.

Social enterprises transcend traditional sector boundaries and have the potential to form a social and solidarity economy with distinct characteristics and language.

Models and diagrams can help to describe and explain the boundaries of the social and solidarity economy, and its link to other economic activities.

Social enterprise is a useful umbrella term for any (democratic) organisational form or activity where 'people are not in it for the money' but still generate a financial surplus.

Social enterprise can be seen as a 'fix' for the ills and addictions of a capitalist system, or as a social democratic movement intent on transforming economic and social relationships.

Questions and possible essay assignments

1. 'Social enterprise concerns the pursuit of particular activities rather than … the democratic transformation of trading organisations.' Critically discuss the limitations of this perspective.
2. Compare and contrast Pearce's three-system model, and the position of social enterprises within it, with other theoretical perspectives on social enterprise. Assess the value of social enterprise theory that constructs it as a cross-sector phenomenon.
3. Critically assess the EMES definition of social enterprise in relation to writings by Greg Dees on social entrepreneurship and Muhammad Yunus on social business.

Further reading

There are some good texts at introductory, intermediate and advanced level. Pearce's *Social Enterprise in Anytown* (2003) has established a good reputation as an entry-level text, and this has recently been joined by Price's *Social Enterprise: What it is and Why it Matters* (2008). A broad and swift journey through the literature up to 2007 can be found in Peattie and Morley's (2008) monograph for the ESRC. Students studying social entrepreneurship will benefit from reading Martin and Osberg's (2007) discussion of the case for definition.

We also recommend three key publications from the EMES Research Network. Firstly, the *Emergence of Social Enterprise* edited by Borzaga and Defourny (2001) is an essential resource for researchers, particularly the analysis of the influence of co-operative and non-profit traditions by Defourny. Secondly, there is further development of the theoretical base for social enterprise in *Social Enterprise at the Crossroads of Market, Public and Civil Society*, edited by Martha Nyssens (2006). Lastly, a new publication *Social Enterprise and the Third Sector* edited by Defourny, Hulgård and Pestoff (2014) provides updated coverage of US–European debates with references to developments in other parts of the world.

For coverage of the field from an Oceania and Asian perspective, see the edited collection by Douglas and Grant (2014) titled *Social Entrepreneurship and Enterprise: Concepts in Context* and Marie Lisa Decanay's (2011) edited volume on *Measuring Social Enterprises*. The former is a more scholarly work, while the latter is aimed at practitioners and will need to be ordered direct from the Institute for Social Entrepreneurship in Asia (ISEA). There is further scholarly coverage on Eastern Asia in a Special Issue (Volume 7, Issue 1) of the *Social Enterprise Journal* and in 'Innovation in Emerging Economies' (Volume 3, Issue 1) of the *Journal of Social Entrepreneurship*.

In addition to the above two journals dedicated to the field, frequent coverage can be found in: *Journal of Co-operative Organization and Management*; *Journal of Co-operative Studies*; *Non Profit and Voluntary Sector Quarterly*; *Voluntas*; *Journal of Business Ethics* and the *Annals of Public and Co-operative Economics*. Furthermore, there have been special issues on social enterprise and social entrepreneurship in *Entrepreneurship, Theory and Practice* (Volume 34, Issue 4), the *International Journal of Entrepreneurial Behaviour and Research* (Volume 14, Issue 5) and *Academy of Management Learning and Education* (Volume 11, Issue 3), and special issues on co-operatives in *Business History* (Volume 54, Issue 6) and *Organization* (Volume 21, Issue 5).

The four additional articles we have selected include two primers suitable for under-graduates: Teasdale's (2012) article 'What's in a name?' which is worth reading together with Ridley-Duff and Southcombe's (2012) critique of the Social Enterprise Mark. For students studying at a higher level, we have selected Domenico, Tracey and Haugh's (2009) theoretical and empirical analysis of cross-sector collaboration and a recent review article on hybridity in social enterprise by Doherty, Haugh and Lyon (2014).

Further reading material is available on the companion website at: www.sagepub. co.uk/ridleyduff.

Useful resources

Co-operatives UK: www.uk.coop/

EMES European Research Network: www.emes.net

FairShares Association: www.fairshares.coop

Global Social Economy Forum: http://gsef2014.org/

Institute for Social Entrepreneurship in Asia: www.isea-group.net/

Intercontinental Network for Social & Solidarity Economy: www.ripess.org/?lang=en

International Co-operative Alliance: http://ica.coop

Social Enterprise Academy: www.theacademy-ssea.org/

Social Enterprise Alliance: www.se-alliance.org/

Social Enterprise Europe: www.socialenterpriseeurope.co.uk

The Social Enterprise Institute: www.sml.hw.ac.uk/socialenterprise/

Social Enterprise Mark: www.socialenterprisemark.co.uk/

Social Enterprise UK: www.socialenterprise.org.uk/

Social Ventures Australia: www.socialventures.com.au/

The Politics of Social Enterprise

3

In this chapter we critically evaluate the global political context in which social enterprise has developed, and give further consideration to the influence of new public *management* and new public *governance*. Key to this chapter is understanding and acting on the tension created by the ascendancy of private sector practices in public and third sector organisations, and the way actors in the social and solidarity economy have responded to those tensions in innovative ways. By the end of this chapter you will be able to:

- explain the concepts of globalisation and localisation
- explain the concepts of *new public management* and *new public governance*
- describe the impact of NPM on public–private–third sector relationships during and after the 1980s
- critically evaluate how local government and organisations in the social economy responded to NPM
- illustrate how social enterprise (internationally) is both an economic and *political* response.

> **The key arguments that will be developed in this chapter are:**
>
> - Attempts to create global markets in goods and services are a recurrent cycle in economic history.
> - Globalisation enables new forms of socially responsible businesses (SRBs), but also triggers charitable trading activities (CTAs) and co-operative and mutual enterprises (CMEs) to limit/resist globalisation.
> - The pursuit of NPM in the 1980s/1990s was a formative influence on the current practice of spinning out social enterprises from the public sector.
> - The social economy response to NPM involved the advancement of employee ownership and support for the solidarity economy.

Introduction

In this chapter, we adopt a perspective that is relatively rare in the study of social enterprise. As we set out in Chapter 2, existing texts advance the idea that social enterprise can take the form of CTAs or CMEs within the third sector. Alternatively, they are framed as a product of interactions between the private, state and third sector actors to produce SRBs. In this chapter, we consider an alternative view that social enterprise is a product of the tensions between attempts to privatise the delivery of *public services* and the radical responses of local politicians and CMEs with socialist sympathies.

We live at a time when the private economy (notionally the *source* of wealth) is the most subsidised sector of the economy. During the 2007–8 economic crisis, the help given to private organisations in the UK and US dwarfed the help given to organisations in the social economy. The **New Economics Foundation** (**nef**) estimated that the UK's 'big four' banks received subsidies to the value of £35 billion in 2012 *in addition to* the 'bail out' investments made by the government (Prieg, 2012). This took the cumulative additional banking subsidy to £193 billion since 2007, six times greater than the value of all grants and donations to the charity sector, and nearly twice the turnover of the co-operative and mutual sector. When considered alongside arguments about the creation of money (Positive Money, 2012), political claims about the 'efficiency' of private markets look (at best) unsound and (at worst) compromised.

The link to contemporary social enterprise is not immediately obvious, so initially we review the way economics developed, then changed, before and after the 1970s.

In particular, we examine the roots, popularisation and impact of neo-liberalism, and the effect this had on 'left-of-centre' entrepreneurship. In outline, the argument runs as follows:

1. A breakdown in the post-war political consensus regarding macro-economic management and full employment coincided with the rise of the 'new right' in politics.
2. The 'new right' advanced a set of principles that led to *new public management* as a way of legitimising SRBs in public administration.
3. The 'new left' (a loose alliance of people holding anarchist, socialist and social democratic beliefs) responded through regeneration activities based on CMEs.
4. New Labour (in the UK) and social democratic parties across the EU adopted *supply-side* economics combined with commitments to social justice, equality and employment protection as a *third way*.
5. The three approaches to social enterprise emerged out of the tensions between *liberal capitalist* ideas embedded in NPM and the *market socialism* that responded to it.
6. By the 1990s, both SRBs and CMEs had prepared institutional challenges to 'old' public, private and third sector development, and this triggered further CTAs in the voluntary sector by the mid/late 2000s.

To appreciate this perspective, it is first necessary to consider the history of global economic systems that led up to the breakdown of the post-war consensus (before and after 1945, up to 1976). We then set out the central tenets of *new public management* (Hood, 1995) and the reactions of progressive liberal and socialist politicians (Chandler, 2008) who initially favoured SRBs and CMEs. Recent analysis links private sector development to growing income inequalities, rates of suicide, community breakdown and endemic health issues, and this has fuelled interest in new models of ownership (Gates, 1998; Wilkinson and Pickett, 2010). We highlight the intersection of SRBs and CMEs with public sector reform, while concurrently highlighting their growing popularity as a way to address inefficiencies in the private sector.

Class exercise: Do you believe in the efficiency of markets?

A significant proportion of adults (both young and old) distrust politics and politicians. The Political Compass is an interesting project that enables a person to find out what their political values are, and how these compare to past and present political parties as well as figures from history. It shows how political parties (including the UK's Labour, Liberal, Conservative and Green parties) have changed their values over time. Most have moved from anti-authoritarian, left-leaning policies to **authoritarian** right-wing policies. According to the Political Compass, most Green parties today occupy the space that Labour parties occupied in the 1970s. Labour parties are now more right-wing and authoritarian than the Conservative/Tory parties were in the 1970s.

Activity: www.politicalcompass.org/

1 Ask your students to take the Political Compass test before the seminar (or bring a tablet, smartphone or laptop to do it in class).
2 Discuss the dimensions of the 'compass': the right–left dimension and the authoritarian–libertarian dimension.
3 Ask students to locate charitable trading activities, socially responsible businesses and co-operative and mutual enterprises on the political compass.

After establishing students' view of the political commitments of different types of social enterprise, play this video to generate further discussion and reflection:

Video: www.youtube.com/watch?v=tskByXRGHjY

The rise of global capital and international markets

Gray (1998) traces the concept of globalisation back to the rise of merchant capitalism, exemplified by the East India Company. In this venture, investors shared the risks of international trade by jointly funding the establishment of trading routes to all parts of the globe to insulate individual ships and crews from local disputes. Today, the concept of globalisation has taken on many shades of meaning, all linked to the technological, business and social institutions that make it possible to trade with people anywhere in the world. As Gray states:

> Globalisation is shorthand for the cultural changes that follow when societies become linked with, and in varying measures dependent on, world markets … Behind all these 'meanings' of globalization is a single underlying idea, which can be called de-localization: the uprooting of activities and relationships from local origins and cultures. It means the displacement of activities that until recently were local into networks of relationships whose reach is distant or worldwide. (2009: 57)

As the scale of ventures increased, so a banking system developed to support them. In the mid-nineteenth century, a group of nations adopted the 'gold standard' to facilitate international trade. The idea behind the gold standard was surprisingly simple.

National governments backed their currencies with reserves of gold and agreed an exchange rate between their own local currency and international gold reserves. This was expected to make it easier to trade internationally as national governments committed not only to using their gold reserves to settle international debts but also to securing the value of their local currencies with something of tangible value.

Gray (2009) regards this period (from 1871 to 1914) as the first of two in recent history when international trade was dominated by institutions that used the rhetoric of free markets to secure advantage for industrialised economies. The first period came to an abrupt end when World War I broke out. As Block writes:

> The gold standard was intended to create an integrated global marketplace that reduced the role of national units and national governments, but its consequences were exactly the opposite. Polanyi shows that when it was widely adopted in the 1870s, it had the ironic effect of intensifying the importance of the nation as a unified entity. Although market liberals dreamed of a pacified world in which the only international struggles would be those of individuals and firms to outperform their competitors, their efforts to realize these dreams through the gold standard produced two horrific world wars. (2001: xxxi)

Important to an understanding of social enterprise movements now, however, is a second period during which international institutions again sought to create a global economy, this time based on fluctuating currencies. According to Gray (2009), the second period occurred from the late 1970s (coinciding with rise to power of Margaret Thatcher in the UK, Ronald Reagan in the US and Deng Xiaoping in China) until the collapse of confidence in global capitalism in 2007–8. In 2008, governments again had to provide financial and social security by taking over major parts of the banking system. Polanyi's words, first published in 1944, are extraordinarily prescient given the situation that developed in 2008:

> The true nature of the international system under which we were living was not realized until it failed. Hardly anyone understood the political function of the international monetary system; the awful suddenness of the transformation took the world completely by surprise ... Not even when the cataclysm was already upon them did their leaders see that behind the collapse of the international system there stood a long development within the most advanced countries that made that system anachronistic; in other words, the failure of market economy itself still escaped them. (2001 [1944]: 21)

Importantly, for contemporary debates on social enterprise, Polanyi argued that liberal economic theory fails to distinguish between 'real' and 'fictitious' commodities. Three items are singled out for discussion: labour, money and land (either in the form of natural resources or the properties we need to live). The assumptions of globalisation extend beyond the trade of tangible goods and services to the commodification of money (through currency speculation), labour (by removing collective bargaining rights and minimum wage protection) and land (through attaching prices to the natural resources required for living). Polanyi argues, in sharp contrast to Fukuyama's (1995) advocacy of high-trust **liberalism**, that during historical periods in which money, labour and land are treated as commodities, commerce destroys social capital and the natural environment. However, he stops short of condemning the market mechanism completely. So long as it trades in 'real' goods, it can be an important part of a mixed economy in which reciprocity and redistribution are also active principles (Hart, 2013).

This clear departure from the followers of Marx meant that Polanyi's work became less popular amongst left-leaning policy makers. But with the rise of social enterprise, his argument that markets can play a limited role (providing they trade in 'real' goods), and work with democratic institutions and member-owned enterprises to generate and distribute wealth, puts his contribution at the heart of social enterprise theory. (Nyssens, 2006)

Gray explains why the commodification of money leads to banking crises:

> Transactions in foreign exchange markets have now reached the astonishing sum of … over 50 times the level of world trade. Around 95 per cent of these transactions are speculative in nature, many using complex new derivative financial instruments based on futures and options. (2009: 57)

As Erdal (2011) would later argue, nearly all transactions in global financial markets produce *nothing of tangible value* (i.e. a product or a service that has direct utility value outside the financial sector). Vast quantities of labour (and money) are engaged in 'casino capitalism', producing 'fictitious' goods and services. If currency values bear little relation to the trading of 'real' goods, they will eventually destabilise markets and increase economic volatility.

However, the situation today is even more entrenched because of the way the commoditisation of money has been taken to extreme levels by fractional reserve banking. This allows the lending (again and again) of an amount of money before the principal has been repaid. The only deduction necessary is the 'fraction' that regulators require the bank to hold in reserve to service their cash flow needs (Positive Money, 2012). Since the switch to digital transactions through online bank accounts and credit/debit cards, banks have started to lend digital money (without anything to underpin its value). The Positive Money movement estimates that 97 per cent of the money now circulating is created 'out of thin air' by private banks (not governments), bears little relationship to the 'real' goods and services in the economy, and increases the volume of money traded as a commodity.

These critiques have a powerful salience today. They highlight how 'fictitious' markets in labour, money and land are implicated in the failure of market institutions and state bodies. In the next section, we examine in more detail the doctrines that led to this commodification and how this changed the balance of power between those with money (banks and corporations) and those with political power (governments and social movements).

The end of the post-war consensus

Polanyi's hopes for a more mixed economy (under state influence) were advanced initially through the application of Keynesian economics. This supported an expansionary policy with the state actively regulating aspects of the economy. The main critique of Keynes came from the **Chicago School** of economists who argued that government intervention is the *source* of the boom and bust cycle by contributing to inflationary policies that make recessions worse (Sloman and Sutcliffe, 2001: 598). They argued that government should limit itself to regulating the supply of money. These views, associated strongly with Milton Friedman (1968), came to be seen as *supply-side* economics. The goal was to regulate inflation and employment by matching the supply of money (monetarism) to the productive capacity of the economy.

Class exercise: Positive money

In the YouTube video at the link below, the Positive Money movement explains how money is created and who benefits from its creation. Watch (the first 10 minutes of) this video and consider the following questions:

1 In a modern economy, who controls the creation of money?
2 Who profits from the creation of money?
3 What issues arise in using this system to regulate the supply of money to the economy?
4 How could the right to create money be changed to finance the public (or community) sectors?

Video: www.youtube.com/watch?v=d3mfkD6Ky5o

Hood (1995) outlines a deep shift in both accounting and management practices that reflected the supply-side arguments of monetarism, leading to a diminishing role for the state as a manager of public enterprises, and ending the state's role as the employer of choice in public services and utilities. Gradually, politicians accepted arguments to withdraw from direct provision and either use taxes to commission services from third parties, or privatise service delivery. Hood argues that this spread gradually, but not completely, across OECD countries. It took root quickly in the UK, Canada, New Zealand, Australia and Sweden, partially in France, Austria, Norway, Ireland and Finland, but not at all in Japan, Greece, Spain and Turkey (until much later).

Klein (2007), however, argues that Friedman's advocacy of monetarism was advanced by capitalising on disasters – both accidental and manufactured – rather than its intrinsic merits. She argues that the private sector spread **New Right** thinking through media empires that were not controlled by the state (Chomsky and Herman, 1988). It was not until the internet age that counter-arguments could be spread rapidly through new democratised forms of communication and publishing.

A persuasive (and amusing) critique of the effects of new right thinking occurs in the work of Harvey (2010). He supports Klein's contention that crises are an important aspect of the capitalist system because holders of larger amounts of capital secure the *benefits* of a fall in market values (through their greater capacity to absorb losses and buy up assets from bankruptcies and insolvencies). Harvey questions whether those favouring a capitalist economy have any satisfactory solution to crises, and postulates that capitalists are shifting the crises around geographically rather than confronting or solving inherent weaknesses of the system. If we consider the Asian crisis in 1997, the South American crisis in 2001, the UK/US crisis in 2007–8, and then the EU sovereign debt crises in 2012, Harvey's argument looks credible.

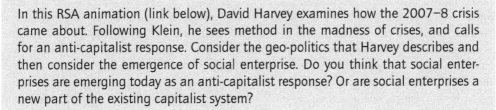

Class exercise: David Harvey's 'The crises of capitalism'

In this RSA animation (link below), David Harvey examines how the 2007–8 crisis came about. Following Klein, he sees method in the madness of crises, and calls for an anti-capitalist response. Consider the geo-politics that Harvey describes and then consider the emergence of social enterprise. Do you think that social enterprises are emerging today as an anti-capitalist response? Or are social enterprises a new part of the existing capitalist system?

1   Which of the explanations of the 2007–8 crisis provided by David Harvey do you find most persuasive?
2   Will CTAs, SRBs and CMEs be able to form an 'anti-capitalist' movement?
3   If yes, what makes these organisations anti-capitalist?

Video: www.youtube.com/watch?v=qOP2V_np2c0

The effects of new public management

Chandler (2008) views NPM as an ideological shift towards new right thinking in the management of public services, leading to arguments for the creation of SRBs and contracts for CTAs. In the short term, this is manifest in programmes to privatise utility companies (gas, telecoms, water and electricity). In the longer term, and perhaps more significantly, NPM manifests itself in 'doctrines' that replace collaborative approaches based on political and professional judgement with target-driven approaches based on managerial control. Hood (1995) set out a number of ideological shifts as well as their operational and accounting implications. In Table 3.1, we examine one of the doctrines to understand the nature of the shifts that took place.

Table 3.1   One of the seven doctrines of new public management

Doctrine	Justification	Replaces	Operational implications	Accounting implications
Transformation of public sector bodies into corporatised units organised to deliver discrete products and services	Makes units manageable; focuses blame for failure; splits commissioning and production to reduce waste	Belief in uniform, inclusive public sector; belief in collaborative approaches to public service provision	Erosion of single service employment; arm's-length management to separate commissioning and provision of services; devolved budgeting	More cost centres; move to activity-based costing (ABC)

Source: Hood (1995), Table 1 © Elsevier

The other doctrines included: more contract-based, competitive tendering with internal markets and fixed-term contracts; a greater emphasis on private sector styles of management; more stress on discipline and frugality in use of resources; more emphasis on visible hands-on top management; formalised standards and measures of performance and success; and a greater emphasis on output controls. Of note here is the move away from long-term employment, collaborative (and uniform) service provision towards decentralised units that compete both with each other and new kinds of service provider (charities, voluntary organisations, employee mutuals, private corporations).

Case 3.1 illustrates how practices associated with NPM influenced public sector reform, and can be linked to the potential development of both CMEs and SRBs. The National Health Service in the UK has been divided into **commissioning** and provider bodies to create a quasi-market. This was encouraged through a 'right to request' policy that allows staff to externalise existing services into discrete social enterprises.

Case 3.1

The 'right to request' in the UK National Health Service

The contemporary expression of NPM in the form of social enterprise can be found in the National Health Service (NHS) of the UK. In November 2008, the

NHS published *Social Enterprise – Making a Difference: A Guide to the Right to Request*. The 'right to request' allows any health professional to put a 'business case' to its primary care trust board to set up a social enterprise. The presentation of social enterprise to health professionals states that it is 'fundamentally about business approaches to achieving public benefit' (NHS, 2008: 6). The focus on innovation, reorganisation into business units providing discrete services, and outcome-driven management is evident in the Chief Health Professions Officer's statement:

> Social enterprise will not be the answer for everyone, but allied health professionals have a long history of providing innovative services in a variety of sectors, settings and throughout care pathways and patient journeys. Consequently, allied health professionals are in an excellent position to take advantage of the 'right to request'. This may be for a particular profession, such as podiatry or physiotherapy, a specialism such as musculoskeletal physiotherapy, a particular care group, or a combination of these. What is most important though is that this is about developing a service that will meet local need and maximise your potential to innovate and ultimately improve outcomes for patients, clients and families, whilst remaining part of the NHS family. (NHS, 2008: 3)

Interestingly, Hood finds it difficult to distinguish between a privatisation agenda and a social democratic reaction to NPM that uses social enterprise to *limit* the influence of the private sector:

> It might be argued that NPM has been adopted in some contexts to ward off the New Right agenda for privatisation … and in other countries as the first step towards realizing that agenda. Much of NPM is built on the idea (or ideology) of homeostatic control; that is, the clarification of goals and missions in advance, and then building the accountability systems in relation to those pre-set goals. (1995: 107)

Concern that 'non-profits' are being sucked into a 'contracting culture' (Dart, 2004) is based on this analysis of the deep shift in management thought and an acceptance of business norms based on commercial contracts. Certainly, there are new providers who adopt a variety of hybrid models, including SRBs that mix employee ownership and private investment (for an example, see www.circle partnership.co.uk). This reflects a change in public policy to take away decision-making from large strategic health authorities and give it to smaller clinical commissioning groups.

However, contracts typically embed new forms of management control and govern-ance that are considerably less 'empowering' than the rhetoric accompanying them (Pratchett and Wingfield, 1996; Curtis, 2008). The increased formalisation (visioning, mission statements, audit), and the outcome-driven character of measurement (targets, service-level agreements and competition), represent a cultural shift to a legal-rational society based on homeostatic controls, rooted in cause–effect assumptions derived from **positivist** research. There are good reasons to question the efficacy of this. Hebson et al. (2003) found that the replacement of bureaucracy with contracting 'partners' decreases opportunities for the collaborative decision-making that can deal with 'complexity' (Stacey, 2007). Transparency decreases and the use of legal remedies increases as service commissioners adapt to their monitoring function, and use their power to adjust rewards (i.e. pay) in line with service-level agreements. Where provid-ers find they cannot meet these agreements (either through their own over-estimation of their capacity, or through unrealistic target setting based on false cause–effect assumptions by commissioners) they may 'walk away' and leave gaps in public service provision. Circle Partnership, two months after receiving a 'business of the year' award from the Employee Ownership Association, cancelled a contract with Lincolnshire NHS Trust to manage Hinchinbrook Hospital claiming that the terms of the agreement were unsustainable (BBC, 2015; Melton, 2015).

The current intention of many governments to allow a proliferation of 'public ser-vice mutuals' (CMEs), public–private partnerships (SRBs) and voluntary sector partnerships (CTAs) poses a challenging question. Is this the continuation of NPM (in a new guise) or a multi-stakeholder turn in which networking and co-production of services signifies a switch to NPG? Osborne (2006) argues that NPM is gradually giving way to NPG by rejecting knowledge rooted in rational-choice theory and management studies in favour of sociological and network theories that provide greater scope for innovation (Coule and Patmore, 2013). Instead of decentralised units that operate in a quasi-market, NPG favours co-design and co-delivery models that create clusters of well-networked providers who have closer relationships with staff and service users (Hazenburg, 2014). Osborne (2006) foresaw this trend as neo-corporatist stemming from growing concerns that *inter*-organisational governance and collaboration in ser-vice design was a key aspect of good quality public services.

An extensive example of this collaboration is occurring throughout the health sec-tor in Italy (CECOP-CICOPA Europe, 2015). According to Restakis (2010), from 1979 onwards the city authorities started to agree contracts with newly formed *social co-operatives* to provide care for people with mental health conditions. Restakis reports that about 8,000 such enterprises now exist in the Bologna region of Italy, in a com-plex network of health organisations that co-design and co-deliver care. By law, beneficiaries must also be co-operative members. Borzaga and Depedri (2014) report on the staggering success of *work integration social enterprises* (helping people find productive work) that report a 65 per cent success rate over three years. This is two to three times higher than has been achieved by either private or trustee-led voluntary sector organisations in the US or UK, and ten times higher than the UK government's work programme (Gilbert et al., 2013).

For Chandler (2008), these developments would be a case of '**local socialism**' that subverts the agenda of NPM to privatise the health care system and transforms it into a set of institutions that follow the norms of NPG. Through new CMEs, those receiving health care can own and control the service that serves them. As Restakis (2010) points out, this 'real' (rather than notional) ownership enables patients, carers and professionals to participate in governance and exercise their voice within the care system. They can also make (and fund, where practical) their own initiatives, increasing innovation and impact.

Advances in employee and community ownership

The rise of local socialism as a political response based on social enterprise development is now acknowledged in historical research into the sector (Sepulveda, 2014). While Friedman's (1962) advocacy of freedom and choice stimulated new attitudes to entrepreneurship throughout the western world, his views were oriented towards a consumer-led, not producer-led, economy. Despite making some persuasive arguments that a vibrant market economy punishes producers who adopt discriminatory practices, Friedman's (1962) rhetoric changes dramatically when talking of the relationship between the workforce, senior managers and shareholders. In this matter, he continued to advocate that the workforce (at all levels) should be subservient to the goal of maximising profit for (institutional) shareholders. While some concessions might be made to workers to align their sympathies with investors (through profit sharing), Friedman continued to argue *against* corporate social responsibility throughout his life (Achbar et al., 2004).

Among American and Australian thinkers, democratisation of the workplace to combine the strengths of SRBs and CMEs countered these attitudes. They advocated 'shared capitalism' (similar to 'social economy' within the EU) that limits the influence of stock market institutions and shares more wealth among producers and consumers (Ellerman, 1990; Turnbull, 1994; Cathcart, 2009; Jensen, 2011). By the late 1980s, employee share ownership plans (**ESOPs**) pioneered in the US were being introduced around the globe. About 35 million employees participate in the US and 2 million in the UK. They hold shares in the company that employs them either directly or indirectly through a trust (**ESOC**, 2014; NCEO, 2014). However, as Melman (2001) discusses, despite Thatcherite rhetoric that share ownership would increase individuals' control over their own destiny, these changes made little impact on the lives of workers or corporate practice in the majority of cases. Where shares do not confer control rights, they make little difference to the pattern of worker layoffs and management practices.

But, where control has passed to member-owners (instead of institutional investors), employee-owned businesses, co-operative companies and societies have started to outperform their private sector counterparts both economically and socially (Perotin and Robinson, 2004; Birchall, 2009; Erdal, 2014). In parts of northern Spain and Italy, the local economies that became dominated by co-operative networks of industrial companies, retailers, schools and universities have become some of the wealthiest regions in Europe. These have been linked to positive health outcomes and increased life expectancy (Erdal, 2014). The MCC in Spain (see Introduction to Part 1 and Case 3.3) provides an example of sustained economic and social development through CMEs. Notable innovations are the rejection of the employer–employee relationship (Ellerman, 1990) and the distribution of power to separate governing bodies representing workforce, manager and owner interests (Whyte and Whyte, 1991; Turnbull, 2002).

The significance of these developments is that they establish pluralist models of ownership where the legitimacy of worker ownership (either individually, collectively or a mix) is accepted alongside arrangements for member and third-party investments. Secondly, the co-operative movement is gradually accepting the argument that practices in SRBs (through recognition of suppliers, consumers and workers as 'strategic stakeholders') should inform the design of multi-stakeholder ownership and governance systems (Lund, 2011; Birchall, 2012; Ridley-Duff and Bull, 2013). In both Italy and Canada, legal forms for 'solidarity co-operatives' are now well established (Lund, 2011), and a coherent articulation based on a FairShares Model of social enterprise is emerging in English speaking cultures (Ridley-Duff and Southcombe, 2014).

The shift towards multi-stakeholder enterprise design comes from the evolution of the social and solidarity economy identified in Chapters 1 and 2. It challenges many of the assumptions in organisational theory that there must be unitary control of operations and decision-making by an executive. In this respect, it furrows a different path from conversions *to* social enterprise where management structures remain in place and only the goals of the enterprise change. In discussions of multi-stakeholder governance, technological changes accelerate, deepen and reduce the cost of applying mutual principles and designing systems for participatory democracy in (networks of) organisations (Murray, 2010).[1]

In this 'sharing economy' (Gold, 2004), the co-ordinating functions of managers can be coded into internet-based software to radically reduce the costs of both management and democracy (Murray, 2010). Wikipedia (which democratises the production and consumption of knowledge) and the mass-movement tool Loomio (which decentralises and democratises decision-making and governance) are current examples of systems that challenge the need for large executive/management teams. Through their adoption, members can re-acquire hegemonic control because the co-ordinating functions of managers and administrators are largely handled in software. It puts members firmly back in control.

Nevertheless, this still leaves open questions of ownership raised by Major (1996, 1998), particularly the issue of 'equity degeneration' – a situation where one or more stakeholders is unable to realise the full value of their past efforts, risk-taking, investments and decisions. In terms of finance, successful mutuals have had to sell equity on the open market to obtain full value for employee or customer owners. For example, Eaga plc, a public sector spinout that sought to end fuel poverty (see Case 3.2), changed itself from a company wholly owned by an employee trust to a plc that permitted external investors. In this configuration, managers bought a minority stake that gave them the balance of power, enabling them to enrich themselves through a private sale to Carillion. The perceived danger – realised in this case – is that 'social ownership' is eroded and replaced by private ownership in the same way that UK building societies and transport companies were demutualised in the 1980s and 1990s (Spear, 1999; Cook et al., 2002).

Case 3.2

Eaga plc: a public service under private or social control?

Eaga plc was formed from a public sector spinoff involving five members of staff who wanted to create an information and advice service for fuel poverty. Initially the company was structured as a CLG, but in 2000 it decided to switch to the model of ownership and control used by the John Lewis Partnership (based on an employee benefit trust, **EBT**). During this period, the company secured public sector contracts and grew rapidly to 4,000 staff. In 2006 the organisation decided that it needed to diversify to reduce dependence on public sector contracts. By floating on the stock exchange, with 51 per cent of shares remaining in the hands of the employee trust and its managers, it secured the finance to establish new operations in India and Canada.

In addition to its original public service goal – to reduce environmental mismanagement and address issues of fuel poverty – the company uses a Partners' Council to discuss personnel issues, company performance and communication with the executive board. In 1993 it also set up the Eaga Partnership Charitable Trust which draws income from the trading organisation and has invested £3 million in projects and research to develop knowledge about fuel poverty.

In 2011, Eaga plc was acquired by Carillion plc and became Carillion Energy Services. This was made possible by trustees who agreed to replace Eaga plc shares with Carillion plc shares. However, many of the decisions relating to the sale of the company were taken without the support or involvement of staff (Mason, 2011). After a petition and staff survey by the Partners' Council revealed widespread discontent, Carillion agreed to share wealth with trust beneficiaries (Tighe, 2011).

(Continued)

(Continued)

Carillion Energy Services continues under private ownership. The Eaga Trust, the EBT run for the benefit of former Eaga staff, still exists and continues to champion employee ownership by providing grants for skill development, and loan/equity finance up to £500,000 to former members of Eaga plc to start their own employee-owned business (Tighe, 2012). However, the case study about Eaga plc on the website of the Employee Ownership Association was removed following the takeover.

Original source: www.employeeownership.co.uk/case-studies.htm#EagaPartnership, updated using press reports by Mason (2011) and Tighe (2011, 2012).

For further international examples, see the companion website at: www.sagepub. co.uk/ridleyduff.

Solidarity enterprises (CMEs) are more dependent than other private sector organisations on a profitable track record or asset base to secure loans that can finance the development of a trust (EBT) (Spear, 1999). In such an arrangement, most (or all) of the shares are initially held in trust, then subsequent annual surpluses are used to buy shares and distribute them to individual share accounts, or permit individuals to buy shares using their own money. In some cases (e.g. Scott Bader, see Case 1.1), a charitable trust rather than EBT owns the company, and staff bonuses are matched by contributions to charitable projects (Paton, 2003). Providing 50 per cent (+1) of shares with control rights remain in trust, and there is an embedded mechanism issuing new shares to individual member accounts, a profitable company cannot be acquired by outside investors against the wishes of its members (SEC, n.d.).

Co-operative transformation of the private sector

The application of these techniques has resulted both in the growth and greater resilience of worker co-operatives and employee-owned businesses that exhibit the characteristics of SRBs and CMEs (Erdal, 2011; CECOP-CICOPA Europe, 2015). In the Basque region of Spain, there is a well-developed approach to acquiring private companies and transforming them into CMEs with SRB characteristics. The journal extract in Case 3.3 is based on findings from a study involving a field trip to Spain (Ridley-Duff, 2005). It describes a meeting with Mikel Lezamiz, the director of the Mondragon Management School, in which he talks about the process of acquiring private companies.

Case 3.3

The Mondragon Co-operative Corporation (MCC)

A longer teaching case and exercise can be found on the companion website at: www.sagepub.co.uk/ridleyduff.

The Mondragon Co-operative Corporation was established in the late 1950s by a priest and five engineers after they were denied the opportunity to invest in the company that employed them. In 2003 the United Nations celebrated the social and economic achievements of the corporation they created. By 2009 this had grown to over 100,000 staff, with over 80 per cent of ownership by staff on the basis of one person, one vote. During a field trip, Mikel Lezamiz – the director of the Management School in Mondragon – described how staff in the MCC work with staff in a newly acquired company to transform it into a co-operative. He discusses this as a gradual transition:

- a move from private to employee ownership
- a shift from employee ownership to participative management
- the introduction of co-operative management (elected councils)
- a vote to transfer the business into co-operative ownership.

Employee ownership is seen only as the start of a much longer process. The main goal is co-operative management and ownership (which can take many years to achieve). As an example, he talked about eDesa, a company the local council asked MCC to buy (to save 1,000 jobs). It took from 1989 to 1994 to educate and prepare the workforce to take a vote on their own future. In 1994, the workforce voted by 87 per cent to 13 per cent to convert to a co-op (via a vote in a General Assembly). At eDesa, the reaction of trade unions was interesting. Two were supportive; two were sceptical but eventually came around. With the backing of all four unions, the company eventually converted to a co-operative. Even now the unions still have an 'ambiguous' attitude to the MCC. Nevertheless, many union members (about 100 people) are active in disseminating information on the values and principles of the co-operative.

Source: Journal transcript, 6 March 2003, Mondragon Co-operative Corporation

Mikel Lezamiz contended that it can take between five and ten years before a workforce develops the readiness to completely take over both ownership and control of their enterprise (i.e. embed co-operative management into an organisation, and then convert to a co-operative legal form). Interestingly, he distinguished the progression process as: *employee ownership* (financial participation); *participative management* (the introduction of **soft HRM** practices); *co-operative management* (putting in place elected governing and social councils to take decisions alongside an executive management group); and *co-operative ownership* (transferring assets and membership to a co-operative legal entity). At Mondragon, development involves a close relationship with the Caja Laboral Popular (Bank of the People's Labour). A *contract of association* setting out the governance arrangements for the co-operative is needed before the bank provides financial support and ongoing business advice (Turnbull, 2002).

These examples raise substantive issues in terms of the politics of social enterprise development. The linking of a charity to a company form does not necessarily involve a fundamental shift in authority relations; both rest on social norms and bodies of law that institute a **unitary** board, top-down authority and rhetorical injunctions to exclude or limit the involvement of employees in both ownership and governance. The transition to employee ownership and control is more radical as it has the potential to restructure authority relations at the level of *class* (Kalmi, 2007; Erdal, 2011). Traditional notions of investor ownership, management control and 'employment' are so deeply embedded in the consciousness of investors, managers and employees that it should not be a surprise that it takes *years* to relinquish and replace them with new ways of thinking. Often, new attitudes cannot be developed without the experience of active participation (or observation) of enterprises with embedded member ownership (Knell, 2008).[2]

But it is not only member-owners that may take years to prepare for such a change. The modes of thought associated with investor-led and hierarchically controlled enterprise are deeply ingrained in the training and professional development of business support staff, academics, accountants, trade unionists, bankers, funders and lawyers. Current course curricula and assessment strategies for professions reinforce dominant approaches to accounting, management, learning and dispute resolution (Johnson, 2003) and this leads to the kind of changes that have occurred at the Co-operative Group (*The Guardian*, 2014b). To support worker, consumer and community ownership, old ways of thinking may need to be relinquished completely, or substantially modified, to provide effective support (Restakis, 2010; Erdal, 2011; Birchall, 2012). If they are not (or cannot), SRBs retain private sector characteristics that limit their capacity to align fully with principles of sustainable development (Novkovic and Webb, 2014).

Moreover, the expectations that spring from worker ownership, as set out by Ellerman (1990), involve the political challenge of a workforce (as a whole) accepting responsibility for both the assets and the liabilities of their enterprises. While acquiring responsibility for assets (cash, investments, property, equipment, etc.) is a psychological barrier relatively easy to overcome, developing the confidence to accept responsibility for *liabilities* is harder (i.e. paying staff, suppliers and creditors, and assuming *legal* responsibility for fellow workers).

The key contribution of Ellerman (1982, 1984, 1990) to the question of whether worker ownership constitutes *social* enterprise comes from his argument that it is a socialised form of entrepreneurship fostered by personal non-transferable member ownership rights, rather than transferable **property rights**.

As Ellerman argues:

> The old public/private distinction is supported by both capitalists and state-socialists. The former use it to argue that the idea of democracy is inapplicable to private industry, and the latter use it to argue that democracy can only come to industry by nationalizing it. But both arguments are incorrect, and the public/private distinction itself must be recast. The word 'private' is used in two senses: (1) 'private' in the sense of being non-governmental, and (2) 'private' in the sense of being based on private property. Let us drop the first meaning and retain the second. Similarly 'public' is used in two senses: (1) 'public' in the sense of being governmental, and (2) 'public' in the sense of being based on personal rights. Let us use the second meaning and take it as the definition of 'social' (instead of 'public'). Thus we have the suggested redefinitions:

> Social institution   =   based on personal rights

> Private organisation =   based on property rights

> By these redefinitions, a democratic firm is a social institution (while still being 'private' in the other sense of being not of the government), while a capitalist corporation is a private firm (not because it is also non-governmental but because it is based on property rights). (1997: 38)

For Ellerman, an enterprise becomes *social* when it rejects private property rights as the rationale for participation in management and governance.[3] Whether an organisation is not-for-profit, non-profit, more-than-profit or for-profit is not the issue. What matters is the *basis on which participation rights are granted*: in a private (economy) enterprise, membership is granted when private property rights are purchased; in a social (economy) enterprise, membership is granted when people are recognised for their labour and trading contributions.

Class exercise: Political norms in private and social enterprise

Find a short video clip of *Dragons' Den* and/or *The Apprentice* that has been broadcast in your country (or use the examples below). These should enable students to consider the assumptions embedded in the neo-liberal formulation of the private sector and write out the 'rules of private enterprise' (e.g. individual

(Continued)

(Continued)

entrepreneurship, equity investments, profit sharing, investor control, absolute owner authority, management hierarchy, business planning, target setting, etc.). If you wish, you can use one or both of the following YouTube clips:

Dragons' Den: www.youtube.com/watch?v=PiEOd7Ks8xk

The Apprentice: www.youtube.com/watch?v=sLVJOmUa3xl

1 Based on these clips, set students the task of 'writing out the political norms of private enterprise' or 'writing out the norms of neo-liberalism' (depending on course context).

Distribute *The Dragons' Apprentice* to students (you can download it from: www.sagepub.co.uk/ridleyduff). Get students to read it (if doing the task in two consecutive classes), or get them to read Chapter 4 'Warren Enters the Dragons Cave', pp. 12–21) if doing the task in a single lecture/seminar.

2 Based on this reading, set the students the task of 'writing out the political norms of social enterprise' or 'writing out the norms of the social and solidarity economy' (depending on the course context).

Do a systematic comparison with the students to help them make connections between political thought and macro-economic systems to the inner workings of individual enterprises. With post-graduate students, you might attempt to write out the 'rules of CTAs, SRBs and CMEs' to gain a deeper insight into the extent that each retains or rejects the 'rules of private enterprise'.

Using producer, worker and community ownership to oppose globalisation

As noted in Chapter 1, the creation of a social and solidarity economy is a conscious political act (Sahakian and Dunand, 2014). In the remainder of this chapter, we consider international examples of social enterprise development that represent political acts using business techniques: the first is **fair trade** in Latin America, Africa and Asia; the second is **micro-finance** in Bangladesh; the third is the **recovered company movement** in Argentina.

Fair trade

Fair trade was pioneered in the 1960s and institutionalised in the 1980s through the creation of a Mexican-Dutch project that resulted in the incorporation of the Fairtrade Foundation. It defines an approach to trading that limits the impact of market prices to increase opportunities for co-operative and community development (Lacey, 2009). While fair trade depends on global supply chains (and operates globally), it modifies market operations and subordinates them to human needs by altering the norms embedded in trading relationships. It does this by advancing a number of fair trade 'principles' (Doherty et al., 2013).

As Jones's (2000) study of Traidcraft reveals, the motive to initiate fair trade enterprises is frequently grounded in political and religious ethics. These incline entrepreneurs to actively limit the influence of the market in the supply and distribution of goods, and also inspires commitments to transforming labour relations through co-operative ownership (Lacey, 2009). Distributors of fair trade products pay a minimum price to ensure they do not fall so low that producers cannot develop their communities (Nicholls and Opal, 2004). Unlike past colonial ventures based on the acquisition of land, and master–servant industrial relations (Melman, 2001), fair trade seeks the creation of local social and solidarity enterprises that produce goods co-operatively for advanced markets. It builds into prices a *social premium* that pays for infrastructure development in producer communities (such as water, health and education facilities).

Davies et al. (2010) discuss the advantages that this ethical form of business accorded Café Direct, and how the ownership of the supply chain came to be shared with producers (who are mostly based in Africa). Doing so not only redistributes financial capital but also creates social capital. Sustainability is achieved through the cultivation of social networks, particularly in public and third sector procurement and retailing activities. Through these approaches, Polanyi's (2001 [1944]) 'fictitious goods' of land, money and people acquire a changed status. Land is treated as a source of wealth, not a commodity: it remains a productive asset under the control of community institutions and producer co-operatives. Working relationships are oriented towards stakeholder engagement with ownership structured to provide both economic and social returns. In place of wage-labour within a private corporation, most income is derived from dividends paid to small (independent) producers based on the amount of produce sold through a co-operative.

Nevertheless, fair trade has encountered a number of problems. Firstly, the quality demands of western retailers can have the effect of imposing high entry costs that are prohibitive. This had led to a proliferation of alternative fair trade standards and limited the geographical reach of the Fairtrade mark (Lacey, 2009). Secondly, and perhaps more significantly, it has proved harder to put some 'principles' into practice than others, sometimes due to the overheads of implementing them (such as transparent sourcing), but also because the market success of fair trade has attracted multinational corporations into the field (Doherty et al., 2013).

Table 3.2   The change in fair trade principles over time

Principle	Change over time
1. Minimum prices	Minimum price higher than market price. Has not always kept pace with inflation
2. Social premium	10% of overall cost, paid over and above market price. Premiums hard to distribute fairly without adherence to principle 7 (democracy)
3. Long-term relationships and supply contracts	Build trust and mutual respect: completely ignored by major retailers who contract only for one season
4. Direct/transparent purchasing from producers	Show full and direct supply chain: never policed and abandoned in 2008 under pressure from multinationals
5. Pre-financial for producers	Advance payments at critical time: suspended in 2008 as a principle, but revived by some large retailers
6. Market information for producers	Improve trust and relationship quality with producers: adhered to in jointly owned ventures; elsewhere poor producer representation
7. Democratic structures	Co-operative production and/or ILO practices: more effective in co-ops; plantations just pay minimum wage – no local democracy
8. Consumer education	Not audited, but frequently practised: still active through Fairtrade mark
9. Sustainable production	Little information on prevalence and practice: not currently enforced

MNCs have successfully penetrated the fair trade movement and secured influence on the boards of accreditation organisations. This increases their lobbying power to dilute the 'principles' by reintroducing plantations that employ labourers (albeit with commitments to ILO labour standards). These changes compromise earlier commitments to co-operative production by limiting the expansion of member ownership and reintroducing the master–servant arrangements of colonial occupation. So the fair trade movement is now split between CMEs that socialise ownership of land and production and who involve local communities in development (as at Divine Chocolate), and MNCs (acting as SRBs) who buy up land and put it (back) under private ownership with wage-labourers running plantations.

Class exercise: Fair trade and endogenous development

Watch the following video clip about fair trade co-operatives in South America: www.youtube.com/watch?v=yu5DhOHLJ-s
    Based on this clip, consider the following issues:

1 What western business norms are modified by the social and solidarity economy?
2 What charitable norms are modified by the social and solidarity economy?
3 How would you explain 'endogenous development' to another person?

Despite challenges, the Fairtrade brand remains widely recognised and highly trusted. The Fairtrade Foundation claims that over 60 per cent of people trust Fairtrade (a level that is as high as charities, co-operatives and SMEs generally) and that nearly 60 per cent of consumers in 24 countries recognised the brand by 2011. Sales (in the UK alone) exceed £1 billion, securing its position as the world's leading ethical brand. (GlobalScan, 2011)

The Grameen Bank and recovered company movements

We now consider two further examples: the Grameen Bank in Bangladesh and the *empresas recuperadas* (recovered companies) in Argentina. These have been selected for different reasons. The Grameen Bank has been particularly effective in transforming the lives of the rural poor (Bornstein, 1996). Academic studies are helpful in problematising and assessing the socio-economic contribution of the Grameen Bank, not just within Bangladesh, but also to the micro-finance movement around the world (Jain, 1996; Dowla, 2006). The Grameen Bank's underlying model not only calls into question the political assumptions that underpin lending (based on property ownership), but also illustrates how a bank can build social capital by organising in a particular way.

The recovered company movement in Argentina has been selected for a different reason. It shows how the industrial working class can respond to globalisation in urban settings (*The Take*, 2004; Klein, 2007). In this case, the concept of *expropriation* underpins a new social arrangement that permits the occupation of an abandoned or idle factory in order to continue or restart production (Howarth, 2007). The political significance is that this challenges business norms regarding the primacy of property rights, and creates an embryonic legal system that permits the protection of jobs and communities against the effects of globalisation (Ranis, 2005). Let us start with the Grameen Bank.

The Grameen Bank was established by Muhammad Yunus as an action research project in 1976 (Yunus, 2007). It was constituted as a bank working exclusively with the 'rural poor' in 1983. There are two key aspects of the Grameen Bank's expansion that are highly significant. Firstly, after 20 years of operation, the bank claimed that it achieved a default rate on loans of only 2 per cent with the poorest sections of the community (Jain, 1996). Such a default rate for credit is extremely low, even in an 'advanced' economy, so this finding alone created interest in the Grameen Bank's approach. It also confounded assumptions that property is needed as collateral (assets that can be turned into cash) to mitigate risks when lending to 'high-risk' borrowers. Secondly, the Grameen Bank's approach to banking has contributed to the creation of social capital and a culture of community-based welfare. In doing so, there have been notable impacts on the social status of women, due to the level of successful lending to them (Dowla, 2006).

Class exercise: The Grameen Bank – a first look

Watch the following video clip about the Grameen Bank in Bangladesh:
www.youtube.com/watch?v=MrUQKuvsmvw&feature=fvw
   Based on this clip, consider the following issues:

1 What are the key challenges faced by the Grameen Bank in Bangladesh?
2 Critically assess the way that 'social collateral' is used to guarantee loan repayments.
3 Critically assess Yunus's political goal of 'creating a world without poverty'.

Jain (1996) explores the institutional arrangements that produce low default rates among borrowers. The bank has been lauded for its use of 'social collateral' (the group guarantees to repay a loan if one group member misses a repayment). Jain argues, however, that the low default rate cannot be attributed to this policy alone. In practice, it was found that Grameen Bank workers and managers do not enforce the group guarantee scheme. The lending policies, he argues, are similar to co-operative banking institutions that have much higher default rates; an explanation has to be found in the internal working arrangements of the bank, rather than its lending policies.

Borrowers are organised into groups of five people. Each group elects a 'chief'. The members of each group cannot come from the same family. They undergo seven days of training on bank policy and the role played by members. Once a group forms – much like any other credit union – they have to establish a track record of saving before being granted any credit. In the first instance, two members of each group receive credit – the creditworthiness of the other group members depends on the first two borrowers' repayment record.

A bank centre comprises ten groups. Each week a bank worker visits the group to collect repayments and consider new applications for credit. Studies reveal that the weekly meeting is vitally important, as it establishes social norms and rituals to reinforce a culture of regular saving and prompt repayment (Dowla, 2006). New applications for credit and regular repayments take place with all members of the centre present (50 people): they are not conducted in private (as is the norm in westernised banking institutions). Jain (1996) reports that these arrangements influence both borrowers *and* bank workers. Financial and procedural discipline comes both from the bottom-up control of members (who will challenge deviations from bank policy) and top-down checks that are routinely carried out by branch and area managers.

Dowla (2006) considers key challenges that were overcome during the growth of the Grameen Bank. Muhammad Yunus, then an economist in Chittagong, encountered resistance from other bankers, as well as political interference from religious groups and politicians.

> When a supportive finance minister proposed a separate bank to expand the Grameen experiment, the commercial bankers put up all possible hurdles [...] When the bank first attempted to introduce housing loans, the Central Bank resisted, arguing that the bank can provide credit only for productive purposes ... Grameen Bank countered by suggesting that a house is like a factory building where all household-based production occurs and as such owning a house is an important input of production in addition to being consumption. On one occasion the bank received a terse letter asking it to justify why the majority of the borrowers of the bank were women. Professor Yunus retorted that the central bank itself ought to justify why the majority of [its] borrowers ... were men. (Dowla, 2006: 105)

Culturally, the struggle was not only to convince political institutions and commercial bankers that the scheme was viable. It also involved convincing the poor:

> The poor could not believe that a government sponsored bank could be seriously interested in their welfare ... [Yunus] had to struggle to convince the eligible women to accept credit ... they would not go in [front] of him because of the purdah norm, so he ended up talking with them with a screen ... Moreover, they were reluctant to accept credit because ... they had been taught that money is something that should be handled by men only. (Dowla, 2006: 106)

Further obstacles came from the spread of local rumours about Christian missionaries, socialist plots and jail sentences for defaulters. Mainstream institutions questioned the business model and accounting practices, claiming that they hid the true level of defaults (Pearl and Philips, 2001).

The progress of the Grameen Bank, however, has been transformative on a number of levels. Firstly, it used share ownership by members to build trust that the bank would not be taken over by governmental or private interests. From registration in 1983, over the course of 20 years, members' share of capital has increased from 40 per cent to over 90 per cent. Dowla (2006: 112) describes this as 'an absolutely new norm of corporate governance for Bangladesh'. Secondly, through successful lending, subsidiary companies (e.g. Grameen Telecom) have contributed to changes in the status and role of women in the community. Bangladesh and Islamic laws enabling women to own property had been limited by social custom (Subramanian, 1998). The Grameen Bank's lending activities have increased not only the property holdings of women, but also the educational opportunities for both their sons and their daughters. A practice of addressing members by name at meetings means that many women are now known by other members of their community as individuals, no longer merely as someone's sister, wife or daughter.

The Grameen Bank rewrites the textbook on risk management by demonstrating that lending against assets and property is a political and ideological choice (to privilege those who possess property), and not one based on intrinsic economic and social benefit or improved commercial performance (Ellerman, 2005). Banking practices using social collateral, backed by processes that deliberately build social capital through participatory economics (Albert, 2003), produce lower default rates on loan repayments than commercial banks' lending to wealthier clients.

The conclusions from the Grameen Bank on social collateral and alternative forms of organisation provide a useful starting point for our second discussion: the development of the social and solidarity economy in Argentina. Unlike Bangladesh, which is one of the poorest countries in the world, Argentina has twice been on the verge of joining the 'first' world. Firstly, in 1910, its GDP per capita was ahead of France and Germany, and second only to the industrial economies in the British Empire (Della Paolera and Taylor, 2004). By the 1970s, it was again the strongest economy in South America, this time interrupted by a military coup (Klein, 2007). Following the 1970s coup, economic advisers, schooled in neo-liberal economic theory, visited Argentina to help establish regimes committed to a policy of 'free' markets. As became the norm during this period, foreign investment (loans from the **IMF** or **World Bank**) was often conditional on making public assets available for private acquisition.

The effects of the 'liberalisation' programme in Argentina have been well documented (Klein, 2007; Howarth, 2007). By 2001, many millions of jobs had been lost and the number of jobless poor had risen from 18 per cent (in 1994) to over 50 per cent (in 2001). In response, both rural and industrialised regions of Argentina have started to establish initiatives that promote self-management.

Class exercise: Recovered companies in Argentina

Additional materials and exercises are available on the companion website at: www.sagepub.co.uk/ridleyduff.
Watch these video excerpts (*The Take*, 2004):

www.youtube.com/watch?v=dMnUkOB4fIE (Part 1)

www.youtube.com/watch?v=ypq1SAvvot8 (Part 3)

Based on a comparison of these clips with earlier clips about Venezuela and Bangladesh, consider the following issues:

1 How do the political contexts of rural and urban social enterprises differ?
2 What is the political significance of the social capital that rural and urban social enterprises develop?
3 What is the political significance of the 'recovered company movement' in relation to the property rights of capital?

In cities, a radical approach based on 'recovered companies' was spreading outwards from Buenos Aires to other parts of South America (Trigona, 2006; Klein, 2007; Hirtz and Giacone, 2013). Hirtz and Giacone (2013) trace the origins of the movement to rebellions against factory closures between 1993 and 2002. Lewis and Klein (*The Take*, 2004) documented how this accelerated after a financial crisis in 2001. Mervyn Wilson, in the introduction to Howarth's report comments that:

> The workers' response was instinctive – to work together to safeguard jobs, and the skills and competencies on which their livelihoods and those of their communities depended. They did not know of, did not work with, and did not draw upon the vast collective memory and experience of the global co-operative movement. They simply organised collectively to take over and keep the businesses running ... As in the early nineteenth century, it is virtually impossible to distinguish between what we would consider today to be the realm of trade union activities and those of a co-operative. (Howarth, 2007: 5)

This study is useful for understanding how and why groups of industrialised workers reacted to the effects of globalisation. It supports Polanyi's (2001 [1944]) argument that whenever 'free' (i.e. international) markets start to dominate, the effect on local economies is highly variable. Industrialised economies (or regions) benefit from a transfer of wealth, while job losses and political repression occur in weaker economies (or regions). In Argentina, this took the form of political action to break up organised labour and protest movements during a second wave of 'liberalisation' in 1994. The effects, however, devastated employment among skilled and unskilled workers, leading to the formation of a 'new co-operative' movement.

Spontaneously, initially without government or international support, workforces started taking over abandoned factories to resume production. They were able to do this under laws that allow a co-operative to secure court permission to use idle equipment for a two-year period. Local courts upheld by-laws that require former owners to negotiate with co-operative members over the rental and purchase of abandoned equipment. In other cases, local government authorities bought the assets and leased them back to the co-operatives.

One high-profile case is Zanon, a ceramics factory that has grown to 300 staff and achieved international recognition. Due to high levels of community support, it has survived six attempts to restore ownership to its previous (private) owners (*The Take*, 2004), and in 2009 members were granted ownership by the provincial legislature (Trigona, 2009). As Ranis points out:

> There are multiple examples of recuperated factories lending their facilities to the surrounding communities for health clinics, art exhibits, theatre evenings, and adult learning centres with university faculty providing courses for credit (the author visited several such factory culture programmes in the city of Buenos Aires). These neighbourhood and community contacts stood them in good stead when threatened with police interventions on behalf of the previous owners. (Ranis, 2005: 106)

Howarth (2007) explains the use of *expropriation*, the legal basis for occupying and claiming the assets of an abandoned factory. In liberal economies, the rights of property dominate: if there is a conflict between defending a person's right to dispose of their property or defending the jobs of a workforce, the rights of the property owner are given priority. In Argentina, the law now recognises – in the case of recovered companies in Buenos Aires – that there are circumstances where the rights of a person to support their family and community can take precedence over the rights of property owners. As Ranis (2005) argues, Argentine and regional governments have constitutional provisions that allow co-operatives (and only co-operatives) to expropriate properties for reasons of 'public utility', or in defence of the 'common good'. This is different both from liberal economies (such as the US and UK) and also from expropriation by the state to nationalise whole industries (as happened in countries dominated by **Marxian** economic thinking).

In summarising the cases of the Grameen Bank and Argentine co-operatives, it is easy to highlight their different development paths and contexts. However, it is the similarities to material in the previous chapters we wish to emphasise. Firstly, both approaches were dependent on the development of community-based social capital that emphasised solidarity. Furthermore, the strength of this social capital empowered the social enterprises to defend their institutional arrangements from interference by powerful commercial and state interests. Secondly, in both cases, the organisations changed the economic 'rules' that govern property and employment rights. At Grameen, consumer ownership of the bank (to invest in their own production activities) led to a different relationship between lenders and borrowers because members were making decisions on both lending and borrowing at the same time. In Argentina, employment rights were superseded by member ownership rights and responsibilities, transforming the relationship between workers and the machinery needed to sustain production. Property was *subordinated* to labour (and public) interest, rather than the reverse. Lastly, in both cases the 'local struggles are a direct result of national and international policies and of the global context' (Ranis, 2005: 115). Social enterprises acted to re-localise control and ownership, and reclaim the wealth generated locally. In Grameen, the struggle was against the poverty created by globalisation in rural communities. In Argentina, the struggle was against urban unemployment created by the 'liberalisation' policies that accompany globalisation. From this, we can draw some conclusions about social enterprise as innovatory work.

Conclusions

In this chapter, we have considered the roots of globalisation and various responses to it. In particular, we have examined social entrepreneurship through the agencies of the state (through enacting the doctrines of NPM) and through private sector reforms (through enacting the principles of fair trade). Both approaches create SRBs and CMEs, rather than CTAs, although there is evidence that CTAs are integral to the fair trade system through their role in allocating fair trade premiums for community development. We have also considered how NPM can trigger 'local socialism' through a community-based business movement that advances both NPG in the state sector and employee-owned/community enterprises that extend participation rights to more citizens through the creation of a social economy.

While the literature on social enterprise from 2005 onwards is well populated with discussions about the impact of 'business practices' on the voluntary and charity sector (Goerke, 2003; Seanor et al., 2013), this chapter has focused on an argument established much earlier in practice that 'social enterprise' comprises commercial activity where ownership and control rights are allocated (primarily) to member-owners, and particularly to producer-owners. The danger, particularly in an Anglo-American context, is that this older CME tradition of social enterprise is weakened by the political power of governments who prefer to control public services through SRBs and CTAs (Peattie and Morley, 2008), and also by the private sector who see more profit potential in SRBs than either CTAs or CMEs. So, while ambiguity in approaches may broaden its appeal, it also reinforces structures that lead to competition over the underlying premises and assumptions that drive social enterprise development. This inherent *pluralism*, however, has been cast as a strength of the sector by a number of writers who – as Polanyi did – see some merit in building a market for 'real' goods, eliminating markets for 'fictitious' goods, and re-enfranchising member ownership as part of a mixed economy (Restakis, 2010; Smith and Teasdale, 2012; Ridley-Duff and Bull, 2013).

Taken together, Chapters 1 to 3 review the full range of social, political and economic changes that are contributing to the emergence of social enterprise as both a concept and process of organising. We see evidence that there is both convergence (on member ownership models) and divergences (in orientations towards profits and markets). However, we close the chapter with an activity based on the words of David Ellerman who believed that localisation through democratic firms could forge something positive irrespective of pre-existing political commitments.

Class exercise: The work and writings of David Ellerman

Materials to support this exercise can be found on the companion website at: www.sagepub.co.uk/ridleyduff.

Read the following statement from *The Democratic Worker-owned Firm* (Ellerman, 1990):

> A capitalist economy within a political democracy can evolve to an economy of economic democracy by extending the principle of democratic self-determination

(Continued)

(Continued)

to the workplace. It would be viewed by many as the perfection of capitalism since it replaces the demeaning employer–employee relationship with ownership and co-entrepreneurship for all the workers. A state socialist economy can evolve into an economic democracy by restructuring itself along the lines of the self-management socialist tradition. It would be viewed by many as the perfection of socialism since the workers would finally become masters of their own destiny in firms organised as free associations of producers.

1 To what extent is the USA extending the principle of 'democratic self-determination to the workplace' through the widespread use of ESOPs?
2 To what extent can 'self-management in the socialist tradition' support new forms of CMEs and SRBs?
3 What factors in neo-liberal doctrine inhibit the development of 'firms organised as free associations of producers' as envisaged by Ellerman?

Summary of learning

In this chapter, we have argued that:

The rise of NPM as a supply-side economic policy replaced Keynesianism. This has accelerated the adoption of private sector accounting and management practices.

The application of NPM in public sector reform has resulted in arguments for social entrepreneurship and employee mutuals in the development of public services.

The concept of 'local socialism' arose to resist NPM by stimulating community economic development: local enterprise networks deploying fair trade, co-operatives and employee ownership are part of the switch to NPG.

Restructuring authority relations at the level of class can take five to ten years because it takes a long time to replace investor-led, hierarchically organised governance with worker-led and/or community-led democratic governance.

A movement for 'economic and social democracy' is being enacted through social enterprises that restructure authority relations in business activities supported by laws that permit the expropriation of private assets for public/community benefit.

Questions and possible essay assignments

1. Using examples to illustrate your argument, explain the basis of Ellerman's contention that all member-controlled businesses are social, rather than private, organisations.
2. 'The switch to new public management was the principal catalyst for social entrepreneurship in the public sector.' Using examples, evaluate the robustness of this claim.
3. 'Social enterprise is primarily about democratising public and private organisations, not transforming charities and voluntary groups into businesses with a social purpose.' Using examples, critically assess this statement.
4. What is the legacy of 'local socialism' to the social enterprise movement?

Further reading

A good place for undergraduates to start is 'Ten big questions about the Big Society' (Coote, 2010) available from the NEF website. Then students will be ready to progress to Hood's (1995) seminal paper on 'new public management', a well-argued distillation of the doctrines of NPM as well as its spread among OECD countries. More recent works by Osborne (2006) and Coule and Patmore (2013) show how NPM is now challenged by the assumptions of 'new public governance'.

Ellerman's (1990) book *The Democratic Worker-owned Firm* is now freely downloadable (as *The Democratic Corporation)* from Ellerman's own website. Parts of the text are challenging to non-economists, but it is notable how many influential people in the world of employee ownership look to Ellerman's initial analysis as a source of inspiration (so it is worth the struggle). Ellerman establishes a clear moral, economic and intellectual justification for worker ownership as the basis of social enterprise. For technical discussions (useful to accountants and solicitors) see Gordy et al.'s (2013) book *Leveraged ESOPs and Employee Buyouts*, available from the National Center for Employee Ownership (in the USA).

A key text to understand how 'economic democracy' is being exported from the US to other parts of the world is Gates's *The Ownership Solution* (1998). Both Gates's work on legal forms, and Shann Turnbull's work on governance practice, have been an influence on the members of the National Center for Employee Ownership (in the US) and the Employee Ownership Association (EOA) in the UK. The EOA's website contains a series of helpful publications, parliamentary reports and case studies on how to implement 'economic democracy' in the UK (see www.employeeownership.co.uk).

A compelling overview of the business trajectory implied by the themes in this chapter is found in the final chapter of Alec Nove's (1983) book *The Economics of*

Feasible Socialism. Despite its age, Nove's final chapter on the potentialities and limitations of a society in which private, social and state enterprise are combined in different proportions to increase human well-being stands the test of time. For a more recent critical debate about the intersection between for-profit and non-profit views on social enterprise, see Bull's editorial in the 2008 Special Issue of the *International Journal of Entrepreneurial Behaviour and Research* (IJEBR).

On the companion website, we suggest four further articles and a novella to stimulate further debate about the politics of social enterprise. Firstly, we recommend Osborne's overview of the switch from public administration to NPM, then NPM to NPG. Secondly, we recommend Smith and Teasdale's arguments for *associative democracy* and its potential role in further reform of public services. Thirdly, we recommend Sepulveda's historical account of social enterprise development in the 1980s and 1990s to provide a political-historical link with NPM/NPG. Fourthly, we recommend Coule and Patmore's paper about the innovations of TSOs responding to the shifts towards NPM and NPG. Lastly, on a more light-hearted note, we provide a satirical critique of neo-liberalism in the form of novella by one of the authors – *The Dragons' Apprentice* by Ridley-Duff (2014).

Further reading material is available on the companion website at: www.sagepub. co.uk/ ridleyduff.

Useful resources

The Corporation (documentary): www.thecorporation.com/

FairShares Association: www.fairshares.coop

Fairtrade Foundation: www.fairtrade.org.uk/

Fairtrade International: www.fairtrade.net/

International Labour Organisation: www.ilo.org/empent/units/cooperatives/

Mondragon (documentary): www.youtube.com/watch?v=2zMvktpKDmo

New Economics Foundation: www.neweconomics.org/

OneWorld: http://us.oneworld.net/

The Political Compass: www.politicalcompass.org/

Positive Money: www.positivemoney.org/

Shift Change (documentary): http://shiftchange.org/

Skoll World Forum: http://skollworldforum.org/

The Take (documentary): www.thetake.org/

Together (documentary): www.together-thedocumentary.coop/

Upside Down World (Latin America): http://upsidedownworld.org/

World Fair Trade Organization: www.wfto.com/

Notes

1 See Loomio.org for an example of a widely used technology that has successfully reduced the need for executive management and which promotes participatory democracy. This video provides an introduction: www.youtube.com/watch?v= Ij0OsRtkl2A.

2 See Chapters 6–9 for teaching cases and discussion on the practical aspects of these debates.

3 In Chapter 11 we discuss in further detail the (legal) property rights defined in the Articles of Association of a company. They can be summarised as rights to: liquidate the company; acquire capital gains; transfer property; derive an income; vote on key decisions; access information; grant public access to information.

Part II

Sustainable Enterprises and Communities

Exemplar Case: Biogas Production in Linköping and Lidköping, Sweden

In 1990, a project to create an energy revolution started in Sweden with the creation of Lidköping Biogas which produces compressed and liquid biogas. The project is exemplary for the co-operation between municipalities in several nations (Denmark, Finland and Sweden), private companies, local farmers, transport organisations, farmers' associations, vehicle suppliers and food companies to produce renewable fuels and low carbon energy products, as well as fertilisers for organic farming.

The biogas manufacturing process starts with the collection of 'substrates' – waste from food production and grain farming – and then goes through two stages: a production stage and a liquefaction stage. The Lidköping plant takes food industry waste (substrates) that is macerated and mixed, then steamed to kill bacteria and warmed up to 38°C. It is then pumped into anaerobic digestion chambers to produce methane. The methane is refined into biogas while the residue is used to create biofertilisers.

Biofertilisers become part of the sustainable organic food industry, and are purchased by associations of farmers to distribute to their members. The biogas is partly distributed to local filling stations for cars and buses (through a pipe network where available), but mostly it is retained for compression into liquid methane so it can be transported to other locations and used in industrial applications. By lowering the temperature to minus 163°C, three times as much biogas can be transported to other locations at the same cost, and in liquid form it makes a good fuel for heavy duty vehicles. Volvo already sells biogas cars, and is now pioneering HGVs that power diesel engines with liquid methane. To provide incentives and create demand, biogas vehicles pay no car tax, do not pay road tolls and get free parking in all municipal car parks.

The potential of biogas production has been exploited by the town of Linköping (Mayer, 2012). Linköping is a city of 100,000 people that sought to reduce pollution from the overuse of diesel. Since 1995, local waste from dairy production (manure) has been combined with crop waste, slaughter-house waste and industrial food waste to provide the raw materials for production. It has created its own local plant, deploying technologies similar to those at Lidköping, and now recycles 100,000 tonnes of organic waste in a continuous production process that takes one month to complete. Linköping residents can purchase biogas cars, and the city's fleet of 70 buses all run on biogas. When biogas fuels are used, carbon dioxide emissions are reduced by 90 per cent. The cost at the pump is 30 per cent lower than petrol (although the level of public subsidy is unclear). Taxis in the city have been installed with a dual-fuel system (biogas and petrol), and the local rail network has the world's first biogas train (with a range of 360 miles before refuelling). The biofertiliser produced is bought by 35 local farms including those that provided the raw materials.

The project has had to face a number of challenges (Mayer, 2012). Mid-project fears about its long-term viability led two of the original partners, including the farmers' association LRF, to sell their shares to a private company TVAB. This means that the wealth now created is not being shared as equitably as was originally envisaged. Nevertheless, local partners had significant input into the project, and illustrate the concept of co-design (Steen et al., 2011), ensuring that many benefits accrue to the local economy, meet local needs and benefit local suppliers. At Lidköping, on the other hand, the production company has remained part of a network of municipal companies owned by Gothenburg City which identifies its owner as 'society's citizens' (www.goteborgenergi.se/english).

Video resources:

For a broad introduction to sustainable development see: www.youtube.com/watch?v=9GorqroigqM

Biogas International, Lidköping: www.youtube.com/watch?v=hIAEe8X41PM

Biogas in Linköping: www.youtube.com/watch?v=0B_9IKfrLJk

Introduction

In 2014, a new textbook – *Principles of Responsible Management* (Laasch and Conway, 2015) – started circulating among business school lecturers around the globe to support the United Nations PRME (Principles of Responsible Management Education) initiative. This textbook is a global academic product: a wide range of researchers, lecturers, practitioners and policy-makers have contributed chapters, case studies, thought pieces and teaching materials in an attempt to transform the teaching of management. By mid-2014, over 500 business schools had signed up to PRME principles and now report regularly on how they are putting them into practice.

It is salutary to examine how the topic of *responsible management* is represented in relation to the theoretical perspectives on social enterprise that we outlined in Part I. We articulated three distinct approaches to social enterprise, each oriented towards influencing existing norms (of philanthropy, mutuality and market trading) so that they align more closely to the values of a fourth approach based on the creation of a social and solidarity economy. The fourth comprises networks of autonomous member-owned businesses – frequently organised to promote multi-stakeholder ownership, governance or management, and which value social and environmental well-being above profit-maximisation (Westall, 2001). We can summarise these transition strategies as:

Philanthropic trading: developing earned income strategies to improve the economic sustainability of social ventures that prioritise improvements to social and environmental well-being.

Co-operatives and mutual: using the principle of solidarity among member-owners to positively impact on the well-being of workers, customers, the local community and environment.

Social business: adapting private sector practices and business models to make the well-being of individuals, communities and the natural environment a higher priority than profit-maximisation.

The field of sustainable development shares a commitment to creating and supporting triple bottom line enterprises (Spreckley, 1981; Elkington, 2004). To do so, public, civil society and market institutions need to be persuaded to meet social needs without breaching the limitations created by environmental and social conditions. In this respect, the fields of sustainable development, responsible management and social enterprise share a theoretical perspective. Examine Figure II-1 and note how the field of responsible management accepts the concept of hybridisation and cross-sector co-operation developed by social enterprise theorists (Billis, 1993; Leadbeater, 1997; Nicholls, 2006; Ridley-Duff, 2008b).

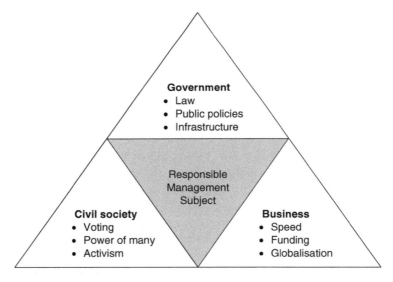

Figure II.1   Representation of responsible management

Laasch and Conway (2015) develop an argument that responsible management is constituted from three sub-disciplines: *sustainability, responsibility* and *ethics*. The way these three sub-disciplines are described provides interesting linkages into the arguments we made in Part I of this book. It demonstrates the relevance of social enterprise to this new paradigm in management thinking, and the relevance of responsible management education to the practices of social enterprise.

Sustainable development is frequently presented as triple bottom line development. In 1987, Bruntland penned a much-quoted statement that:

> Sustainable development is development that meets the needs of the present without compromising the ability of future generations to meet their own needs. It contains within it two key concepts:
>
> the concept of **needs**, in particular the essential needs of the world's poor, to which overriding priority should be given; and
>
> the idea of **limitations** imposed by the state of technology and social organisation on the environment's ability to meet present and future needs. (Bruntland, 1987: 43)

Sustainable development, therefore, depends on not using resources more quickly than they can be re-created, substituted or replenished. While this is conceptually straightforward in relation to the physical environment, it is more challenging to conceptualise its application to economic and social domains.

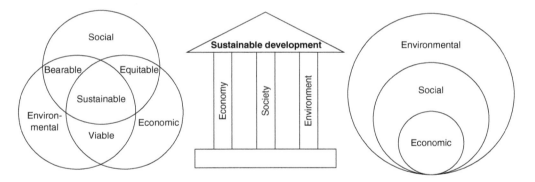

Figure II.2   Representations of sustainable development

In economics, sustainable development depends on enterprises spreading economic capital equitably without harming any enterprise stakeholder's ability to generate the income they require to meet current and future needs. This necessarily includes each stakeholder's capacity to pass on the skills and resources needed by the next generation to create economic capital. In the social domain, sustainable development depends on enterprises that improve interpersonal trust among the members of a community (i.e. which create social capital). Enterprises need to both create (and avoid disrupting) social networks on which stakeholders depend to meet their needs and secure a good quality of life. In the environmental domain, sustainable development translates more straightforwardly into actions that ensure natural resources are not used more quickly than natural systems can replenish them, or for which safe substitutes can be invented when natural resources will not last indefinitely (Barbier, 1987; Giddings et al., 2002).

The University of Massachusetts offers something interesting here. In their research on sustainable products, they build a model that encompasses five aspects of a journey towards sustainability. The five categories are: environmentally sound, economically viable, healthy to consumers, beneficial to local communities and safe for workers. The section on economically viable is surprisingly interesting to us here, as within the criteria they state:

The firm is stable in terms of ownership and philosophy.

The company reinvests in the facility to improve its capacity for further production.

This is relevant to our argument as social enterprise is aligned with (and can meet the criteria for) sustainable development more readily than mainstream businesses (University of Massachusetts, n.d.).

A holistic perspective is challenging because it is relatively easy to recall examples where single bottom lines are satisfied without considering the other two, but harder to recall cases where two or three are achieved at the same time. As both historic and recent analyses show, private ownership and labour management techniques have traditionally been combined in a way that enables one social group (capital owners) to acquire a disproportionate share of economic, social and environmental capital (often against the wishes of an overwhelming majority) (Marx, 1887; Norton and Ariely, 2011). In contemporary analyses, corporate operations and economic policies that increase consumption are also widely criticised for harming people and the environment (Achbar et al., 2004; Leonard, 2007; Hawken, 2010). A counter-view – but one increasingly hard to evidence – is that organised labour uses social capital to extract ever larger shares of economic capital from capital owners without considering the environment (Rathzell et al., 2012). As we learned in Part I, practitioners of the social economy envisage a solution by removing the barriers between capital owners, employees and consumers so that workforces and consumers become co-owners or common owners of the 'capitals' needed to meet their needs.

Seeking financial profit from economic development can have both positive and negative effects on other forms of capital (creating more jobs, displacing existing jobs, creating facilities but also destroying resources). The case of the fishing industry highlights some of the challenges. Environmental agencies come into conflict with local fishing industries on the question of who best protects economic, social and environmental capital. As the following press report illustrates, the bureaucratic application of policies designed to protect the environment from the action of large corporations can destroy the economic and social capital of local communities that have already worked out how to live sustainably.

Paul Joy, a local fisherman and co-chair of Nutfa (the New Under Ten Fishermen's Association), spoke to the *Guardian* for a film [...]. 'If we were drug smugglers we'd understand it,' he told the *Guardian*. 'But we're just fishermen trying to earn a living, and with the quotas as they are, we can't.' At the height of the cod season, in early winter, each boat's catch limit has been set at about 1.4kg a day, which represents less than half a fish. 'What we're allowed to catch doesn't even pay for the fuel to go out there and catch it,' said Joy [...]. Local fisherman John Griffin, 52 said, 'You can't run a business like this. It'd be nice to tick over – but for the last few years, we've been on a deficit. Eventually, something's got to give. We've got enough car parks and amusement arcades [...] *This fishery's been here for thousands of years and generations of people. To lose it would be crazy.*' (Harris and Harvey, 2012, emphasis added)

For this reason, the concept of 'responsibility' has a specific meaning in the discipline of responsible management. Laasch and Conway (2015: 26) articulate responsibility as the capacity to consider the needs of *multiple* stakeholders so that choices 'lead to the optimization of overall stakeholder value (SV), instead of the narrow focus on maximizing shareholder value'. They suggest that achieving this depends on building up competencies in *labour relations*, *consumer relations* and *supply chain relations*, in addition to *investor relations*.

To do so requires the development of *ethical* reasoning – the capacity to make good decisions when faced with moral dilemmas, the working out of which interests need to be protected in a given situation, and the developing of procedures that are regarded as fair and just. In moral philosophy, the rights and responsibilities of the individual (liberalism) are debated alongside the rights and responsibilities of the communities to which those individuals belong (communitarianism). In the context of social enterprises, working out just systems for recruitment, promotion, reward, conflict resolution, wealth allocation and distribution represent a few of the challenges where ethics can help stakeholders to navigate the dilemmas they face.

The structure of Part II

In Part II, we firstly examine the concept (and marketing of) social value (Chapter 4, Measuring Social Value: Outcomes and Impacts). Without a conceptual understanding of social value, the social auditing processes needed to inquire into it, and the social reporting needed to evaluate its impact, there will be little opportunity to turn social value into economic value (Bourdieu, 1986). Furthermore, based on the argument that all environment protection activities depend on changing human behaviour, there is a possible role for social marketing as a tool for achieving both social and environmental goals (Kolter and Zaltman, 1971; Stern, 2000; McKenzie-Mohr et al., 2012).

In Chapter 5 (Income Streams and Capital Management), we turn our attention to generating income. We identify different streams of income, the social and financial capital needed to establish them, and the modes of trading that can sustain them.

New in this edition is a chapter that considers the role and rise of social investment as both a concept and a practice (Chapter 6, Social Investment and Crowdfunding). Each approach to social enterprise gives rise to a different set of investment institutions. A social investment industry is developing to support both philanthropic trading and social businesses, but co-operatives and mutuals have started to favour various forms of crowdfunding: member shares, community shares or crowd (investment) funding. We consider how each type of social investment constructs the concept of 'value' and consider the way each approaches the management of their investments.

We round off Part II with Chapter 7 (Social and Ethical Capital). In this chapter, we not only consider the conceptualisation of these terms, but also consider them as 'products' of social enterprise. We examine whether social enterprises are sites for the creation of social and ethical capital, and whether it is the rate at which they fulfil this act of creation that can serve to differentiate them from private and state enterprises.

Measuring Social Value: Outcomes and Impacts

Mike Bull, Rory Ridley-Duff and Pam Seanor

4

Learning objectives

In this chapter, we explore the marketing and measurement of **blended value** in social accounting practices in order to generate a dialogue about their impact. By the end of this chapter you will be able to:

- explain how 'social auditing' in social enterprises is the equivalent of 'marketing' in private enterprises
- compare and contrast **social accounting and auditing (SAA)** and **social return on investment (SROI)**
- explain the differences between outputs, outcomes and impacts
- critically assess 'performance' as a concept
- critically evaluate how a social auditing mind-set affects ownership, governance and management.

The key arguments that will be developed in this chapter are:

- Establishing the value that social enterprises create, and communicating it to a community of interest, makes social auditing/reporting integral to the marketing of social enterprise.

(Continued)

(Continued)

- Social enterprises measure their effectiveness in terms of outcomes and impact, not output or profit.
- Two dominant approaches to measuring social impact have emerged: one based on 'bottom-up' SAA; the other based on 'top-down' SROI.
- Developing an understanding of systems theory helps to understand and conceptualise both SAA and SROI.
- Social accounting emphasises inter-disciplinary skills in collecting, interpreting and reporting qualitative and quantitative data.

Introduction

Up to here, we have considered the macro influences that shape social enterprises as they form and develop. In the Introduction to Part II, we began to explore the process of building a business system that links social enterprises committed to sustainable development, and which distributes value created throughout supply chains to stakeholders, rather than shareholders. This chapter asks some challenging questions. How can members, managers and governing bodies know if their organisation is contributing to sustainable development? How can they assess impact on the communities in which they are embedded: their workforce, customers, service users and physical environment? This might be summed up in a single question. What is it to 'perform' *socially*?

This chapter tackles these questions. We will argue that different assumptions about the quality and quantity of evidence needed to assess 'social impact' affects *what* gets measured, and *how* it gets measured. Charitable trading activities (CTAs) may need different measures to a co-operative and mutual enterprise (CME), and CMEs may need different measures to a socially responsible business (SRB). Each approach to social enterprise (see Chapter 2) makes assumptions about the role that stakeholders will play in contributing to, receiving information about, and taking action to create positive social impact. In line with previous chapters, we adopt a constructionist approach to emphasise how philosophy and ideology influence both conceptualisations of social value, and the way it gets measured and communicated.

Social reform in a neo-liberal world, as critiqued in other chapters, creates a socio-political system in which 'the market' is positioned as the best provider of the goods and services we need, including public services funded partly, mainly or wholly by taxes. This system relies on an audit trail of where and for what money is spent. The high status accorded to accounting has both positive and negative consequences for organisations in the social economy interested in delivering public services. What outcomes might governments be interested in? What issues are being addressed with public money? The expectation is that public money will be spent on caring for society. Therefore traditional measures of (financial) reporting employed by mainstream businesses are less relevant when accounting for public money. This is where social accounting has developed a niche. Social accounting provides an evidence base that directly acknowledges the way resources are used and the non-financial value they create. Simply put, social outcomes funding is accounted for by *impact reporting*. However, in theory and in practice, capturing evidence of social impact is at best problematic and, at worst, near impossible.

In order to bring the chapter to life, we intersect the discussion with a case study about 'Hazel', a project of the Wooden Canal Boat Society. We present it in small chunks throughout the chapter to highlight how the journey towards social accounting can unfold.

Case 4.1

The Wooden Canal Boat Society (Part 1)

In a case study, Wilson and Bull explain the public funding sought by the Wooden Canal Boat Society (WCBS) for the restoration of a wooden canal boat used to improve community health and well-being. WCBS engage people recovering from mental ill-health by offering skippering, rides and short breaks. In the case study, the local authority in the Tameside borough of Stockport (UK) became involved in the project from its infancy. The adult social care commissioning team began to explore new ways of commissioning in a political climate of social care personalisation. After the introduction of personal budgets, service users have the financial resources to control their own care provision. When the commissioning team met WCBS, there was a focus on illness prevention and care diversification to lighten the load on traditional care centres.

Source: based on Wilson and Bull (2013).

We continue to encourage a critical approach to the conceptualisation of performance and social impact. Firstly, we discuss the nature of marketing activities in social enterprises, the impact of having multiple goals and an ambiguous relationship to markets (Moreau and Mertens, 2013). We then examine two approaches that help with the discovery and articulation of the social value that social enterprises create: SAA and SROI. The former is advocated by members of the Social Audit Network, while the latter, based on work in the mid-1990s at the Roberts Enterprise Development Fund in the US, has been adapted in many countries, including the UK (Emerson, 2000;

Pearce and Kay, 2008; Nicholls, 2009a). Towards the end of the chapter, we critically discuss the implications for practice, and then introduce a framework that connects '**social rationality**' to 'performance management' (Ridley-Duff, 2008b).

While recognising the political significance of rhetorical claims that SAA and SROI are 'objective', we do not regard either qualitative or quantitative measures as objective in an absolute sense. Instead, we regard them as interpretive frameworks that stakeholders deploy to argue for (or against) the allocation of resources. The reporting of social outcomes cannot sit outside this. Indeed we go as far as to suggest that social accounting and reporting are *marketing* tools to discover and promote the social value created by social enterprises. For this reason they are likely to grow in importance as business systems for deciding where to invest time, energy and money (Flockhart, 2005).

How is marketing different in social enterprises?

Ever since Kolter and Zaltman (1971) coined the term *social marketing*, the idea that marketing techniques can address the needs of organisations with social goals has been accepted in marketing theory (MacFayden et al., 1999). The most commonly articulated approach is to reproduce the planning and processes of a conventional marketing campaign, but use it to bring about changes in human behaviour. However, these assumptions have drawn criticism on the grounds that marketing in social enterprises pursues different aims (Dholakia and Dholakia, 1975). While there may be 'segments' of a population that a social enterprise wishes to 'target' (either to provide a benefit to a defined group or to change their behaviour), social enterprises may alternatively be committed to undoing the social damage created by the continual segmentation of populations by the private and public sectors. They may seek to undo the damage created by stereotyping or the dividing of people into classes, to resurrect the idea of universal access (to water, to medical care, to work, to food, to education). Universalisation may drive the logic of a social enterprise's marketing efforts, not segmentation. At the very least, the Ps in a marketing mix (product, place, price, promotion, people, process and physical evidence) need to expand, not limit, the market for goods or services, or place limits on impact.

There are some commonalities, however. While the popular perception of marketing is the 'action or business of promoting and selling products or services' (Google Search result), the Chartered Institution of Marketing (CIM) advances an academically grounded definition that marketing is 'the management process responsible for identifying, anticipating and satisfying customer requirements profitably' (CIM, 2009: 2). By highlighting processes for the identification and satisfaction of needs and wants, the CIM's definition deals effectively with the misperception that marketing is about advertising and selling. However, this is not sufficient for the social economy because it is more stakeholder, and less customer, driven. Secondly, social enterprises will prioritise blended value and impact over profit. Consequently, we define marketing for the purposes of this chapter as:

> The management process responsible for identifying, anticipating and creating goods and services needed by stakeholders through actions that efficiently redistribute, mutualise or market their availability.

This definition acknowledges that anticipating and meeting stakeholder needs is integral to marketing a social enterprise. However, doing this 'profitably' may be over-ridden by the desire to provide goods and services on a 'non-loss' basis to maximise access, rather than profits. In the rest of this chapter, we focus on accounting, auditing, returns and performance because these concepts frame how members of a social enterprise learn about, and monitor, the value they create for each stakeholder.

Social audit and accounting practices

Early approaches to social auditing and accounting can be traced to work undertaken at Beechwood College, Leeds (in Yorkshire, England). This is evidenced by *Social Audit: A Management Tool for Co-operative Working* (Spreckley, 1981) in which a triple bottom line is clearly articulated (see Chapter 2, Definition 1). This started nearly a decade before the Bruntland Report on sustainable development (Bruntland, 1987), and a full 15 years before Elkington took credit for its popularisation (Elkington, 2004). Spreckley was involved in the development of fair trade and worker co-operation (see Chapters 2 and 3).

Principles underpinning early social auditing in the UK

- It must be multi-perspective, i.e. include views from key stakeholders, staff, customers, beneficiaries, funders and investors, etc.
- It should be comprehensive, i.e. cover all activities of the social enterprise.
- The organisation should learn from the exercise by comparing performance over time with other, similar, organisations.
- Social audit should be undertaken regularly and become embedded in the running of the social enterprise.
- The social accounts prepared should be checked by an independent panel or assessor.
- The findings of the verified (i.e. audited) social accounts should be circulated and discussed.
- The process should underpin a philosophy of continuous improvement.

A social audit, therefore, starts with two inter-related questions:

1. What questions do you need to ask to evaluate the organisation's social impact?
2. How will you know if your organisation is 'successful'?

The first question can be enlightened by examining a clause from Geof Cox's Stakeholder Model Ltd (see Table 11.4). One clause (shown here in Case 4.2) sets out the perceived purpose of social audit by providing a way to assess governance processes and their internal and external impacts. A social audit, therefore, delves into deeper questions of what and why the enterprise does what it does, and who it is done to (or for), and the value it creates. Clause 28 mentions 'employees', 'customers', 'suppliers', 'people living in areas where the Company operates' and the 'natural environment' as stakeholders in a social audit.

Case 4.2

Stakeholder Model Ltd, Articles, Clause 28

28.2   A social audit of the Company's activities may, by resolution of the Directors, be undertaken annually in addition to the financial audit required by law.

28.2.1 The role of the social audit shall be to identify the social costs and benefits of the Company's work, and to enable an assessment to be made of the Company's overall performance in relation to its objects more easily than may be made from financial accounts alone.

28.2.2 Such a social audit may be drawn up by an independent assessor appointed by the Directors, or by the Directors, who may submit their report for verification or comments to any independent assessor.

28.2.3 A social audit may include an assessment of the internal democracy and decision making of the Company; the wages, health and safety, skill sharing and education opportunities of its employees, or other matters concerning the overall personal or job satisfaction of employees; and an assessment of the Company's activities externally, including its effects on customers and suppliers, on people living in areas where the Company operates, and on the natural environment.

The second question (How will you know if you are 'successful'?) extends into the domain of research philosophy. 'Success' is itself a socially constructed concept, and the issue is whether the quality of the evidence and the interpretation by an 'independent assessor' meet the criteria of 'success' established by the members of the enterprise being audited, or the lens that the assessor has been trained to use during auditing. The Stakeholder Model (see Table 11.4) relies on an independent assessor to prepare the social audit, or to verify one created by an enterprise's directors.

Paton (2003) observes that the current trend towards social auditing is part of an 'audit explosion' (Powell and DiMaggio, 1991). Organisations use audits to demonstrate their efficiency and effectiveness. Paton emphasises a number of differences between social audits and regular 'institutionalised' financial audits: they are undertaken voluntarily; they involve certification by a third party; they apply to governance and management *systems* (not just outcomes); and they offer scope for interviews and observation alongside documentary evidence. As Mook et al. (2007) point out, 'reporting and auditing' is the preferred lexicon of non-profit and social organisations, and the term 'accounting' may be avoided. The rationale for this 'alternative' language is explained by Pearce:

> Social audit is best understood as a reaction against conventional accounting principles and practices. These centre on the financial viability and profitability of the individual economic enterprise. By contrast, social audit proposes a broader financial and economic perspective, reaching far beyond the individual enterprise … which may not be amenable to quantification in monetary terms. (2003: 124)

Part of this reaction is linked to a different philosophical outlook. Mook et al. contrast the way the accounting profession is viewed by social auditors and **'rationalist'** accountants. In mainstream accounting, 'concepts such as profit and loss are viewed as a reality rather than a particular way of constructing reality' (2007: 3). In contrast:

> Social organizations can be understood more fully if they are studied contextually as organisms that affect and are affected by their communities. Within this context, accountants are active participants in shaping reality, a point of view that runs counter to the widely held perception of accountants as passive recorders of information. (2007: 7)

Having set out the history and terrain that social accounting aims to cover, we now consider two approaches. The first (SAA) is becoming the method of choice for CTAs and CMEs seeking to use accounting practice to engage stakeholders. The second (SROI) is becoming the method of choice for CTAs funded by the public sector and social businesses (SRBs) funded by social investments, particularly in the field of housing (McBurney, 2014).

A qualitative approach: social accounting and auditing

Social accounting and auditing is a flexible framework for capturing (and affecting) social impact. The framework is predominantly *qualitative* in nature, and according to the Social Audit Network it enables organisations to:

- account fully for their *social, environmental* and *economic* impacts
- report on performance
- provide essential information for planning future action and improving performance.

The process (see Figure 4.1) involves social enterprises following a cycle to develop their understanding of the impact they have on their community of interest and (where relevant) beneficiaries. Integral to the process is the opportunity to consult and account to stakeholders identified in the governance statement, and provide an honest assessment of the 'worth' of the enterprise.

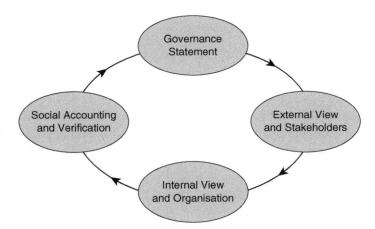

Figure 4.1   The process of social audit

Source: Spreckley (2008: 8)

The Social Audit was part of the initial development of social enterprise in 1978 at Beechwood College.

Pearce and Kay state:

> The first step is about organisations clarifying their mission, objectives and related activities, and the values and principles that underpin all their actions, as well as

identifying their key stakeholders. The second step involves recognising the quantitative and qualitative indicators that enable the enterprise to report effectively on its performance and impact against its stated mission, objectives and values through data collection and consulting appropriately with its key stakeholders. The third step is about bringing all the collected information together into social accounts that are then verified by an independent panel that, once satisfied, issues a social audit statement. Most organisations keep social accounts for a period which usually runs concurrent with their financial year. (2008: 9)

The SAA framework, available through the Social Audit Network, has a considerable following and is supported by a network of approved auditors. Gordon (2009) claims that the SAA framework is much cheaper to implement than SROI – with direct costs of £2000–£3000 against £19,000–£25,000 for SROI projects. External verification is a key selling feature that matches financial accounting practice, and the final report will have both marketing and management value.

Case 4.1 (continued)

The Wooden Canal Boat Society were made aware of funding from their local authority for health and well-being services. Dave Wilson of the Commissioning Team explains that WCBS had estimated the restoration at £128,000. A bid was rejected by the funders, because the social benefits were unclear. The WCBS were boat people while the commissioning team were care commissioners. There was little common language shared between them. The commissioning team required evidence in a language they understood and the WCBS needed to prove impact to persuade funders to invest public money outside of their comfort zone. Interest within Tameside Council in the SROI model was growing and so the team got directly involved with WCBS to develop an SROI forecast – both sides were able to learn something from the exercise.

Quantitative measures: social return on investment

The SROI approach, originally developed by the Roberts Enterprise Development Fund, is adapted from more traditional economic tools of **cost–benefit analysis** (Nicholls, 2009a). It aims to translate social impacts into financial values and is a predominantly (but not exclusively) *quantitative* approach. It is promoted in both the US and the UK, with the New Economics Foundation adapting the model for use in the UK. The SROI Network outlines the approach as follows:

> SROI is an approach to understanding and managing the impacts of a project, organisa-
> tion or policy. It is based on stakeholders and puts financial value on the important
> impacts identified by stakeholders that do not have market values. SROI seeks to
> include the values of people that are often excluded from markets in the same terms
> as used in markets, that is money, in order to give people a voice in resource allocation
> decisions. SROI is a framework to structure thinking and understanding. It's a story not
> a number. The story should show how you understand the value created, manage it
> and can prove it.
>
> *Source*: www.thesroinetwork.org/content/view/31/1/ (accessed 20 May 2010).

NEF acknowledges that there are limitations if systems are not in place to collect data,
and that the process is time consuming and demands a diverse range of 'soft' and 'hard'
skills. Nicholls (2009a) also points out that SROI can rarely benchmark effectively and
has to use proxies that can be directly linked to monetary values. Furthermore, in
practice 'operating costs' are difficult to discern from 'core costs', and where organisations use goodwill, volunteer efforts and grant funding, these may not be factored into
the 'true cost' of a project. We add another consideration. The approach is based on an
a priori model of change (inputs, activities, outputs, outcomes and impacts). While this
enables comparisons to be made, and gives the process a structure, it inhibits an
organisation from benchmarking against its own change model (as captured in a
'governance statement', for example).

Table 4.1   SROI impact analysis

Inputs	Activities	Outputs	Outcomes	Impacts
• Service contracts • Grants • Sales revenues • Volunteer time	• Training • Work placements • Jobs	• Number of people involved in training • Number and level of qualifications obtained	• Job skills learned • Soft skills learned • Well-being, social and personal development • Life satisfaction • Increases in income • Reduced dependence on benefits • Reduction in reoffending and crime	• Subtract what would have happened anyway to estimate impact • Check that each column leads to accomplishing the mission

Source: based on nef (2006)

The key innovation in the NEF approach is to move beyond 'outputs' and consider
'outcomes' and 'impacts'. While outputs are amenable to quantitative measurement,
outcomes are *qualitative* changes in the lives of the people affected by the social enterprise's employment practices, products and/or services. Impacts, however, require

further quantitative analysis. An assessment is made whether the outcomes would have occurred anyway, or whether they are a result of contributions by the social enterprise (Table 4.1). If the latter, the monetary impact of the qualitative changes can be assessed and aggregated, then presented in such a way that the value of each £1 invested can be demonstrated to potential funders or investors.

SROI frames the issues it is going to address in terms of 'desired outcomes', and (in the NEF implementation) has sufficient flexibility to allow stakeholders to define these. While adopting a quantitative approach, it is justified on the basis that the social sector needs a method of accounting that can bridge into the world of public sector procurement and social investment (Flockhart, 2005). SROI, therefore, is designed primarily to meet the needs of social investors (just as statutory accounts are designed primarily to help financial investors). Also, just as management accounts are needed to supplement statutory accounts, an SAA report may be needed to supplement SROI to provide the 'internal' view needed for management activities.

Nevertheless, the attribution of financial values to outcomes in order to calculate savings to wider society *is* an accounting innovation. Where organisations need to demonstrate value to commissioning bodies, charitable trusts and social investors, SROI offers an advantage. Arguably, SROI is more than an accounting tool. It is also a way of thinking that enables a social enterprise to identify the value of their service to any other party (expressed in both non-financial and financial terms). As such it can be an effective sales tool (in individual tender situations) and a marketing tool (for sector-level knowledge creation) by setting out how social value gets created.

Case 4.1 (continued)

At the WCBS a three-person working group set about an SROI forecast. The trio represented WCBS, the Council and a sector support agency. From the outset it became clear that rigour was an issue; time constraints, proxies and attribution issues might undermine the credibility of the forecast. The team planned for people with mental health issues to be involved in every step, from restoration of the boat, working alongside boat restoration engineers (boat builders) as well as passengering (boat users) once restored. The numbers were too great to count, the mental health issues too varied, the impact too unwieldy. They decided to focus on one type of person – the boat users – disregarding boat builders in the forecasting process. Upwards of 30 stakeholders were invited to be part of the analysis. This compromised the forecast ratio, but made the plan more manageable.

SAA and SROI: similarities and differences

The SAA and SROI approaches share the aim of benefiting people by clarifying and measuring social impacts. Nonetheless there are tensions between these two approaches. In our experience, support agencies appear to promote one, or the other, but rarely both approaches. An exception to this trend is social housing where McBurney (2014) found 58 per cent prepared SROI reports, and 18 per cent used SAA. SAA emphasises a bottom-up community development approach focused upon building capacity and producing a bespoke social auditing framework. The SAA approach emphasises social rationality by prioritising relationships with stakeholders, soliciting and reporting their views, and using the process to stimulate further discussion. While stakeholders play a role in SROI, their involvement is more instrumental. They provide 'data' on 'outcomes' to support econometric calculations.

A criticism of SAA's approach, however, is that it produces reports that are not (easily) comparable to those of other organisations (Nicholls, 2009a). Because SROI is focused on external relationships, it is driven by government and social policy agendas (mission is matched to the fundholder's objectives), and seeks to measure the effect of service delivery (tasks are matched to fundholder's service requirements). This 'task based' view encourages a level of standardisation in which individual organisations act as suppliers of data so that commissioners and policy-makers can use it to decide their priorities. Secondly, as SAA is a report and SROI contains a single financial ratio, the appeal to funders is instant. As Pearce and Kay write:

> SROI is attractive to investors, funders and contractors, especially in the public sector, because it speaks the language of business and gives them a number. However, a related concern is that such interest can tend to make the SROI process funder and investor led. (2008: 18)

Pearce (2009) comments that SROI is over-emphasised by government and warns of the danger that the UK and Scotland governments are expressing a 'worrying trend towards control' rather than acting as enablers of community-led enterprise.

Another difference is in the steps each approach requires: the Social Audit Network has devised an infrastructure to support quality assurance, which is lacking in SROI. Pearce points out that the verification process for a social audit involves three to five persons, normally chaired by someone with experience, and drawn from a register of approved social auditors. The independence of the panel underpins a 'rigorous' and 'tough' day-long process of analysis that is concurrently 'creative and constructive'.

In practice, there is room for both frameworks, each serving different needs. Pearce and Kay (2008) report progress towards this by members of both networks (Table 4.2). Interestingly, practitioners in both networks also agreed how their approaches differ:

> One difference is that SROI is predicated on the notion that a financial indicator may be found for a change that is achieved (sometimes using a proxy if no actual indicator is available). While SROI argues that 'the number is not as important as the story' the reality

is that most people (and SROI reports) tend to focus on the number and the basis on which it is calculated. SAA by no means rejects the importance of numbers and indeed advocates the use of financial indicators when this is appropriate. However, SAA believes that there are some outcomes and impacts which can only be described and reported using the views and perceptions of stakeholders – in effect the 'story'. (Pearce and Kay, 2008: 15)

Table 4.2   Common principles underpinning SAA and SROI

Principle	Definition
Stakeholder engagement	Engaging with, and consulting, stakeholders is central to the process of social accounting in order to understand the impact of the organisation
Scope and materiality	Acknowledge and articulate the values and objectives of stakeholders before agreeing which aspects are to be included in the social accounting process, so that stakeholders can draw conclusions about performance and impact
Understanding change	Articulate clearly how activities work, and how they contribute to the social and charitable objectives of the organisation and its stakeholders. Evaluate these on the basis of the evidence gathered
Comparative	Make comparisons of performance and impact using appropriate benchmarks, annual targets and external standards
Transparency	Demonstrate the basis on which the findings may be considered accurate and honest; show they will be reported to and, where appropriate and feasible, discussed with stakeholders
Verification	Ensure appropriate independent verification of the social accounts
Embedded	Ensure that the process of social accounting and audit becomes embedded in the life cycle and management practices of the organisation

Source: based on Pearce and Kay (2008)

Pearce and Kay (2008) view the starting points for the two approaches as different. SAA is focused on the need for organisation members to be clear about their vision, mission, objectives and activities, and the identification of stakeholders who are either affected by, or can affect, the organisation. These stakeholders become partners in the process of social accounting and are consulted on how they view the organisation's performance and impact. While SROI starts from a similar point, it identifies the stakeholders' objectives in relation to their engagement with the organisation (as 'inputs', 'activities', 'outputs', etc.) and develops financial indicators to assess the value of their involvement.

The emphasis on and use of financial indicators places SROI within a positivist discourse linked to mainstream economics, without presenting any serious challenge to it. While the two frameworks appear to prescribe different paths for organisations – the SAA approach is presented as 'bottom-up' and 'grassroots', while the SROI community reflects a 'top-down' approach (Nicholls, 2009a) – both make claims to be objective representations of reality. However, those undertaking an SAA audit are advised to consult stakeholders on how performance should be evaluated: there is scope for stakeholders to *construct* criteria and shape their organisational reality. SROI advisers, on the other hand, seek to present performance in predefined ways (as outcomes and impacts) by deploying an *a priori* theory of social change. Measurements are presented in ways that meet the needs of public commissioners and social investors, rather than the organisation's stakeholders. This being the case, SAA emphasises the access, information and emotional needs of stakeholders and demonstrates commitment to social rationality. SROI requires access to information (in a one-way exchange), and then uses this to undertake an intellectual task that measures material value. It deploys social rationality instrumentally in order to pursue an **economic rationality** 'end'.

Case 4.1 (continued)

The WCBS SROI project was complex, their Excel skills were put to the test to develop a meaningful ratio and 'there was a certain amount of manipulating the figures as the working group went through the analysis. Foremost in the minds of those in the working group was a final ratio that looked reasonable and realistic' (Wilson and Bull, 2013: 322). Despite a flawed and somewhat compromised impact assessment, they arrived at a ratio of 1:4. For every £1 of investment, there would be £4 worth of savings across state services. The team acknowledge and are clear that the ratio would not stand up to close scrutiny. The exercise highlighted the challenges of proportionality and attribution. But they also concluded that the learning process was as important as the ratio itself. The SROI project turned out to be the tipping point in the bid. After a second proposal, they secured funding for the project.

Class exercise: Analysing approaches to impact measurement

Further materials (Cases 4.1, 4.2 and 4.3) are available on the companion website at: www.sagepub.co.uk/ridleyduff.

Organise the seminar participants into groups of three (members A, B and C).

- Give cases 4.1 and 4.3 to group member A.
- Give cases 4.2 and 4.3 to group member B.

- Give an evaluation grid to group member C.
- Ask group member A to explain the types of performance that are stimulated and measured by SROI.
- Ask group member B to explain the types of performance that are stimulated and measured by SAA.
- Ask group member C to show their analysis to members A and B. Discuss and, if necessary, amend the interpretation.

Critical perspectives on social reporting

In research using the Balance Tools (Bull, 2006, 2007), the diagnostics provide an opportunity for organisations to highlight their social impact (see Table 4.3). This could potentially be used as a promotional technique for audited standards (externally verified SAA, SROI), performance evaluation, social aims, non-financial reporting or social accounting. Balance captures evidence of engagement with SROI and SAA in a number of its sections. Based on findings from 751 assessments, social enterprises were found to be between stage 2 ('thinking but not doing') and stage 3 ('currently working on'), with results for social accounting that indicate they are at stage 2 ('thinking but not doing'). Furthermore, on average the social enterprises in the sample are starting to engage with social impact management, but are only at the start of the process. This is interesting given that the sector is so reliant on public funding as the press give the impression that the trend is towards proving the value of contracts under the Social Value Act 2012.

Table 4.3 Balance results (related to marketing and measuring social value)

Section	Topic	Mean (stage 1 low to 5 high)
Marketing	Promotion techniques	3.2
Internal activities	Audited standards	2.3
	Performance evaluation	2.9
Multi-bottom line	Social aims	3.5
	Non-financial metrics	2.8
	Social accounting	2.2
	Mean	2.82

Nicholls (2009a) outlines the importance of reporting social value creation as part of a search for sustainable solutions to social change. By evidencing it using a dialogic process (like SAA), it can become more than this. It can become integral to a relationship marketing strategy (Berry, 1983; Buchanan and Gilles, 1990) that builds and retains both individual and collective commitment by soliciting stakeholders' perceptions of performance. Paton (2003) hints at this motive when he reports that practitioners engage in performance measurement for many reasons. They may wish: to develop relationships with (different) stakeholders; to demonstrate competitive advantage; to improve performance; to satisfy funders' requirements. Each motive influences what is counted, how it is valued, and the level of willingness to change measures in the future. While it is unsurprising that social enterprise members will not be enthused in equal measure by social reporting activities, the evidence from 751 Balance assessments shows that there is a disparity between rhetoric and reality in the sector. Of 28 measures that Balance tracks, social auditing and social reporting were found to be the two practices that were *least* developed, while the *four* most developed (in order) were cash flow management, sustainability, participation and stakeholder governance.

Coule (2008) suggests that these discrepancies can be partly explained by accountability 'pulls' that influence stakeholder relationships and strategic priorities. This may explain why – in the wake of a decade consulting and promoting community interest companies – there has been a 'pull' towards community engagement. Since 2008, in the wake of events triggered by global banking institutions, and subsequent cuts in public services and jobs, there is more interest in the democratisation of capital ownership and workplace management (Dunning et al., 2015; Social Economy Alliance, 2015). Alternatively, the climate debate moves in and out of political discourse, and may yet form the dominant alternative discourse to the status quo (Baudhardt, 2014). Whichever is the case, social accounting provides a means to explore (and critique) such questions as: who is setting the agenda? How much attention is paid to member, public and beneficiary interests? How much voice is given to each stakeholder?

The proxies chosen to assess social impact *do* matter. The following items, for example, are presented as proxies for 'performance' at different points in this book:

- 50 per cent 'earned income' as a watershed for recognition as a social enterprise
- the number of social enterprises reported in sector surveys
- the level of member ownership (particularly worker ownership) in a social enterprise
- the number of jobs created (relative to investment levels) by social enterprises
- the number of people who benefit from the services of social enterprises.

While we can acknowledge that the above numbers superficially indicate significance and impact, these are quantitative, *income* or *service*-related measures and do not measure entrepreneurial innovation or well-being throughout society. In short, these are what NEF would call outputs, *not* outcomes. This, however, is not to suggest that qualitative measures are the most appropriate or without their own limitations, or that quantitative measures are irrelevant. Rather, we argue that there is a false dichotomy when qualitative and quantitative measures are separated from each other. They both need collection and interpretation to produce knowledge.

As Light (2008) comments, most measurement systems for social enterprise and entrepreneurship do not offer information on social change and impact. They offer a means for evaluating the effectiveness and efficiency of service delivery or the level and sophistication of internal organisational development (see Case 8.4, Balance).

Performance as a concept

How can we reframe 'performance' to capture higher level outcomes and impacts more effectively? During lecture tours to Indonesian universities, Rory developed four questions to promote debate about the nature of social entrepreneurship and value creation.

- Is it the pursuit and fulfilment of a social goal/mission (through CTAs)?
- Is it the inclusive way social enterprises are organised (through CMEs)?
- Is it the way the wealth is distributed and reinvested (for the benefit of many, not a few)?
- Is it the pursuit of sustainable development (protecting/enhancing natural, human and social capital)?

If the creation of social value is a key performance measure, consider the way performance is viewed by the following interviewees (from Exercise 4.2 on the companion website). Every participant interviewed in this study had been working under target-driven contracts in the field of healthcare. They express increasing awareness of the limitations of quantitative performance measures. To navigate the ambiguity in their statements, a multi-dimensional model of social and economic rationality was developed to interpret findings from this study of performance coaching (Ridley-Duff, 2005, 2009). The framework in Table 4.4 clarifies constructions of 'performance', and how they link to each other and social impact.

Class exercise: What is social performance?

Exercise 4.2 on the companion website contains further materials to undertake this as a seminar activity.

(Continued)

(Continued)

Example 1

Performance can be shown as hard evidence, but you would surely want some qualitative change? If people are performing their job correctly, they are showing some change in their ethics ... their broad values and approaches which aren't open, or only with great difficulty, to hard facts.

Example 2

It's not about efficiency, not about tasks, it is about being effective ... and personal happiness and goals and things. If people aren't happy, they don't perform ... Happiness is the key to it all for me. Sounds a bit on the hippy side, but there you are.

Example 3

I get frustrated ... while I like the debate ... I like to move forward to action and achievement as a result. That will be different for different people ... The other thing that comes into it ... this is the bit where I hesitate because it is so difficult to measure ... it is someone who achieves what they've got to do, but also achieves growth and has a good attitude. Now how do you measure a good attitude?

Example 4

It's keeping that cycle of learning and ongoing movement ... not stagnating ... when you talk in all those [competency] terms that are the 'in' terms ... it switches people off ... it's good stuff, it is, but people think of all these manuals, and forms they have to fill in. I like to keep the free flow, something that you don't feel strangled by. That helps you to get through the competency framework.
(Health sector manager interviews, February/March 2009)

Questions:

1 Can social dimensions of performance (ethics, attitude, happiness and learning) be measured?
2 What proxies might indicate 'good' social performance?
3 What impact does social performance have on the development of social, ethical and human capital?

Table 4.4 **Theorising links between performance and social impact**

Type	Characteristics	Performance and social impact
Social performance (supported by social rationality): 'developing a community of interest' using skills at getting and giving attention in order to form, develop, maintain and end relationships		
Emotion	Giving and getting access or information that clarifies emotional commitments	Performance as the ability to interpret social network dynamics and clarify emotional commitments in order to help people process emotions and make decisions about their relationships
	Giving and getting access or information that stimulates emotion, and communicates emotional attitudes and intentions	
Information	Giving and getting information about people, ideas and tasks so that access to people can be organised or direct assistance offered	Performance as the ability to obtain, organise, analyse and use information to develop human relationships for their own sake (rather than in pursuit of a task)
	Giving and getting attention through sharing knowledge, story-telling and joking	
Access	Giving and getting access to people, ideas and resources	Performance as the ability to create, use or shape tasks in such a way that they contribute to the formation and development of satisfying relationships
	Giving and getting attention (verbal and non-verbal) that conveys personal interest	
	Presenting oneself in ways that induce others to communicate and commit to ongoing relationships	
Economic performance (supported by economic rationality): 'getting the job done' using skills in getting and giving assistance in order to complete tasks		
Physical	Giving and getting commitments to meet face-to-face, travel and relocate. Facilitating meetings and providing direct assistance with physical tasks	Performance as the capacity to motivate oneself to arrange and attend meetings with others, and adopt or model behaviours that support the effective and efficient completion of tasks
	Physical behaviour that fuels commitments to care for (and economically support) colleagues and dependents	
Intellectual	Giving and getting (sharing) conceptual ideas that provide alternative ways of understanding how to go about tasks	Performance as the capacity to develop and disseminate expertise, and apply it in ways that bring about the effective and/or efficient performance of tasks
	Knowledge of how to give and get assistance in ways that induce and maintain mutual commitment	
Material	Giving and getting non-physical and non-intellectual support (e.g. money, time, contracts) that leads to material gains in pay, cost-effectiveness and service or trading opportunities	Performance as the capacity to manage money and time effectively in the acquisition, delivery and completion of tasks and contracts

Source: adapted from Ridley-Duff (2009: 42), Table 5

The framework was developed during a three-year study of social enterprise governance to highlight competing rationales for enterprise that recursively shape each other (Ridley-Duff, 2005). It was revised further during a 12-month study of 'performance coaching' (Ridley-Duff, 2009). The model outlines a *relational* perspective on organisations in which people – usually outside the management group – are viewed as the *primary* source of satisfaction (and dissatisfaction) at work. Relationships constitute the 'ends' of enterprise, rather than the 'means', and are valued for their own sake. This view competes with a task-based view in which people – more often managers or entrepreneurs – pursue goals (status, income, recognition) and organisational objectives (missions, targets). From this view, relationships are 'means' and not 'ends', subordinated to the pursuit of individual or collectively determined 'goals'. Exercise 4.2 (on the companion website) highlights that people as well as processes matter, and that performance can be viewed through many lenses. Different people have different views on what they perceive is important (to themselves and to others).

Emerson (2000) frames this as a difference between 'interactive social capital' (social value created through the interactions of people with each other) and 'transactive social capital' (social and economic value deriving from the transactions that social interaction makes possible). The relational view of organisation is shaped by social rationality, a decision-making model that supports the formation, development, management and maintenance of relationships. Gates's (1998) critique of Anglo-American societies suggests that skills in social rationality have been lost while technical competence (economic rationality) is still developing. Competing with this perspective is the task-based view that organisations (and therefore the people in them) serve a mission, goal or 'higher purpose'. In this case, economic rationality dominates by elevating the pursuit of a 'task' or 'goal' above the individual members of the organisation (and even the organisation itself) so that they are regarded as subservient to it. This world view has been strengthening in western corporations, reshaping business practice (Miller and Rice, 1967), influencing public administration (Hood, 1995) and – despite resistance – affecting notions of management in the social economy (Dart, 2004).

As Turnbull (1994) claims, social interaction necessarily *precedes* any economic transaction, and therefore provides more scope for economy (in the broadest sense). This being the case, economy depends *primarily* on understanding efficient and effective 'social interaction' in which financial management is just one of many elements. This reverses the dominant logic of economics based on income–expenditure analysis, and has profound implications for social accounting practice in social enterprises. Social rationality not only acquires equivalent status to economic rationality, it reframes economic competence as just one of many forms of social rationality that captures only a small part of performance in an organisation – and therefore only a small part of its 'impact' (Paton, 2003).

Ridley-Duff's model (2005, 2009) makes clearer how the greatest potential for impact occurs when all aspects of social and economic performance can be 'blended'. Anything that decreases the ability of people to assist each other inhibits social performance (i.e. limits their capacity to develop sustainable satisfying relationships). Similarly, anything that inhibits relationship development potentially decreases economic performance (i.e. limits capacity to collaborate to achieve goals or 'missions'). Consequently, the need for a holistic approach that interprets, analyses and reports blended value continues to grow (Nicholls, 2009a).

Implications for social enterprises

In the drive to make enterprises more efficient and/or business-like, there is a point made by Stacey (2007: 39) that systems have 'paid little attention … to ethics, ordinary human freedoms and the unknown nature of the final state towards which human action tends'. Though issues of ethics and human freedoms are talked about in social enterprise practices, both SAA and SROI are oriented towards the idea that organisations are systems of rational causality, with inputs leading to outputs, which can be 'objectively' assessed.

Grenier (2002) highlights that within this discourse, opportunity is presented as a 'fact' that the social enterprise needs to recognise or frame in order to take effective action. However, our experience is that this process does not begin by identifying a clear opportunity. Instead, there is a 'fuzzy' or 'trial-by-error' process guided by the desire to change something for the better. Goldstein et al. (2008) note that there is a decreasing tolerance for the emergent or unexpected outcomes that Mintzberg et al. (1998) see as a vital part of strategy development. There is less attention to the quality of network dynamics, and less discussion of the way structures and power relations are changed by regimes of measurement and control. A potential problem is that organisation members may fail to question and challenge the thinking in which they become embedded, and be unable to relate this thinking to their own failure to achieve particular outcomes.

Stacey (2007) sees this as a legacy of naïve cause-and-effect models in the natural sciences that social scientists have rejected as inadequate as a theoretical base for organisation and management studies (Burrell and Morgan, 1979; Morgan, 1986; Grey, 2005). A more promising line of thought is one based on holistic thinking about management systems, to organising them as *dialogic* exchanges between sentient actors, in which every participant can provide and obtain feedback to assist critical and 'generative' thinking (Beer, 1966, 1972; Stacey, 2007; Coule, 2008; Cooperrider et al., 2014).

Conclusions

The private sector, as well as politicians on national and international stages, frequently talk of the need for 'competitive advantage'. This chapter suggests that the marketing slogan used by co-operatives is equally apt for the social enterprise sector. There are also benefits from seeking a 'co-operative advantage' by modifying accounting practices and emphasising the value of collaboration in knowledge development, not just within the boundaries of a single organisation, but at the level of a social network that spans organisational boundaries. As Paton argues:

> Performance (particularly in social enterprises) is what … people more or less agree, implicitly or explicitly, to be performance. (2003: 5)

Where programme outcomes do not have a market, or a monetary value, but are valued within a community, it is difficult – perhaps impossible – to assess value using a commercial framework. The evidence in this chapter suggests that these programmes can be valued through new forms of discursive democracy, and through research and audit processes that give a voice to stakeholders commensurate with their interest in a change process.

Commercial frameworks marginalise social impact by emphasising discussions on what Emerson (2000) calls 'transactive social capital'. Social auditing has a different focus: 'interactive social capital'. As Pearce (2003) argues, the value of social auditing is that it supports the development of social rationality to 'empower the many' rather than a few individuals. By deviating from traditional accounting practice, it becomes possible to envisage a business community where *any* group or individual who can affect or is affected by an organisation's business activity can decide how to influence the future direction of that business. They might be an employee, a volunteer, a customer, a client or a member of a geographic or interest-based community. Social audit and reporting provide an institution for capturing and acting on their feedback.

Summary of learning

In this chapter, we have outlined issues in social audit, reporting and investment and the debates regarding the reporting of social performance. Principally, we have argued that:

A constructionist approach is useful to understand the diversity of language and approaches in social accounting, and the role of the accountancy profession in shaping the 'reality' of social enterprise.

Marketing for social enterprises involves the identification, anticipation and satisfaction of stakeholders' needs.

Two approaches to assessing social performance have emerged, one based on auditing the views of stakeholders, the other based on monetising the 'impact' of the organisation's activities.

The two approaches come together in the concepts of 'integrated accounting' and 'blended value' that seek to report both economic and social outcomes together.

Both approaches stress their 'objectivity', although SAA is more clearly oriented towards the development of a 'relational' approach to organisation development.

The concept and measurement of performance are hampered by an under-theorisation of the 'social' dimensions of performance.

Social performance can be assessed by developing performance indicators for social rationality.

Questions and possible essay assignments

1. 'Social accounting and auditing should be oriented towards the satisfaction of a social enterprise's internal stakeholders.' Critically assess the benefits and limitations of this view, and assess whether social auditing could also act as a marketing model for social enterprise.
2. Describe the analysis framework that underpins social return on investment. What advantages does this offer when tendering for public sector contracts or seeking social investments?
3. 'Neither SAA nor SROI fully address the issue of social enterprise performance.' Critically assess the concept of performance, and the extent to which SAA and SROI support the development of social rationality.

Further reading

The debates surrounding the measurement of performance are well framed in Rob Paton's research into the topic in *Managing and Measuring Social Enterprises* (2003). The book is useful for its analysis of the way practitioners vary their engagement with performance measurement, and a **constructivist** perspective that 'gets inside' the different outlooks that inform practice. There are several lengthy and accessible reports that refer to the development of practice. The first is a report from the Social Audit Network by Pearce and Kay (2008). Although somewhat partisan in its recommendations, it articulates findings from 70 organisations who have undertaken social accounting. Detailed practitioner guidance on social audit is available in the fourth edition of Spreckley's *Social Audit Toolkit* (2008) published by Local Livelihoods, while guidance on SROI produced by the Cabinet Office in 2009 has been updated by members of the SROI Network (2012) (www.thesroinetwork.org/sroi-analysis/the-sroi-guide).

We also recommend four articles to support study. For undergraduates, we recommend starting with Flockhart's (2005) paper about the rising influence of SROI in public procurement, and then following this with Wilson and Bull's article on SROI in practice. For more advanced study, we have suggested Mook's (2007) article which presents accounting as a socially embedded activity, not a technical profession. Lastly, we recommend Nicholls's (2009b) scholarly critique that deploys three different theoretical perspective to make sense of five cases that inform the field of 'blended value accounting'.

Further reading material is available on the companion website at: www.sagepub. co.uk/ ridleyduff.

Useful resources

Balance diagnostic tool: www.socialenterprisebalance.org/

FairShares Diagnostics: www.fairshares.coop/wordpress/diagnostics/

Impact Measurement: impactinvesting.marsdd.com/social-impact-measurement/

Prove and Improve: www.proveandimprove.org/

Social Audit (India): http://ibsa.cgg.gov.in/Books-SocialAudit/1.pdf

Social Audit (UK): www.locallivelihoods.com/cmsms/index.php?page=publications

The Social Audit Network: http://socialauditnetwork.org.uk

Social Reporting Blog: http://ifad-un.blogspot.com/

SROI Network: www.thesroinetwork.org

Income Streams and Capital Management

5

Learning objectives

In this chapter we discuss the idiosyncrasies of generating an income and managing capital in social enterprises. Different sources of finance are outlined, providing the reader with an awareness of how many social enterprises differ from traditional charities and for-profit businesses. By the end of this chapter you will be able to:

- critique the idea that social enterprises are non-profit
- distinguish between forms of income (donation, grants, contracts and market trading)
- explain restricted, unrestricted and designated funds
- critically assess arguments for the diversification of income streams to sustain a social enterprise.

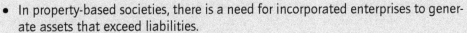

The key arguments that will be developed in this chapter are:

- In property-based societies, there is a need for incorporated enterprises to generate assets that exceed liabilities.
- A contract mind-set is different to a grant aid mind-set. There is a heightened sense of accountability to funders for outputs and outcomes.

(Continued)

(Continued)

- Income generation may be based on a 'whole economy' (all trading) or a 'mixed receipts' (partial trading) strategy.
- The legal form of a social enterprise affects its ability to raise capital and trade effectively.

Introduction

In previous chapters we have introduced the contexts of social enterprise development (Chapters 1, 2 and 3), the challenges of sustainable trading (Part 2 – Introduction), and the creation, monitoring and development of social value (Chapter 4). Each is connected to strategies that are adopted to generate income and raise capital for social investment. In this chapter we consider the different forms of economic capital that a social enterprise can access, and how trading improves economic sustainability. We do this to present the breadth of choices available, and to assess the strengths and weaknesses of each.

We deal firstly with terminology by myth busting the term 'non-profit'. We show how the term 'profit' is used differently in charitable trading activities (CTAs), co-operative and mutual enterprises (CMEs) and socially responsible businesses (SRBs). We explore the nuances surrounding the terms 'surplus' and 'profit', and how the latter is frequently imposed on the social economy to conform to private sector accounting norms. Secondly, we look at changes in the balance between trading activities, grants and donations, and how successful trading provides greater access to **debt finance** (loans). We conclude the chapter by preparing the ground for Chapter 6 in which we examine the growth of social investment. By the end of this chapter, you will be able to explain and critique financial strategies that aim to maximise blended value (Emerson, 2000).

Surplus, profit, non-profit and the production of blended value

It can be argued that the mix of income streams defines a social enterprise. One aspect of the definition of social enterprise we outlined in Chapter 2 was the level of trading, and we will return to this shortly. Before we do that, we want to stress how the delicate balance between different kinds of capital (economic, social, human, intellectual, natural) are the lifeblood of any organisation. Social enterprises are no different in this respect. This said, economic capital – the machinery, tools and financial resources available to an enterprise – have a far reaching influence on its potential to generate impact and it is this type of capital that we focus on in this chapter.

Brinckerhoff (2000) sums up this attitude well: 'no profit – no mission'. We think there is a grain of truth in this statement. At the same time, we need to be mindful that 'profit' and 'mission' are socially constructed concepts that are interpreted differently in various cultural settings. The way private businesses use the words 'profit' and 'mission' may have a different logic to the way they are used in social businesses. Moreover, social entrepreneurs may accept or reject private business norms, prompting Emerson (2000: 23–4) to comment that '[economic rules are] the constructs of social perception … fully imbedded within our social systems [that] act upon each other in an endless interplay'. As we discuss elsewhere in this text, social entrepreneurs frequently 'rewrite' economic and social rules. The same can be true of social enterprises and their strategies for generating income. Consider the term 'surplus'. Surplus – the balance of income over expenditure generated by members – is a term used by many but not all social enterprises. SRBs would probably express this as 'profit' because they exist entirely within the market system, as do many consumer co-operatives. But other social enterprises do not, and educational material for worker co-operatives in the USA differentiates 'surplus' from 'profit' on the basis that surplus is generated by the work of members, while profit describes the acquisition of financial capital from the employment of labour.

The closer organisations are to the private economy (Pearce, 2003) the more comfortable they are expressing income over expenditure as 'profit'. The closer organisations are to the social economy, the more comfortable they are expressing income over expenditure as either 'surplus' or 'profit' depending on the audience they talk to (see Table 5.1). As we have discussed in Chapter 3, social enterprises that have member-owners (co-operative shareholders) and which are permitted to distribute surpluses may be required by local laws to express distributions of surplus as a 'profit-share' or 'dividend' for tax purposes. Social enterprises closer to the third sector stick to the term 'surplus' within their legal entity, particularly where the members are guarantors or trustees (not shareholders). In this case, surpluses cannot be distributed as a profit-share, as it is illegal to do so.

Class exercise: Distinguishing surplus and profit

Watch the following video: www.youtube.com/watch?v=qbZ8ojEuN5I
Based on this clip, consider the following issues:

1 What justifications are offered for worker control and ownership of enterprises?
2 What is a '**patronage refund**'? Who receives it?
3 What is 'profit' according to the Democracy at Work Network in the USA? Who gets it?

Table 5.1   Expressing the difference between income and expenditure in social enterprises

Legal format	Ownership	Terminology
• Company Limited by Shares or Community Interest Company (CLS Incorporation)	• Shareholders	• Profit/Loss
• Co-operative Society • Mutual Society • Employee-owned Business	• Members • Employee shareholders or employee trusts	• Surplus/Deficit or Profit/Loss
• Voluntary Association • Community Benefit Society • Credit Union • CIO Association	• Members	• Surplus/Deficit
• Company Limited by Guarantee or Community Interest Company (CLG Incorporation)	• Volunteer	• Surplus/Deficit
• Charity/Foundation • CIO Foundation	• Volunteer	• Surplus/Deficit

Whatever the terminology, it is not the case that social enterprise members are uninterested in trading profitably or generating a surplus. The key difference with private enterprises is not whether they seek to trade profitably, but the role that trading plays in achieving *social* goals, and how profits from trading are invested by members to maximise well-being.

In property-based economies (where ownership of the means of production is organised as a property right), an incorporated organisation needs to acquire or generate assets that exceed liabilities over its lifetime (i.e. to generate a cumulative net surplus or profit). Any that cannot do this will become *insolvent* and are legally obligated to cease trading. This economic imperative is, however, not without its critics. Yunus (2007: 5) claims that placing profitability above all other considerations creates an economy that 'exacerbates poverty, disease, pollution, corruption, crime and inequality'. So what is Yunus challenging? We need to clarify some finer points of the economic imperative as well as rethink the implications of labelling non-market driven enterprises as non-profit.

'Non-profit' is a term that has become common within the voluntary sector, and is a legal term in the US. However, it is worth clarifying that this means non-profit *distributing*, rather than non-profit *making*. The sector has been perceived as negative about economic viability (non-profit taken as *no*-profit, and therefore loss-making). Clarifying that there are profit-making, but non-profit distributing, organisations within the field of social enterprise (engaged in CTAs) crystallises why paying dividends to private individuals and firms is seen as a boundary marker in social enterprise culture.

But non-profit distribution is not a defensible boundary because it does not distinguish private from social enterprises. Some social enterprises (CMEs and SRBs) may create social value through their approach to distributing surpluses to members and/or beneficiaries. What if the boundary was reframed in terms of whether an enterprise was 'for-purpose' (purpose-driven) or 'not for-purpose' (profit-driven) (McCulloch, 2013)? Would it be reasonable to label all private enterprises as 'not for-purpose'? Or would some 'private' enterprises share characteristics with for-purpose enterprises (i.e. social enterprises)?

Social enterprises engaged in CTAs either aim to generate a surplus/profit or miti-gate a loss. By reducing the amounts siphoned off from surplus/profits, they reinvest more in social value creation. Figure 5.1 outlines the continuous production of value. Income (from philanthropic or commercial sources) is invested in the production of goods and services. These are then sold to generate 'blended returns' (Emerson, 2000). The economic surplus feeds back into further product and service development, creat-ing further blended value. The outputs are goods and services. The outcomes are economic, social and ethical capital (see Chapter 7). If needed, social and ethical capital can be used to attract more philanthropic, co-operative or private capital (Bourdieu, 1986).

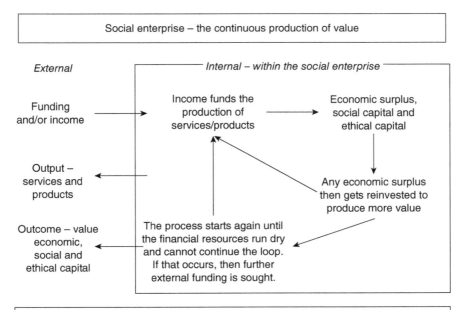

Figure 5.1   The continuous production of value

In terms of Yunus's (2007) challenge, there is a subtle, yet crucial, difference here between for-profit organisations and (for-profit) social enterprises. Private busi-nesses are profit centres for shareholders whereas social enterprises are profit centres (or surplus generators) for stakeholders. Private businesses are primarily driven by institutions and laws that require them to maximise the creation of financial capital for shareholders – they are required by law to be profit-*maximising*. Social enterprises are primarily driven by institutions that seek to create stakeholder value (as outlined in Chapter 4). They are profit-*making* or surplus generating mechanisms that support community development or which fulfil a social mission. The argument that you can do more good with an increased income is rooted in the assumption that improvements in well-being can be secured for more people.

As Price (2008) argues, increases in income may create more social value by:

- employing more marginalised people (minority groups, people with disabilities or health problems)
- speeding up regeneration of a local economy (in post-industrial, rural and deprived areas)
- creating more 'low-profit' businesses to increase the availability of much needed goods and services
- creating more value-driven businesses that pursue sustainability (recycling, renewable energy, fair trade)
- creating more goods and services for a specific community (geographically-based or interest-based groups).

Balance diagnostic data

We will discuss how Bull developed the Balance diagnostic tool in Chapter 8 (Bull, 2006, 2007). It is used to collect data from organisations that self-define or are defined by others as social enterprises. In the section below, we consider data collected from 354 social enterprises over a decade (2004–14). Research participants were asked to rate themselves against five key developmental stages:

Stage 5 ('A thriving social enterprise with 100 per cent trading income, with surpluses to reinvest, develop the organisation and shape/self-fund new services, sometimes in collaboration or partnerships with others'). A Stage 5 enterprise can compete with private firms in open markets.

Stage 4 ('Self-sufficient from own trading income, but surpluses are negligible'). A Stage 4 enterprise is surviving, but is not yet thriving or able to take full control of its future. This is also the state of many SMEs in the private sector.

Stage 3 ('Some mix of grant (or other non-self-generating income) and trading income'). A Stage 3 enterprise aligns with Dees's (1998) conceptualisation of mixed trading and charity income.

Stage 2 ('Partially dependent with some trading income – in need of grant income to be maintained'). A Stage 2 enterprise is more reliant on grant income than trading income.

Stage 1 ('Totally grant (donation – or other non-self-generating income) dependent'). A Stage 1 enterprise is – arguably – not a social enterprise for reasons discussed in Chapter 2 (and below).

The findings from Balance (Table 5.2) indicate that the majority of the 354 social enterprises in the sample saw themselves as partially dependent with some trading income, and in need of grant income to be maintained (42.4 per cent). There is an even spread between those that were currently totally grant dependent (20.9 per cent) and those that were self-sufficient using trading income, but which had negligible surpluses (23.7 per cent). Only 2.3 per cent of the sample saw themselves as being at Stage 5 (thriving with 100 per cent trading income). In total, 74 per cent of the sample (at Stages 1, 2 and 3) were mixing income sources, blending grants, donations and trading income. When we look at their *goals*, the findings are of interest. Only eight of the 354 wished to remain completely grant dependent, all the others wanted to undertake some trading. Interestingly, 59 per cent (at Stages 1, 2 and 3) wished to retain a 'mixed receipts' approach with both trading and grants/donations. Only 40.9 per cent wanted to be self-sufficient, with a surprisingly low number (4.5 per cent) striving to generate profits commensurate with private business norms.

Table 5.2   Current and future aspirations of a sample of social enterprises

Balance diagnostic tool data. Social entrepreneurs' opinions of their organisational income position in relation to the following 5 stages:	Business stage now		Business stage aim	
	Number	Percentage of total	Number	Percentage of total
1. Totally grant dependent (on donations, or other non-self-generating income)	74	20.9%	8	2.3%
2. Partially dependent with some trading income – in need of grant income to be maintained	150	42.4%	60	16.9%
3. Balance of grant (or other non-self-generating) and trading income	38	10.7%	141	39.8%
4. Self-sufficient using trading income, but surpluses are negligible	84	23.7%	129	36.4%
5. Thriving social enterprise with 100% trading income, with surpluses to re-invest, develop the organisation and shape/self-fund new services, may be in collaboration or partnerships with others	8	2.3%	16	4.5%
	354		354	

Theorising income and investment activities

There are many terms used to describe the financial sources on which social enterprises rely. Table 5.3 sets out a classification and the order in which we will consider them.

Table 5.3   Generating income and capital for social enterprises

Classification	Accounting norm	Description	Regulated by
Trading	Revenue	Revenues and surpluses/profits from the sale of goods and services, and contracts for services	Contract law
Fees	Income	Member dues and subscriptions	Contract law Co-operative law* Association law
Donations	Income	Individual and corporate giving	Trust law Charity law Association law
Grants	Cost recovery	Monies received or paid to run a project that achieves a specific (charitable) aim	Trust law Charity law Association law
Loans	(Social) investment (debt finance)	Loan finance, overdraft facilities, debentures, (fixed interest) bonds	Contract law Financial services law
Shares	(Social) investment (equity finance)	Preference shares, member equity, social investments, community share issues	Company law Co-operative law*

*Inside the UK, it is now covered by a mixture of the Co-operative and Community Benefit Societies Act 2014, and – in the case of credit unions – the Financial Services Authority.

Funds, profits and accounting

Before we consider trading further, let us clarify the subtle differences between 'income', 'receipts', 'surplus', 'profit', 'revenues', 'costs' and 'investments' in accounting practice. Income is not the same as profit, nor is it necessarily helpful to regard it as revenue. While income, revenues and receipts *may* be the same, the variation in language reflects different institutional and accounting environments. In the US, non-profit organisations engaged in CTAs use Form 990 or Form 990-EZ to declare total receipts, while for-profit SRBs report their income as sales revenue (total turnover from the sale of goods and services). In the UK, smaller charities use cash accounting based on receipts and expenses, while larger ones have to produce a profit and loss statement.

Perhaps for this reason, there is ambiguity in accounting for grant income. While grant payments are 'receipts', they usually cover expenses that have already been incurred. For this reason, it can be problematic to regard grant income as 'revenue'. In audited accounts, grants may be presented as income or allocated as a (negative) cost against items for which a claim has been made. Grant income is also subject to trust law, not contract or company law. When money is 'granted', a 'trust' is formed between the donor and the recipient regarding the purposes for which the money can be used (Morgan, 2008).[1] If none are specified, the monies can be used for any purpose defined in the 'objects' of the recipient's organisation. Hence, there are unrestricted grants that support an organisation's mission and restricted grants that support an agreed activity. Grants are allocated to *funds* so that any donor can inquire how their money has been used. Figure 5.2 is taken from the **SORP regulations** (Charity Commission, 2005).

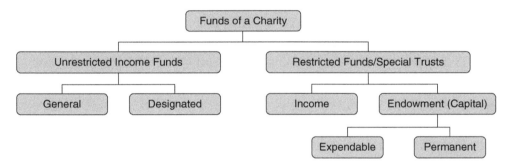

Figure 5.2   Fund management in a charity context

Source: 'Accounting and Reporting by Charities: Statement of Recommended Practice' (Charity Commission, 2005: 11), Figure 1, reproduced under the terms of Crown Copyright Policy Guidance issued by HMSO. © Crown Copyright 2005

The presence of **restricted funds** (of any kind) indicates that the organisation is managing charitable funds under trust law. The scale of this activity affects its status as a social enterprise. The **Social Enterprise Mark (SEM)** (see Chapter 9) expresses its award criteria in terms of how the applicant uses 'profits', *not* how it manages 'funds'. The assumption is that profits (in the generally accepted sense of the word) are used to make social investments. This encourages the *investment* mind-set favoured by Emerson:

> To move from charity to investing in change requires those who 'own' that future … have the ability to track its performance over time – and tie that transformation back to the capital support and community resources that made it possible. (2000: 18)

Emerson's view is that the generation of profits, and then the tracking of their reinvestment, increase learning and understanding of blended value (i.e. deeper knowledge of the relationship between social investments and economic and social impacts). The Social Enterprise Mark, therefore, is not making a mistake using this language: it is tied to a discourse that prioritises the generation of profits to make investments, and which de-emphasises the raising of funds to recover costs. There is, inevitably, an overlap – and potential for greater blended value – when an organisation pursues social objectives through trading activities.

It is also worth commenting on the way CMEs adapt their accounting practices. They deviate from norms by maintaining detailed records of member transactions for reasons other than market intelligence or legal requirement. This is most apparent in retail chains where members' financial transactions are tracked *for the purpose of calculating their share of the surplus*. This can apply also to the provision of financial services (based on the value of products purchased). It is also a standard practice in worker co-operatives: wages paid and hours worked are not tracked simply to calculate tax payments to the Inland Revenue, but also for the purposes of calculating an employee's share of the surplus.

In summary, income (receipts) may come from trading, subscriptions, donations, grants, loan finance and **equity capital**. All (at different times) can have a role in developing a social enterprise depending on its legal form (see Chapter 11).

Trading

In this section we discuss the differences between mission-related and mission unrelated trading. At present, the primary discourse in social enterprises is encouraging them to behave like businesses who trade (Dart, 2004). Trading is selling products and services. Social enterprises may share characteristics with other businesses when they supply goods and services to consumers. In these situations the end user, the customer, pays for the product/service. In some cases social enterprises may feel they need to undercut their competitors to survive, while others feel that their added value is worth a premium price (Bull and Crompton, 2006).

As Price states:

> social enterprise is about making money rather than spending it – and that means trading the products and services or the value created with the enterprise for remuneration that generates the income to survive. (2008: 40)

Pearce concurs when he comments:

> it is a *sine qua non* that social enterprises engage to some degree in trade by providing goods and services for which customers pay. Engaging in such economic activity is how social enterprises achieve their social purpose. (2003: 34)

The alternative, as Price (2008) states, is grant (or contract) dependency characterised by periods of secure income followed by financial famines that thwart efforts to sustain innovations in service delivery. Social enterprise (allegedly) offers more stable financial resources that are less reliant on the whims of grant holders. For charities, trading also constitutes a source of **unrestricted funds**. A strategy that is *over*-reliant on trading, however, can also weaken the enterprise. Pharoah et al. (2004) suggest that a failure to secure trading income may *not* reflect a lack of entrepreneurial effort but may arise out of the diverse and difficult challenges that social enterprises take on. These challenges include: establishing local resources; navigating highly complex contracting arrangements; plugging gaps in service provision; and slowly *creating* markets that make further trading possible.

The association between trading and for-profit businesses carries some rhetorical baggage. For-profit trading is labelled 'opportunistic', 'entrepreneurial', 'market focused', 'creative', 'customer driven' and 'risky' (Bull and Crompton, 2005). Social enterprises and other third sector organisations have now created their own language to describe trading in a social economy (Bull, 2006, 2007). In doing so, it is clearer that income generation is not the preserve of the private sector.

In the UK, over half the income of voluntary and community sector organisations now comes from trading (NCVO, 2014), outstripping all income from grants, gifts and donations. As Jim Brown confirms in reports to the Finance Hub, earned income from open market trading is the most valuable source of income, and contributes most to unrestricted funds. It is increasingly seen as a route to independence and growth potential. Wei-Skillern et al. (2007: 135) draw on the Johns Hopkins Comparative Non-profit Sector Project to show that the same is true globally (53 per cent fees, 35 per cent government, mostly contracts, and 12 per cent philanthropic giving). In some countries trading income is particularly high: Kenya (81 per cent), Mexico (85 per cent), Philippines (92 per cent).

Table 5.4   Streams of income by source (%)

	Fees (trading)	Government	Philanthropy
Latin America	75	15	10
Scandinavia	59	33	7
USA	57	31	13
Asia	56	22	12
Africa	55	25	19
Eastern Europe	49	31	19
Europe	38	56	6

Source: Wei-Skillern et al. (2007: 136)

Table 5.4 provides insight into political and cultural influences on the propensity of social enterprises to trade. In some countries, income is more accessible from philanthropic sources (compare Africa at 19 per cent to Europe at 6 per cent). In other cases, government contracts offer more opportunities (compare Europe at 56 per cent to

Latin America at 15 per cent). Hence, the income streams influence both the number and the nature of social enterprises and fluctuate over time.

Pharoah et al. (2004) add that large voluntary sector organisations have been generating trading income for some time, but maintain a clear separation between mission-related activity and 'business' activity. For example, sales of Christmas cards and items from gift catalogues are examples of business activity that support mission-related investment. It is possible to base an income strategy on *primary purpose trading, ancillary trading, beneficiary trading* and *mixed trading* linked to an organisation's charitable objects.

Trading is also income from contracts for services. Neo-liberal economies have seen a shift from government grants and local authority public funding to *contracting* organisations in the social economy (as outlined in Chapter 3). The Civil Society Almanac (NCVO, 2014) shows how the position has changed (Figure 5.3). In 2000/1, public authorities and trusts issued grants worth £4.8 billion and contracts worth £4.6 billion. In 2011/12, £2.6 billion was issued in grants and £11.5 billion in contracts. Grants decreased 54 per cent while contracts rose 240 per cent.

Contracts are competitively tendered, with the funder shaping their requirements and the bidder offering a price for the delivery of the service. The power to shape service delivery moves from the grantee to the contractor. Prices are fixed and the bidder (in theory) can add a profit margin, so some surplus can be generated. With a restricted grant, every penny has to be spent on delivering a service. This leaves no

Voluntary sector grant and contract income from government, 2000/01–2011/12 (£ billions, 2011/12 prices)

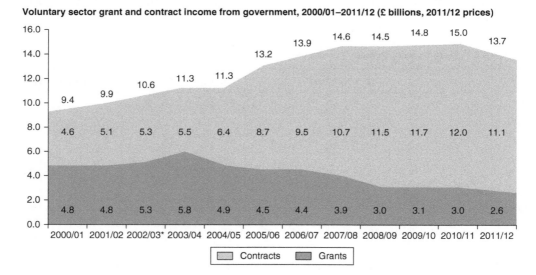

Figure 5.3   Changes to grant and contract income in the voluntary sector

Source: http://data.ncvo.org.uk/a/almanac14/how-has-the-funding-mix-changed/

money to develop infrastructure, buildings, fittings and equipment as this cannot be bought with restricted grant money, nor is it permissible to generate a surplus. Conceptually, contracts *buy* service delivery, while grants *fund* service delivery. Moreover, contracts buy specific *outputs* detailed in a tender specification, shaped and determined by the funder, and may include service level agreements (SLAs) that require the achievements of results against targets (see Chapter 3 for further discussion).

Empirical research suggests that 100 per cent trading income is an unrealistic goal for those social enterprises working with severely disadvantaged groups (Pearce, 2003; Wallace, 2005). Mike's Balance data shows this (Table 5.2). Only 4.5 per cent of the organisations that have used Balance aim for 100 per cent trading income. Is 50 per cent more realistic? A mixed receipts approach is the most observed arrangement with 39.8 per cent of organisations suggesting that they aim for a balance between grant and trading income. Those below a 50 per cent trading threshold can be regarded as on a journey towards social enterprise, as observed by Smallbone and Lyon (2005). On closer inspection, we found that the situation is more fluid (Seanor et al., 2007). Social enterprise income changes with grant cycles and peaks and troughs of consumer spending. Seanor et al. (2013) suggest that there are also times when organisations fluctuate between grants and contracts, and between debt and equity – a kind of tidal movement. So, we are interested in the mix of income streams and acknowledge the way they fluctuate from one period to the next. These tidal movements are hard to pin down, but classification of those above 25 per cent, 50 per cent and fully trading is helpful to make a distinction between **whole economy** social enterprises (100 per cent trading in markets) and **mixed receipts** social enterprises that combine a number of income streams and move some 10–20 per cent above and below the tide line of 50 per cent trading income (Coulson, 2009: 21).

Bev Meldrum (formerly a member of the Tool Factory in London) explained to us that delivering contracts is different from selling goods and services. She believes like Wallace (2005) that long-term sustainability is built through a strategy of diversification based on mixed grants and contracts. Diversification is the operative word as an over-reliance on one source of grant or contract income leaves the enterprise vulnerable, by becoming too beholden to one constituency, unable to spread risk, or achieve autonomy in their business decision-making. The Big Society discourse has framed grants as bad because they encourage dependency, whereas commerce is seen as good because it encourages more business-like behaviour (see Chapter 1). Just as individuals have been encouraged to 'self-help', so have voluntary sector organisations. The other side of this debate involves co-operative finance. Unlike charities that may be seen as over-reliant on grants, co-operatives may be over-reliant on trading to generate capital, and have long been advised to raise more in the form equity from members (Cornforth et al., 1988).

Wei-Skillern et al. (2007) offer a useful starting point for assessing how an organisation might reflect on certain products/services in relation to social impact and surplus (profit).

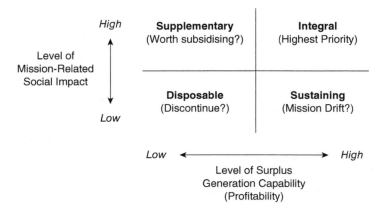

Figure 5.4   Classifying activities

Source: Wei-Skillern et al. (2007) Figure 4.1 and Table 4.1, with permission from SAGE Publications Inc.

Figure 5.4 shows four categories of income. Bottom left (*disposable*), neither meets the organisations' social or financial targets. Top left (*supplementary*), achieves social, but not financial goals. *Supplementary* activities achieve high levels of social impact, but generate low surpluses. Nevertheless, *supplementary* activities may be desirable as they may be core to the mission. Bottom right (*sustaining*), may generate a surplus, but deliver little social impact. Top right (*integral*) – the sustainability sweet spot – secures both social and surplus generating activities. In many organisations we come across, *integral* and *sustaining* type products and services may well subsidise *supplementary* products and services (Bull et al., 2010). Tensions, however, arise when the organisation is stretched diagonally between *supplementary* and *sustaining* activities, which can lead to **mission drift** that risks demotivating staff (Seanor and Meaton, 2008) and damaging the reputation of the enterprise (Coule, 2007). A strategic goal, therefore, is to find trading opportunities that are *integral* to the achievement of both social impact and **surplus** generation.

All activities, as Wei-Skillern et al. (2007: 138) warn, 'are initially, and on an ongoing basis, capital absorbing'. For example, selling goods and services to service users requires investments in marketing, not just in terms of devising and implementing strategies, but also in terms of the staff time to make them happen. Similarly, bidding for contracts takes time and commitment. If successful, the contract also needs servicing by monitoring outputs, outcomes and impacts and reporting them back to commissioning bodies. Consequently, experience and know-how are needed to identify ancillary and project management costs (including rents, building maintenance, office services and management time) so that bids are based on the principle of full-cost recovery. However, as Bull and Crompton (2005) have found, it is a precarious process vying for public sector contracts. Some social enterprises forego **full cost**

recovery as contractors (predominantly local government/authorities) negotiate down the differences between direct cost and full cost recovery.

Charities and trading

In the UK, a charity can engage in trade, and not be subject to tax on its earnings, if:

- It is *integrated with the primary purpose*, specified by the charity's objects. Currently, there are 12 categories of charitable objects (see Charities Act 2006, Section 1, Clause 2(2)).
- It is *ancillary to the primary purpose*, but linked. For instance, an educational charity might sell books.
- It is *beneficiary trading*. For example, a charity teaching disabled people horticultural skills can then sell the horticultural products made by the beneficiaries.
- It involves the *sale of donated goods*, given for that purpose.
- It is *mixed trading* involving a single trading activity which has both primary purpose and non-primary purpose, but where the non-primary element is under £50,000 and less than 10 per cent of the total trading income.
- It is *occasional trading* (for any purpose) and is only a small part of the annual total income, defined by the Charity Commission as:

  - up to £5000 if total income is less than £20,000
  - up to 25 per cent of total income between £20,000 and £200,000
  - maximum of £50,000 if total income is over £200,000.

- It *qualifies as an extra-statutory concession* which applies to fundraising events such as barbecues, auctions, festivals and concerts. The events are supposed to be one-off, but up to 15 such events at the same venue within one year can be exempt.

Source: www.gov.uk/charities-and-trading

If an activity is likely to attract corporation tax, it may be cost-efficient to set up a **trading arm** and gift the profits back to a parent charity (to reclaim the tax). Trading arms can also take on contracts that fall outside the charitable objects of the parent charity, and so protect against undermining its autonomy or ethos. By developing trading arms, charities can obtain the benefits of both charitable and commercial trading. However, there is a question over whether the trading arm constitutes a social enterprise. The rationale for creating a trading arm is to gift profits back to the parent organisation, but there is more than one way of doing this.

Typically, a charity trading arm is a CLS, with 100 per cent ownership of share capital by the charity. However, it is not uncommon for the trading arm to be constituted as a CLG with an independent board. The use of a CLS trading arm raises the question of whether the subsidiary satisfies the criteria for the social aspects of enterprise. Is the trading arm 'social' in the sense of being subject to democratic control? Is it 'social' in the sense of being able to exercise autonomy? While a trading arm has autonomy from the state, the parent charity can impose management controls that remove its autonomy and internal democracy. This being the case, it can simultaneously satisfy 'social purpose' criteria but fall well short of 'socialisation' criteria that depend on the democratisation of production methods and wealth distribution (Ridley-Duff and Southcombe, 2012).

To illustrate this point, it is worth comparing the trading arm perspective to arrangements in the Mondragon Co-operative Corporation. Member co-operatives are free to vote themselves in and out of the co-operative network, and internal democracy ensures they take their own decisions on profit distribution (Ridley-Duff, 2005). Aside from co-operative laws that require 10 per cent of profits to be invested in social and educational projects, members can exercise democratic control. The theorisation of 'social', therefore, matters. Prioritising 'social purpose' can undermine autonomy and democracy (i.e. the 'socialisation' of the entrepreneurial process). The reverse is also true: democratisation can subvert the 'social purposes' of the organisation's founders if not regulated by an external body.

The case of Ealing Community Transport (ECT) further clarifies this. Established in 1979, it provides transport for people with disabilities and the elderly in the Ealing borough of London. ECT became a flagship, award-winning social enterprise, and its former CEO (Stephen Sears) was a key contributor to the development of CIC legislation.[2] We pick up the story 30 years on in Case 5.1.

Case 5.1

Anna Whitty, current ECT Chief Executive

Ealing Community Transport started life as an industrial and provident society (exempt charity) providing community transport to local organisations using grant funding from its local authority. Over the years a variety of other grant opportunities allowed the organisation to grow. A grant to develop furniture reuse and later paint exchange was integral to ECT's development of its environmental services. The drying up of these grants with changing political priorities led ECT to use its enterprising spirit to develop innovational recycling opportunities which its local council contracted as part of a pilot scheme. This also roughly coincided with the award of a handful of home-to-school contracts to the core transport business.

Read the full case on the companion website at: www.sagepub.co.uk/ridleyduff and consider the following questions:

- How did ECT go about raising funds to develop different community services?
- What role did contracts play in the development of ECT?
- How would you characterise the mix of income streams at ECT?

Ealing Community Transport created the ECT Group as a wholly owned subsidiary and converted it to a CIC in 2005. The case provides an outline of the ravelling and unravelling of income sources and opportunities for social enterprise through their 30-year history (from 1979 to 2009). Its first six years was dominated by grant funding (as a charitable project) before it was established as a legal entity that was 'both commercial and charitable' (SEC, 2005: 37). It engaged in a period of diversification, using opportunities to blend social enterprise activities with income from gifts (grants), trading (contracts) and finance (debt). By 2009, it had 24 separate companies. Many had been converted to CICs to embed the social mission more deeply in each company. As Case 5.1 highlights, ECT moved from traditional sources of grant income to trading opportunities, using contracts with the public sector.

In the ECT case, its reliance on debt finance meant it was hit hard by the economic downturn of 2009. By selling its recycling subsidiaries, it was able to inject £15 million into its community transport services. The sale of various trading arms within ECT Group attracted controversy both for the valuation placed on a £47 million turnover business generating about £2 million profits a year, and also because the sales seemed to confirm that the asset lock in the CIC regulations was not secure (Schwartz, 2008). While the CEO Stephen Sears viewed this as an 'opportunity' that demonstrated the 'flexibility' of the CIC, others raised substantive questions about the integrity of the asset lock, and the likely backlash from funding bodies which may now avoid awarding contracts to CICs because they fear them being sold to private sector companies (Gosling, 2008).

In ECT's case, the regulator confirmed that ECT operated within its own rules and that the money raised from the sale of subsidiaries enabled ECT to service debts in its parent businesses. The events surrounding ECT, however, highlight two things about CICs and income streams: firstly, income can be generated *for* social enterprises by selling CICs as assets to the private sector; secondly, the asset lock does not effectively prevent CICs from transferring their *income streams* to organisations outside the social economy.

To conclude our discussion of trading activity, we summarise the options open to social enterprises in Table 5.5.

Table 5.5   Trading choices of social enterprises

Direct sales (charging customers for products and services that are core activities)	If a social enterprise can earn income from direct sales linked to their mission, this is the 'holy grail'. Direct sales opportunities tend to be most available to organisations that can operate in viable markets by satisfying unmet needs, forging new market opportunities or working in established markets
Indirect sales (charging customers for products and services that are non-core activities)	This approach involves selling products and services made by the organisation (such as training or consultancy) to offset the cost of providing other (core) services that deliver the social objects of the enterprise
Contracts for services	This involves entering into contracts to provide specific services, goods or support for specified activities. The caveat here is that the contract may be written by the funder to support their social agenda (which may or may not be compatible with the objects of the social enterprise)
Retailing (selling products or services not made by the organisation)	This may involve selling products/services, some of which are mission related. As Hudson (2002) points out, environmentally friendly washing machines and fridges can be bought from Friends of the Earth, Oxfam can supply furniture, Amnesty provides ethical investment plans. The UK's largest charities for blind and deaf people (RNIB and RNID respectively) have multi-million-pound trading arms selling products from catalogues geared to the needs of blind and deaf people
Running a charity shop	Retailing can be further supported by establishing dedicated retail outlets. Shop income is counted as earned income rather than gift income, and can contribute to unrestricted funds

Gifts and donations

Gifts have been a successful source of income for charities and voluntary organisations for centuries. At the same time, grants can be less flexible than trading income, particularly if they do not meet the full cost of an activity, or are tied to a restricted fund. A culture of grant dependency increases the pressure *for* social enterprise (see Case 8.1, Seedley and Langworthy Trust). For example, a grant to work with homeless people may cover the costs of short-term accommodation, but not food or other support. Unless other income streams are put in place, then financial sustainability is at risk because support is delivered without fully recovering the cost. As a result, the concept of 'full-cost recovery' is gaining ground as an accounting practice in not-for-profit organisations (Doherty et al., 2009: 114).

In an organisation dependent on restricted funds, the organisation could have money in the bank, but be unable to use it (even as collateral for raising loans). There is always a risk that funds may have to be paid back ('clawback') if the grant is not used for the specific purpose of the award. The holding of funds, therefore, may create a balance sheet that shows a positive amount which obscures issues of sustainability. Seeking financial sustainability through grant funding involves careful financial management that may (possibly) be seen as more of a burden than an opportunity. Kenton Mann of Music Unlimited – a social enterprise based in Greater Manchester in the UK – states:

I think for us, as soon as the grant stopped I said, 'We're not going to do that again' – because spending other people's money is really hard. (Bull and Crompton, 2005: 23)

This said, unspent funds can be carried over from one financial year to the next with the agreement of the funder, and may be transferable to other projects.

Social enterprises can gain considerable benefits from acquiring charitable status. As Price (2008) points out, there are approximately 2,500 grant giving trusts in England and Wales, and acquiring charitable status increases access to them. Charities get 80 per cent relief on business rates and exemptions from corporation tax on primary purpose trading. One area for caution, however, is the nature of services that might be provided with grant funding. Grants may be tax free, but there may be VAT (value added tax) to pay (on supplies or on the provision of services that attract VAT). For example, while education services do not attract VAT, consultancy services do. A social enterprise needs to be clear that funds are being used to further their mission (primary purpose trading) and not for other services (secondary trading). If the organisation delivers VATable services to a value above the VAT threshold (£81,000 in 2015), it will have to register for VAT and face a bill that cannot be recovered from a funder.

Whatever the benefits and pitfalls, Pharoah et al. (2004) point out that grants remain a major source of funding for both charitable and non-charitable social enterprises, and continue to benefit a 'mixed receipts' strategy in support of social and charitable objects. Moreover, Pearce (2003) contends that the problems created by grant dependency cannot be solved by the recipient organisations. Funders *create* a culture of dependency through the way they attach conditions to their grants. Ellerman (2005) believes they must share responsibility for the effects of the way they make social investments.

An alternative to grants is *donations* from private individuals or organisations. One advantage is that they are received in advance of expenses, improving cash flows and providing opportunities for investment income. There are different types of donations: time, skills and personal resources. While non-financial donations do not add to income, they can reduce the cost of providing services. Case 5.2 highlights a particularly innovative development for increasing donations to non-profit and charitable organisations.

Case 5.2

MissionFish

MissionFish is a technology that adds value to eBay auctions. eBay is a global community undertaking a large number of auctions all around the world. Sellers can use MissionFish to donate part of their sales revenue directly to a recognised charity or non-profit organisation. eBay calls this the Giving Works program. It also allows

(Continued)

(Continued)

non-profits to sell their goods on eBay and raise funds. In addition to facilities that are attached to sale items, a 'Donate Now' button can be added to allow direct donations from a PayPal account without affecting an auction.

A fuller teaching case can be found on the companion website at: www.sage-pub. co.uk/ridleyduff.

Questions:

1   What governs the way the income passing through MissionFish can be used by the non-profit or charity that receives it?
2   If a non-profit or charity sells goods on eBay and uses MissionFish to allocate all the income, are the funds raised 'earned income' or 'gifts'?
3   If people use the 'Donate Now' button, what type of income is this?

Donations made through MissionFish are a source of unrestricted funds (if not given in response to a charity appeal). The money can be used for any expenditure or held as a reserve and can be used to make *social investments*. While schemes like these are welcome, donations are often insufficient to generate the funding required for capital expenditure (in buildings or machinery), or the development of new products, services and viable markets. As Cadbury comments:

> The third sector … will need access to finance to expand its activities and to adapt to … ever changing demands of communities it serves. At the same time, the people managing these organisations will have to accept that borrowing and a certain degree of financial risk will enable them to achieve far more than if they take more restricted views of their capacities. (Cadbury, 2000, cited in Bridge et al., 2009: 148)

The above view now seems dated in light of the successes in crowdfunding charitable projects (see Chapter 6). However, it will remain the case that some TSOs will see value in using loan finance to develop their activities. In the next section, we consider financial instruments that make this possible.

Loans and the debt–equity ratio

Taking out a loan requires a sufficient level of income (or increased income) to service repayment of the debt including any additional interest. This can create some barriers for organisations that generate little surplus. Doherty (2011) stated that in 1998, when Divine Chocolate set up, they struggled to attract start-up finance. Only a government loan guarantee scheme helped them to secure a loan. The reasons for these difficulties can be partly explained by understanding the concept of **gearing** (the ratio of total capital to debt finance), demonstrated in Figure 5.5.

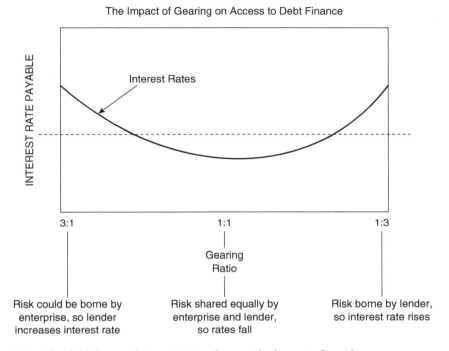

The Impact of Gearing on Access to Debt Finance

Figure 5.5   Why debt finance interest rates change: the impact of gearing on access to debt finance

The reason that many social enterprises pay higher interest rates or struggle to obtain finance is not, as is commonly supposed, that they focus on non-profit activities; it is because their capital structure is unattractive to lenders.[3] As Ridley-Duff (2009) reports, lenders may want the facility to convert loans to shares as a condition of lending (i.e. turn low-risk debt finance into high-risk equity finance *in order to lower their own risks*). Non-profits constituted as a CLG cut themselves off from some sources of debt finance, and *encourage dependence on grants and donations* whether conscious of this or not.

This information is helpful when negotiating with banks. Faced with questions like 'So you are not primarily interested in profit?', 'What are your assets?', 'Who are your guarantors?', 'So no one owns the enterprise as such?', what response can a social enterprise make? If the organisation is a CLG, one response is to develop a plan for trading that will generate regular surpluses, then return to the bank with evidence that surpluses are being made. This 'chicken and egg' situation, however, will be uninviting for those ideologically opposed to increasing profit margins or raising prices to service a loan. However, such activities do not imply profit-maximisation, only the making of profits to service a debt (effectively keeping the finances of the enterprise 'in balance'). If opposition to profit-making cannot be overcome, the best income strategy remains one based on fundraising in order to acquire assets. Debt finance, however, will remain inaccessible while the organisation has no assets or trading surpluses.

Conclusions

We have discussed strategies for acquiring economic capital and the financial practices of social enterprises. While UK policies on social enterprise emphasise trading levels based on the sale of services and contracts with government bodies, we have also discussed the ongoing relevance of grants and donations. In the next chapter, we consider the emergence of the social investment industry and crowd-sourcing, which is changing the landscape for raising philanthropic, co-operative and private capital.

The income streams for voluntary and charity organisations based on gifts (grants and donations) are being replaced by a growing reliance on trading (sometimes unrelated to mission). There are two questions to ask about this move to contracting. Firstly, can social enterprises delivering services under contract radically reshape society? Secondly, will contracts provide sufficiently robust resources for long-term capacity building, growth and sustainability when commissioning bodies tend to use them as a way of reducing their own costs? Co-operatives, on the other hand, have the reverse challenge of ending over-dependence on trading by developing capital structures that enable them to re-engage their members through community share issues, and build new relationships with social investors (see Chapter 6).

The social enterprise movement has encouraged a more business-like approach to income generation, increasing the focus on market trading, entering into contracts for outsourced public services, and developing institutions to increase social investment. Alongside these efforts is the continuation of fundraising to generate funds that can increase social impact. In the final part of the chapter, we discussed the potential difficulty of obtaining loans where there are no trading surpluses, assets or rules to cover the issue of equity. We used case studies to clarify the ebb and flow of practice, and the shifting sands of the social economy, as organisations move from grants to contracts to market trading and back again. We finish, therefore, on a note about the diversity of practices and the benefits of retaining an open mind on the optimum mix of income streams in social and economic development.

Class exercise: Analysing income streams and investments

Materials to support this exercise are available on the companion website at: www.sagepub.co.uk/ridleyduff.

This exercise involves using Table 5.3 and Figure 5.4 to analyse three further cases (Cases 5.3, 5.4 and 5.5 available on the companion website).

- Organise seminar participants into groups of three, and provide them with the three cases.
- Use Table 5.3 and Figure 5.4 to analyse each case.
- Identify the income streams and investment activity.
- Identify the types of funds that each organisation uses and/or creates.
- Report your findings and compare them to the rest of the group.

Summary of learning

In this chapter, we have argued the following:

Social enterprises (ideally) operate profitable trading activities for the purpose of generating surpluses that can be recycled into value creating activities.

A contract mind-set is different from a grant aid mind-set. It involves a heightened accountability to funders for the outputs and outcomes of results against targets.

Social enterprises have a wide range of trading options open to them (direct sales, indirect sales, contracts for services and retailing).

Some social enterprises continue to rely on grants and donations as part of a 'mixed receipts' strategy that contributes to sustainability.

Social enterprises may need to carefully consider the impact of their constitution and income generating strategy when seeking to raise debt finance (loans).

Questions and possible essay assignments

1. Using examples, describe and critically assess the contribution of *integrated, supplementary* and *sustaining* income generation strategies to the development of a social enterprise.
2. Social enterprises can balance both contract and grant income, what are the complications for sustaining both strategies within an organisation? Critically evaluate the strengths and weaknesses of each.
3. What factors make it hard for a social enterprise to obtain loan finance? Critically assess the strategies that can be adopted to make it easier to obtain loan finance.
   Further reading material is available on the companion website at: www.sagepub. co.uk/ ridleyduff.

Further reading

Income streams and capital management are under-researched areas in the social enterprise literature. For those focused entirely on charitable trading, we recommend Lloyd and Faure Walker's (2009) book *Charities, Trading and the Law*. The further reading we suggest for students includes Wallace (2005), an article from the first edition of the *Social Enterprise Journal* on financial sustainability. For a general introduction to finance for social enterprises, we suggest Foster's chapter in Doherty et al. (2009) is a good read. For more advanced reading we recommend Wei-Skillern et al.'s (2007) book on social entrepreneurship.

Useful resources

Blendedvalue.org: www.blendedvalue.org

Charity Bank: www.charitybank.org/

Co-operative Bank: www.co-operativebank.co.uk

Cooperative Capital Fund: http://cooperativefund.org/coopcapital

Key Fund Yorkshire: www.thekeyfund.co.uk/

KnowHow NonProfit: www.knowhownonprofit.org/

Unity Trust Bank: www.unity.co.uk/

UnLtd: http://unltd.org.uk/

Notes

1 This is why the word 'trustee' is used to describe the member of a charity board.
2 One author attended the launch of the CIC at Social Enterprise London, at which Stephen Sears spoke about his own role in the development of the legislation.
3 This said, a general scepticism that social economy organisations can repay loans plays a part. One student, a banker turned social enterprise adviser, commented that there was a further substantive reason. The reputation of a bank could be severely damaged if it withdrew overdraft or loan facilities from a charity. This creates a culture of caution among bank managers when lending to charities.

Social Investment and Crowdfunding

6

Learning objectives

In this chapter we discuss the emergence of social investment as an industry, and the rise of numerous internet-based crowdfunding projects. By the end of this chapter you will be able to:

- distinguish between different types and sources of social investment for different approaches to social enterprise development
- understand and explain investment logics and investor rationalities
- critically assess choices that social entrepreneurs face when choosing between crowdfunding and institutional funding
- think creatively about philanthropic, co-operative and private capital so that you can design a capital structure attractive to stakeholders.

The key arguments that will be developed in this chapter are:

- The social investment industry comprises philanthropic, co-operative and private capital mediated by social/commercial investment funds and crowdfunding technologies.

(Continued)

(Continued)

- Social investment is underpinned by a wide range of rationalities and logics that affect the design choices for a social enterprise's capital structure.
- Crowd-sourcing provides an alternative approach to social investment that suits the logic of the social and solidarity economy.

Introduction

In Chapter 4, we considered the nature of social value and measurement of 'social performance' through the lenses of social auditing and social return on investment. In Chapter 5, we turned our attention to the management of capital, strategies for generating income during charitable trading activities, and how to conceptualise income and expenditure for the purposes of accounting and distribution. We also examined links between trading strategies and the achievement of social goals.

In this chapter, we switch the focus from income generation to investment capital. We explore how each approach to social enterprise – through co-operative and mutual enterprises (CMEs), socially responsible businesses (SRBs) and charitable trading activities (CTAs) – is reflected also in various approaches to social investment. In 1999, the UK Treasury published the *Enterprise and Social Exclusion* report that brought the issue of social investment to the fore. As a result, the then Department for Trade and Industry established the Phoenix Fund, which ran from 1999 to 2006. This was the forerunner to community development finance initiatives (**CDFIs**) providing loans for ventures in disadvantaged communities. Doherty et al. (2009: 15) state that by 2003 there were 23 CDFIs supporting social enterprises in communities across the UK. However, when these CDFIs are examined more closely, they can be found to operate in a particular way that shows their public sector/philanthropic origins. The ethos is quite different from mutual approaches that are emerging in the field of community shares (Brown, 2006), crowdfunding and investing platforms (Lehner, 2013). As social investment institutions operate with a range of different 'rationalities' (Nicholls, 2010), we need to grapple with the motivations and logics that arise in different parts of the social investment industry.

In this chapter, we start by considering the logics that underpin social investment activities, and how these are (or are not) aligned with the logics of the social and solidarity economy. Based on the application of a theoretical framework developed in earlier chapters (Westall, 2001), we identify institutions aligned with voluntary sector principles (community finance, crowd*funding*), the social and solidarity economy (mutuals, credit unions and community shares) and private sector (loans, equity and crowd-*investing*). We will examine in more detail the rationalities and logics of the institutions in Figure 6.1 to clarify the choices faced by social entrepreneurs, and the optimum choices for policy-making.

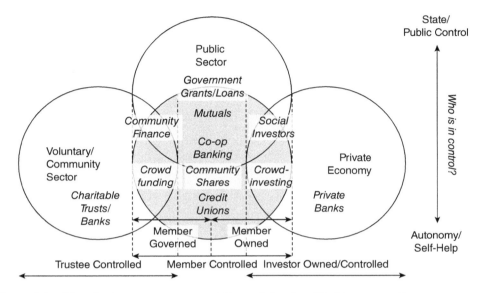

Figure 6.1   Where's the money to support the social and solidarity economy?

Shifting from a cost recovery to an investment mind-set

The shift from grant seeking to an *investment* mind-set has been a feature of Emerson's work on blended value:

> To move from charity to investing in change requires those who 'own' that future … have the ability to track its performance over time – and tie that transformation back to the capital support and community resources that made it possible. (2000: 18)

Emerson's view is that tracking which resources support successful investments will increase learning and understanding of blended value (i.e. develop a deeper knowledge of the relationship between social investments and economic and social impacts). This discourse prioritises the study of how profits are generated by investments and moves away from the logic of raising funds to recover costs. There is, potentially, substantial areas of overlap when social entrepreneurs create CTAs, CMEs and SRBs to create blended value. Nicholls's (2010) foundational paper on the logics of social investing explore these areas of overlap. In doing so, he separates the *outcomes* of investing (i.e. changes in social and economic value creation that occur after an investment is made) and the *objectives* behind a social investment (the benefits to the investor who provided capital). In the case of a philanthropic investment, the only objective is a social or environmental outcome without any consideration of a financial return. In the case of 'pure' social investing, the only objective is a market (or above-market) rate of return (ROI). The issue of social or environmental benefits is incidental rather than central (e.g. trading carbon quotas on a commodity market, or investing in infrastructure for the community, because the returns are as good as or better than other commercial opportunities).

Nicholls, however, identifies blended value for both investor and investee as the logic that underpins the most innovative approach to social investment. As he states:

> In the middle – blended – space, entirely new organizations are emerging that seek hybrid deals that mix various types of return ... lucrative social venture capital investments that may return market (or above market) Internal Rates of Return whilst also achieving a clear social or environmental objective ... as well as opportunities for many small-scale individual social investors that seek different blended mixes of social and financial return (for example by buying shares in Cafédirect). (2010: 76)

In addition to the logics of the investment, Nicholls discusses the rationalities of the investor in terms of Weberian ideal types (Weber, 1978). He differentiates *mean-ends rationality* (the intention to create a secondary effect as a result of a primary action) from *value-rationality* (the intention to act in a way consistent with ethical and moral frameworks). The value of such a distinction is conceptual clarity between investments made to achieve, for example, greater 'efficiencies' in the production of sustainable goods (means-ends investing) and investments that are made to be consistent with an investor's own personal values (McGoey, 2014).

However, here also, Nicholls sees (in practice) the blending of the two rationalities in which investors seek to improve the 'efficiency' of social innovation, driven by personal values that incline the investor to invest in 'sustainable' technology. A straightforward example from a study by Outsios (2013) suffices to illustrate the point. Eco-entrepreneurs in his study were often influenced by a commitment to 'deep ecology' (Naess, 1983), which created an 'environmental habitus'. This inclined entrepreneurs to screen investment opportunities and select only those where financial objectives would be secured through sustainable development outcomes. He cites an example of a straightforward business proposition pursued by the owners of Calder Cabs who bought a taxi firm then replaced all the vehicles with hybrid (petrol + electric) engines. This blend of rationalities is labelled '*systemic*' by Nicholls (2010) to reflect instances where the *objective* of the investor is to advance both efficiency and values of a social system at the same time.

From this foundation, Nicholls generates nine distinctive approaches to social investment, based on the intersections between investment logics and the investor rationalities (see Figure 6.2). In summarising his work, we can distinguish between investments that provide financial, blended and social/environmental returns *for the investor* (e.g. clean energy, socially responsible investing, venture philanthropy), and investments that provide financial, blended and social/environmental return *for the investee and society* (philanthropy, mutual/mission related, social change investments). In between, Nicholls identifies investments that blend investor and investee benefits (e.g. impact investing, social enterprise investment, government investment). Interestingly, he finds – in practice – that there is far more social investment capital at the *values* end of the spectrum (£3.6 trillion), a much smaller but substantial amount for *means-ends* investing (£900 billion), with the smallest amount devoted to integrating the two (£19 billion).

		Financial	Blended	Social-Environmental
	Means-End	Clean energy investment	Socially responsible investment	Venture philanthropy
Investor rationality	Systemic	Impact investment	Social enterprise investment	Government investment
	Value-Driven	Philanthropy	Mutual investments/ mission-related investments (MRI)	Social change investment

Investment logic

Figure 6.2   The institutionalisation of social investment

Source: based on Nicholls (2010), Figure 2

Critical perspectives on the logics of investment

A number of issues arise in the evaluation of Nicholls's (2010) matrix. Firstly, we need to consider work by Piketty (2014) that highlights the structures and processes that create and sustain inequality. Secondly, as Web 2.0 technologies have matured, there has been a growth in crowdfunding reviewed by Lehner (2013). Lastly, there has been a rise in venture philanthropy, something that McGoey (2014) regards as a form of philanthrocapitalism. Perhaps the most central of these is Piketty's finding that – historically – any period during which the rate of return to capital is higher than the growth rate of the economy systematically enriches capital at the expense of labour. Given that Nicholl's matrix highlights social investment logics seeking 'market-rate' and 'above market-rate' returns, social investment institutions might *exacerbate* poverty and inequality, even if social or environmental benefit is achieved.

Based on Piketty's analysis, two clear priorities emerge as important in the design of social investment institutions and instruments. Firstly, Nicholls identifies 'blended returns' in which both investor and investee (and wider society) can share. For Piketty, only if the returns to the investee and society are greater than returns to the investor will social investments eliminate structural inequality. Secondly, as capital is more unevenly distributed in society than income (and contributes more substantially to inequality), social investment strategies can alternatively socialise capital ownership, and not depend entirely on low-interest loans (Gates, 1998; Yunus, 2007; Ridley-Duff and Bull, 2013). These two characteristics, the *spreading of capital ownership* and *blended returns* from investments meet the criteria we set out for social enterprise (see Chapter 2). In the first case, a rapid increase in the number of investors can spread wealth to lower income households. In the second case, investees (workers/consumers/wider society/environment) can divide the benefits from an investment with the providers of capital. These logics can be combined to stimulate additional benefits to society by reducing the social and economic costs of inequality (Wilkinson and Pickett, 2010).

Some of these issues came to the fore in a series of heated exchanges on social investment at the 'Alternative Commission on Social Investment' that took place at the School for Social Entrepreneurs (Huckfield, 2015; Ward, 2015). The investment logic of most CDFIs, investment funds and private institutions is to ensure a return to capital that is higher than the growth rate of the economy (and which will – if Piketty's argument is robust – actually make inequality worse). Nicholls cites ambitions among many social investors to achieve rates of return between 5 to 10 per cent. Piketty's study reports that these aspirations fit the historical rates of return achieved by investors over hundreds of years. They achieve (on average) 6 to 8 per cent from stock market speculation, and 4 to 5 per cent from property ownership (land, buildings etc.). However, because overall economic growth (over the same period) has averaged just 1.5–1.7 per cent, these economic practices *continually* transfer wealth from producers to owners of capital. On this basis, a number of the combinations of logics and rationalities in Nicholls's matrix will further *impoverish* rather than *enrich* most people.

This contrasts sharply with the logics of other investment systems that are yet to be studied seriously by a scholarly community. For this reason, it is worth briefly introducing views from advocates of Islamic Banking and the Positive Money movement. Swan and Pidcock (2009) start by examining the western context. With extensive reference to the *General Theory of Employment, Interest and Money* (Keynes, 2008 [1936]) they argue that interest rates on loans need to be capped at *2 per cent* to prevent money (and bankers) from becoming too dominant. They then proceed to cite Islamic teachings by Iman Al Gazzali as the foundation of Islamic Banking principles:

> Whoever effects the transactions of interest on money is, in fact, discarding the blessings of Allah, and is committing injustice, because money is created for some other purpose, not for itself [...]. If it is allowed for [a person] to trade in money itself, money will become [their] ultimate goal, and will remain detained ... like hoarded money. (Swan and Pidcock, 2009: 35–6)

This position, taken as a foundational value that guides Islamic Banking, is not only being picked up by 'eastern' or Islamic scholars in the wake of repeated financial crises, but also by Positive Money, started in London by economics students disillusioned with the way the subject is taught at university.[1] The movement campaigns for three things (www.positivemoney.org/our-proposals/):

- To remove the right of private banks to create money and give this right to a new democratically controlled institution, protected from private banks, but accountable to parliament.
- To create 'debt-free' money (money that commands no interest rate) which can be 'spent' rather than 'lent' into the economy to reduce both government and personal debt.
- That money should always start its life by being spent into the 'real economy' to prevent it from being used for financial speculation or the fuelling of property bubbles.

Explore these three rationales further at: www.youtube.com/watch?v=eHQ7wvWzUW0.

These critical perspectives on social investment differ from the *mind-set* emerging from debates at the School for Social Entrepreneurs (Ward, 2015). Even the 'alternative' social investment community comprises people who think it would be crazy to permit loans or transfers that gave capital only a 2 per cent (or lower) return to capital. And yet, Piketty's (2014) study shows that the long-term impact of this approach (see Figures 5.1 and 5.5 in his book) will enrich those with capital, and not those without it. The alternative (understood by Keynes) is the kind of stimulation of the 'real economy' that the Positive Money movement seeks to support. In Piketty's study, the only period of economic development during which inequality was *reduced* coincided with national governments engaging in social investment outside the control of international banking institutions (between 1950 and 1975). While the IMF and World Bank were too weak to dictate national policies, structural inequalities across society were reduced for the first time by peaceful (democratic) processes of social investment organised by governments. It took a 'shock doctrine' to scare people and governments into giving influence back to the private sector, after which the rate of return to capital once again exceeded the rate of return to labour (Klein, 2007; Piketty, 2014).

The report of the Alternative Commission on Social Investment (2015), as well as reports from government backed advocates of social investment (Brown and Swersky, 2012), both report on the mismatch between social enterprises who want to pay 3 to 6 per cent interest for sub £250,000 loans and social investors who want to lend larger amounts or have double-digit interest rates for small loans. At present, they propose tax incentives to bridge the gap. This perpetuates transferred wealth (over the long term) from taxpayers to private investors and demonstrates how both social entrepreneurs and social investors are still trapped in a neo-liberal discourse. It is with some justification that Huckfield (2015) argues that this mind-set has the potential to kill social enterprise.

However, the low take up of Big Society Capital's social investment funds could indicate that knowledge of this paradox is already well understood across the sector.

If we are to take Piketty's analysis seriously, there is a conundrum that the advocates of 'pure' social investment need to address. Logically, there can be only two strategies that will lead to the enrichment of the wider population over time. The first is that the investment logic of blended value must be designed to enrich the investee at a *faster* rate than the investor (while ensuring investors' capital is not depleted). The second is that *distributing capital* (rather than acquiring it) is an equally good strategy for reducing poverty (because asymmetries in the ownership of capital entrench inequality more than asymmetries of income).

Reassuringly (from a social and solidarity perspective) the evidence from Nicholls (2010) is that blended social investments through mutuals is already the most established part of the global social investment industry. Of the £4.5 trillion estimated to be available for social investment in 2010, £3 trillion (66 per cent) is invested through mutuals and co-operatives (by an estimated 143 million people worldwide). Nicholls argues that these investments are 'blended' in both senses: co-operative and mutual members are both investors and investees as the same time, and their investments provide them with both economic and social returns.

Furthermore, the members of the Social Economy Alliance are unequivocal that crowdfunding and community shares are its preferred engine for social investment. In 2015, it launched a document calling for 'The Right to Invest', questioning why the value of overseas investment in the UK is worth two-thirds of GDP in the UK (63.3 per cent) while in Germany it is under one quarter (23.4 per cent). They describe opportunities for community ownership of renewable energy companies, football clubs, housing projects, the press, railways and banking. They claim:

> We have the money here in the UK ready to invest, with £1.2 trillion of cash holdings in UK households. Meanwhile, crowdfunding and community shares are on the rise. Globally, crowdfunders contributed $2.7 billion in 2012, helping to fund more than one million projects. The UK alternative finance market grew by 91 per cent in 2012 to £939 million in 2013 – and is predicted to be worth £1.6 billion in 2014. This includes peer-to-peer lending, worth nearly £300 million in 2013, invoice trading platforms funding worth nearly £100 million and equity crowdfunding worth £28 million. (Dunning et al., 2015: 3)

For this reason, we now focus on understanding the distinctions between philanthropic, co-operative and private capital, and examine the creative ways in which mutual institutions can reshape the future of social investment.

Philanthropic, co-operative and private capital

Emerson (2000) clarifies the ownership implications of different capital investments. Large donations of philanthropic capital (donations and grants) may entitle a person or organisation to exercise voting rights in board meetings, but CTAs are structured to eliminate capital ownership so investors cannot withdraw their capital and cannot give their voting rights to another party (unless such a right is agreed in advance, or permitted by **Articles of Association**). Private capital (stocks and shares) on the other hand, invested in an SRB will have both voting and ownership rights linked to the size of the investment. Depending on the Articles (plus any additional shareholder agreement and regulation) private investors can sell shareholdings to whoever they choose at any price they agree. They cannot withdraw private capital, only sell the rights (and benefits) of ownership to another investor.

Co-operative capital (in CMEs) has a different set of characteristics. For co-operative shares, the norm is to limit *transfer* rights so that neither voting rights nor economic returns can be passed to another party without the intervention of an elected **governing body**. Co-operative capital, however, can be withdrawn (subject to any rule requiring a minimum investment period or limits on withdrawals within an accounting period). In practice, members can redeem their co-operative capital (or sell it to a trust, in the case of an employee-owned businesses), and then the co-operative (or trust) can decide whether to reissue, sell on or cancel the shares.

Emerson (2000: 16) argues for a 'social capital market' to end the 'schizophrenia of capitalism' in which charitable trusts separate their economic and social investment activities. Even though they generate funds for social investment through economic investment portfolios, Emerson found that 75 per cent of them gave little consideration to the *social* impact of their *economic* investing. Blended value, as a proposition, seeks to end this dichotomy by encouraging investors to balance the generation of social and economic returns through investments in social enterprises. But where might such behaviour already exist? Are there any large-scale examples of 'ordinary people' (i.e. people who are not 'high net worth' individuals) saving and lending their money to each other in a more equitable way? Are there large-scale examples of people offering philanthropic or **patient capital** at low interest rates (or as interest-free loans) in support of social ventures?

Case 6.1

Zopa and Kiva: two examples of mutual finance

Further materials and exercise activities are available on the companion website at: www.sagepub.co.uk/ridleyduff.

Zopa (www.zopa.com) started in 2005, is a peer-to-peer lending institution that enables its members to save and borrow from each other. According to *The Guardian* (2014a), it 'uses the internet to cut out the banks entirely' to give both savers and

(Continued)

(Continued)

borrowers a better deal. The only money available to borrowers are the savings of Zopa's members (so money comes from the 'real economy' and there are no fractional reserve banking practices). By the end of 2014, Zopa's website claimed it had lent £753 million to more than 54,000 members, and had received the 'most trusted' MoneyWise Customer Service Award for four years running.

In peer-to-peer lending, the lender's money is at risk, but this risk is mitigated by dividing each person's deposits into small amounts (e.g. £10 units) and lending it to a large number of borrowers. Zopa claims that most of its lenders and borrowers are *not* 'high net worth' individuals, but are credit worthy middle-income earners. Its credit-scoring system does mean that marginalised members of a community who have a poor credit record could be refused a loan request (or have to pay much higher rates of interest). Despite this, the Zopa system shows that a large group of 'ordinary people' who would otherwise not have access to loans and savings rates enjoyed by the 'rich' can organise this for themselves through a mutual.

To put this to the test, one of the authors (Rory) borrowed a loan at 5.9 per cent to buy a second hand car (this was between 2 and 6 per cent *lower* than car loans available from banks and car dealers). He also tested out Zopa's claims about lending using some of his savings. In the two years to February 2015, he received 5.1 per cent interest (after charges) on the money lent (3 per cent higher than the interest received on his bank's individual savings account (ISA)). This practical test shows that mutual saving/lending clubs like Zopa can enable people who are not 'high net worth' individuals to achieve rates of return on their capital similar to professional investors. However, it also highlights that people with poor credit ratings are still better served by **credit unions** (fully mutualised saving/lending institutions like the Grameen Bank designed to provide banking services for low income households).

What about interest-free loans to start new businesses? Kiva claimed (in 2012) to have helped 800,000 entrepreneurs in 60 countries through an international peer-to-peer lending network. Kiva means 'unity' in Swahili. It invites members of the public to invest small amounts (starting from $25) in projects listed on their website. By 2015, Kiva was raising $1 million dollars every three days ($122 million a year). Kiva loans are interest-free – the lender charges no interest, but does expect to get their capital back. To see how this works, Rory gave a $25 Kiva voucher to his nephew in 2010. Five years later, his nephew was still lending it out to new projects. After one default, his capital shrank to $21, but it has been recycled several times to support projects of his nephew's choosing.

In 2009, Kiva's practices came under close scrutiny when it was discovered that they *recover* capital already paid to social entrepreneurs so the appearance of making a direct investment in a social entrepreneur's project is an illusion (Roodman, 2009).

However, once a local micro-finance provider *raises* capital to reimburse their expenditure via Kiva, they do establish a direct link and the repayments collected from the micro-entrepreneur are used to reimburse Kiva lenders.

Class exercise: Zopa and Kiva

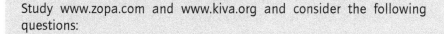

Study www.zopa.com and www.kiva.org and consider the following questions:

1 Do Zopa and Kiva provide a blueprint for member-owned banking in the social economy?
2 Are there other internet-enabled technologies (mobile phones, PayPal) that can further democratise banking?
3 Is this approach to social investment better able to meet the needs of social entrepreneurs than social investment bodies established by private foundations and governments?

Find out more about peer-to-peer lending in the UK at: www.youtube.com/watch?v=Qe-HogbHvOo

Hear about the start of peer-to-peer lending in South Africa at: www.youtube.com/watch?v=FaCORZlLLmc

Find out about peer-to-peer lending in the US at: www.youtube.com/watch?v=BLmvlNNoGpA

Find out more about Kiva micro-finance at: www.youtube.com/watch?v=TLQX_5kQHyo

For Kiva Labs see: www.youtube.com/watch?v=v2vetkuQivw

Every Zopa lender can see who has borrowed their money (and what their money has been borrowed for). On Kiva, lenders choose who to support based on the blended value created, and not on the basis of the financial returns (because there are none). At Zopa, borrowers can borrow at rates substantially lower than high street banks (if their credit rating is acceptable), and also get savings rates higher than private banks can offer. This helps to improve their lives (social) and saves them money (economic). Kiva shows that individuals *are* willing to support social investments with interest-free (debt-free) loans in a way that is consistent with the goals of Positive Money, and which conform to the 'type one' approach to social business advocated by Yunus (2007).

Case 6.1 (Zopa and Kiva) illustrates how social investment can operate on a different model to meet needs left unmet by institutional social investors. It deviates from the norms of private sector banking institutions (Brown and Swersky, 2012; Lehner, 2013) by providing loans at rates, in amounts, and with repayments terms that meet more of a (social) entrepreneur's needs. While Big Society Capital does provide capital for blended value investments, how will the blend of social and economic returns for both investors and investees compare to those provided by a mutual saving/lending institution?

The success of new forms of mutual saving/borrowing during the financial crash of 2008 has – at last – stimulated academic interest. Lehner (2013) has produced a paper that sets out a series of theoretical propositions to guide research. He also highlights four arguments that provide a basis for understanding why crowdfunding linked to the tenets of 'new co-operativism' (Vieta, 2010) may be preferred by both social entrepreneurs and crowdfunders alike (particularly those firmly within the social and solidarity economy). The four arguments are rooted in:

- The ambiguity and diversity of a social enterprise's goals: crowdfunders are more likely to be diverse and therefore more likely to (collectively) support a range of social and economic goals.
- The 'alternative' models of social enterprise governance and management: while member ownership (democratic governance) is alien to private investors, crowd-funders will see democratic governance as legitimate, or even desirable.
- The 'cultural-distance' between private investors and social entrepreneurs: crowd-funders engaged in mutual lending will be more familiar with the cultural norms and preferences of social entrepreneurs.
- The lack of 'management-speak' in the business narratives of social entrepreneurs: while this can lower credibility with private investors, it can raise credibility with crowdfunders.

He identifies a number of mediators of the relationship between 'the crowd' and the 'business model' that require further empirical research. Foremost among these are: information economics; Web 2.0 technologies; the ethical legitimacy of business ideas and; the legal-regulatory framework (see Figure 6.3). Lehner's schema for researching crowd-based social investment highlights the key concepts of control, participation and reward to function well.

New sources of capital

In the last two decades, banks more sympathetic to social enterprise have emerged or rebranded themselves. Significant among these (in the UK) are Charity Bank, Co-operative Bank, Triodos Bank and Unity Trust Bank who all offer support for CTAs, CMEs and SRBs. While they aim to support blended value creation, they do not necessarily assess risk in ways that are fundamentally different from mainstream banking institutions, and are not necessarily a cheaper source of debt finance. They are, however, more likely to offer expertise and networks of investors who are ideologically sympathetic, and who are able to see the blended value created by a social enterprise.

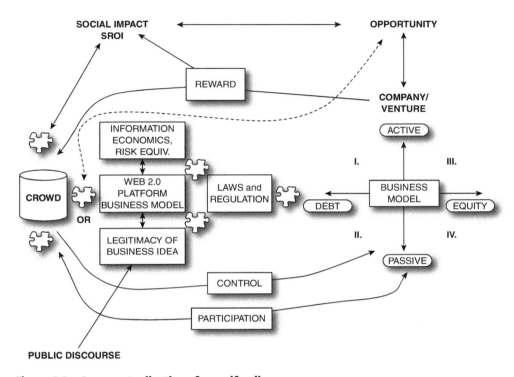

Figure 6.3 A conceptualisation of crowdfunding

Source: based on Lehner (2013), Figure 1

Alongside these banking institutions are new social enterprise investment funds. Examples discussed in Case 6.2 (on the companion website) include:

- The Social Investment Business: www.sibgroup.org.uk/
- Key Fund: http://thekeyfund.co.uk/
- Big Issue Invest: www.bigissueinvest.com/
- Bridges Ventures: www.bridgesventures.com/

However, institutional investors (banks and private/government investment funds) now face competition from a range of crowdfunding platforms. The following are some of the more popular platforms that provide different types of capital for CTAs, CMEs and SRBs in the UK and US.

- Philanthropic Capital (for CTAs, CMEs or SRBs):
  - www.crowdfunder.co.uk
  - www.indiegogo.com
  - www.kickstarter.com

- Co-operative Capital (for CMEs):

  ○ www.microgenius.org.uk (community shares crowdfunding platform)

- Private Capital (for SRBs and some CMEs):

  ○ www.fundingcircle.com
  ○ www.crowdcube.com

The amounts raised through these platforms put into perspective the limited success of the Social Investment Taskforce in the UK to work with City institutions on the creation of a social investment industry. We are faced with a division between social investment schemes favoured by regulators and private investors, and those that the wider public are willing to support.

To illustrate the differences in impact, consider the following. Twelve years after the UK government convened a Social Investment Taskforce (in 2000) to outline how to acquire and invest over £400 million in dormant bank accounts, it finally created Big Society Capital. Its 2013 accounts show that deals for £47.9 million have been signed and £13.1 million has been paid to investees. In 2013, it reported a loss of £2.9 million, had staff costs of £2.1 million, paid salaries above £60,000 to ten staff, and above £100,000 to two further staff (Big Society Capital, 2014; Huckfield, 2015). In contrast, the idea for Kickstarter first formed in 2002, and eventually went live in 2009. At the time of writing, it has been supported by over 8 million people who have made more than 20 million pledges totalling $1.56 billion towards 79,074 'creative projects'. Similarly, Indiegogo currently reports 15 million visitors *per month*, with 150,000 funded projects in 224 countries. Both Indiegogo and Kickstarter provide 'rewards' rather than 'returns' to funders, making the capital donated philanthropic in the sense that investors do not buy a financial stake or get a traditional financial return.[2] The UK's largest philanthropic crowdfunding site (www.crowdfunder.co.uk) has only operated for two years. In that time it raised £2 million from 70,000 followers to fund approximately 3,000 projects.

- Watch this 'History of Kickstarter' video released on its fifth anniversary in 2014: www.youtube.com/watch?v=qcR_UHV0tKE
- See current Kickstarter funding summary here: www.kickstarter.com/help/stats/
- See current Indiegogo funding summary here: www.indiegogo.com/about/our-story

The speed at which crowdfunding/investing is developing is rapid. These two sector leaders demonstrate some of the qualities that Lehner highlights as being aligned with the social solidarity economy. Kickstarter is a B-Corp (a for-benefit private company). It commands high levels of public support and user participation, transparently reports on every project, provides impact reporting and has funded small (less than $100) as well as multi-million dollar projects (greater than $10 million).

This type of philanthropic capital, however, sits alongside **venture philanthropy** (Price, 2008). McGoey (2014) has coined the term 'philanthrocapitalism' to describe the relationship between people like Bill Gates (The Gates Foundation) and the governments they can influence. McGoey acknowledges that The Gates Foundation provides more investment in health (worldwide) than the World Health Organisation (WHO). However, he also puts this into perspective by pointing out that a *single programme* of the US President's Office on HIV/AIDs prevention provides more funding than the Gates Foundation provides to all its projects. Philanthrocapitalism describes two inter-related tendencies. Firstly, the state acts as philanthropist (and, according to McGoey, uses its capacity to support the development of private capital more than the social economy). Secondly, successful businesspeople take it upon themselves to engage in philanthropy and utilise the business practices of capitalism to plan and execute social projects (following Rockefeller, Carnegie, Ford and Gates). For McGoey (2014: 122), the current constellation of activities propagates a 'dubious belief' that private philanthropy does more to address 'gaps' left by the state than the reverse. He concludes, 'it is often governments [who are] subsidising philanthrocapitalists'.

The contentious aspect of philanthrocapitalism is the extent to which individuals who have made private fortunes in business will acquire hegemonic control over even more domains of activity. Their hands-on approach means they can acquire voting rights if they invest in a for-profit social enterprise. The upside of granting shares, according to Emerson (2000), is that it promotes a *learning culture among social investors* by encouraging them to track the social and economic value they create. This learning will, in cases of investor satisfaction, increase the funds available for social investment. But this consideration might equally apply to *employee and community investors* who will take a keen interest in how their savings support the social economy, but prefer to do so through mutual ventures that crowd-invest in CMEs and SRBs (Brown, 2004, 2006; Erdal, 2011). A key question for both social entrepreneurs and policy-makers is 'which controlling interest provides the best "blended-value" return?'

The rise of community shares, credit unions and employee ownership

As Brown (2004) highlights, CMEs are rediscovering the concept of community share issues (a form of co-operative equity) to raise capital for social enterprise development. As far back as 2002, Triodos Bank helped the Ethical Property Company raise £4.2 million. In 2004, it helped Café Direct raise £5 million. In both cases – despite limited returns on equity – the launches were heavily oversubscribed. Brown further highlights the values of its (social) investors:

in 1990 the Centre for Alternative Technology (CAT) raised £1 million by selling shares to investors who have no voting rights, have never received a dividend and who cannot easily sell their shares. Traidcraft has raised nearly £5 million through four successive share issues over the last twenty years, but up to 2004 had never paid a dividend to shareholders. Until the most recent share issue in 2002, Traidcraft shareholders had no voting rights, and even now voting rights are restricted. (2006: 74)

Brown (2006) estimated that only 1 per cent of ethical investments were directed towards social enterprises in 2004. If growth of 10 per cent per annum could be achieved, it would increase the capital available by £1.2 billion (in the UK alone). Locality's 2013/14 Impact Report highlights that it helped 61 members raise £8.47 million in investments, and issued a further £2.56 million in grants. Locality is a partner in the Community Shares Unit of Co-operatives UK. The co-ordinator of the unit, Simon Borkin, reported that community shares in 2013 raised £35 million from 30,000 co-operative members, with individual projects ranging from £100,000 and £1.1 million. A new crowd-*investing* platform (www.microgenius.org.uk) enables Co-operatives UK to track the creation of co-operative capital. The average investment is currently £750 per investor, from members who are in lower/medium income households, and the average number of members backing each project is 175. This strategy for community ownership also provides low cost capital (at levels that Keynes and Piketty would approve) to buy local pubs, shops and space for local businesses. Members typically get 3 to 5 per cent return, but have to wait some years before dividends are paid at all. Just as important is that this form of social investing gives the investor membership and representation in the running of the project they invest in. Both the interest received on capital contributions, and the voice that such contributions gives social investors, differentiates community shares from crowdfunding.

With changes in credit union law to make more co-operative capital available to social enterprises (through a new right to provide business banking services), the legal framework for co-operative capital is now more aligned with the successful model of Mondragon (see Part 1 – Introduction). During its early development, Mondragon's Caja Laboral (Bank of the People) secured over 300,000 members in a region half the size of Wales to provide start-up and development capital for its network of co-operatives (Whyte and Whyte, 1991). With UK credit union membership continuing to rise (from 343,155 to 704,535 in the five years to 2009, rising to 1,173,299 by December 2014), there are now assets exceeding £1 billion in the UK credit union system (www.abcul.org). This, however, is still small by international standards. ABCUL's 2014 Annual Report claims there are 208 million credit union members worldwide, contributing assets of $1.7 trillion, with market penetration of 47 per cent in the US, 43 per cent in Canada, 30 per cent in Australia and an impressive 75 per cent in Ireland (the UK is less than 2 per cent).

Case 6.3

The Indonesian concept of 'Arisan'

The following is based on Rory Ridley-Duff's report to the British Council Indonesia after a visit to Jakarta in 2012.

Consider the case of social entrepreneur Yoos Lufti, whose credit union movement in Indonesia was studied by Dr Maria Radyati at Trisakti University in Jakarta. Indonesian saving/borrowing clubs are based on the concept of Arisan (mutual interaction), and Yoos Lufti helped to establish the Tanggung Renteng (a savings/loan co-operative). Yoos has established over 500 groups where people initially socialise together, then apply for loans by providing each other (and other institutions) with a 'mutual liability guarantee'. Under a mutual liability guarantee, a group of people apply for a loan together and agree to pool their repayments to repay the lender. If one member cannot make a repayment, the other borrowers cover it while they help the defaulting borrower deal with the issue that led to their default. This form of financial management ensures each person helps and supports others in their immediate community.

Lufti claims that Muhammad Yunus visited her in the mid-1970s to discuss the model, and Yunus then adapted it for the Grameen Bank. In western writings, Muhammad Yunus's approach has been labelled 'social collateral' for the purposes of a loan guarantee (see Chapter 3). Important in the tradition of Arisan is building the ability of people to speak before their peers, improve their capacity to articulate their circumstances, improve their negotiation skills and increase their confidence as part of a supportive community. Lufti also reports that loan default rates are 'almost zero' (confirmed by Dr Radyati) and this means money can be lent at interest rates of 1–2 per cent – the level at which Keynes suggests economic development can be optimised.

Tanggung Renteng is organised entirely around women in Indonesian communities, but there is potential to apply it to other contexts: a) groups of employees entering into a 'mutual liability guarantee' to capitalise a CME; b) groups of CMEs entering a 'mutual liability guarantee' to develop a joint venture. Trust issues in western cultures may be a barrier, but the economic advantages of mutual liability may be sufficient to justify investigation. Tanggung Renteng, however, reported barriers to the participation of organisations (from Indonesian Law) so they will require changes similar to those just introduced in the UK. Both the UK and Indonesians

(Continued)

(Continued)

can learn from the linkages established in the Mondragon co-operative network between savings/loans co-operatives, industrial enterprises, social insurance schemes, education and research to strengthen their social economies.

I was particularly taken with the concept – and achievements – of the 'mutual liability guarantee'. The reduction in the cost of capital alone produces millions (billions?) of additional investment capital for the social economy over time.

Investigate this idea in your own national context and consider carefully:

1   What are the cultural and legislative enablers and barriers to a 'mutual liability guarantee'?
2   Could 'mutual liability guarantees' help credit unions and crowd-investing schemes to develop more rapidly?
3   Can you devise a 'mutual liability guarantee' scheme for your country that would enable more workers to make social investments in worker co-operatives and employee-owned business?

To round off this section, we also need to consider the position of employee-owned businesses (see Chapter 3). At the 2014 Working Capital Conference (Wakefield, 28 February), Nick Donahoe, CEO of Big Society Capital, responded to Bill Birch's[3] inquiry on capitalising a Yorkshire coal mine that would invest a substantial percentage of its profits in community development. Birch was initially told 'there's no reason it can't be supported if it is a co-operative structure'. However, on further questioning, Donahoe confirmed that 'being a co-operative alone is not sufficient to be eligible, but if it is a co-operative with a social purpose then it would be eligible'. This prompted a further question as to why co-operative values and principles were insufficient to establish credentials as a 'social purpose' enterprise (see Chapter 1). It took a one-to-one conversation with Donahoe to establish *how* Big Society Capital evidences 'social purpose' – it requires a conventional charity-like asset-lock and 'social objectives' in Articles of Association. As a consequence, the very CMEs and SRBs that contributed to the initial wave of social enterprise development face the same barriers accessing Big Society Capital as they face qualifying for the Social Enterprise Mark (Ridley-Duff and Southcombe, 2012; Teasdale, 2012). As Big Society Capital supports only one of the three approaches to social enterprise, its impact on the wider social economy will be limited (Huckfield, 2015).

However, employee-owned enterprises *are* receiving social investments from two other sources (EOA, 2013). Firstly, employee-owned businesses can receive internal investments from their own members (Bill Birch and 11 other people each invested £5,000 in their venture). Secondly, tax regimes are being reworked to enable the state to play the role of philanthrocapitalist (McGoey, 2014). In the US, in addition to tax benefits for workers investing in their own ventures, US federal (and sometimes state) authorities reduce corporation tax based on the level of employee ownership (NCEO, 2015). The higher the level of employee ownership, the lower the level of corporation tax. Within Nicholls's (2010) matrix, this could be seen as an indirect 'government investment', providing blended returns for both employees and local/national governments.

Similarly, there is a new tax regime for employee ownership in the UK (HMRC, 2014). Any individual, trustee, person or company disposing of a controlling interest to an employee benefit trust can receive full tax relief on their capital gains. In effect, a government 'social investment' equal to the amount of the tax due from an outgoing investor is used to incentivise the mutualisation of private enterprises. This encourages the *transfer of capital* from private-owners to member-owners (through individual and trust-based employee shareholding) and enables more people to share in the returns to capital (Piketty, 2014).

The impact this can have on the lives of working people is already known in the EU from studies of Mondragon in Spain and Bologna in Italy (Whyte and Whyte, 1991; Erdal, 2011). In the US, however, recent press reports that over 400 'cashiers, shelf-stackers, clerks and others' at WinCo (an employee-owned supermarket) have become millionaires is leading to a proliferation of social media that communicates how employee mutuals can impact on the lives of both workers and the wider community. *Time Magazine* has called WinCo 'Walmart's Worst Nightmare' (Tuttle, 2014) (for more on WinCo see: www.youtube.com/watch?v=shnE0IPDa3E#t=216 and www.ryot.org/winco-foods-grocery-employees-millionaires-walmart/883593).

These tax schemes – both in the US and UK – are rooted in reframing the use and allocation of *private* capital so that it operates for *mutual* benefit. From a social investment (and tax system) perspective, the investment is still a *financial* investment with the modification that capital is held in trust for the benefit of the workforce and/or community. In the next – and final – section, we highlight further ways in which CMEs are becoming creative in designing and allocating capital in the spirit of 'new cooperativism' (Vieta, 2010). We give three examples of circumventing bankers and financial investors completely by looking at capital in a new way – as *the product of labour*.

Creative approaches to creating and allocating capital

In this section, we provide three examples (from New Zealand, Indonesia and the UK) of organisations who regard labour (and the products of labour) as a form of equity. We present this to illustrate that 'capital' does not have to be 'money', but it must have value to the enterprise and its users to become the basis of a member's equity. These examples come from small-, medium- and large-scale enterprises to show that size is not a factor in changing to a different paradigm of thought.

The first example is *New Horizons Music Ltd*. This small company (five members, including Rory) operated from 2006 to 2009 to distribute income from music sales to rock band members. The capital structure chosen would later influence the FairShares Model (Ridley-Duff and Southcombe, 2014; Ridley-Duff and Bull, 2014). The company had two types of capital: Labour Shares and Investor Shares. Four people bought Investor Shares (250 at £1 each) on incorporation, and then each musician was allocated Labour Shares in proportion to the music they had written (one share for each minute of music). A three-minute track composed by one member led to an allocation of three Labour Shares. An eight-minute composition by four band members led to each band member getting two Labour Shares. The money raised by Investor Shares paid for the initial manufacture of CDs. Later, CD manufacturing was paid out of sales revenues.

As a result, each social enterprise member was able to earn income in three ways: 1) royalties based on the established norm of rewarding artists with a percentage of revenues from the sale of their creative works; 2) Labour Share *dividends* calculated by dividing half the surplus among Labour Shareholders in proportion to their Labour Shares, and; 3) traditional dividends based on sharing the remainder of surplus in proportion to Investor Shares held. Each member had only one vote, irrespective of how their shareholding was made up. Applied more widely, the *New Horizons Music* model could create a mutual enterprise in which surpluses are shared (after payment of royalties) among a much larger group of artists, but on the basis of both *labour* and financial investments.

Our other examples come from a trip to Indonesia in 2012, and peer-reviewing a paper for the *International Journal of Co-operative Organisation and Management*. In 2012, Rory met Silverius Oscar Onggul (Onte) during a trip to Indonesia. Onte is an Ashoka Fellow who organised JAUH, a logging co-operative. In 2012, it had 1,500 members who had built up a business to export sustainably produced eco-timber. At the outset, the logs had limited value and were being illegally felled. After securing certification for their quality, JAUH increased the value of its members' logs ten-fold. Increased income meant that fewer logs needed to be felled to have a sustainable income (and this improved the sustainability of the forestry operation as well). At JAUH, capital was provided in the form of *logs* – the products of labour – and not financial capital.

The same was found in our large-scale example, Fonterra, in New Zealand. This is a producer co-operative – the country's largest – producing dairy products for export. Fonterra's constitution defines each farmer's contribution as follows:

> [Shares] shall be one Co-operative Share for each kilogram of milk solids obtainable from the average quantity of milk determined by the Board in relation to that supplied to the Company by a Shareholder in that Season … (Fonterra, n.d.)

Put more simply, each farmer is require to provide *milk* to purchase their membership, and will receive one share (co-operative capital) for each kilogram of milk solids that can be made from it. In effect, each farmer pays their membership dues (and investment capital) in the form of milk. This also affects their voting rights – they receive one voting share for each 1,000 kilograms of milk solids created from their milk supply. Voting power, therefore, is linked to the *produce* of each member, and not a financial investment.

In all cases (UK, Indonesia and New Zealand) shares are created and allocated to recognise the production and labour power of members (for their music, their logs and their milk). No member is *required* to make a contribution of money to become a member, so their entry is linked to the socio-economic value of what they can produce, and not the financial value of money they can invest. In an earlier study, Rory found a case of voluntary labour for two months being used as the capital contribution of new workers in an employee-owned businesses (Ridley-Duff, 2009). Similarly, the FairShares Association – following this same paradigm of thought – recently defined its 'qualifying contributions' for membership in terms of the *creation* and *use* of FairShares IP (FairShares Association, 2014).

Conclusions

In this chapter, we have introduced a wide range of options for social investment. We have differentiated blended value for investors from the blended value that is created by investees in their community (Emerson, 2000; Nicholls, 2010). We also reviewed the argument of Keynes, Piketty and Positive Money that exposes how rents, interest rates and private capital enriches capital owners at a faster rate than providers of labour (Keynes, 2008 [1936]; Swan and Pidcock, 2009; Piketty, 2014). This problematises the assumption that all anyone needs to do to become wealthier is to work harder. Wealth is spread by social investments that achieve one or both of the following outcomes: either interest rates are kept low enough to ensure that investees grow their incomes at a faster rate than investors grow their return on capital, or – alternatively – social investments pay for the mutualisation of private capital so that producers share in the higher rates of return enjoyed by private investors.

From this starting point, we explored two examples. The first (Zopa) illustrated how 'ordinary people' could participate in higher returns to capital by creating savings/lending mutuals, or – alternatively – joining a credit union. The second (Kiva) demonstrated the willingness of people to provide interest-free loans (from as little as $25) and then choose which entrepreneurs to support through crowd-investing technology. The potential of crowdfunding to scale quickly, focus on impact and innovation, and fund projects of all sizes – was considered against more sluggish, inflexible institutions that are framing 'mainstream' social investment (e.g. Big Society Capital).

In the second half of the chapter, we switched from a discussion of philanthropic and co-operative capital to the way *private* capital can be mutualised by philanthrocapitalists, governments and employee-owners to provide blended returns. Tax regimes that incentivise employee mutuals were discussed and compared. In the final section, we illustrated how capital can be framed as a *labour* investment that has socio-economic value, rather than as a *financial* (monetary) investment. Moreover, voting rights can be linked to labour investments just as easily as financial investments to secure blended returns for labour (Emerson, 2000; Nicholls, 2010; Ridley-Duff and Bull, 2014).

Class exercise: Comparing approaches to social investment

Cases 6.2 and 6.3 are available on the companion website at: www.sagepub.co.uk/ridleyduff.

Part 1 (approx. 40 minutes)

Divide your seminar group into three sub-groups (5 minutes).

Distribute Case 6.1 (Zopa and Kiva) to members of group 1, 6.2 (Social Investment Funds) to members of group 2, and 6.3 (Mondragon) to members of group 3. If they have not read the cases in advance of the seminar, give them a short time to prepare (10 minutes).

Ask all group 1 members to convene and debate how to make Emerson's idea of a 'social capital market' work in practice (25 minutes).

Ask all group 2 members to convene and clarify the innovations of the Mondragon banking system, and how this might be used to critique and improve Emerson's 'social capital market' (25 minutes).

Ask all group 3 member to convene and clarify the innovations in crowdfunding/investing that could improve the workings of a 'social capital market' (25 minutes).

Part 2 (approx. 30 minutes)

Identify the investment logic and investor rationality behind each of the cases discussed using Nicholls's 'logics' framework (25 minutes).

Following the seminar, write a 500 word blog or essay answering the question:

'Is social investment safer in the hands of "professional investors" operating social investment institutions, or "ordinary people" selecting projects listed on crowdfunding/investing platforms?'

Summary of learning

In this chapter, we have argued the following:

A social investment mind-set is different from a fundraising mind-set. It involves tracking and learning from the investments made in order to increase understanding of the economic and social value created for both investors and investees.

Social investing advances the concept of 'blended value', and the practice of investing in a way that creates social and economic returns for both investor and investee.

Social investments are underpinned by an 'investment logic' and an 'investor rationality' that varies across different social investment institutions.

Mutual finance, in which both investor and investee share the benefits and outcomes of social investment, is currently the dominant type across the world.

Capital (and investments) can be conceptualised as the *outputs of labour* to provide a viable alternative basis for issuing shares that does not require monetary contributions.

Questions and possible essay assignments

1. Using examples, describe and critically assess the concept of 'blended value'. How does blended value for the investor differ from blended value for the investee?
2. 'Social enterprises should not issue shares or accept equity finance.' What are the limitations of this statement? Illustrate your answer by evaluating a creative 'alternative' strategy for attracting capital.
3. What factors make it hard for a social enterprise to obtain social investment? Critically assess the factors that make an organisation 'investment ready'.

Further reading

The primer for this chapter is Emerson's 'The nature of returns' (2000), easily found by typing the article title into Google. While sometimes polemical, the paper grapples with the nature of social and economic returns, and articulates the case for blended value as a strategy for social investment.

Perhaps the best current example of blended value is the social investment system at Mondragon. Chapter 8 of Whyte and Whyte's *Making Mondragon* (1991) describes the history of the co-operative banking system, and the contract of association that underpins the relationship between the member co-operatives and the bank. Chapter 16 examines the 'changing role' of the bank as it finds ways to defend and rescue organisations facing trading difficulties.

Further coverage is provided by two contributions from Jim Brown. The first is a practical 'toolkit' written for the Finance Hub (Brown, 2007) that helps voluntary sector organisations to prepare for funding applications. The second is 'Designing equity finance for social enterprises' (Brown, 2006). This will be of particular interest to co-operative social enterprises and mutual societies. Empirical research on the link between structure, management practices and finance can be found in Rory's paper 'Co-operative social enterprises: company rules, access to finance and management practice' (Ridley-Duff, 2009).

Further reading material is available on the companion website at: www.sagepub. co.uk/ridleyduff.

Useful resources

The Association of British Credit Unions: www.abcul.coop

Baxi Partnership: www.baxipartnership.co.uk/

Big Issue Invest: www.bigissueinvest.com/

Blendedvalue.org: www.blendedvalue.org

Bridges Community Ventures: www.bridgesventures.com/

Charity Bank: www.charitybank.org/

Co-operative & Community Finance: www.coopfinance.coop/

Cooperative Capital Fund: http://cooperativefund.org/coopcapital

The Key Fund: http://thekeyfund.co.uk/

The Social Investment Business: www.sibgroup.org.uk

SOVEC: www.sovec.nl/

Triodos Bank: www.triodos.co.uk/uk/business_banking/

UK Social Investment Forum: www.uksif.org/

Unity Trust Bank: www.unity.co.uk/

UnLtd Advantage: http://unltd.org.uk/

Notes

1 See this biographical note by one of the founders of Positive Money: www.bendyson. com/about/.

2 For a quick comparison watch: www.youtube.com/watch?v=gTRZh1ZK000. There's a discussion by the founder of Indiegogo at: www.youtube.com/watch?v=twDfSogk1Tg.

3 Based on verbatim notes made by Rory Ridley-Duff at the Working Capital Conference, 28 February 2014.

Social and Ethical Capital   7

Mike Bull, Pam Seanor and Rory Ridley-Duff

Learning objectives

In this chapter you are encouraged to consider the implications of social and ethical challenges in social enterprise. By the end of this chapter you will be able to:

- explain and compare theories of social capital and their role in community development
- describe the ways in which people analyse social capital
- critique the roles of social networks in developing social capital and social enterprises
- articulate the role of ethical values in the formation of enterprises
- apply ethical theories to understand the nature of ethical capital in social enterprises.

The key arguments that will be developed in this chapter are:

- Social and ethical issues are of central importance to members of social enterprise.
- Social capital encompasses numerous ideas including trust, civic spirit, goodwill, reciprocity, mutuality, shared commitment, solidarity and co-operation.

(Continued)

(Continued)

- Perceived power affects the development of social capital.
- Social capital offers a useful theoretical framework for conceptualising the value of social enterprises in community development and public policy debates.
- Ethical capital offers a useful theoretical framework for conceptualising the motivations and orientation of social entrepreneurs, as well as members of social enterprises.

Introduction

In this chapter, we discuss different theories of social capital and ethics. Laville and Nyssens (2001) argue that social enterprises generate greater amounts of social capital than public or private sector organisations. Not only does this provide them with a competitive edge in the market, it becomes a public policy argument for supporting them (Birch and Whittam, 2008).

In Part 1, we examined in detail the role of social enterprises in challenging the dominant assumptions of business and bringing about different attempts at transformation in the private, voluntary and public sector. In this chapter, we consider the ethical dimensions of attempts to transform business culture. There are some writers who focus on social and environmental dimensions of change (Preuss, 2004; Krueger et al., 2009), others examine how social entrepreneurs can gain a competitive edge from their 'entrepreneurial virtues' (Sullivan Mort et al., 2003), their 'ethical fibre' (Drayton, 2005) and the 'ethical capital' they are able to create (Bull et al., 2010).

A survey by Social Enterprise UK (SEC, 2013) attempted to quantify social motives in social enterprises in the UK. The top five motivations were: 'improving a community' (37 per cent); 'improving health and well-being' (31 per cent); 'creating employment' (27 per cent); 'helping vulnerable people' (21 per cent); and 'supporting social enterprise and third sector organisations'. This helps with understanding the social value that people working in social enterprises wish to create. In Chapter 4, we introduced some questions that were developed during social enterprise lecture tours in Asia. Of these questions, three touch directly on the creation of social and ethical capital, and their deployment to promote sustainable development.

Is social value creation:

1. The pursuit and fulfilment of a social goal/mission (ethical)?
2. And/or the inclusive way enterprises can be organised (social)?
3. And/or the pursuit of sustainable development (ethical and social)?

The first question links to the priorities of charitable trading activities (CTAs) and socially responsible businesses (SRBs). The second and third questions link more to the priorities or SRBs and co-operative and mutual enterprises (CMEs). In this chapter, we will consider the concept of social capital first and then develop the argument to include ethical capital.

Understanding views on social capital

The 'social' component of social enterprise is often interpreted as an organisation's social purpose or mission. According to Sullivan Mort et al. (2003), a social enterprise's primary purpose is to create social value for its stakeholders. But which type of social value? And for which stakeholder groups? Is it the provision of a particular good or service that will improve community or beneficiary well-being (a consumption perspective), or is it through the reorganisation of patterns and practices of work (a production perspective)? Both perspectives need consideration and will contribute to an optimum outcome.

The concept of *social capital* is a metaphor found across numerous fields of study. Similar to the term 'social enterprise', it welds together two disparate concepts. Tan et al. (2005) define 'social' in terms of *altruistic* motives, while Smith and Kulynych (2002) discuss how the term 'capital' was originally used to discuss a *reserve* and a *provision for the future*. The question posed by Chell (2007) is whether combining these terms creates a contradiction. Is it possible to develop a 'reserve' of 'altruism'?

While we need to consider these issues, there is agreement among writers that social capital implies the development of *trust, civic spirit, goodwill, reciprocity, mutuality, shared commitment, solidarity* and *co-operation*. It offers a way to recognise resources that are difficult to quantify in economic theory, but which are recognised as important (Coleman, 1988; Putnam, 2001; White, 2002). Adler and Kwon (2002) frame these aspects, despite their ambiguous and elastic meanings, as things that make it easier to achieve a common goal or action.

Hanifan is credited as being the first to use the term in 1916 while writing about 'goodwill, fellowship, mutual sympathy, and social intercourse among a group of individuals and families' to enhance education (Smith and Kulynych, 2002: 154). Social capital also evolved as a concept in discussions of Coleman's (1988) *social exchange theory* to argue that communities benefit when children and young people grow up in similar school networks, supported by parent and teacher associations.

Fukuyama (2001) discusses how social capital may also be viewed as the 'cohesiveness' of relationships at the inter-organisational level, especially at stressful times. In this respect his theorising differs from Coleman who emphasised relationship stability as a condition for social capital to develop. These differences have prompted authors to seek explanations for divergent conceptualisations of social capital. For example, Law and Mooney (2006) argue that those on the political left use the term to describe solidarity and collective action, while those on the political right use it to denote specific ethical, community and family values (see Figure 7.1).

Figure 7.1   Political spectrum and social capital

Source: Law and Mooney (2006)

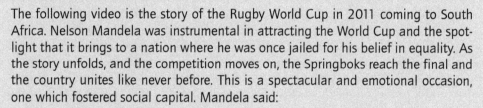

Case 7.1

More than a game

The following video is the story of the Rugby World Cup in 2011 coming to South Africa. Nelson Mandela was instrumental in attracting the World Cup and the spotlight that it brings to a nation where he was once jailed for his belief in equality. As the story unfolds, and the competition moves on, the Springboks reach the final and the country unites like never before. This is a spectacular and emotional occasion, one which fostered social capital. Mandela said:

> Sport has the power to change the world. It has the power to inspire. It has the power to unite in a way that little else does. It speaks to youth in a language they understand. Sport can create hope where once there was only despair. (Sport Matters, n.d.)

Watch the video: www.sportanddev.org/en/newsnviews/news/?3634/Nelson-Mandela-the-Rugby-World-Cup-and-social-change

The story highlights that sport is a vehicle for the development of social capital. The United Nations highlights this when they suggest:

> Sport has historically played an important role in all societies, be it in the form of competitive sport, physical activity or play. But one may wonder: what does sport have to do with the United Nations? In fact, sport presents a natural partnership for the United Nations (UN) system: sport and play are human rights that must be respected and enforced worldwide; sport has been increasingly recognized and used as a low-cost and high-impact tool in humanitarian, development and peace-building efforts, not only by the UN system but also by non-governmental organizations (NGOs), governments, development agencies, sports federations, armed forces and the media. Sport can no longer be considered a luxury within any society but is rather an important investment in the present and future, particularly in developing countries. (UN, n.d.)

Putnam (1994, 2001) popularised the concept by exploring the importance of rela-tionships, especially membership of voluntary associations, in Italy and the USA. Putnam is critical of Coleman's approach, as focusing upon the family restricts the usefulness of the concept to explain access to wider social networks. As Preuss comments:

> The most common function of social capital … lies in its ability to provide network-mediated benefits *beyond* the immediate family. (2004: 157) (emphasis added).

Bourdieu (1986) uses the term to discuss class relations. He argued that social capital can empower members of a group to take social action that brings about political change. However, when Putnam discusses Bourdieu, he emphasises how social capi-tal can benefit all members of society without reference to political power (Edwards, 2004). White (2002), therefore, theorises that Bourdieu's approach to social capital is a polar opposite to Putnam and Coleman. Figure 7.2 summarises White's contention that Bourdieu uses the term to describe the pursuit of social justice and empowerment through voluntary social action, while Putnam and Coleman view social capital as a way to strengthen traditional family and community organisations.

Critically questioning dominant assumptions highlights that interpretations of 'social capital' perpetuate different understandings of 'good society'.

Figure 7.2   White's view of Bourdieu's approach to social capital

Critics of Putnam's approach point out that he does not consider power dynamics in relationships, or issues of advocacy and resistance to the state and market (Smith and Kulynych, 2002). Nor does Putnam consider the civil rights movement, the women's movement, gay rights and anti-war protests as products and builders of social capital. Edwards (2004) critiques Putnam's approach as an attempt to re-create 1950s nostalgia, a 'Rockwell perspective', depicting the 'good old days' and not the civil rights cam-paigns that challenged inequality throughout American society. For Putnam, the 1960s and 1970s are periods during which social capital was *lost* rather than developed.

Cope et al. (2007: 215) comment that research has an 'almost evangelical faith in the gains from social interaction'. They draw attention to findings that 'collaborators may cheat or free-ride on goodwill leading to a breach of trust and a breakdown in relations'. A similar critical edge is apparent in the comments of Law and Mooney who see the use of the term 'capital' as something that increases the hegemony and pen-etration of 'business-speak' in social ventures:

> Social capital is one of those elusive terms that provide think tanks, academics, journalists, politicians and policy-makers with a way to speak as if something meaningful is under discussion. Talk of social is permitted so long as it is accompanied by an orthodox emphasis on capital. (2006: 127)

Despite this, Putnam's views are gaining prominence internationally in community development, and now actively drive policy initiatives such as the Big Society (Rowson et al., 2010). This stemmed from a Cabinet Office report in which it was claimed that:

> Social capital consists of the networks, norms, relationships, values and informal sanctions that shape the quantity and co-operative quality of society's social interactions. (2007: 5)

'Third Way thinkers' use social capital as a concept in social policy and regeneration programmes to promote stakeholder involvement and partnership approaches (White, 2002). The UK government's *Social Enterprise: A Strategy for Success* (DTI, 2002) and subsequent papers about empowerment advocated developing social capital to stimulate the third sector and social enterprises. Through the policy of Big Society, new policies for giving ownership and control to local people, and encouraging local authorities to ensure that social enterprises have the social capital to compete fairly for public sector contracts are part of a mainstream debate (Evans, 2011; Social Economy Alliance, 2015).

However, as we discussed in Chapter 1, it is unclear who the UK coalition government sought to empower through this policy. If, as Corbett and Walker (2012) claim, the Big Society agenda is intent on furthering neo-liberalism through delivering 'uneconomic' services using volunteers (and putting 'economic' services out to tender in the private sector), this suggests a much stronger alignment with Putnam's notion of social capital than Bourdieu's notion of social justice and community empowerment.

Nevertheless, this leveraging of social capital in the community – a policy of greater reliance on the self-organising capabilities of citizens – is spreading across cultures. In Japan – a country previously hostile to non-profit organisations – over 30,000 non-profits formed after a major earthquake near Kyoto in 1995. This size of the civilian response prompted new statutes to legitimise local associations. More recently, commissioning rules have changed to permit 'certified' organisations to work in partnership with the state. In short, the state now wants to leverage the social capital created by local associations to improve the cost-effectiveness of public service delivery (Laratta et al., 2011).

Class exercise: Social capital and community empowerment

Social capital is believed to promote political and social reform through civil engagement and co-operative working. Governments see social enterprise as a way to unlock 'hard to reach' communities so that social capital can be rebuilt.

This discourse emphasises being 'civil', with an implicit expectation that third sector organisations and social enterprises will be 'good citizens' (i.e. non-disruptive). Yet, conversely, social entrepreneurs are described as disruptive change agents and mavericks.

In light of Bourdieu's views on social capital, what are the implications for social enterprises when they work with disadvantaged groups? Consider:

1 How social capital affects the 'voice' of groups in society (will they be heard?).
2 How charity law – requiring the board of trustees to be unpaid – might affect the development of social capital among individuals on low incomes (will they participate?).
3 How Bourdieu's views on social capital might form the basis of community action.

Additional questions:

4 How might social entrepreneurs play a role in building (different types of) social capital?
5 How might this affect their ability to secure contracts to deliver local services?
6 How might a social entrepreneur's motives and actions be interpreted using social capital theory?

In this section, debates in the social capital literature have been summarised and linked to recent developments in public policy. In the next section, we consider how people have sought to analyse levels of social capital.

Structural approaches

The study of social capital, and attempts to measure its strength, are approached through either *structural* or *contextual* analysis. Writers utilising the structural approach concentrate on connections and ties between people. The cliché for this approach is that 'it is who you know, not what you know', reflecting a view that network structures and the connections between people enable network members to get ahead. Another useful metaphor is that social capital acts as the 'glue' that holds people together (see Granovetter's 1983 study on weak and strong ties in securing employment). The dominant metaphors of a structural approach are 'ties', 'bridges' and 'bonds' (Bridge et al., 2009; Doherty et al., 2009). Social entrepreneurs rely heavily upon the structural context of the environment to create situations for co-operative action. Network interactions are based upon 'strategic alliances' giving improved access to ideas and information. These interactions are often portrayed as networking spaces facilitated at **hubs**, workshops, conferences and events. Based on empirical work, Cope et al. comment that:

> Since economic activity is embedded in society, the innovative entrepreneur develops social capital through building networks which provide external sources of information, support, finance and expertise allowing mutual learning and boundary crossing. (2007: 214)

The 'boundary crossing' of entrepreneurs represents 'bridging capital' where people can use their social capital to work with people in different groups to gain access to resources and ideas. In contrast to this is the concept of 'bonding capital' that 'glues' people together in a group, often by establishing shared norms and social rituals. Hosking and Morley (1991) talk of the number and position of connections and ties to explain levels of access to network resources.

Latour (2005) criticises the structural approach for metaphorically representing a network as a series of connections through which information 'flows' like water. He argues that information does not flow in this fashion among a group of people, and that the number of connections cannot explain how information is communicated. The *quality* of relationships at interpersonal and inter/intra-group level, as well as the number of dimensions on which relationships operate, all affect the amount and quality of the information communicated among network members (Ridley-Duff, 2005; Ridley-Duff and Duncan, 2015). For this reason, we need to consider the *contextual* approach that focuses on the way that social norms and values develop, and their impact on interpersonal trust.

Contextual approaches

The alternative view is that network structures do not adequately capture the importance of the *quality* of relationships in a network. Table 7.1 summarises Adler and Kwon's (2002) analysis of the two approaches to analysing social capital.

Table 7.1   Structural and contextual approaches to social capital

Structural	Contextual
Networks	Trust
Connections	Norms
Weak and strong ties	Values
Bridges or bonds	Attitudes
Actions	Reciprocity
Responsibilities	
Accountable decision-making processes	

In social enterprise development, Amin et al. (2002) argue that local context is a crucial factor. The context and content of communications, and the relationships themselves, affect how information is understood and acted upon. A contextual approach focuses upon the development of trust, the process by which organisational norms and ethical values are established. As Smith and Kulynych comment, Putnam does not:

> distinguish among different kinds of trust – interpersonal, organizational, governmental – or adequately specify the relations among them. (2002: 159)

Various authors have focused attention on civic commitment, mutual trust, the promotion of collective action and social equity. As Evers states:

> Taking social capital building as a term of reference offers the advantage of making it possible to take account not only of the social and economic goals of the organisations, but also the other dimensions and effects of activities, which are specific to social enterprises. This may also help to sensitise us to the organisational challenges linked with the aim of balancing multiple goals and commitments that have an economic, a social and a civic dimension. (2001: 303)

Contextual approaches to social capital theory, therefore, help us to understand how communities develop competencies beyond contracted outputs, through the nurturing and valuing of social networks as ends in themselves.

Fenton et al. (1999) warn of the potential damage to trust, confidence and an altruistic culture from becoming more (big) business-like. Surveys of trust show that big businesses generate low levels of trust. The public have much higher levels of trust in social economy organisations, but this can be explained as much by organisation size as legal form.

For example, in a 2010 survey of 1,054 adults comparing trust in co-operatives and shareholder companies (Simon and Mayo, 2010) less than one in five adults associated public limited companies with the terms 'fair' (18 per cent), 'honest' (15 per cent), 'open' (13 per cent) and 'democratic' (14 per cent). Co-operatives were seen as 'fair' (75 per cent), 'honest' (63 per cent), 'open' (59 per cent) and 'democratic' (53 per cent). However, Gallup's (2014) poll (in the US) shows that 'small businesses' secure high levels of trust (62 per cent), particularly compared to big business (21 per cent). So survey results comparing co-operatives and companies need to show the intervening variable of size and local ownership to fully investigate whether legal forms impact on trust. The same consideration will be true of charities. In a similar UK survey (nfpSynergy, 2014) trust in charities stood at 56 per cent. This is *lower* than small businesses (who achieved 62 per cent) but much higher than multinational companies (at 20 per cent).

So, while it is tempting to associate trust with particular *types* of business, the finding that small (local) community businesses are just as trusted as charities and co-operatives suggests that a connection to (and embeddedness within) a community is the most important factor. In short, charities and co-operatives are more trusted than big businesses, but it is the *social capital* (community connection) rather than their legal form that provides the most persuasive explanation for that result. Schumacher (1993) may be right – when it comes to trust, small is beautiful.

Social networking

In considering the issue of relationships between sectors, the role of intermediate agencies is important. Cohen and Prusak (2001) stress the need for organisations to place trust in support agencies. Attempts to develop social capital are often supported by government action to create social networks. Table 7.2 outlines two sets of views offered by UK government documents on the value of networking to social enterprise. The reports, however, omit mention of: trust; the role of networks in helping to understand complex situations; and the opportunities that networks offer to alter balances of power and influence. In short, their view is limited to a structural view of social capital.

Doherty et al. state that the advantages for social enterprises from networking derive from the fact that:

> Relationships are established with existing and potential customers and a level of familiarity, trust and recognition of professional competency may lead to commissioned or negotiated contracts and invitations to tender. (2009: 159)

Table 7.2 UK government views of the benefits of social enterprise networks

View	Benefits
Office of the Third Sector	Opportunities to share knowledge and experience
	Shared approach to accessing external funding
	Mutual support and encouragement
	Opportunities to share good practice
	Easier access to structured support
	Reduction in costs allows general networking
Department of Trade and Industry	Useful in building contacts
	Widening access to support
	Building broader understanding and knowledge

They report that networks are used to influence opportunities and actions and that this is a 'reciprocal process' where actors gain an understanding of complex situations by sharing ideas about what is important and what is necessary to do. This contextual approach emphasises mutual learning, creates reputations and influences perceptions of trustworthiness in the development of partnerships. Murdock speculates that this trust comes from 'a shared set of values or beliefs':

So far the literature offers some evidence that trust is founded in values and beliefs and it is important because it facilitates collaboration, but trust depends on reciprocity and engagement. (2005: 3)

The last part of this comment raises the question of whether or not reciprocity and engagement are found in practice. Murdock comments that social enterprise network characteristics:

embrace the idea of a group identifying a number of individuals sharing common values, where knowing and relating are important elements, where reciprocity is an important function and where peer pressure may shape processes and rules. (2005: 9)

In doing so, Murdock implies there is an expectation that motivations are based upon more than a utilitarian motive (e.g. mobilisation of resources) and that social enterprise networks are not only held together by their instrumental value, but also by common goals, shared values, mutual respect and peer pressure to remain loyal to a cause (Pearce, 2003).

There is surprisingly little research examining trust, or perceived trust, between social enterprises. While Sydow (1998) has asserted that the frequency and openness of inter-organisational communication increases the possibility of trust, empirical studies of local support networks produce mixed findings. Interesting, Sydow concludes that even if trust is a vital mechanism to absorb the complexity of interactions between organisations, *distrust* serves the same function. Unfortunately, distrust depletes the *quality* of social capital throughout the community even if it is an effective way of dealing with complexity. Seanor and Meaton (2008) lend support to this finding. They found that interactions were coloured by mistrust between organisations, community users and agencies within a regional network.

Nevertheless, this finding looks context dependent. Outsios's (2013: 197, 201) compared commercial and social entrepreneurs engaged in eco-entrepreneurship. He found that 'social entrepreneurs use their social capital to a higher degree than commercial entrepreneurs' and that all entrepreneurs studied benefited from 'affiliating with entrepreneurial networks and utilizing them to overcome constraints'. This means there is a difference in the findings of Seanor and Meaton (2008) and Outsios (2013). Seanor and Meaton's found poor *quality* social capital in social networks of charities and public bodies within a region (irrespective of the number of 'connections'). Outsios's market-oriented study found good quality social capital, particularly among social entrepreneurs. They were willing to share knowledge and resources to develop 'green' markets.

In concluding this section, it is worth asking whether the ability to generate trust and social capital is contingent on the political and economic environment. In light of Hebson et al. (2003), who found that a 'contracting culture' with large commissioners is not conducive to the development of trusting relationships (and therefore the development of social capital), we need to consider how the competitive environment influences the development of trust relations. While social capital may be a useful concept to describe a co-operative culture that develops under a regime of decentral-ised governance and wealth sharing (Restakis, 2010), it is more problematic in economies where there are huge wealth inequalities or large numbers of suppliers competing for contracts and funding (in either the private or public sector).

Values, ethics and sustainability

Pearce (2003) argues that people in social enterprises are motivated by ethical values of co-operation, doing good work and trust. This imagery was reflected in the first version of the Social Enterprise Quality Mark (*c*. 2009) showing a halo above the words 'social enterprise'. To evaluate ethical standards, it is first necessary to prob-lematise ethics itself. Granitz and Loewy (2007) identify six ethical theories that influence human action (see Table 7.3). This framework enables the debate to move beyond simplistic discussions of whether social enterprises (or social entrepreneurs) are 'more' ethical, to a consideration of *how their ethics differ* from those developed in other contexts.

The theories in Table 7.3 cover a range of perspectives. The first two are associated primarily with the negative and positive aspects of self-interest (*individualist*). The third and fourth theories focus on normative positions that aim to advance collective interests (*collectivist*). The final two are rooted in ethical strategies geared towards the manage-ment of complex social situations and cultural diversity (*relativist*). In the discussion that follows, these theories are used to clarify different ethical values and their likely impacts.

In this and previous chapters, we highlighted that the commitment to a social mission (and the definition of a social purpose) is one of three broad approaches to social enter-prise (Chapter 2). This makes social enterprises *values-led*, irrespective of the importance they place on market trading (Westall, 2001). But what is the nature of the values that guide their action? And what impact does the application of these values have?

Table 7.3 The implications and underlying philosophies that inform theories of ethics

Ethical theory	Implications	Philosophy
1. Machiavellianism	Emphasis on the effectiveness of any proposed action, irrespective of alternative moral or political considerations. It has come to be associated, perhaps unkindly, with selfishness and unfettered self-interest. An action is 'ethical' if it achieves its objective, irrespective of process. In its corrupted form, it has been linked with the use of deceit and lying for personal or political gain.	Individualist/ Liberal
2. Rational self-interest (rationalism)	Emphasis on pursuing self-interest through a series of 'fair exchanges', and assessing whether particular 'trades' are fair to both parties (a fair exchange of 'benefits'). Proposed actions will be evaluated in terms of procedural justice that maintains the autonomy of parties, and the fairness and equity of processes.	

Ethical theory	Implications	Philosophy
3. Deontology	Emphasis on understanding belief systems, developing agreement on what is 'right' and 'wrong', and cultivating moral sensitivities through reinforcement of the 'right' behaviours. Proposed actions are influenced by the perceived 'rightness' and 'wrongness' of the proposed behaviour.	Collectivist/ Unitary
4. Utilitarianism	Emphasis on achieving the best outcome for the greatest number of people, and calculating the balance of costs and benefits in order to achieve the 'best' overall outcome. Proposed actions will be influenced by evaluations of whether more people will benefit from (not) taking a proposed action.	
5. Situational ethics (consequentialism)	Emphasis on the level of opportunism and opportunity costs, with consideration of the situation or circumstance that prompts different behaviour. Proposed actions will be evaluated in terms of the benefits/ costs of taking action, and whether any action is 'reasonable' given the specifics of the situation.	Relativist/ Pluralist
6. Cultural relativism	Emphasis on *cultural* norms of 'right' and 'wrong', and the different cultural settings that impact on beliefs. Proposed actions are evaluated in terms of sensitivity to others' cultural awareness: will they have the ability to participate fully, or will the action enhance cultural understanding and awareness? Is the proposed action culturally appropriate?	

A statement that social enterprises are *values*-led needs further qualification. It could be taken to imply that commercial organisations have *no* values. However, it is more a question of *which* values guide decision-making. Is decision-making guided only by a consideration of our own access to (financial, social, human, natural) capital (*individualist*)? Or is it guided by a desire that 'our' community should be able to obtain the capitals it needs (*collectivist*)? Or is it framed by the goal of reconciling different groups' need to secure sustainable access to different types of capital over time (*relativist*)?

Ethics are not easily objectified, so the challenge of assessing them is one of evaluating statements of ethical or social values. For example, Mook et al. argue that:

> An ethical accounting statement provides measures of how well an organization lives up to the shared values to which it has committed itself. [It] is not objective. It does not prove anything, but draws a rich and informative picture of how stakeholders perceive their relationships with the organization. (2007: 55)

Mook et al. also argue that ethical values characteristic of 'business' are changing management practice in the social economy. They cite Campbell (1998: 28) that:

> Once upon a time [voluntary organisations] were called non-profit organisations to emphasise that the provision of service took precedence over the permanent amassing of funds. The breakeven philosophy was the dominant management ethic and adherence to that ethic demanded honest and diligent management ... if management is entirely relieved of the public obligation inherent in the breakeven philosophy [from

changes experienced over time], what alternative ethic will emerge to prevent undue hoarding of resources? With tacit approval for an 'ok-to-profit' ethic, is the final and irrevocable 'must-profit' phase far behind? (Mook et al., 2007: 6)

The assumption in this extract is that *profiting* from a social or economic exchange is unethical, based on utilitarian reasoning that 'profit-seeking' harms more people than it benefits because it leads to the 'hoarding of resources'. However, does this apply to mutual 'profits', economic exchanges in which more than one party can obtain the benefits they seek from a 'solidarity enterprise' (Lund, 2011)?

Leadbeater (1997) describes the ethical qualities of the individuals in social enterprises as a key difference between them and people in other organisations. Sullivan Mort et al. (2003) supports this view by arguing that virtue (e.g. integrity, love, empathy, honesty) is a key difference between members of social and other enterprises. These are deontological judgements based on an assumption that people have relatively fixed character traits that determine their level of 'virtue'.

By way of example, Bill Drayton of Ashoka speaks of 'ethical fibre', qualities such as honesty, trust and commitment to serve others, which are deemed essential characteristics in the selection of social entrepreneurs. To test for such qualities Ashoka uses an 'intuitive test' that asks an interviewer to imagine themselves in danger, and to assess how comfortable they would be in getting out of their situation if an applicant was with them. They are asked to give a high mark (10) if they feel secure and a low mark (1) if the new applicant leaves them feeling insecure. This is their test for 'ethical fibre'.

Ashoka's approach requires all senses and human faculties to be used in evaluating potential social entrepreneurs. While this suggests a deviation from a rational approach to recruitment, it can be challenged on the basis that intuition is an insufficient way to evaluate 'ethical fibre'. How can you, for example, counter the effects of stereotyping and prejudice (Aronson, 2003)? A case in point is described in Ridley-Duff (2010) who found that, between 1999 and 2003, a values-driven approach to selection and induction at School Trends Ltd resulted in turnover four times *higher* than the industry norm. The goal may have been the development of a 'community company' with 'shared values', but the effect was a dramatic *increase* in social exclusion.

Bull et al. (2010) explore the utilitarian link to happiness in a critical appraisal of ethical systems that influence social enterprise development, and note that only some social enterprises have overt goals and actions that promote the utilitarian concept of 'the common good'. A 'common good' perspective, however, is a useful way to evaluate notions of 'public interest' (required for CTAs) and 'community interest' (required in SRBs and CMEs). Utilitarian ethics influences the evaluation of social enterprises that seek to adopt particular legal forms. Support may not be given to organisations if the purposes they specify are not accepted by funders as being consistent with broad public or policy-makers' notion of the public good.

Lastly, Sen (2000) argues for a pragmatic approach that is not based upon a theory of happiness, well-being or love. In doing so, he steers debate towards *situational ethics* that take account of *cultural relativism*. Sen, like Edwards, emphasises how meaning is interpreted and negotiated. He argues that it is pluralism and critical reflection that contributes to a 'good society' (Edwards, 2004). So, they are responding to Pearce's (2003: 34) calls to 'contribute to the common good, to benefit society and, more widely, the planet'. The goal may be clear, but the pathway needs to be learnt through deep reflection about the *impacts* of applying ethical values.

In short, ethical values are used to both justify and appraise approaches to social enterprise. In seeking to understand and theorise social enterprise (and social entrepreneurship), we cannot ignore the ethical frameworks that underpin different approaches as these encourage particular management practices that have different social impacts. This consideration of *critical ethics* (a useful umbrella term for all ethical reasoning that considers situational, historical and cultural factors) returns to Kant's (1998 [1788]) argument about the difference between noumena ('things in themselves', separate from human perception) and phenomena ('things that have meaning for us', only knowable to us through our perception). Kant's categorical imperative is that ethical actions should be grounded in the premise of *treating others as you wish them to treat you*. While this has been erroneously presented as a 'universal' code of good conduct (on the basis that it postulates a universal ethical law), Kant leaves open the possibility that ethical values may change as we develop new perceptions and understandings about the outcomes from treating each other in different ways.

On this basis, Edwards (2004) argues that an important aspect of ethics is *the willingness to discuss the meaning and value of difference*. He argues that it is not diversity *per se* that constitutes a significant difference between civil society and other sectors, but that civil society norms emphasise human rights, peaceful negotiations, tolerance, trust, co-operation and freedom from want. These norms are difficult to negotiate with large public agencies who want political control and corporations that want market dominance. However, such norms are possible in dense networks of co-operatives, mutuals, charities and small-scale socially responsible businesses (Schumacher, 1993; Restakis, 2010). As a result, while members of smaller organisations may struggle to trust larger and more powerful organisations (on account of the asymmetries in power), they will have a much higher chance of developing a good quality of life, with high levels of trust in their communities (Simon and Mayo, 2010; Gallup, 2014; nfpSynergy, 2014).

Class exercise: Ethics as the capacity for critical reflection

Critical theorists have evaluated the 'social' aspect of enterprise by drawing upon the works of:

Karl Marx, who advocated social and communal ownership and control of the means of production.

(Continued)

(Continued)

Anthony Giddens, who argues that human agency can modify entrenched social structures.

Jurgen Habermas, who argues that asymmetries in social power distort decision-making.

Habermas is credited with reviving interest in democratic forums to create 'ideal speech' situations as a way of improving decision-making. These perspectives argue that asymmetries in power need to be addressed before meaningful empowerment at both individual and organisational levels can take place. All three authors consider historical contexts and cultural influences. This being the case, they draw on situational and cultural ethics to expose the fallacy that individual reflection on rational self-interest can ever be 'fair' and 'equitable'. Habermas argues that all 'rationality' is a social product of 'communicative action'. Without democratic control, those who control resources (a 'ruling class') organise communication to their own advantage and determine which thoughts, ideas and concepts will be taught. Democratic forums are seen as the fairest (and most rational) way to debate and make social and economic decisions.

1 To what extent do members of social enterprises follow their own, or their community of users', concerns in making strategic decisions?
2 To what extent is the notion of consensus used to guide social action?
3 What are the ethical challenges in deciding a course of action if there are numerous and complex views of a particular problem?

Ethical capital as a framework for understanding social enterprise

In 2007, Tim Smit (the CEO of the Eden Project) gave a speech at the Voice conference on social enterprise in which he spoke about society, his team of people and the types of characters they were:

One of the most interesting things I have come across recently is that a lot of people in the city reckon that corporate life as we know it is going to be dead in thirty years. And I would say that Eden would be a good example of why. When I look at my top executives, the top eight people who work for me are all people who have decamped from very successful jobs in very successful organisations, because they no longer want to work for corporations where there is no *ethical capital*, and this is happening all over the place. Nowadays 40% of school leavers apparently do not want to work for a corporation. (Smit, 2007, emphasis added)

Gupta et al. (2003: 979) set out a view that *ethical capital* is created when particular ethical values are used to guide the creation of social capital. In particular, this occurs in the context of:

> Investments and institutional arrangements that may be governed by ethical norms of accountability, transparency, reciprocity and fairness to both human and non-human sentient beings.

They suggest that in working relationships, cultural norms to nurture co-operation and social networking are not well established. Ethical capital arises when a *contextual* approach to social capital development takes priority. For Preuss (2004), this means that ethical capital is not so much a subset of social capital, but a *product* of the trust that can be engendered when high *quality* social capital spreads through a community (Putnam, 1994).

In Table 7.4, we summarise Wagner-Tsukamoto's (2007) view that levels of ethical capital in commercial practice can be analysed. Wagner-Tsukamoto stops short of considering the ethical values of the social economy, so in Bull et al. (2010) we contributed to extending the debate. We theorised a fourth level of active, intentional

Table 7.4   Levels of ethical capital

Level 1

Passive unintended moral agency – accumulated through Adam Smith's 'invisible hand' of the free market – where the accumulation of wealth and distribution achieves some level of ethical capital, such as through rising living standards. However, the core belief and responsibility is managing an organisation to maximise financial profit.

Machiavellian ethics moderated by rational self-interest.

Level 2

Passive, intended moral agency – accumulated through following the rules of the game, obeying the codes of conduct in the norms and customs of society, operating without deception or fraud (for example, regulations set by governments and local authorities). This rule-following behaviour achieves the lowest intended moral code. Bull et al. (2010) describe this level as the bottom end of corporate social responsibility: 'Good must be done for reason of profit' (Friedman, 2003). Hence, it could include more consideration of the environment so long as it is profitable to do so.

Rational self-interest evolves into deontological ethical standards.

Level 3

Active, intended moral agency and the creation of ethical capital. Bull et al. (2010) describe this as organisations at the top end of the corporate social responsibility spectrum – John Lewis, Ben and Jerry's, Café Direct, Divine Chocolate – and organisations that go beyond the minimum rules of market morality. Hence, profit is an outcome of ethical thinking linked to market opportunities.

Deontological norms subjected to utilitarian ethical reasoning.

Source: based on Wagner-Tsukamoto (2007); Bull et al. (2010)

'blended value' (Emerson, 2000) where social and economic factors are combined to develop ethical capital. Creating blended value involves a consideration of *situational* and *cultural* factors, moving beyond a universal notion of 'utility' or 'common good' to one that is socially and historically embedded.

While the first three levels of ethical behaviour (Table 7.4) focus on 'profitability' in terms of economic capital, at level 4 (see Table 7.5) it is reconceptualised as a way of building social capital. At level 4, business ethics are reframed so that explicit consideration is given to the development of social *and* economic capital: double bottom line accounting. Where the environment is also considered, triple bottom line accounting occurs. Level 5 embraces the concept of 'charity', where economics is subordinated to social and ethical reasoning, and financial management is guided wholly by social and charitable objectives.

A useful way to visualise this involves adaptation of Alter's (2007) sustainability equilibrium (Figure 7.3). Levels 1, 2 and 3 represent the ethics of traditional private businesses that are primarily based on economic value creation. Level 1 represents the traditional 'for-profit' business (based in individualistic assumptions of Adam Smith's 'invisible hand'). This aligns with passive unintended moral agency. Level 2 represents corporations passively practising social responsibility, while level 3 involves active, intended moral agency and the conscious creation of ethical capital (a more collectivist/unitary perspective). At level 4, the balance between purpose and profit switches, with purpose becoming more dominant as a rationale in trading decisions, while level 5 shows a situation in which trading in markets is supplanted by other forms of public or charitable funding with investment decisions made entirely on ethical grounds (a wholly *values*-led approach). Hence, these levels act primarily to provoke debate about the relative importance of different kinds of ethics in organisational decision-making, and which combinations of ethics are needed to maximise sustainable development.

Table 7.5   Levels 4 and 5 of ethical capital

Level 4
Active, intended moral agency that moves beyond corporate social responsibility to actively create social capital through ethical trading and management practices. Examples include the Mondragon Co-operative Corporation (see Chapter 2) and Grameen Bank (see Chapter 5). Profitability is an important but secondary goal, a by-product of ethically informed action that accelerates the conversion of social capital into economic capital that is distributed to advance equity and solidarity.
Utilitarian goals contextualised and localised using situational ethical reasoning.
Level 5
Active, intended moral agency that subordinates entrepreneurship and business activity to the creation of social and ethical capital using the highest level of ethical reasoning. Business practices are culturally sensitive and grounded in situational reasoning. Profitability is acceptable only for a social purpose, and both social and economic capital are placed at the disposal of a democratically accountable polity that considers community benefit. Capital is used to foster a tolerant, culturally diverse and socially cohesive economy that is responsive to civil society.
Utilitarian goals contextualised and localised using both situational and cultural reasoning.

Source: Bull et al. (2010)

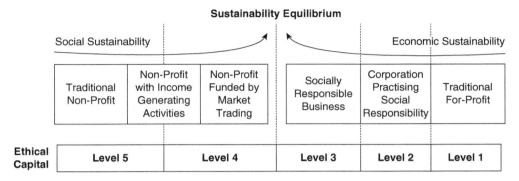

Figure 7.3 Ethical capital and Alter's sustainability framework

The implication of the theoretical perspective in Figure 7.3 is that a socially sustainable society requires charitable and social economy organisations that balance (and limit) the effects of for-profit entrepreneurship. All three approaches to social enterprise (CTAs, SRBs and CMEs defined in Chapter 2) are 'middle-range' approaches at levels 3–4. These combine economic and social value creation through different strategies that make changes internally/externally through the agency of a democratically organised CME, or focus on changing the operations on markets through the creation of CTAs and SRBs.

Conclusions

The purpose of this chapter has been to explore social and ethical capital, in order to offer another perspective on the contribution of social enterprises to a modern economy. The contribution of social capital theory is to provide a (socially constructed) language for discussing the intangible aspects of organisation, enterprise and societal development. The experience of people involved in regional and economic development confirms that the number of connections in a social network does not wholly explain long-term social and economic outcomes. The quality of the connections, and the ethical values that guide them, also affects rates of development. Social capital provides an imperfect, but useful, framework for discussing the efficacy of social networks and the relationships that develop within them. As Westall and Chalkley (2007: 17) argue:

> In order to fully grasp the implications of these visions and realise the potential of social enterprise, we need to break out of our usual ways of looking at the world, particularly about the 'natural' business model or the narrow but hugely powerful concepts and implications of mainstream economics.

Deploying concepts like social and ethical capital represent a way to break out of conventional ways of examining the world and to challenge the notion that there are 'natural' business models. There are a variety of business models in which the role of ethics can play a larger or smaller role. If, as various studies suggest, creating and sustaining social capital and expressing ethical values enhance business success (Collins, 2001), should collaborative rather than competitive market models inform the future development of social enterprise networks? Will social networking sites built with Open Source software, licensing content with Creative Commons, integrating democratic decision-making tools (like Loomio) provide practical ways to spread social and ethical capital? Or will private business capture the sector's users, acquire their content, and seek to privatise its contents and protect it for their own commercial use?

This chapter has not offered a normative approach to the creation of social and ethical capital. Instead, it has sought to clarify different perspectives so that readers can re-evaluate notions of trust, accountability, transparency, reciprocity and fairness. In doing so, we have aimed to problematise the idea that social enterprises 'have' ethics while other enterprises do not – all enterprises are expressions of societal ethics, and they all affect (and are affected by) the social capital of their host communities. Going forward, we see greater value in asking 'what theories of ethics, and what levels of ethical reasoning, should we aspire to as we develop the enterprises of the future?'

Summary of learning

In this chapter, we have argued that:

Social, community, ethical and environmental issues are considered important to those creating and working in social enterprises.

UK policy is framed by Putnam's approach to social capital, while Bourdieu's notion of power has been neglected.

Writers mean different things when they discuss *social value* and *social capital*.

There are two approaches to conceiving and analysing social capital: *structural* (based on 'ties', 'bonding' and 'bridging') and *contextual* (based on trust, values, reciprocity and mutuality).

A contextual approach to social capital requires detailed consideration of the way ethical values influence the *quality* of communications within a community.

There are different theories of ethics that can be linked to different approaches to organisational development and management practice.

The ethical values that sustain social enterprise are different from those that sustain private enterprises, and tend towards utilitarian reasoning, culturally sensitive and situational reasoning.

Questions and possible essay assignments

1. 'A "structural approach" to social capital is an inadequate way to understand the development of a community and the enterprises that operate within it.' Using examples, critically assess this statement.
2. 'We just want to deliver a service people need; we don't want to challenge the way the system works.' By cross-referencing theories of social enterprise with theories of ethics, critically assess how much social value an enterprise that 'just delivers a service' can create.
3. 'An important factor in recruiting good staff to social enterprises is the attractiveness of their ethical capital.' Critically assess the concept of ethical capital and the role that it plays in attracting good staff and satisfying its product and service users.

Further reading

For background on social networks, see the debates surrounding Granovetter's work in the 1970s and 1980s on the 'strength of weak ties' (Granovetter, 1973, 1983). A good starting point for social enterprise is Chapter 6 in Pearce's *Social Enterprise in Anytown* (2003). For clarifications of the concept see Evers and Syrett's (2007) paper on social capital in economic regeneration. There have been a number of foundational discussions on the contribution of social capital to social enterprise (and vice versa). See two chapters in *The Emergence of Social Enterprise* by Evers (2001) and Laville and Nyssens (2001) that focus squarely on perspectives within the social enterprise research community. For a public sector perspective, see the paper in the journal *Regional Studies* by Birch and Whittam (2008). New textbooks on the social economy (Bridge et al., 2009) and social enterprise (Doherty et al., 2009) have useful introductions to business ethics and social capital in the context of social enterprise. For more radical coverage, and the conversions between forms of capital, see Bourdieu's (1986) 'The forms of capital', and for a discussion of mistrust see Seanor and Meaton's (2008) paper on the companion website. For a perspective that connects relationship dynamics (social rationality), social capital and social enterprise see 'Social enterprise as a socially rational business' (Ridley-Duff, 2008b), and a development of the ideas in this paper in Bull et al. (2010), which can be downloaded from http://shura.shu.ac.uk/2618/. Lastly, we recommend chapters from *Principles of Responsible Management* (Laasch and Conway, 2015) on 'responsibility', 'ethics' and 'sustainability' which include information about the way ethical thinking has developed in business over the last 50 years.

Further reading material is available on the companion website at: www.sagepub.co.uk/ridleyduff.

Useful resources

Ethics Survey Tools (SurveyMonkey): www.surveymonkey.com/mp/ethics-survey/

FairShares Diagnostics: www.fairshares.coop/wordpress/diagnostics/

Social Capital in Asia: www.apo-tokyo.org/00e-books/IS-16_SocialCapital.htm

Social Capital Benchmarking: www.hks.harvard.edu/saguaro/communitysurvey/

Social Capital Gateway (EU): www.socialcapitalgateway.org/index.htm

Social Capital Guide (ONS, UK): www.ons.gov.uk/ons/guide-method/user-guidance/social-capital-guide/index.html

World Bank Social Capital Assessment Tools (SOCAT): http://go.worldbank.org/E2UHFCJP00

Part III
The Practice of Social Enterprise

Exemplar Case: Management Practice – The Monkey Business

'I wanted to run a place that had the values of sustainability, but also explored what it is to be a great place to work in terms of its neighbourliness – we do fantastic local sourcing (90% of what we consume is locally sourced, and our waste strategy is highly regarded – waste neutral). It's a lot easier than people say. We also wanted to ask the question, "What does a great place to work feel like?" Now, I've never worked for anybody in my entire life and I had this real problem with my chair of trustees. After we got to 500 staff he said, "Tim, you've got to grow up. You're a maverick – you haven't got any corporate structures to run this place." So I said, "Like what?" And he said, "Damn it man, you haven't even got any KPIs!" And I said, "What are they?" And he looked at me thinking that I was pulling his plonker. He explained what KPIs were and I said, "Why – if you've employed the right people – would you want them? They know what to do so why do we need to do this to tick [off] at the end of the year?" He said, "Look. If you don't do it, one of us will have to go." I said, "I'm going to be really sorry to lose you." He made me go away and said, "If you can't do it my way, can you at least come up with something that the trustees can recognise as a system of management that is vaguely plausible?"

So I went away at the weekend with two fine bottles of wine and wrote a management manual called *The Monkey Business*. This doesn't start from the proposition of line management. I take line management with a pinch of salt – you have to put it down so the banks think you are doing it their way. Ultimately, Eden isn't run like that. *The Monkey Business* had a series of rules to it and these may be useful to you because what it is about is how to create a culture for yourself where you are deliberately ripping the blinkers off your head. So rule number 1 is that you can't come to work until you have said good morning to 20 people. Rule number 2 is that you've got to read two books that everyone you know would say were completely outside of your experience, and review them for your colleagues. Rules 3, 4 and 5 are that you have to see one movie, one concert, and one piece of theatre – same rules as number 2. Rule 6 is that once a year you have to make a speech about why you like working for me – if you can't you've got to resign. I find it concentrates the mind. Rule 7 – I don't have the comfort of religion, but I'm very superstitious – I believe that if good fortune lands in your lap and you don't share it with others then not only will you lose it, but it will never return to you because you've shown yourself not worthy of it in the first place. So Rule 7 is that you have to conduct a guerrilla act of goodwill to someone you do not know, once a year, and they must never know you've done it. And my team love doing that – it's such a gas […] and what a country this would be if we were all doing that, wouldn't it? Fantastic. We also have two other rules. One is that you have to break bread with 40 people who make it worth coming to work … the breaking of bread together, and working at night, has led to every single strategic decision Eden has ever taken. Think about that. Day time person is different to night time person. You only get working person during daylight hours. You don't bring in all the experience, so that's why we do a lot of work at night. Lastly, all my people from the most junior to the most senior has to learn how to play samba drums [because] most people are very shy of looking foolish. So, if you can put them in a position where they thought they were going to look foolish and they discover that they are not foolish […] then they get very excited […] We have another funny system. All our senior team have to do what are called "tricky days" – we have to spend 15 days working on the front line to learn respect for where the business is rooted. And also we have projects that are done on a voluntary basis.'

Source: Smit (2007), audio recording transcribed and edited by Rory Ridley-Duff

Introduction

Tim Smit's speech to the Social Enterprise Coalition 2007 conference describing a management system at the Eden Project has become part of the folklore of social enterprise in the UK. In 2010, we contributed to its status by publishing a paper about 'ethical capital', one of the concepts advanced in that speech (Bull et al., 2010). In this introduction, we'd like to add another – the rules behind *The Monkey Business*. Smit questions both the need for, and value of, hierarchical management. He also acknowledges that many people seeking finance from banks have to *pretend* that hierarchies exist to secure funding, indicating a disjuncture between the practices that they use to create and spread wealth and the way bankers imagine it is created. Smit's 'rules' are underpinned by a desire to 'rip blinkers off your head'. We see this as part of a growing call for critical, rather than conventional, management studies.

In Part III, we explore the importance of advances in **critical management** studies to social enterprises aiming to achieve triple bottom line outcomes (Adler et al., 2007; UN Global Compact, 2007; Laasch and Conway, 2015). The case of Eden is not the only exemplar case we could choose, but we chose it for its combination of commitments to sustainable development, social goals and non-hierarchical management. We might have chosen the Grameen Bank, the Mondragon co-operatives or John Lewis Partnership – they would also be good places to start. However, a particular case from South America competed with Tim Smit for pride of place and it is worth examining why.

SEMCO was transformed from a conventional private company to a partnership with employees who co-ordinate autonomous, self-managed operating units. These have been re-organised into 'a confederation of small, freestanding units' where 'there are no job titles and no personal assistants, people set their own salaries [and] everybody shares in profits' (Bock, 2005). Bock claims that the development of SEMCO – in contrast to the story of leadership propagated by a major shareholder (Semler, 1993) – was triggered by multiple factors including Semler's own ill-heath, two financial crises, and numerous proposals from worker-led committees and trade unions. He denies that any 'master plan' existed, but does credit Semler with a 'genius' for making empowerment work by giving up power. Instead, he looks to various systems theories to offer a different perspective.

> There are two models for the kind of changes we have seen at Semco. One is the biological model of punctuated equilibrium. Things go along fairly smoothly with minor changes, then there is a sudden burst of change and things settle down again. The other model comes from chaos theory. In chaos theory major change happens when an organism faces a threat that moves it away from equilibrium and stability, and out toward the edge of chaos. The major changes at Semco over the last two decades have created a company that is a confederation of small, freestanding units. That 'structure' is part of why Semco can adapt so quickly today to deal with threats or to seize opportunities. Semco's units are limited to 150–200 people. That's something of a magic number in sociological, management and anthropological studies. (Bock, 2005)

Introduce yourself to SEMCO with this video:

www.ted.com/talks/ricardo_semler_radical_wisdom_for_a_company_a_school_a_life

This observation is a good starting point for Part III of this book as it draws attention to the issue of scale (Schumacher, 1993). In Part I, we explored the mixed history of social enterprise informed not only by charitable, co-operative and voluntary sector traditions, but also by experiments in economic democracy within the private sector and attempts to 'spin out' parts of the state to deliver public services more effectively. SEMCO contrasts with the Eden Project in respect of its heritage, development and industry, but what it has in common is an ideology based on small self-organising units and projects that aim to forge partnerships for mutual advantage.

As Turnbull's (2002) work on governance argues, species survive and grow by reproducing, not consuming themselves. He argues that this logic also pervaded Mondragon's early development. Restakis (2010) and Amin et al. (2002) note that this was also the case – albeit less consciously – in the co-operative economy of Northern Italy. As we discussed in Chapter 3, the Grameen Bank was built out of self-managed bank branches, each with 50 members (Jain, 1996). Biological metaphors emphasise the incubation and nurturing of new offspring (start-ups and spin outs), not the rapacious consumption of them (acquisitions and mergers). The change of mind-set has profound ramifications for the theoretical base of management theory, and it transforms the advice likely to be given to managers of social enterprises regarding the practices of ownership, governance and management.

In Part III, therefore, we engage in debates to consider which theories and practices might form the basis of the discipline of social enterprise management. We will further examine issues in initiating, developing and expanding organisations in a 'fourth' sector (Westall, 2001) as well as the management choices faced in the transformation of organisations in the third, public and private sectors (Ridley-Duff and Bull, 2015). Before we explore this in more detail, it is worth considering the impact of metaphors on management thought.

Management studies has been criticised for deploying metaphors linked to the world of machines more than living beings, offering up analyses of the functions performed by different parts of an organisation (Morgan and Smirich, 1980; Morgan, 1986). This is characterised by discipline-specific discussions of the expertise needed to achieve management competence *over* these functions. This **functionalist** approach to organising (Burrell and Morgan, 1979) renders organisations as a series of discrete but inter-related tasks over which 'management' needs to exert 'control'. It ignores the question of how management itself develops organically, and the political and social contexts that influence the development of a management style.

We have, therefore, avoided putting the cart before the horse by adopting a position that organisations are more like organisms or collections of narratives that interact in ways that affect their survival (a more biological or narrative perspective). There is a precedent for this. Paton's (2003) thoughtful study of managing and measuring social enterprises noted that in addition to groups of managers who adopted functionalist or cynical attitudes to management systems, there was another group who were critical and pragmatic, using management systems to initiate dialogue with staff and stakeholders, using them to clarify understandings and co-construct narratives, or – alternatively – developing systems that build trust and which cement strategic relationships. Figure III.1 outlines business

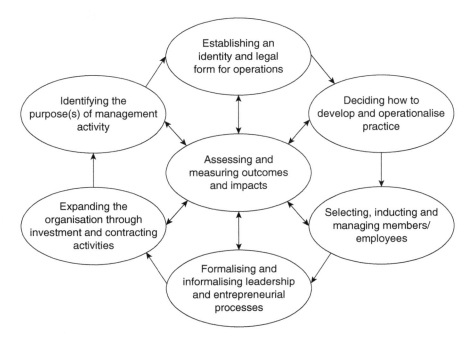

Figure III-1   Cyclical business development

development as a cyclical and recursive process rather than a set of business functions (Cornforth, 1995). This makes more explicit the constructed and evolving nature of 'management' so that its role(s) and purpose(s) become visible and amenable to debate.

Outlining a perspective on social enterprise management education

Chapters 8 and 9 consider the linkages between strategy-making and ideologies of management. How are the purpose(s) and goal(s) of founders embedded in new organisations? Can organisations be structured in a way that supports the pursuit of social, environmental and economic goals? In Chapter 10, we consider how social enterprise activities may be set up by collegial groups of people as well as 'visionary' entrepreneurs. As a result, there is often a first phase of organisation development that is more dependent on mutual commitments and trust relations before the challenge of building formalised systems of management. In Chapters 11 and 12, we consider how informal systems of trust are reinforced (or undermined) during the processes of constituting and governing a social enterprise. How do legal forms and business contexts reinforce (or undermine) cultures of governance and human relations?

As organisations evolve, they are faced with a range of choices on how to develop the relationships that support their work. This increases the active consideration of the rights and responsibilities of each stakeholder group. As the speech by Tim Smit acknowledges, external parties (funders, banks, investors, support organisations) seek to impose or find satisfactory evidence of formal management and leadership capabilities. Engaging professional institutions usually means evidencing the values of various professions to meet *their* criteria for financial and social support (Dart, 2004; Ridley-Duff, 2009). In the field of social enterprise, there could be two responses. Firstly, there is the task of re-educating the finance sector about the socio-economic benefits of more participatory management systems. Another way (described in Chapter 6) is to re-create financial institutions so that crowdfunding is the dominant principle. This way, more decision-making power rests with a wider range of owner-members and stakeholders so that professional investment managers exert less influence.

Processes of change can increase tensions between different stakeholders who compete with each other over the practical and ideological aspects of sustainable development. Often there is an increased need to manage the disjuncture between the informal and formal policies and values propagated by different stakeholder perspectives (Wallace, 2005; Bull, 2008). Maintaining a business-cycle perspective not only highlights how these tensions continually (re)construct the narratives of 'management', but also (re)construct the notion of a 'manager' (Watson, 1994). As case studies will reveal, some social enterprises tend to employ people in recognised management roles while others tend to divide management functions up and distribute them among organisation members. These practices are linked directly to their outlook on building 'social purpose enterprises' or 'socialised enterprises' (see Chapter 2).

In the 1980s, Bradley and Gelb (1983: 54) surveyed both co-operative and conventional private businesses and found that 33 per cent of Mondragon's owner-workers felt they participated in 'important decisions', and that 60 per cent had some level of influence. This compared to findings of 7 per cent and 21 per cent respectively in similar size private businesses. Given Mondragon's track record in Spain, SEMCO's record in South America, and the continued good fortunes of the John Lewis Partnership in the UK, it is no longer credible to argue that participatory democracy is an inefficient approach to managing enterprises. So, what has changed? Was management theory wrong, or just 'of its day'? Is participatory management easier than it used to be, or are the cultures of these organisations happy accidents that are hard to reproduce?

As we finalise this text, there is early evidence that barriers to participation are becoming fewer and less costly to address. The Enspiral network of management consultants and software engineers has piloted software applications that make collaborative budgeting and decision-making straightforward with nothing more than a smart phone, tablet or laptop computer connected to the internet. Enspiral itself has over 100 contributors – a peer-network of consultants and software developers, plus a much larger army of volunteers. Like Wikipedia, there is no human 'boss' because technology regulates the creation of co-authored, peer-reviewed content (www.enspiral.com/). Inspired by the needs of the Occupy Movement, they created Open Source software called Loomio (www.loomio.org/) to enable groups of people (located anywhere in the world) to have conversations on specific topics, develop proposals, record debates and track decisions collaboratively online. Even in its Beta version, 30,000 groups started to use the software, and the software has been translated into 22 languages by a volunteer support network.

Introduce yourself to Loomio with this video: www.youtube.com/watch?v=Tl1GcHnnVNw.

It is striking to read the list of 'organisation types' offered in Loomio Beta (which reflects the nature of the organisations that have discovered it). The choices are littered with the activities and organisations of the social and solidarity economy and civil society:

Advocacy Group

Arts

Activist

Business

Collective

Community Group

Co-operative

Democratic Organisation

Economics

Education

Environmental Group

Family

Local Government

Online Community

OpenSource Software

Religious/Spiritual

Political Initiative

Social Enterprise

Social Justice

So, technology for collaborative budgeting and decision-making is set to revolutionise management practices in a way that is conducive to the creation of socially responsible businesses (SRBs) and co-operative and mutual enterprises (CMEs). Loomio itself is a charitable trading activity (CTA), built through crowdfunding and cross-funding from consultancy work, and then distributed free to everyone as 'infrastructure' for the future of organising. If the first industrial revolution automated control of physical production processes, rendering many production workers obsolete, the second industrial revolution looks set to automate the management of knowledge production, bringing into question the need for traditional management hierarchies. In this context, we begin our exploration of the practices of management, leadership and entrepreneurship in social enterprises.

Strategic Management and Planning 8

Learning objectives

In this chapter, we consider the nature, role and process of strategic management. By the end of this chapter you will be able to:

- describe the principal themes and challenges of strategic management in social enterprises
- distinguish between prescriptive, descriptive and critical-appreciative theories of strategic management
- critically appraise the application of complexity theory to strategic decision-making processes
- analyse different approaches to strategic management using a theoretical framework
- explain the likely outcomes that arise out of the application of rational (structured) planning and ecological (systems) thinking in the practices of strategic management.

> ## The key arguments that will be developed in this chapter are:
>
> - Strategic management aims to elicit the medium- and long-term goals of organisational stakeholders, and then devise a strategy to fulfil them.
> - Both *intended* and *emergent* strategies affect what can be realised in practice.
> - Strategic management involves planning, but does not necessarily involve written plans.
> - Approaches to strategic management can be radically affected by social philosophy, legal form and economic conditions.
> - Strategies can be 'rational' or 'ecological' in their orientation giving rise to centralised (logical) and decentralised (systems) thinking in strategy-making.

Introduction

> Organizations that succeed, organizations that thrive, organizations that are going to be the providers of services in the next century all know where they are going. (Brinckerhoff, 1994: 130)

> The behaviour of people is not driven by unchanging rules. The 'rules', if that is what they are, change as people learn. (Stacey, 2007: 222)

The comment from *Mission-based Management* goes to the core of this chapter. Do 'successful' organisations know where they are going? Mintzberg et al. (1998), in their entertaining book *Strategy Safari*, argue that the first view is a *partial* truth. Using the story of the 'The Blind Men and the Elephant', they argue that managers are mostly like 'blind men' and strategy is an 'elephant' that no one can see without carefully listening to, and co-operating with, others. As the poem concludes:

> So oft in theologic wars,
>
> The disputants,
>
> I ween,
>
> Rail on in utter ignorance Of what each other mean,
>
> And prate about an Elephant Not one of them has seen!
>
> (Jon Saxe, 1816–87, cited in Mintzberg et al., 1998: 3)

In this chapter we discuss the challenge of conceptualising the 'elephant', and the processes by which stakeholders can reduce their blindness and contribute to sense-making and future planning. However, we also go further by drawing on Stacey's work to problematise the field of strategy-making and its relevance to social enterprise development. In the case of Mintzberg, we draw attention to two groups of theories (*prescriptive theories* and *descriptive theories*) that capture *intended* and *emergent* aspects of strategic management (Mintzberg et al., 1998). We build on this by adding perspectives from the field of *critical management studies* that strategic management can also be seen as the vehicle by which owners (and their agents) maintain their control over (others') economic, social and human capital (Alvesson and Deetz, 2000; Alvesson and Willmott, 2003). In the case of Stacey, we draw attention to his analysis of problem-solving and the insights this provides for managing 'wicked' problems through social enterprises (Curtis and Bowkett, 2014). Given the complexity of the challenges that social enterprises can *choose* to face, the application of complexity theory to the field of strategic management helps social enterprise managers to reflect on the limitations of traditional planning systems and design complex adaptive systems that are fit for the socio-economic contexts in which they work.

With this in mind, we explore the conceptual side of strategic management and planning, and why it is believed to be important. We also take a critical look at the process of strategic planning using three case studies. These focus on how the strategic goals of individuals and collegial groups can be elicited and constructed into workable planning documents (artefacts). Lastly, we introduce readers to a diagnostic tool called Balance that provides a self-help approach to analysing the performance of a strategic management system.

Class exercise: Planning challenges

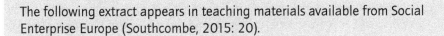

The following extract appears in teaching materials available from Social Enterprise Europe (Southcombe, 2015: 20).

> When it comes to planning a social enterprise the requirements and thinking can be very different to that needed to put together a traditional business plan. For example you may have to consider that the enterprise:

- Will be shaped by agreed ethics and shared values
- Will be governed by social or 'socialised' objectives
- That success will be measured through the contribution to a better community society/world
- That governance may be a shared and inclusive 'process'
- That finance will be through many different sources
- Will want the engagement and involvement of different and diverse stakeholders at all levels

(Continued)

(Continued)

- Will see management as an open and democratic process
- Will look more to co-operation and partnership working rather than competition
- Profits either re-invested or distributed to 'social' shareholders
- Will consider complex legal structures to accommodate the social objectives, ethics and values and shared ownership
- Will be committed to creating social wealth and not private capital
- Where beneficiaries may be diverse and varied
- Whose workers and volunteers are also owners, partners or beneficiaries
- Where sustainability is measured through achieving permanent social change
- Will issue social licences extending the scope of the enterprise
- Will use a social audit as a public judgement of the enterprise.
  The plan can therefore look very different and may be called a *social enterprise plan* rather than a 'business plan'.

Discussion questions:

1 Is the phrase 'business plan' or 'social enterprise plan' more meaningful to you?
2 What would you expect to see (or not see) in a 'social enterprise plan' compared to a traditional 'business plan' for a profit-maximising business?

An EU project to establish the educational needs of social enterprise managers (Moreau and Mertens, 2013) found that they seek to become competent at mixing social, environmental and economic objectives using a multi-stakeholder governance system. They saw their social enterprises as *multi*-purpose, consciously meeting the needs of more than one constituency at the same time. This increases the likelihood that they will need to become skilled at eclectically drawing on and integrating techniques in private, mutual and voluntary sector organisations to create charitable trading activities (CTAs), socially responsible businesses (SRBs) and co-operative and mutual enterprises (CMEs).

As there is no single approach to social enterprise, the variety of strategic choices presents a significant challenge. The diversity of organisational forms (linked, in many cases, to different strategic goals) represents an additional challenge. What will happen in a large (or small) social enterprise when the owners are members of staff and/or users of their organisation's services? What happens if beneficiaries and/or staff are prevented from participating in strategic decisions? If multiple stakeholders are involved in strategic decisions, how does it work effectively? While the *concept* of strategic management spans all types of organisation, *practice* is neither predictable nor uniform.

Third sector organisations have been affected by changes in both the public and private sectors (see Chapter 3) because – paradoxically – they are being encouraged to trade through contracts funded directly (or indirectly) by public sources and/or corporate sponsors (Alter, 2007). According to Hudson (2002), substantive changes that started in the 1980s have accelerated after a series of private sector scandals increased the attention given to 'corporate governance' (NCVO, 2005; Ridley-Duff, 2007). The rise of NPM in the 1990s and NPG in the 2000s has acted as a normalizing influence on strategic management practices in the third sector (Coule and Patmore, 2013).

What we offer here falls short of an overview as it represents our ongoing reflections on how strategic management theory can help social enterprise managers engage with the challenges they face in practice. The chapter's purpose is to aid students to navigate the choices they face, and to understand how the process of strategic management influences the development of a management ideology (Chapter 9). Our starting point, therefore, is establishing how guiding principles for different types of social enterprise are developed. It can be a formal process, a deliberate act of planning to guide an organisation or institution on how to articulate its: vision and objectives; purpose and motivation; direction; route map for followers; risk parameters for decision-making; and (where helpful) its 'business' plan. Formal planning holds out the possibility of encapsulating an organisation's vision for the future using formal statements about values, missions and action plans, linked to evaluation frameworks and management systems for tracking them (Fujitsu, 2010).

However, we also bear in mind the critique of Alvesson and Willmott (2003) who argued that strategic management has – in the hands of private business and governments – often obscured and mystified management processes in order to marginalise and disempower strategic stakeholders (the workforce, customers or service users and suppliers). As such, strategic management may not be organised to simplify and clarify the choices facing an organisation, or to promote effective discussion. It also presents as an opportunity to devise rhetoric and arguments that alter (or maintain) asymmetries of power and wealth so that elites can continue to acquire control over workers, customers, service users and suppliers for the private benefit of shareholders. In this case, strategic management processes may deliberately use complex arguments to make it harder for other stakeholders to shape emerging discourses on management.

The context for strategic management and planning

Before we get deeper into theories of strategising, let us consider a case that highlights the challenges faced by social enterprises. Seedley and Langworthy Trust (SALT) is in the city of Salford, in the north-west of England. It runs a busy drop-in centre for the community, providing: services that support local residents; help with domestic issues; support to settle neighbourhood disputes; and spaces for community cohesion. This organisation is typical of many striving to become social enterprises delivering a wide range of services with limited (financial) resources (Case 8.1).

Case 8.1

Seedley and Langworthy Trust (SALT)

Seedley and Langworthy Trust was established in 1997. It was set up to develop effective links between people who live and work in Seedley and Langworthy and partners from the public, private and voluntary sectors. Seedley and Langworthy are neighbouring areas within the City of Salford, near Manchester in the north of England. Both are labelled 'deprived wards', suffering a decline in manufacturing and high unemployment, and coping with the knock-on effects to the social, economic and cultural fabric of their communities.

You may find it helpful to read the short history of SALT at: www.sagepub.co.uk/ridleyduff. With single regeneration budget funding at an end, SALT needs to develop a social enterprise plan to secure new sources of income.

1 If you were tasked with helping SALT think about their future, what would you do?
2 What approach would you adopt to help SALT?
3 Where would you start?

Conceptualising strategic management

Strategic management involves reflective thinking within an organisation or institution about its place within its environment (political, economic, socio-cultural, technological, legal and environmental). Mintzberg et al. (1998) describe how a 5Ps approach can assist in:

adopting various *p*erspectives ...

... to identifying *p*atterns...

... so you can determine your *p*osition ...

... and develop a *p*lan ...

... or a *p*loy.

We argue that strategic management is (potentially, but not necessarily) a unifying and motivationally important process because it involves the application of ethical reasoning in framing, shaping, articulating and communicating ideas, decisions and norms (see Chapter 7). The conventional view is that strategic management processes bring people together for planning and making decisions while operational management is concerned with managing activities and projects (Stacey, 2007). At the same time, strategic management is still 'socially constructed', by which we mean that the processes and outcomes are (subjective) agreements between people – managers, board, staff and stakeholders – represented through artefacts that communicate their authors' understanding of their context. During strategic management processes, these understandings are translated into concepts (ideas) that are enacted through 'theories in use' that are believed to produce tangible outcomes and impacts (Wenger, 1998; Cooperrider and Whitney, 2005).

A level of scepticism, however, regarding the rationale for complex strategic management processes is worth retaining. After the takeover of the Zanon factory in Argentina (see Chapter 3), one of the new worker-owners commented that:

> We pay ourselves a fair salary. We discuss how much money we have, how much to save, and how much to take. For us as workers, accounting is easy. I don't know why it [was] so hard for the bosses … (*The Take*, 2004)

Similarly, Muhammad Yunus (also Chapter 3, Grameen Bank) talks about the way poverty is *represented* as a complex 'intractable' problem, but the solutions to it can be straightforward once institutional assumptions about banking and people are challenged. From a social enterprise perspective, complexity may continue to exist because practitioners attempt to solve 'intractable' issues that are *created by* the dominant (neo-liberal) paradigm using the *modes of thoughts* that support it. So, in developing a strategic management process some space is needed to consider whether switching to a different paradigm might offer up solutions that are more straightforward and less complex.

In short, how can we keep our minds open to the differences between technical complexity (economic rationality) and social complexity (social rationality)? From an economically rational point of view, the question of poverty looks solvable ('Can wealth producing assets be redistributed to people who are "poor" to solve the problem?'). Yes – they can. But from a socially rational point of view (Ridley-Duff, 2008b) it looks more complex ('Can you get wealthy, powerful people to desire reciprocal, equitable, meaningful relationships with people they have exploited to acquire their wealth and power?'). The lens of 'social rationality' highlights that there are no *technical* solutions that can transform people's *ethics* in the way a new technology can transform our capacity to manufacture goods (see Chapter 7). Social innovation is – in Stacey's (2007) terminology – 'complex' because legal-technical solutions and economically 'rational' thought can only play a supporting, and not a leading, role in the process. To reconfigure social relations (so that wealth can be distributed more fairly) requires substantive changes in *social* rationality which – in turn – will produce a new economic paradigm.

Class exercise: Stacey's view of complexity

Materials to help with this exercise can be found on the companion website at: www.sagepub.co.uk/ridleyduff.

Obtain the Articles of Association/Governing Document for one charity engaged in CTAs, one SRB and one CME linked to the field your students are studying.

Write down the 'objects' stated in their Articles/Governing Document.

Watch this video by Professor Robert Geyer about Ralph Stacey's 'complexity theory': http://vimeo.com/25979052.

1 Using Stacey's theory, characterise the 'objects' of each enterprise as:

- issues that are 'traditional' and solvable using 'evidence-based policy-making' (actionable through practices over which there is a high degree of agreement and for which the impacts are known)
- issues that are 'complex', 'wicked' or 'chaotic' (actionable through a wide range of alternative actions over which there is limited (or no) agreement about the likely impacts).

2 What are the implications for strategic management if objects address 'complex' or 'wicked' problems?
3 If 'evidence-based policy-making' is applied to 'complex' or 'wicked' issues, what outcomes would you expect to occur?

Table 8.1 shows a meta-theory of strategic management choices identified by Mintzberg et al. (1998) and Alvesson and Willmott (2003). In each case, 'strategising' is framed in a different way. Firstly, there are *prescriptive* theories – formalised processes of conceptualising and analysing the issues faced by an organisation. These are aimed at facilitating discussion in management events, away days and planning activities, and are guided by handbooks, guidance, policy documents and quality management processes.

While recognising the contribution of consultants and business schools to the dissemination of 'prescriptive' theories, Mintzberg et al. (1998: 6) identify five additional schools that 'have been concerned less with prescribing ideal strategic behaviour than with *describing* how strategies do, in fact, get made'. These are 'configured' through:

- entrepreneurial 'visioning'
- cognitive 'mental processing'

Table 8.1   Three groups of theories about strategic management

Group	School	Primary characteristic
Prescriptive theory Concerned with how strategies *should* be developed	Design school	Strategising is a *conceptualising* process
	Planning school	Strategising is a *formal* process
	Positioning school	Strategising is an *analytical* process
Descriptive theory Concerned with *actual* descriptions of strategic management	Entrepreneurial school	Strategising is a *visioning* process
	Cognitive school	Strategising is a *mental* process
	Learning school	Strategising is an *emergent* process
	Power school	Strategising is a *negotiating* process
	Cultural school	Strategising is a *collective* process
	Environmental school	Strategising is a *reactive* process
Critical-appreciative theory	Critical-appreciative management school	Strategising is deconstructing the *mystifying*, *marginalising* and *obfuscating* narratives of powerful elites to reveal how they have *colonised* power, followed by the co-construction of new narratives that emphasise the sharing and spreading of power and wealth
Concerned with the *social and political objectives* of management and managers	Configuration school	Strategising is a generative process of selectively combining any of the above approaches to test and refine a 'theory of change' that guides the development of a social enterprise plan

Source: Mintzberg et al. (1998); Alvesson and Willmott (2003); Cooperrider et al. (2014); Ridley-Duff and Duncan (2015)

- negotiation of power
- collectively evolving a culture
- adapting to the environment.

He links these processes to *emergent strategies* that occur outside formal pre-planned events. They may be embedded in social practices rather than written down, and may be realised by accident or design, manifesting themselves in a '**community of practice**' that arises in a particular context (DiMaggio and Powell, 1983; Wenger, 1998).

In the field of social enterprise management, the critical thinking that underpins emergent strategising is at a premium because of the 'complex' nature of the issues that social enterprises address. Critical management is advanced in two senses: firstly, as the capacity to *deconstruct* social systems that impoverish a community (so they can be avoided and, if necessary, challenged); secondly, in the *constructionist* sense of establishing a dialogue that constructs a 'theory of change' which advances sustainable development (Curtis, 2008, 2014; Curtis and Bowkett, 2014; Ridley-Duff and Duncan, 2015).

An oft cited example of a social enterprise that deconstructed the problems inherent in post-World War I capitalism (and then co-constructed a viable alternative) is the John Lewis Partnership (JLP). In his 1954 exposition of the management strategies at

JLP, Lewis (1954) sets out the partnership's 'principal management' (a *partially* elected commercial board, a chairman's committee and a *mostly* elected central council). However, he also identified, designed and ensured both social and financial support for JLP's 'critical side' comprising: an auditor; a counsellor; a financial adviser; a registrar; a general inspector; a journal called *The Gazette*, all of which provided partners with information to feed into the 'principal management' bodies. The *strategic aim* of the business – embedded in two irrevocable trusts – became 'the happiness of all its members' (JLP, 2013). This, in turn, rests on three management strategies that inform contemporary co-ownership: sharing gains (trading surpluses and assets); sharing information (through 'unlimited rights of discussion'); and sharing power (through principal management bodies that each have 'considerable spending power') (Lewis, 1954: ix). As Lewis writes:

> Producer-cooperation may perhaps be defined to be profit seeking enterprise upon the independent initiative of two or more persons without any exploitation of some by others so that all the workers, managers and managed alike, will be sharing fairly, that is to say as equally as is really possible, all the advantages of ownership ... These may be grouped under three heads, Gain, Knowledge and Power. The sharing of gain does not necessarily involve the sharing of knowledge or power. Where gain is not shared reasonably, knowledge will create more or less serious discontent. Hence the volcanic ferments of our present-day world. Knowledge in fact must tend strongly to lead sooner or later to a more or less reasonable sharing of gain and power. (1954: 25)

Affirmative strategic management and planning processes

Prescriptive theories tend to focus 'business needs' and *organisational* questions about 'best practice'. Descriptive and critical approaches are more focused on processes to find the 'best fit' between individual skills and aspirations and agreed organisational goals (Storey, 2001). Table 8.2 shows auditing questions in FairShares Level 1 Auditing instruments. They are a product of research to stimulate a critical-appreciative dialogue about the nature of social enterprise (see Chapter 2). Some questions stimulate collective deliberations, but others stimulate individual and small group reflection. The questions in Table 8.2 are a product of a more *affirmative* approach to strategic management. There is still a 'critical' goal (in the Freirian (1970) sense of emancipating individuals from dominant discourses) but the process relies less on deconstruction and more on the identification of 'strengths' on which individuals in the organisation can build.

Cooperrider and Srivastva (1987) argue that *appreciative* questioning is underpinned by the tacit question 'what gives life?' Early practice was articulated as appreciating, envisioning, co-constructing and sustaining social change by eliciting positive stories (see Figure 8.1). It has been popularised through a 4I model (initiation, inquiry, imagination and innovation) and a 4D model (discovery, dream, design and destiny) that describe phases of inquiry (Watkins and Mohr, 2001; Cooperrider et al., 2008).

Table 8.2 FairShares Diagnostics – Level 1 Auditing Questions

Initial Social Audit (collective process)	Initial Participation Audit (individual and collective process)
Purpose and Impact	*PRME Principle – Sustainability*
• What is the purpose of your enterprise? • How is the social, environmental and economic impact of your trading assessed?	• How do you want to participate in designing new products and services? • How do you want to participate in getting products and services to the people who need them? • How do you want to participate in staff (member) appraisals? • How do you want to participate in ensuring products and services are sustainably produced?
Ethics and Values	*PRME Principle – Ethics*
• What values and principles guide the choice of goods/services that you offer? • What values and principles guide the way you produce and/or sell those goods and services?	• What would encourage you (and those around you) to participate in learning new skills at work? • What ethics should be applied to the process of appointing/electing staff (members) to new positions? • How would you like to be treated (and others to be treated) while you are doing your day-to-day work?
Socialised and Democratic Ownership, Governance and Management	*PRME Principle – Responsibility*
• Who are your primary (secondary and tertiary) stakeholders? • How do the ownership, governance and management systems ensure an equitable distribution of wealth and power to all primary stakeholders?	• How do you want to participate in planning for the medium and long term? • How do you want to participate in setting wages, hours and leave entitlements? • How do you want to participate in allocating surpluses (profits) and deficits (losses)?

Source: FairShares Level 1 Diagnostics, www.fairshares.coop

The constructionist commitments at the heart of appreciative inquiry (**AI**) are evident in the contention that 'we human beings create our own realities through symbolic and mental processes' and that these processes can change both biological and organisational destinies (Cooperrider, 1999: 92). Based on these assumptions, AI has expanded beyond organisational development (OD) to projects in schools, community organisations and development bodies (van der Haar and Hosking, 2004; Grant, 2006). Backed by questions and processes that elicit strengths and competencies, AI researchers embrace a 'positive lens' in the belief that this stimulates change more quickly and effectively than focusing on deficits and problems.

There are some parallels with Stacey's work on complexity in which strategic management seeks to root itself in an ontological assumption that the world is complex, rarely reducible to a cause–effect model, and for which there are no single interventions that can produce predictable results (Stacey, 2007). Stacey's work is more

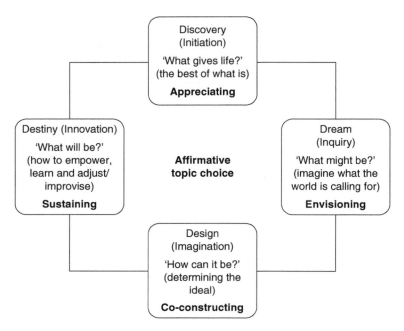

Figure 8.1   Early framing of appreciative inquiry

Source: Ridley-Duff and Duncan (2015)

accepting that social systems also present 'wicked' problems where it is hard to agree what the presenting problem is, and for which people will try a range of alternative solutions before settling on a stable approach.

Class exercise: Co-ownership, entrepreneurship and peace

In 2014, a spokesperson from United Nations announced at the International Co-operative Summit that their research group had established a statistically significant link between social economy development and the UN's 'social progress indicators'. This showed a correlation between higher densities of CMEs and lower levels of social conflict (Ridley-Duff and Hurst, 2014a). In light of these findings, watch this video of a 'positive' account of the contribution of co-ownership to peace in an Arab-Israeli community. Consider how David Cooperrider links outcomes to the 'strengths revolution' in strategic management (appreciative inquiry), and then consider the impact of repeating this story as a strategy for using SRBs/CMEs to build peace in regions affected by conflict.

Video: www.youtube.com/watch?v=V8n1BsbW-0I

1 Identity the elements of the story that make up this 'positive' narrative.
2 'Focusing on strengths is more effective than focusing on weaknesses.' Discuss.

While a formal (or written) strategic plan may be a useful way for members of an organisation to present their perspective(s) on future development to key stakeholders, the principal lesson from the above is that a lot of strategising takes place in small steps. Collins (2001) reports that 'great' companies rarely undertake launches of new strategies devised by senior managers. Instead, their performance 'takes off' when multiple strategic choices at all levels of organisation fit together in a way that provides a competitive (or collaborative) edge. Critical-appreciative processes catalyse the taking of small steps and provide an environment for them to align and influence 'performance' (Grant, 2006; Cooperrider et al., 2014; Ridley-Duff and Duncan, 2015).

Cases of strategic management in practice

Now we have set out what strategic management aims to achieve, and possible processes for bringing it about, we discuss three cases to explore the extent to which they are achievable (Table 8.3). SALT (Case 8.1) introduced earlier, illustrates how a strategic away day can support the development of a written business plan that fulfils the planning needs of an organisation. This took place at a venue (and with the equipment needed) to create a 'space' where the participants had time to reflect on, and develop, a sense of direction.

Table 8.3 Strategic management case studies: Cases 8.1–8.3

SALT (Case 8.1)

Seedley and Langworthy Trust (SALT) was established in 1997. It was set up to develop effective links between people who live and work in Seedley and Langworthy (areas within the City of Salford, near Manchester in the north of England) and partners from the public, private and voluntary sectors.

Broomby CIC (Case 8.2)

Broomby CIC was established by Mark Powell – a specialist in the development of social firms – after his previous employer (IMBY, a registered charity) changed its policy on social firm development. As Mark was committed to employing disabled people in social firms, he set up Broomby CIC in 2006 to take over projects started by IMBY.

SoftContact (Case 8.3)

SoftContact was founded in 1979 by six friends who met at college. The founders wanted to create an egalitarian place to work where they were free from management supervision. The company grew to 15 staff in the 1980s by fulfilling the social objective of providing IT training, advice and support services to third sector organisations.

The case studies, with international alternatives, are on the companion website at: www.sagepub.co.uk/ridleyduff

In Case 8.1 the issues for discussion were decided by interviewing people at all levels in the organisation to formulate workshops. The away day agenda for SALT was organised to develop:

Purpose: vision, mission and values.

Position: where is the organisation compared to others working in this field?

Plan: where the organisation wants to be?

Performance: milestones, achievements, monitoring, management and evaluation.

Alongside these four key Ps, teams were encouraged to follow a formula to guide the preparation of the business plan:

1. Review current status.
2. Identify goals.
3. Agree initiatives.
4. Set targets/objectives.
5. Agree assessment and evaluation.
6. Reflect and continuously improve.

While the agenda set for SALT focused almost wholly on the needs of their organisation, the other two cases (8.2 and 8.3) adopted an approach that focused on the intersection between individual and organisational aspirations. In Broomby CIC (Case 8.2), participants were initially provided with a questionnaire that gave them 24 'scenarios' and asked them to assess which of five choices most closely reflected their organisation. The questionnaire was an **heuristic**, designed to introduce people to the *diversity* of choices, and multiplicity of relationships, that are managed through a strategic management process. Following this, the framework was used to conduct one-to-one (coaching-style) interviews. These were written up and provided to each participant: they brought questionnaire responses and the interview transcript to a workshop in which they analysed and planned actions with other members of their organisation.

The process sought to identify 'issues' (that needed resolution) and 'actions' (that people wanted to undertake together). While the process was designed to aid people in understanding their own and others' values, the process did not involve *establishing* shared values. Nor was the 'output' a formal business plan: it was a one-page document that sought to summarise the issues/actions that future management and/or board meetings wanted to address, plus a one-page document for each individual that summarised their own issues/actions.

At SoftContact (Case 8.3), an 'annual review' took place each year at self-catering accommodation rented by the company. In this case, the annual review was organised to reflect the strategic goal of the founders to generate and reinforce an egalitarian culture:

Members were expected to share responsibilities for cooking and washing up, coffee making, house cleaning, minute taking, chairing sessions, preparing and presenting papers, and writing up minutes. These policies promoted member interaction and supported equality policies and objectives ... Saturday night usually involved a meal out, followed by drinks and various games at the self-catering accommodation. Watching TV was discouraged but not prohibited. Members usually played card games (poker, bridge), or other games that involved a lot of interaction. Alcoholic drinks were always available. Opportunities to chat informally were highly valued and viewed as an integral and vital part of the induction of new members.

As with Case 8.2, there was a strong focus on identifying *individual* goals and reflecting on these during discussion of business proposals and organisational goals. On the Friday evening, several hours were devoted to *personal reports*, a process by which all members (based on previously undertaken peer appraisals) made others aware of their career aspirations. The whole of Saturday was devoted to business proposals which were introduced, discussed and voted upon by all members (on a one-person, one-vote basis). On Sunday, annual budgets were discussed and revised in light of the decisions taken the previous day.

Class exercise: Appraising different approaches to strategy-making

Additional materials to support this exercise are available on the companion website at: www.sagepub.co.uk/ridleyduff.
In groups of three or six:

- Allocate Cases 8.1, 8.2 and 8.3 to group members.
- Read and carefully consider the case you have been given (10 minutes).
- Using Table 8.1, find examples of each school of strategic management in the cases you have read (20 minutes).
- Establish the 'configuration' of schools of strategic management in each case (15 minutes).
- In what contexts might one configuration be preferable over another? (15 minutes).

In the case of SALT (Case 8.1), the consultation was guided by a management/consultant-led approach in which the content (i.e. section headings) of the business plan was *designed* in advance. The away day was *planned* so that it would create statements on the vision, mission and shared values of the organisation (so that they could be added to marketing materials and business plans). Next, there was a focus on socio-economic *analysis* (using a PESTLE),[1] market *analysis* (using a SWOT), the identification of sources of income, and the *design* of services.

The Broomby CIC case (Case 8.2) was also management/consultant led, but there is no evidence that the goal of the development process was the production of a formal business plan. Instead, there was a focus on *emergent learning* and *analysis*. This was supported by a diagnostic questionnaire to generate questions for face-to-face discussions; participants developed their *cognitive* skills through *reflection* on questionnaire responses and interview summaries. The content of a plan was developed through *analysis*, but no cultural 'normalising' (vision, mission or value statements) was attempted. Instead, there was an attempt to establish 'critical success factors' (a form of *visioning*).

Lastly, the SoftContact case (Case 8.3) represents an *informalised* and institutionalised strategic management process devised over many years (DiMaggio and Powell, 1983), without any external support and not driven by the need to write a formal business plan. There is evidence of *collectivisation* through the proactive establishment of behavioural norms (playing games, self-catering, etc.) that are intended to reinforce *cultural values* (e.g. an egalitarian culture, workplace democracy). It is, perhaps ironically, a highly structured process (with months of advance planning, peer appraisals, minute taking, voting). It is *critical* in the sense that it is *designed* to increase individual participation and minimise dominance by powerful actors.

Doherty et al. (2009) suggest that 'strategic workshops' (such as away days) can be detached, singular events that may fail to embed changes in day-to-day practice. Once people return to their everyday worlds very little changes. They also express concerns that, unless everyone in the organisation is on the away day, the resentment and suspicion of those who did not attend creates barriers to implementation.

Strategic planning, therefore, can be viewed both as an expression of management philosophy and as a process of inquiry. Beinhocker, in his book *The Origin of Wealth* (2007: 323–8), suggests that strategising is less concerned with outlining a course of action and more concerned with *negotiating an understanding of uncertainty*. Even if this is so, that is not to say that the effort is wasted: it becomes a learning process that supports the development of both individual and group strategies. The words on the pages of a business plan may matter less than the process through which it is produced (Berry et al., 2005). Weick, echoing the sentiment of the 'generative' approach advanced by Cooperrider's appreciative inquiry advocates a 'sense-making' process in which:

> The likelihood of survival goes up when variation increases, when possibilities multiply, when trial and error becomes more diverse and less stylized, when people become less repetitious, and when creativity becomes supported. (Weick, 2001: 351)

These arguments favour emergent, appreciative approaches and cast doubt on tightly controlled strategy formation in support of written plans. Strategic management enacted through analysis, planning and evaluation is replaced by organic, flexible and adaptable practices that create a culture of strategising. This orients the process towards preparing and flexing the mind, developing an adaptive culture where strategies, scenarios and alternatives can be meaningfully compared and evaluated. It becomes more of a process of gazing for options than gazing for a set of answers (Beinhocker, 2007).

Mintzberg et al. (1998) also expresses a preference for strategising by drawing out strands of thinking to configure a preference. As Weick implies, this comes close to acknowledging complexity theory and a capacity for 'thriving on chaos' (Peters, 1989), deploying the management equivalent of freestyle jazz or improvised theatre as a way of generating ideas. Once generated, they can be selected, honed and crafted until they produce the results desired (Weick, 2001: 351). With this in mind we now turn our attention to ways in which strategic management systems might themselves be assessed and evaluated.

Assessing strategic management performance

Strategic management performance analysis tools for the private sector are common-place. There are business 'excellence models' (**EFQM**), Balanced Scorecard (**BSC**) adaptations, centres for total quality management (**TQM**), often drawing extensively on the work of Deming (Mann, 1989); or you can choose between strategies based on management by objective (**MBO**) and business process re-engineering (BPR). Adapting these for the social (enterprise) sector is an option, but given vehement criticism of business schools after the financial crisis of 2007–8 (James, 2009), it is appropriate to consider the implications of doing so.

Anheier (2000) claims that business-focused strategic analysis tools cannot be easily adapted by social enterprises because the latter have *multiple* bottom lines (not just multiple key performance indicators (KPIs) supporting a single bottom line). Paton also highlights the conundrum of performance management in his comment that:

> The very reasons why activities are undertaken in the non-profit sector are also the reasons why performance measurement will be deeply problematic. (2003: 49)

In stating this, he draws attention to the social costs of private (and public) sector management. It makes no sense (business-wise, or otherwise) for the social economy to uncritically accept practices until they have identified root causes of the problems they seek to resolve. So, at the very least, the drive towards 'contracts' and adopting 'business-like' behaviour requires social performance indicators (and forms of social organisation) that do not reproduce the social costs created by the practices of private and public sector management.

Strategic management tools designed and created from the perspectives of large profit-maximising businesses or well-resourced public authorities need to be carefully critiqued to establish their value to social enterprises (Spreckbacher, 2003; Alter, 2007). Several authors also draw attention to the issue of differences between large and small businesses (Scase and Goffee, 1980; Schumacher, 1993; Storey, 1994; Jennings and Beaver, 1997). Small businesses are less driven by formality. Given the high levels of trust in SMEs (Gallup, 2014; nfpSynergy, 2014), it could be that informal approaches – rather than formalised planning and control systems – are one of the key sources of efficiency in SMEs, co-operatives and charities. Could this explain why Dandridge (1979) and Wynarczyk et al. (1993) both argue that strategic management for small businesses needs re-theorising?

An unavoidable difference is that performance measurement and quantification in social enterprises is geared towards evidencing *social value* creation in line with a *social purpose* that deals with 'complex' situations in a community. Social returns may depend on levels of trust, or similar unexpressed, unquantifiable or hard-to-measure 'returns' (Paton, 2003). As Thomas (2004) notes, measuring social returns is likely to be expensive, both in terms of generating data, and also in terms of staff time and investments in information technology. Given this, both the economics and impacts of performance measurement will be different.

A case that illustrates this is a study of community development practices in Sheffield that started in 2007 (Duncan, 2009b; Duncan and Ridley-Duff, 2014). Duncan had been enthused by early social enterprise writings and the use of 'springboard stories' by Denning in international development. He wanted to create new employee-owned catering businesses with Pakistani women. However, the use of 'prescriptive' planning tools failed because Duncan and the women belonged to different 'communities of practice' (Wenger, 1998). The approaches he adopted had no resonance or cultural meaning for the women, and Duncan underestimated the impact of cultural differences regarding men's and women's capacity to engage in commerce. On realising this, he turned to appreciative inquiry to deepen his research team's[2] understanding of the barriers to commerce by Pakistani women. He needed to generate 'new narrative possibilities' by gathering stories from both Pakistani men and women (Duncan and Ridley-Duff, 2014). After generating a narrative supporting change, a new project led by community leader Nadia Asghar started in 2013 to document commercial practices in the community. These 'appreciative' stories are an integral part of a process that now stimulates micro-enterprises based on Pakistani women's interests (see www.stmaryschurch.co.uk/community/appreciative-inquiry/).

One of the issues here is that for performance to occur, the parties working together need to co-construct an understanding of the performances they want. Thomas highlights the problem of perception and interpretation:

> The performance captured by a particular set of measures will always be partial and contextual, reflecting the fact that the measures have been selected, analyzed and interpreted through the lenses of the organizations and individuals involved with the process. (2004: 11)

The upshot of this is that performance management tools need to be deconstructed and reconstructed for the social enterprise sector if they are to work effectively. One such tool for which there have been successive attempts at adaptation is the Balanced Scorecard. This adopts a holistic approach to performance measurement that steers thinking away from economic indicators (Kaplan and Norton, 1992). As Bennett et al. claim:

> The concept of the BSC is based on the assumption that the efficient use of investment capital is no longer the sole determinant for competitive advantages, but increasingly soft factors such as intellectual capital, knowledge creation or excellent customer orientation become more important. (2003: 19)

Kaplan and Norton (1992) suggested that the BSC is appropriate for transfer to non-profit organisations, and two sector-specific projects have provided some early progress towards this goal. Firstly, Social Firms UK constructed an online 'Dashboard' intended as an integrated management performance tool based on the principles of the BSC. Secondly, the New Economic Foundation worked with the Social Enterprise Partnership (SEP) to pilot the BSC in social enterprises. Their research highlighted that the BSC needed to be adapted to incorporate the commercial practices of social enterprises by including: multiple bottom lines; multi-stakeholder and social objectives; social goals; a broader financial perspective focused on sustainability; and a broader relationship perspective that goes beyond the customer to capture a larger group of stakeholder perspectives (Somers, 2005). Case 8.4 describes a further project funded by the European Social Fund (**ESF**) to create a practical tool for use in social enterprises.

Case 8.4

Balance: developing a strategic management tool for social enterprises

Balance is an on-line strategic management diagnostic tool for social enterprises and other third sector organisations (Bull, 2006) (www.socialenterprisebalance.org). The tool aids strategic analysis, priority setting and critical reflection in assessing organisational competencies. It was developed in 2005 by Mike Bull during a research project that involved Dilani Jayawarna, Helen Crompton, Alison Wilson and Robin Holt at the Centre for Enterprise, Manchester Metropolitan University. The original version had five sections and subsequent research by Mike Bull has extended the tool to seven sections. The tool was originally the outcome of three years' research (between 2004 and 2007) on the management practices of social

(Continued)

(Continued)

enterprises (Bull and Crompton, 2005, 2006; Bull, 2007). It was funded by a regional ESF grant. It identified language and concepts appropriate for use in social enterprises. The tool is divided into seven sections, covering: (1) stakeholder perspectives, (2) multi-bottom line, (3) internal activities, (4) learning, (5) income diversification, (6) governance, and (7) visioning. Across the seven sections there are 38 questions. The tool presents statements, such as: 'Our board understands their responsibilities in terms of the legal issues, policies and governing rules of the organisation and conducts themselves accordingly.' The assessor then reviews a scale of possible responses from five levels, as to where they feel their organisation best fits – level 1 being weak, level 5 being expert. The assessment is undertaken in a subjective spirit, evidence and objectivism are replaced with gut feel, instinct and honesty within the assessment.

After completion of the diagnostic the website generates a snapshot histogram bar chart that outlines the opinions of the assessor in terms of the maturity of the organisation (immature, being an organisation that has no knowledge, intentions or strategies to engage with the topic – to mature, being an organisation that has experience, knowledge and a strategy to engage with the topic). The benefit of Balance is not only in using the findings of the analysis to reflect on the individual findings, but to get others involved, a board and management team. If people individually assess in isolation from one another and bring their snapshots to a meeting, then the conversations and opinions about the results add another rich level of evaluation to the exercise.

The final part of the diagnostic is once a user has evaluated their current position, they may seek to focus their attention on some organisationally weak areas of their business and management competencies. The 'Action Plan' is a PDF document that provides a breakdown of suggestions and tips for developing the skills required to develop the business should the assessor consider it important to do so.

A teaching case with questions, and an academic article on the reformulation of the BSC into Balance, is available on the companion website at: www.sagepub.co.uk/ridleyduff.

The basis of Balance is shown in Figure 8.2. Essentially the tool is premised on developing under-developed areas of an organisation's business and management structures in order to balance out and support organisational maturity.

One of the early advocates and users of Balance was Unlimited Potential in Salford. They have used the tool annually since 2004 to monitor their progress. Case 8.5 provides a summary of the outputs to illustrate how progress can be monitored. Results can be compared not just against the organisation's own previous results, but also against the average for all organisations that have used the Balance tool.

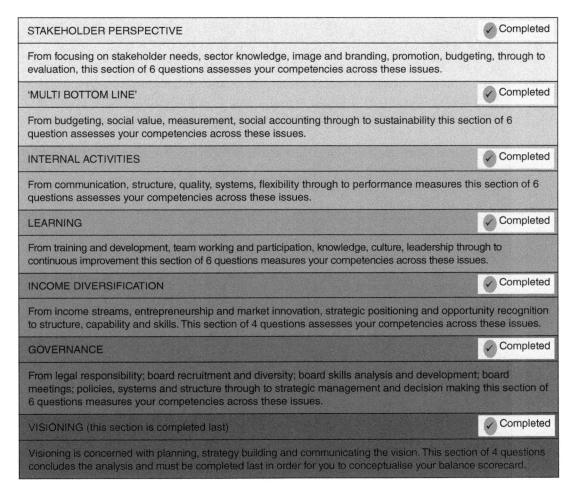

Figure 8.2 Balance

Source: generated with www.socialenterprisebalance.org

Case 8.5

Unlimited potential

At the launch of the Charlestown and Lower Kersal New Deal for Communities (NDC) in March 2000, local people who wanted to be involved in planning the new health services started identifying themselves. Six months later, they were meeting

(Continued)

(Continued)

on a regular basis, analysing data, shaping the plan and forming themselves into the Community Health Action Partnership and subsequently Unlimited Potential. In 2009 they undertook a further self-assessment using Balance and compared it to their findings from 2008. The results were:

- stakeholder perspective: good progress (was 76.7 per cent, now up to 86.7 per cent); above average
- internal activities: light decline (was 96.7 per cent, now down to 90 per cent); well above average
- multiple bottom line: good maintenance (was 100 per cent, now down to 96.7 per cent); well above average
- learning: excellent progress (was 83.3 per cent, now up to 93.3 per cent); significantly above average
- visioning: maintained (was 100 per cent, still 100 per cent); well above average.

Read the full case on the companion website at: www.sagepub.co.uk/ridleyduff and then answer the following questions:

1 Using Table 8.1, critically evaluate whether Balance is a *prescriptive*, *descriptive* or *critical-appreciative* management tool.
2 Critically assess the language deployed in the Balance tool. To what extent is the language (and its implicit assumptions) appropriate for the organisation(s) in which (or for which) you have studied or worked?

Balance findings

Balance has collected 751 individual assessments since 2006. While we cannot consider that level of detail in this chapter, it is worth considering the overall level of maturity reported by participants who have used Balance. The data is representative of self-certified and identified social enterprises, predominantly in north-west England, who have been supported by a network of agencies in the region. The data was gathered over six years and excludes 'income diversification' and 'governance' as these are recent additions after user feedback in 2012.

The snapshot represents average scores within the database. They highlight that internal activities are least developed (56 per cent). This section includes: communication, structure, quality systems, flexibility and performance measures – essentially qualities of the internal structure. Scoring highly was the 'multi-bottom line' section (66 per cent), which includes: budgeting, social value, measurement and social accounting. Although the section scored highest overall, there is a hidden finding that social accounting (at 40 per cent) remains in its infancy (something we discuss in Chapter 4).

These findings suggest that the average social enterprise is 'beginning to' implement practices that will address organisational issues. What this means is that organisations are beyond 'thinking about doing', but are not mature enough to have 'already done', and certainly the average suggests they feel they are far from 'experts in' various aspects of strategic management. This reflects the age of many of the sample – either because they are new start enterprises or because they have been in transition to social enterprise after establishing themselves as voluntary sector organisation or charities. Put simply, the results reflect that the social enterprises in the sample are new to social entrepreneurship, but are maturing.

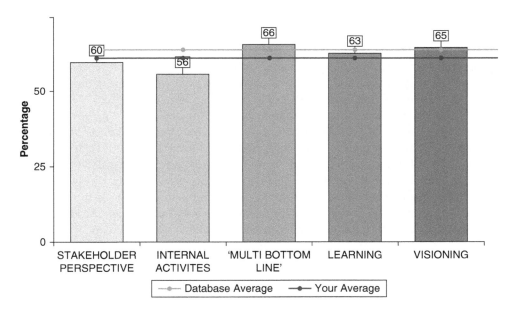

Figure 8.3   Balance findings

Source: generated with www.socialenterprisebalance.org

Having identified that there may be value in using strategic management performance tools, we conclude the chapter by adding our own thoughts on the distribution of power and responsibility between employees, members, managers and the governing body (board of trustees or directors).

Critical reflections

Our experience as researchers, lecturers and practitioners suggests that theory is both useful and limited. Devising strategy is messier than theory would suggest. It also varies across the social economy depending on the philosophical assumptions that are dominant among organisation members (Ridley-Duff, 2007). In the case of CTAs, boards are (by law) required to be voluntary and *external* (in the sense that they comprise people who are not paid employees). This may also be the case in CMEs owned by consumers, as the members are primarily customers rather than members of the workforce. In both cases, employees either cannot be board members, or are elected to represent consumer or charitable interests rather than labour interests. The *reverse* is true in CMEs that are staff-controlled (employee-owned businesses and worker co-operatives). In this case, members of the workforce may be the *only* people permitted to serve on the board,[3] and may be 'voluntary' in the sense that no additional payment is made for their services as a director (BBC, 1980; Ridley-Duff, 2005). This reflects a cultural (rather than legal) norm within the social economy. As for the new legal form of the CIC, insufficient research has been conducted to establish if directors are paid regularly. Legally, however, there is no obstacle to doing so.

The size and structure of organisations both matter. In co-operative organisations, even though they are formally democratic, member control gets more limited as size grows, particularly if the enterprise takes on debt finance (Kasmir, 1996; Bounds, 2014). Furthermore, executives can acquire power over co-operative governing bodies through their control of information and processes, and then use this to influence the outcome of strategic management decisions (Whyte and Whyte, 1991). Interestingly, the JLP counter this tendency in three ways: firstly, they have a 'free press' (*The Gazette* journal) – any letter written to the *Gazette* must be published and answered by a manager; secondly, they have a 'registry' to which members can go if their concerns are not acted on by their line manager; lastly, they can raise issues through elected representatives able to influence the Partnership Council and chairman.

In CICs, the legal form has been designed (as is the case with US B-Corps and 'social purpose' companies in the EU) so that a managing director can also be a full member of the governing body (Low, 2006). This follows the private sector norm, popular in SRBs, of supporting founding entrepreneur(s) who wish to maintain control over the organisations they create.

With this variety of possible relationships between members, managers and directors, the crucial question arises: who is involved in strategic management? Is it the paid management staff? Or is it the responsibility of the board or management committee? Legally, strategising is the responsibility of the board (or management committee). Research suggests that there are negotiating spaces between paid managers and board members (and between *worker-owners* in co-operatives). For example, Coule's (Coule, 2008; Chadwick-Coule, 2011) study of sustainability in the voluntary sector found that this negotiating space is itself a stabilising influence. Organisations become *more vulnerable* if they follow advice from private sector reviews of governance (NCVO, 2005). In three of four cases, Coule found that organisations most at risk were over-reliant on the relationship between the chair and the CEO. This resulted in the marginalisation of members, managers, trustees and directors in decision-making, through the non-disclosure of information needed by them to make strategic choices.

Figures 8.4, 8.5 and 8.6 highlight new ideals of strategic control that reflect progressive 'private' and 'co-operative' thinking (Turnbull, 2002). Norms in the private sector can be traced back to a study by Berle and Means (1932). They produced a theory that organisational growth results in a gradual separation of ownership (by shareholders) and control (by professional managers). The powers given to shareholders (and board members) to control executives, therefore, stem from the assumption that executive are *agents* of the owners, employed to follow owners' wishes. Figure 8.4 reflects this 'rationalist' perspective, and hints at the link between *prescriptive* theories of strategic management and the assumption of control by founders who internalise the concept of 'management prerogative'.

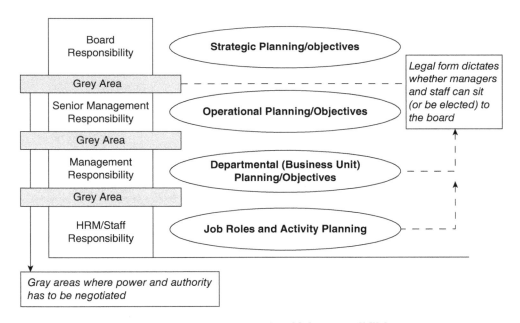

Figure 8.4   Strategic, operational, departmental and job responsibilities

Charities and organisations that pursue CTAs frequently operate on the basis of trust law (rather than company law). This leads to a justification that trustees must be empowered to ensure that donated monies are used in accordance with the donors' wishes (or for stated charitable objects). While the rationale for top-down control is different from a private enterprise, the management control system is still designed to separate the governing body (responsible for strategic management) and executive management (responsible for operations). Executive managers are still, in law, subordinate to the board.

From a critical-appreciative perspective, the 'rationalist' argument for top-down (line management) is much weaker. In parallel with Beer's (1966) argument for *systems thinking*, Deming encouraged organisations to devise quality management systems that continually improved processes to cutting out everything that is wasteful. Deming's system thinking fits well with the philosophy of sustainable development through its commitment to reducing waste (Mann, 1989; Fujitsu, 2010; PEX, 2013). Moreover, Crawford (2011) applied the logic of Deming's *production* system to the relationships that drive civil society (and a more social economy).

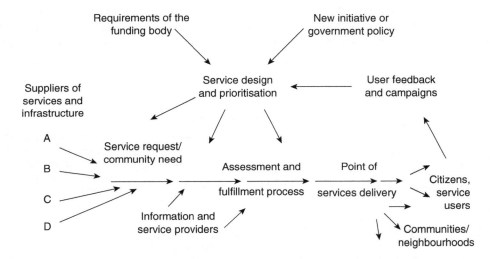

Figure 8.5   Adapting Deming's system of profound knowledge to the needs of civil society

Systems thinkers point out how living organisms, as well as cybernetic/robotic inventions, thrive on control *loops* and *localised feedback mechanisms* for effective governance, and do not rely on long chains of command. Living organisms (right down to the individual cell) have multiple feedback and communication systems that increase their resilience and enable them to function even when one part of a system stops working (Dobson et al., 2015). This has, over time, strengthened the argument for co-operative governance rooted in an **ecological perspective** in which network relations replace hierarchies to allow parties to learn about (and influence) each other's behaviour (Turnbull, 2002). Drawing on a range of written works (by Birchall, Cornforth, Gates, Ellerman, Erdal, Pateman, Lewis, Turnbull and Vanek) Ridley-Duff and Southcombe (2014) have evolved a FairShares Model in which systems thinking is applied to the question of social enterprise design. In this case, strategic questions are resolved by **enfranchising** the stakeholder groups best able to answer them.

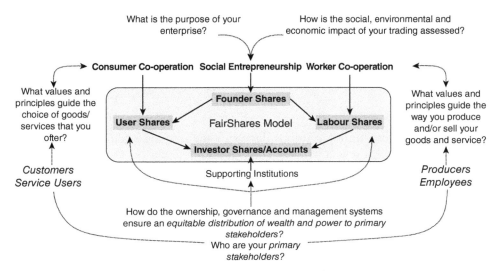

Figure 8.6   Towards a multi-stakeholder view of strategic management

Gates (1998) and Turnbull (2001) claim that enfranchising key stakeholders (either through ownership or forms of social auditing) can remove the communication barriers that hierarchies *create*, and replace them with a **network governance** system that reduces exploitation and makes collaboration easier. Applied to social enterprise, this means that an enterprise's workforce (whether voluntary or paid), its product/service users (whether freely given or chargeable) and its suppliers all become *strategic stakeholders*. Looked at this way, investors (or public funders) are optional extras important for accelerating development, but not a *fundamental* necessity. Ecological perspectives, not least because of their link to evolutionary thinking, are more strongly linked to Mintzberg et al.'s *emergent* perspective on strategic management and Stacey's writings on complexity (Mintzberg et al., 1998; Stacey, 2007).

Strategic management in organisations based on the thinking shown in Figure 8.4 may be viewed positively as a partnership between the board (governing body) and the management team, with the grey areas indicating areas of interaction to negotiate authority and control (Carver, 1990; Hudson, 2002). Unlike the assumptions that underpin Figure 8.5 and 8.6, authority is conceptualised as being at the 'top' of the organisation, exercised *downwards* through various 'controls' (sometimes to ensure **legal compliance** against a standard or statutory requirement). There are well-developed quality management systems that fit this mould, such as the popular PQASSO system (www.ces-vol.org.uk/PQASSO). In Figure 8.5 authority is *necessarily* dispersed (as it is recognised that no single organisation can control a social system), while in Figure 8.6 authority is *deliberately* dispersed. In both cases, the metaphor for the governing body is to act more like the 'heart' of a living being, ensuring that resources are continually flowing to all parts of a (complex adaptive) system so they can select what they need, and contribute what they can to strengthen the whole.

Conclusions

In this chapter, we have introduced the concept of strategic management, and explored different approaches that reflect different contexts and outlooks on management itself. In the absence of management experience, it is not surprising that *prescriptive* theories are sought as a starting point from which to develop practice. When these prescriptions fail, however, it is necessary to consider *descriptive* theories that focus on sense-making, reflection and appreciative questioning that encourages the critical review of experiences. Descriptive theories – which avoid the fallacy of the 'quick fix' – enhance cognitive and learning skills, enabling managers to progressively engage with *critical-appreciative* management processes. This is a pre-requisite for dealing with 'complex' and 'wicked' problems (Curtis and Bowkett, 2014) that need intensive and prolonged engagement with a community. Critical-appreciation and systems thinking also mitigate the effects of over-centralised power by promoting strategic management that 'configures' strategies to meet the needs of particular situations, and which draw in those parties best able to answer key questions. Over the long term, this equips managers with the cognitive awareness to assess which 'tools' are designed to increase economic or social opportunities for their designers, and which contribute to organisational learning and the well-being of members and beneficiaries.

Summary of learning

In this chapter, we have explained:

Ways of reducing our 'blindness' to the way strategic management is developed and enacted in different types of social enterprise.

That theories of strategic management can be *prescriptive*, *descriptive*, *critical* and *appreciative*.

The challenge of assessing the effectiveness of strategic management (in a social enterprise context), through attempts to create sector-specific adaptations of the Balanced Scorecard.

How strategic management arises out of 'rational' and 'ecological' approaches to enterprise design, which – in turn – lead to centralised (unitary) and decentralised (pluralist) management practices.

Questions and possible essay assignments

1. 'Private sector theories of strategic management are of limited use to social enterprises.' Using examples, critically assess the applicability of this statement to charitable trading activities and socially responsible businesses.
2. Drawing on *prescriptive*, *descriptive* and *critical-appreciative* theories of strategic management, assess the way that strategic aims evolve in a social enterprise of your choice.
3. Using any combination of Figures 8.4, 8.5 and 8.6, critically assess how relationships between citizens, governing bodies, consumers, producers and investors are developing in an SRB or CME of your choice.

Further reading

If you have insufficient time to read the whole of Mintzberg et al.'s *Strategy Safari* (1998), we heartily recommend the first chapter which provides an overview of *intended* and *emergent* strategic management, and the contribution of different schools of thought. Another excellent introduction that considers a wide range of perspectives on studying organisations as organisations is Christopher Grey's *A Very Short, Fairly Interesting and Reasonably Cheap Book about Studying Organizations* (2005). We have also found Ralph Stacey's book *Strategic Management and Organisational Dynamics: The Challenge of Complexity* (2007) a good resource.

Doherty et al.'s *Management for Social Enterprise* (2009) has a chapter entitled 'Strategic management for social enterprises' that takes a different approach to the topic. Hudson's *Managing Without Profit* (2002) also provides useful chapters on managing strategy and the concepts of vision, mission and values from an executive perspective. For more critical coverage, we recommend Chadwick-Coule's article 'Social dynamics and the strategy process' (2011), and Coule and Patmore's work on institutional logics (2013).

In addition to Mike Bull's published reports on the ESF Balance project (downloadable from www.socialenterprisebalance.org/Publications.aspx) we commend his 2007 article on the development of Balance in the *Social Enterprise Journal* (Bull, 2007). In the same journal, we also recommend Clifford Conway's (2008) article on business planning training in social enterprises.

Further reading material is available on the companion website at: www.sagepub. co.uk/ridleyduff.

Useful resources

Appreciative Inquiry Commons: http://appreciativeinquiry.case.edu/

Balance: www.socialenterprisebalance.org

Balanced Scorecard Institute: www.balancedscorecard.org/

CoCo (The Cooperation Commons): www.cooperationcommons.com/

The Deming Institute: www.deming.org/

FairShares Model: www.fairshares.coop/wordpress/fairshares-model/

Free Management Library: http://managementhelp.org/plan_dec/str_plan/str_plan.htm

ISEA (Strategy Configurations): www.isea-group.net/initiativesstratconf.php

Nash equilibrium: https://en.wikipedia.org/wiki/Nash_equilibrium

Open Space Technology: www.openspaceworld.org/

PQASSO: www.ces-vol.org.uk/PQASSO/pqasso-the-basics

Third Sector Performance Dashboard: www.proveandimprove.org/tools/socialfirm.php

Venture Navigator: www.socialenterprisewm.org.uk/help-advice/venture-navigator/

Notes

1 A PESTLE analysis is similar to a PEST analysis (political, economic, socio-cultural and technical), but adds legal and environmental impact analyses.
2 The research team – without whom this project could not have proceeded – included bilingual English, Urdu and Punjabi speakers able to conduct workshops and produce translations of interviews. They were Nadia Asghar, Aroose Uppal, Saffeina Kahn, Sobia Shafique, Khalida Ayaz, Shamim Khan, and Zeeshan Khattak.
3 For more on co-ownership (including research publications) see the website of the Employee Ownership Association. Election and remuneration practices vary a lot in co-owned/co-operative businesses. John Lewis and the Co-operative Group pay the directors that are elected/appointed, but other co-operatives and mutuals see it as normal for members to make themselves available if elected to a governing body.

Management Ideologies

9

Rory Ridley-Duff, Tracey Coule and
Mike Bull

Learning objectives

In this chapter, we go more deeply into the way ideology affects management practices during charitable trading activities (CTAs), social business development (in
socially responsible businesses, SRBs) and co-operative management (in co-operative
and mutual enterprises, CMEs). We do this to study how different management decisions and choices influence the culture that prevails within a social enterprise. By the
end of this chapter you will be able to:

- critically assess the ambiguity surrounding management as a concept in social
  enterprises
- critically evaluate attitudes to democratic management, ownership and governance
- outline **unitary**, **pluralist** and **radical** perspectives on employee relations
- critically evaluate the impact of theoretical perspectives on the management of
  stakeholders

> ### The key arguments that will be developed in this chapter are:
>
> - The concept of 'best practice' changes depending on the stakeholder perspective adopted.
> - Different bodies of knowledge compete to shape thinking on how people are managed.
> - Management ideology emerges from the interplay between individual value commitments, the cultural ecosystem that shapes decision-making, and dominant discourses on stakeholder management.
> - Social enterprises are diverse in the way they interpret and enact a management ideology.

Introduction

In this chapter, attention is focused on how management ideologies develop to establish norms in the social relationships between people at work. Frequently, the development and control of people at work is studied as 'human resource *development*' when the focus is on learning (Harrison, 2005), and 'human resource *management*' (**HRM**) when the focus is on social control and employment law (Clegg et al., 2008). We resist the temptation to approach the subject from the perspective of 'human resources'. We also resist what we believe to be an unnatural separation between the study of 'human resources' and 'governance'. The justification for this is based on a rejection of the idea that control necessarily emanates from the top of the organisation (Grey, 2005; Jackson and Parry, 2008). While there may be periodic attempts to run organisations in this way (or present this as the model of control to various stakeholders for political advantage), we argue that the development of people, and attempts to control them, can be usefully studied by seeking to understand the way they interact and shape each other's activities (Watson, 1994; Darwin et al., 2002). In social enterprises, this is particularly important because there may be deliberate attempts to subvert traditional management practices through the introduction of participatory democracy. With the advent of the internet, and social networking technologies, the costs of participatory democracy are now negligible (compared to a generation ago). This means that workplace democracy – once seen as either inappropriate or highly desirable but too costly – is now so affordable that the cost–benefits of traditional management practices need re-evaluation (Ellerman, 1990; Johnson, 2006).

Class exercise: Subverting management control in decision-making

In September 2011, a movement to 'occupy Wall Street' spontaneously triggered activists all around the world to occupy key financial institutions to protest the power of the 1 per cent (the richest people in the world). The legacy of the Occupy Movement has been a new set of protocols for participatory democracy, and the development of technology by activists that make participatory management easy (and cheap) to practice.

A group of software experts at *Enspiral* (www.enspiral.com/) took the social practices that developed in the Occupy Movement and created Loomio (Jenson, n.d.). Loomio is a collaborative decision-making tool that is now used by over 30,000 groups around the world. In Spain, the political party Podemos has used Loomio to develop (in just 12 months) from an unknown political party to a party that leads national opinion polls. It has created 900 Loomio groups for branch members to contribute to policy-making (Blitzer, 2014).

- Watch this video about Loomio: www.youtube.com/watch?v=B1gLEAKPkOc
- For help with creating Loomio groups, watch this video: www.youtube.com/watch?v=TbnuUT8j6tw
- Create a Loomio Group, invite your students/colleagues into the group, then start a discussion about social enterprise management practices.
- Make a proposal that: 'Loomio should be the decision-making tool of choice in the social economy'.
- Set the end date to just before you give this lecture (or set it one week ahead if there is no lecture). When the vote has completed, report the outcome to your Loomio group members.
  During the discussion, consider the different approaches to social enterprise based on charitable trading activities, socially responsible business practices and co-operative and mutual principles described in Chapter 2. Evaluate Loomio's suitability for all three approaches before committing your vote.
- Write a 500 word essay (or blog) about your experience of Loomio. How do you rate its potential as a management tool? What are the implications of using it? Could it subvert established management practices?

Our own research supports Stewart's (1983) view that close study of management, and attempts to proactively manage people, produces a picture quite different from that propagated by the founding texts of scientific management (Fayol, 1916; Taylor, 1917). In these texts, organisations are dissected and managers learn how to plan, organise, command, co-ordinate and control their financial, human and physical resources (Clegg, et al. 2008). In contrast, **ethnographic studies** of management reveal something different:

> The picture that emerges ... is of someone who lives in a whirl of activity, in which attention must be switched every few minutes from one subject, problem, and person to another; of an uncertain world where relevant information includes gossip and speculation. It is a picture, too, not of a manager who sits quietly controlling but who is dependent upon many people, other than subordinates, with whom reciprocating relationships should be created; who needs to learn how to trade, bargain, and compromise. (Stewart, 1983: 96)

This view, cited as part of Watson's study of managers' lived experience, indicates that managers engage in reciprocal and interdependent relationships, but have to manage these within the context of law and regulation that assumes hierarchy. Frequently, a 'softer' approach to management rooted in a desire to treat people with dignity, as capable of reflecting on and learning from complex and difficult situations, comes into conflict with a much 'harder' world of authority, embedded in constitutional rules and employment laws. This chapter is important for developing a fuller understanding of the way that entrepreneurs, managers and staff can approach the implicit conflict between 'soft' approaches that emphasise understanding, reflection, emotional intelligence and group working, and 'harder' approaches that rely on the enforcement of rules, deference to authority and evaluations of individual competence.

Class exercise: First look at the ideologies of management

Ridley-Duff and Ponton (2013) undertook a study to develop a theoretical framework for investigating workforce participation in co-operatives (CMEs) and SRBs. Their framework has been adopted by Social Enterprise Europe and the FairShares Association for an online diagnostic tool that facilitates explorations of management ideology. The diagnostics explore the depth of participation (both at present and desired in the future). During the study, participants learnt how to critique and distinguish passive and active employee involvement, managed and member-led participation practices. In 2013, participants at Viewpoint Research CIC voted to end control by a single owner-manager and implement elected works council to negotiate working practices with managers.

- Ask students to bring a smart phone, tablet or laptop to class.
- Get each student (and tutor) to fill out the diagnostic survey: www.quicksurveys. com/s/y4GJd.
- Explore results from this (and previous) surveys at: http://tolu.na/1vCapFm.
- Based on the *questions* and *answers* put in the diagnostic tool, get students to critique the boundaries between:

  - *a unitary* ideology that is management controlled and driven (depths 1–3)
  - *a pluralist* ideology based on negotiated agreements between staff and managers (depth 4)
  - *a radical* ideology based on self-regulated participation by member-owners (depth 5).

- Get each student to evaluate their own preferred management style.

You can find further supporting materials (including a paper version of this survey instrument) on the companion website at: www.sagepub.co.uk/ridleyduff.

Taken together social practices are expressions of the social (and legal) rules that guide management behaviours. In the following section, we delve further into this issue by outlining unitary, pluralist and radical perspectives on management. These were developed by Fox (1974) to describe relationships that develop between employers and workforce members. To help study these relationships, we use four case studies to explore the diversity of practices. In the final section, we critically evaluate the cases and locate them within Purcell's (1987) framework for management styles.

Unitary, pluralist and radical management

The definition of unitary, pluralist and radical workplace cultures are derived from studies of industrial relations (Fox, 1966; Salamon, 2000) and have been redefined in the context of social enterprise and voluntary sector management practices (Ridley-Duff, 2007; Chadwick-Coule, 2011). Fox defined three perspectives on employer–workforce relationships within the workplace. Firstly, he set out a *unitarist* view that reflects the outlook of those who have acquired (or who defer to) executive power. This is supported by rhetorical strategies that justify increased management control to produce harmony in working towards common goals. Implicit in this view is managers' 'right to manage' and the suppression of challenges to managerial authority.

Secondly, Fox identified a *pluralist* perspective in which organisations comprise competing groups that have different values, interests and objectives. In employee relations and governance, this surfaces in the establishment of negotiating and debating forums through which collective bargaining can take place (i.e. agreements reached between *groups* of people based on their collective, rather than individualised, interests). From a pluralist perspective, conflict is inevitable, requiring employer and employee representatives to devise and utilise conflict resolution processes. In considering the social enterprise sector, pluralist perspectives can be extended to volunteers, beneficiaries and the community in which the enterprise is located, and becomes manifest in governance and social auditing arrangements that involve these stakeholders.

Lastly, Fox (1966) outlined a *radical* perspective in which conflict is viewed not simply as inevitable, but as a product and driver of *social transformation*. As Hunt (1981: 90) argues, conflict is 'desirable and constructive in any social system' as it can open up different solutions to a problem, encourage creativity and surface emotive arguments. Indeed, as Collins (2001) notes, the presence of open conflict is a hallmark of 'great' companies. Conflict itself is not inherently destructive – it is the way conflict is managed that becomes destructive. Positive approaches to managing conflict involves recognising the value of challenges to organisational norms and the empowerment that comes from respecting the widest possible range of opinions (Cooperrider et al., 2014). This radical perspective surfaces regularly in calls for more participative management cultures at work (Lewis, 1954; Pateman, 1970; Willmott, 1993; Johnson, 2006).

The question is: which of these perspectives (and therefore which associated ideology for managing people) is best geared towards the socialisation of business ownership and management and/or pursuing the social purpose defined in an organisation's constitution? Table 9.1 outlines the practical impacts of adopting different ideologies of management on management practice, conflict resolution and democratic debate.

Table 9.1   Applying Fox's perspectives to social enterprise practice

Unitarist	Pluralist	Radical
Management prerogative		
Absolute right	*Curbed*	*Challenged*
Board/CEO is sole source of authority and meaning	Shared decision-making on limited issues	No automatic right of managers to manage
Board and senior managers establish values, policies and practices	Some co-determination on 'employee' and 'stakeholder' issues	Authority delegated to managers by workers' or members' assembly, or by an elected governing body
		Values and attitudes are emergent, based on informally accepted social practices

Unitarist	Pluralist	Radical
	Attitude to conflict	
Not valid	*Accepted*	*Endemic*
Pathological, irrational	Within limits. Rejected if managers' right to manage is challenged	Provides opportunity for creative discussions on how to transform working arrangements. Based on the goal of embedded member ownership principles
Managed through disciplinary and grievance procedures to reassert management prerogative	Managed mostly through disciplinary and grievance procedures using 'natural justice' principles to ensure fairness. Openness to alternative dispute resolution (ADR) in the form of arbitration, conciliation and mediation where it may help	Managed primarily through debate in democratic forums (group) and mediation (one-to-one), with disciplinary and grievance procedures (or arbitration) used only where mediation fails
	Debating forums and collective bargaining	
No or limited role	*Accepted/tolerated*	*Embedded in culture*
If used, managed by board members or executives, or limited only to strategic decision-making at board/ management level	Limited scope within agreed 'boundaries'. Managers seek to limit to 'business' matters, rather than matters of management control	Continuous and active learning in co-operative management bodies and/ or trade union meetings. Joint councils and/or sub-boards are embedded in the organisation culture and constitution
No collective bargaining on terms and conditions of employment, or strategic management	Avoids joint decision-making on business and strategic management decisions	Agreements reached through collective bargaining and mediation processes

In the next section, therefore, we explore the application of these concepts. Two cases are based on studies of CTAs in the voluntary sector (Coule, 2008), and other cases involve an SRB and a CME (Ridley-Duff, 2005). The cases are summarised in Table 9.2.

Table 9.2   Case studies: Cases 9.1–9.4

Custom Products (Case 9.1) – SRB Case

Founded in 1990 by a school teacher and one of his pupils, the company provides goods and services to schools. In 2004, the founders and 130 employees voted (separately) to convert to a trading company (CLS) owned by an employee trust; 100 per cent of income comes from trade.

Trading Trust (Case 9.2) – CTA Case

Founded in 1930, and registered as a charity in 1960. The organisation has a strong faith-based ethos and over a third of the organisation's income is earned through sales: vocational courses that satisfy charitable objectives. In 2007, there were 80–100 volunteers and 40–45 staff.

(Continued)

Table 9.2   Continued

Rights Now! (Case 9.3) – CTA Case

Founded in 1998 as a charitable company (CLG), the organisation fights for the rights of people with learning disabilities, including those who have a sensory impairment, and generates a third of its income through sales. The organisation has 20 staff and 10 volunteers.

SoftContact (Case 9.4) – CME Case

Founded in 1979 by six friends, the company grew to 15 staff in the 1980s providing training, advice and support services to third sector organisations, then shrank after the GLC was closed. The company, a co-operative society, helped found Social Enterprise London.

The case studies and additional teaching materials are all available on the companion website at: www.sagepub.co.uk/ ridleyduff.

Class exercise: Identifying an ideology of management

Materials to support this exercise can be found on the companion website at: www. sagepub.co.uk/ridleyduff.

- Divide the class into groups of four and distribute Cases 9.1, 9.2, 9.3 and 9.4 to group members.
- Give the students 10 minutes to read and make notes about their case.
- Invite each student to spend 5 minutes explaining their case to the other members of their group.
- Discuss and locate each case on the ideological map of management styles shown in Figure 9.1.

Consider the following:

1 What management style would you advocate for (your) social enterprise?
2 Is it possible to have a culture that both is radical and uses 'soft HRM' practices?

Recruitment, selection and induction

Differences are apparent in the way each organisation recruits board members. At Custom Products, all directors had connections through family or friends. The conversion to an employee-owned company has changed this. Any permanent employee (with over two years' service) is now eligible for election to the board, subject to conditions initially set by executive managers. This contrasts with Trading Trust where a separation of governors from staff was preserved to satisfy charity law. Recruitment at Trading Trust was based on professional expertise and commitment to a faith-based ethos. Rights Now! took a different approach, combining trustees with a disability and others possessing specialist management skills. Of the four organisations, however, only SoftContact has an identical recruitment process for both staff and directors. This was a product of its legal form (a co-operative society) whereby all members passing their probationary period became full members (and directors).

In the other three organisations, only Custom Products was evolving in a similar direction (a by-product of its conversion to a CLS majority-owned by an employee trust). Nevertheless, the executive group imposed its own criteria to limit candidates who could stand for board membership, and required them to go through 'culture management' training as a *precondition* of eligibility. This potentially enables executives to control which employees can be elected governors. At Rights Now! and Trading Trust, the separation of trustees and staff under charity law meant there was no progression path to the board unless staff gave up their employment.

Rotation practices for board members differed. At Custom Products, elected members of a governing council serve four years (two change every two years). A similar situation existed at Rights Now! with policies ensuring a turnover of board members. While Trading Trust and SoftContact did not rotate directors, the rationale was different. At Trading Trust, there were no formal mechanisms for the re-election of trustees and some had served over ten years. At SoftContact, rotation was not needed because all members acquired voting rights at general meetings after completing their probation period (no separate board meetings took place).[2]

In employment, Custom Products had a two-stage interview process that assessed behavioural characteristics (values and philosophy) before invitation to an interview to assess job skills. Applicants were required to fill in an application form (CVs were not accepted). This was similar to SoftContact where formal applications were processed in accordance with a carefully designed equal opportunity process, including interviews that assessed both job skills and suitability for co-operative management. These formal approaches were less in evidence at Trading Trust where paid staff were selected, at least in part, on the basis of their faith. From a staff perspective, however, this was regarded as a key benefit of working there. Rights Now! also had relatively informal processes that sought to employ and develop people with learning disabilities. Recruitment aimed to pair able-bodied and disabled persons, with the disabled person leading (in accordance with charity objects).

Dispute resolution

Rights Now! and SoftContact were both characterised by vibrant debate, with social norms that facilitated dialogue between staff. Despite the 'official' separation of trustees and employees at Rights Now!, a CEO who withheld information triggered a transformation in the culture when their actions threatened organisational survival. In the wake of this, trustees and staff started taking lunch together. As one staff member reports:

> I think that relationship makes the board less detached from the workers on the ground, because they're not sat up in this hierarchy. I don't feel like it's all going on and I'm not contributing … and decisions are just being made. I feel that if it came to it, I could walk in there [the board meeting] and say 'this isn't ok', not that I've ever needed to, but I wouldn't feel frightened to do that or intimidated. (see Case 9.3)

Similar sentiments existed at SoftContact, and members reported strong exchanges in general meetings. However, in this case, all members had a constitutionally defined role in shared decision-making, leading to different reflections:

> The practicalities of exercising [democratic] 'choice' … led to heated arguments that made SoftContact – in the words of one founder – 'a hell of place to work'. Solutions to conflict, however, were inventive. Disputes over product choice were resolved by allocating each member free time to devote to his [sic] own projects … Counter-intuitive management practices arose (voluntary self-suspension, voluntary termination of contract) that challenge strongly held beliefs that 'management' is necessary to enforce discipline. In one case, a member left voluntarily after severe criticism by a client. Far from needing to discipline him, workers 'felt guilty about not "supporting" their colleague'. (see Case 9.4)

The absence of formal 'management' did not result in indiscipline: as Jackson and Parry (2008) note, self-management can lead to extraordinary levels of self-discipline on the part of members, and this can impact (negatively) on innovation. During downturns in trade, members would defer making expense claims, defer taking wages, take unpaid leave, take out loans to support either their families or the organisation, take temporary jobs in order to work fewer hours – anything that ensured organisational survival and prevented the need for redundancies. As trade improved, staff would return and claim the monies owed to them.

In contrast, at Trading Trust there was a deep-seated and underlying expectation that management, and their instructions, must always be respected. Because management-led change was constructed as a technical necessity – for the 'common good' – any conflict, disobedience or resistance to change programmes was portrayed as irrational behaviour, ignorance or stupidity, and an illegitimate challenge to managerial authority. Trading Trust's chair comments:

> I think the main challenge I've had is … bad relationships with staff. Occasionally you get someone who's not quite fitting and it causes unhappiness. I think that's been the main challenge because the difficulty is … it's hard to sack people so you might think someone's the source of a problem but you can't just say, right, you're out mate. You've got a procedure to go through. (see Case 9.1)

Those who did not comply left the organisation, or were ostracised until they did. Similar processes of ostracism were noted in findings at Custom Products, although this was managed through a 'softer' approach to dispute resolution with HR staff following disciplinary and grievance procedures learned during **CIPD** courses. After 2003, HR staff at Custom Products decided not to enact formal disciplinary proceedings against staff. Instead they provided support for unhappy staff to leave the company. Staff reports of Custom Product's HRM practices, however, do not suggest that managers always sought solutions based on compromise.

These dispute resolution strategies can be related back to the ideologies of unitarism, pluralism and radicalism. In the case of the unitarism, a single system of authority exists and is codified to guide notions of right and wrong. In *authority-driven* cultures, the process of dispute resolution involves making judgements on whether discrete actions conform to the norms established by people in positions of authority. In contrast, radicalism tends to eschew rules that the parties in dispute did not create for themselves. In radical cultures, dispute resolution is a more *experience-driven* personal affair, to be resolved locally, rather than a normative affair to be resolved by reference to the norms of previous generations.

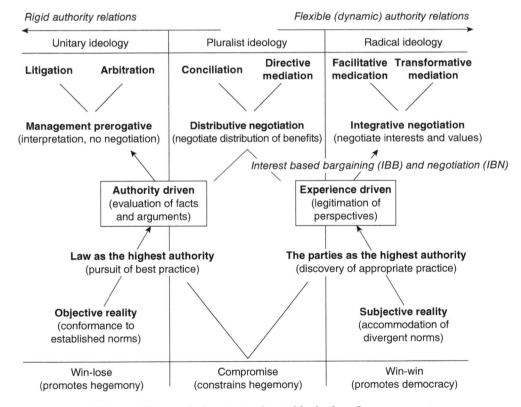

Figure 9.1   Linking conflict resolution strategies to ideologies of management

Source: Ridley-Duff and Bennett (2011), Figure 1

In relation to management ideology, the unitary approach frames authority structures and rules as an abstract but objective reality within which organisation members exist. Management style is geared to propagating and protecting authority structures so that no single person can subvert them. In contrast, pluralistic and radical approaches favour a more agile and dynamic response when management systems are challenged. Here, there is more bargaining, negotiating and sensitivity to constructed (subjective) realities. The preferred style of management is one that favours (rapid) evolution to survive in a changing environment.

Figure 9.1 summarises these options and show the links between the approaches to conflict resolution observed and the ideologies of management we have discussed.

Critiquing the case studies

Further insights into above cases can be achieved by assessing them using Purcell's (1987) theory of management styles. This further clarifies the range of choices made by social enterprise practitioners and facilitates a critical evaluation of their approach (see Figure 9.2). It could be argued that the legal form of organisation that members choose, and the organisational structures subsequently adopted, steer it towards a particular approach. However, the cases presented suggest a level of **pragmatism** and ambiguity.

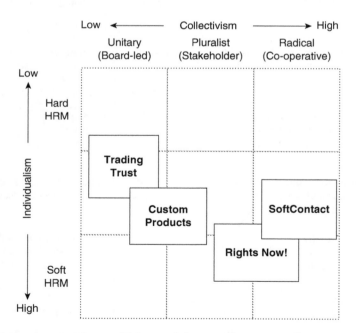

Figure 9.2   Management styles applied to social enterprise case studies

Source: Purcell (1987), reprinted with permission of Wiley Blackwell

We have argued that the logic of charity law reinforces the view that employees are subordinate to board authority, taking on the role of servant in the master–servant relationship. Codes of good practice recommend a clear separation of governance and management functions (NCVO, 2005) so it follows that a charitable social enterprise would be encouraged (through law and codes of practice) to adopt a unitary approach to governance and management in the domain of employment. Case evidence suggests that this only has a limited impact. Trading Trust and SoftContact show a high degree of consistency between legal form and ideology, while Rights Now! and Custom Products have an ambiguous relationship to the discourses encouraged by their legal form.

Trading Trust is characterised by a unitary structure and ideology. Staff assume everyone in the organisation will benefit from decisions made at a senior level and tend to ignore or hide conflicts of interest. Its charity model and history are entrenched in operations and mechanisms for legitimising the authority of a select group of leaders (the trustees and chief officer) over a group of subordinate followers (staff and volunteers). While Custom Products has adopted a legal form that will more easily allow for democratic governance and management practices, it is taking time to change its culture. Proposals for a social council, and direct democracy in executive appointments and business planning, were rejected by an executive management group before they could be put to staff.

At Trading Trust, this orientation produces a 'hard' approach to HRM: practices focus on maximising control; jobs are considered to be relatively easy to fill and high turnover is not regarded as a problem; learning and development tend to focus on vocational courses of direct relevance or benefit to the organisation; and supervision is primarily a mechanism for holding staff to account for implementing board and management plans. Though Custom Products takes a softer approach, close scrutiny of the recruitment, induction and socialisation processes revealed deliberate use of psychological techniques to reinforce desired behaviours and beliefs. This screens out those who will not subscribe (or conform) to the company's stated social values. The appearance on the outside is 'soft', but internalised values have a distinctly 'hard' edge.

Moreover, within Trading Trust, board members were strongly motivated to meet legal obligations through the development of formal operational policies. The unitary approach to governance and management is thus manifest in a heavy bias towards written contracts, with the foundations of psychological contracts receiving little explicit attention. Again, although framed within a 'softer' approach to HRM and a stronger focus on psychological contracts, Custom Products created policies, procedures and practices that actively reinforced particular values through the exclusion of those who would not conform.

Our research suggests that acceptance and legitimisation of certain approaches are associated with the coherence between governance and management practices and the social values expressed in an organisation's management ideology. It is, therefore, incoherent for an organisation espousing egalitarian social values to employ a **totalitarian style** of governance and management. Nevertheless, it appears in the case of

Trading Trust that such an approach is adopted. Unfortunately, for employees in Trading Trust and Custom Products who can envisage an alternative to the status quo, their alternatives are seen as subversive, and their treatment is at odds with rhetorical claims about social values. In relation to conflict and dispute resolution, both organisations lean towards a unitary (authority-driven) approach, which ultimately promotes **hegemony**, though the means by which this is achieved varies.

In contrast to Trading Trust, the organisational members of Rights Now! have made a deliberate decision to challenge the dominant norms suggested by the charity form. While there was no indication that board members or managers in Rights Now! would knowingly flout legal requirements, they created practices that transcended the boundaries of a traditional charity model and share similarities with SoftContact. Unlike SoftContact, whose legal form is arguably more amenable to a radical management ideology, Rights Now! – as a charitable company – is, by necessity, characterised by a unitary structure. Nevertheless, it has created and sustained a radical ethos as a pragmatic response to a former chief officer withholding vital information.

Organisational members in Rights Now! and SoftContact see organisations as being constituted by diverse groups 'whose pursuit of disparate sectional interests inevitably produces manifestations of conflict' (Darwin et al., 2002: 97). Even though SoftContact had no CEO, it evolved a highly formalised recruitment and induction process, giving its culture a slightly harder edge than Rights Now!. Within this, there was constitutional support for conflict between various organisational stakeholders, including employees, rendering conflict itself as 'normal', and producing regular creative transformations in practice.[3] Power is thus a central concept within these organisations, as it is used to explain relationships between people (Ridley-Duff and Ponton, 2013).

The complex decisions made by trustees and managers occur within a moral framework where 'managers have to judge their actions not only in terms of their efficiency but also by whether or not they are morally correct' (Garvey and Williamson, 2002: 7). The moral and social values of Rights Now! and SoftContact are thus embedded in practices throughout the organisations, and they are explicit about how there is an environment conducive to sharing ideas and helping each other to solve problems. A critical factor appears to be recognition that the workplace – and involvement in decision-making – is potentially a rich learning opportunity. Clawson (1996: 8) describes this as a shift away from a 'bureaucratic way' where 'the boss knows best' to a 'process way' where 'the process owner knows best'.

Such an approach is characteristic of soft HRM (see Chapter 12) that *also* promotes the possibility of alternative modes of practice located in **democratic** discourse. Here, the importance of the psychological contract surpasses that of written contracts and procedures. This undermines and displaces **technocratic**, top-down management through asking ethical questions about collective priorities (Forrester, 1989). Its purpose is to 'open up radically new understandings of organisational life that have potential to promote new modes of work that give voice to, and promote, critical reflection and autonomy' (Alvesson and Willmott, 1996: 114).

A Foucauldian view of management ideology and discourse

In critical management studies, there is a much greater emphasis on studying (and recognising) the power of language in determining who is included and excluded, and who is silenced or rendered invisible. In terms of management ideology, discourse renders visible or invisible any one or more of the following in various management discussions: member, employee, trustee, volunteer, director, manager, customer, volunteer, supplier, client, governor. Discourses construct them, influence their status, and shape how they are regarded in relation to each other (Foucault, 1970). Talk determines the rights that each will acquire, and the responsibilities that they will be expected to uphold. Discourse influences how people are defined and accepted into social entrepreneurial processes, and the power they have within them to shape other people's lives. While this linguistic approach may be considered a 'soft' perspective, it is experienced as 'hard' when encountered during enterprise development.

As Curtis (2008) argues, the power of one party or group to prevent social and economic activity on the basis that another person or group has not conformed to their social conventions reveals the power of discourse. It also illustrates how dominant groups impose their world view on others, and make support conditional on acceptance of their own **discursive reasoning**. One role of social enterprise education, therefore, is to make this explicit so that it is visible, amenable to debate and open to challenge.

In establishing an ideology of management that is fit for purpose in a social enterprise setting, it is important to consider whether the context within which a social enterprise is operating is chaotic, complex or predictable (see the discussion of Stacey's complexity theory in Chapter 8). In light of the context, decisions can then be taken about which people and processes will need to be involved to manage the context. It can also give clues to the institutional obstacles and enablers that a social enterprise many encounter. This applies to both 'soft' issues regarding philosophy, culture and the engagement of community members, staff, customers, suppliers and investors, and the 'hard' issues of access to technology, buildings, infrastructure and space for development.

However, managers of social enterprises need not be passive when presented with cultural norms that create obstacles to the pursuit of a social goal. By defining what is meant by terms such as 'social enterprise', 'social purpose', 'social value', 'social ownership', 'social innovation' and 'social return on investment', power is acquired over the legitimacy of social enterprise as a field of endeavour. Control of the terms provides control of the tacit rules that underpin different approaches to enterprise development. Moreover, if these definitions are accepted and spread, power shifts to the people who control access to, and use of, the new terms (Parkinson and Howarth, 2008; Dey and Teasdale, 2013).

Class exercise: The Social Enterprise Mark and Co-operative Marque

In 2010, the Social Enterprise Mark Company launched a certification process for social enterprises to increase their brand value. The initiative created some controversy when it was found that worker co-operatives involved in the formation of the social enterprise movement were unlikely to satisfy eligibility criteria (Floyd, 2011; Ridley-Duff, 2011; Ridley-Duff and Southcombe, 2012). The International Co-operative Alliance provided a solution in 2013 by launching a Co-operative Marque. In any award system, management ideologies are embedded in eligibility criteria. Study the standards below and critically assess the management discourses they are committed to advancing.

Preparation

Examine the six criteria for the Social Enterprise Mark and supplementary documentation provided by the Social Enterprise Mark Company (further details can be found at: www.socialenterprisemark.org.uk/assessment/):

> To prove your social enterprise is creating social value, you should apply for Social Enterprise Mark certification. As agreed by the social enterprise sector in 2009, you must meet the social enterprise definition represented by the criteria:

- have social or environmental aims
- have own constitution and governance
- earn at least 50% income from trading (new starts pledge to meet this within 18 months)
- spend at least 50% profits fulfilling social or environmental aims
- distribute residual assets to social or environmental aims, if dissolved
- demonstrate social value

(As we write this chapter, The Social Enterprise Mark Company is launching its Social Enterprise Gold Mark too – see www.socialenterprisemark.org.uk/socialenterprise-goldmark/. You may like to study the 'gold' standard instead of the basic standard.)

Examine the ICA definition of a co-operative and the eligibility criteria for the Co-operative Marque (details at www.identity.coop):

- A co-operative is an autonomous association of persons united voluntarily to meet their common economic, social, and cultural needs and aspirations through a jointly owned and democratically controlled enterprise.
- Co-operatives are based on the values of self-help, self-responsibility, democracy, equality, equity and solidarity [and] believe in the ethical values of honesty, openness, social responsibility and caring for others.

Organisations are eligible for the Co-operative Marque if they are:

- a co-operative or group of co-operatives
- an organisation committed to the seven co-operative principles (see Chapter 1)
- an organisation dedicated to serving co-operatives.

Activity

On your own, then as a group, consider the eligibility of each of the following social economy projects for both awards. What advice would you give them about the match between their ideology of social enterprise and the ideology embedded in the Social Enterprise Mark and Co-operative Marque?

1 An enterprise incorporated as a company limited by shares, structured to ensure that each workforce member has one vote when there are decisions about distribution and reinvestment of trading surpluses.
2 A trading charity with social and environmental projects, in which strategic decisions are taken by an independent board after proposals are submitted to it by an appointed manager.
3 A network of educators, researchers and consultants organised as an unincorporated association to create and distribute Open Source software, and Creative Commons IP to voluntary groups, charities, co-operatives, mutuals and social businesses.

Further materials for seminars are available on the companion website at: www.sagepub.co.uk/ridleyduff.

In the case of the Social Enterprise Mark, a paradox exists that a commitment to shared ownership and participatory management implicit in a CME is not regarded as evidence of a social goal or benefit unless it is written into the constitution as the organisation's 'social purpose' (Finlay, 2011). The latest information from Balance (Bull, 2007), which now contains 751 assessments (see Chapter 8), indicates that 'participation' and 'stakeholder governance' are the third and fourth most developed management skills. Why are they only part of a 'gold standard' when it is regarded as such a high priority among actually existing social enterprises?

The SEM requires that implicit (embedded) values evidenced by incorporating as a co-operative must be made explicit in Articles of Association. Bearing in mind growing evidence that 80–90 per cent of populations in Anglo-American cultures are being impoverished by the operations of private corporations (Achbar et al., 2004; *Capitalism: A Love Story*, 2009; Norton and Ariely, 2011), any business approach that reverses the trend (through a statutory commitment to socialised ownership and control) is surely a *de facto* social enterprise? The intention to be social is made crystal clear by the corporate form adopted rather than the inclusion of an 'object' in Articles of Association.

Devising enterprise forms, structures and processes that actively *prevent* the impoverishment of working people and consumers is not only a management competence but also a management ideology. How important is it that management education for social enterprise goes beyond techniques to *relieve* impoverishment to include enterprise designs and management processes that *prevent* impoverishment? In short, what contribution does management ideology play in reproducing or ending the processes of impoverishment at work (Piketty, 2014)?

Class exercise: Reversing exploitation using the FairShares Model

Read the short article 'The case for FairShares' on the companion website at: www.sagepub.co.uk/ridleyduff, then answer the following questions.

1 Define the term 'primary stakeholders' for the purpose of this discussion so that students are aware of the interests of: social entrepreneurs (founders); producers and employees (labour); customers and service users (users); social and community investors (investors).
2 In the private and voluntary sectors, how is power and wealth *accumulated* by managers and owners?
3 How can enterprises be redesigned so that power and wealth is *distributed* to primary stakeholders?
4 Apply the FairShares Model to an enterprise of your choice: what aspects of its ownership, governance and management would need to change before it could claim alignment with the FairShares Model?
5 Introduce students to the FairShares Model Enterprise (Example) on Loomio at: www.loomio.org/g/ugICXanW/fairshares-model-enterprise-an-example.

So, is it sensible for the *language of private enterprise* (embodied in concepts such as 'purposes/objects', 'incorporation', 'business', 'accounting' and 'profits') to be at the heart of the definition of *social* enterprise? One of the key contrasts between the two awards is the language. In place of 'purposes and objects' (Social Enterprise Mark) are 'needs and aspirations' (Co-operative Marque). In place of 'incorporation' is 'voluntary association'. Furthermore, Social Enterprise Mark charges people to be assessed against its criteria, while the Co-operative Marque is free to applicants who meet the criteria. In this act alone, the Social Enterprise Mark Company belongs to the economy of market relations while the Co-operative Marque belongs to the mutual economy (see Part 1 – Introduction).

However, the language of the Co-operative Marque is also based on terms that the *philanthropic* community would criticise. It is based on Big Society type language (self-help, self-responsibility and autonomy), the values of liberalism (democracy equality, equity, solidarity) and normative ethical values (honesty, openness, social responsibility and caring for others). Only some commitments (social responsibility and caring for others) are fully aligned with philanthropy, while others (self-help, self-responsibility, autonomy) align with Big Society rhetoric. Does this imply that the Social Enterprise Mark supports a management ideology more oriented towards CTAs and non-mutual SRBs, rather than CMEs? And is the Co-operative Marque more oriented towards CMEs and SRBs constituted as mutual enterprises?

Both award systems are gaining support, but which offers a better framework for the development of the social economy? For the Social Enterprise Mark, trading, incorporation and profitability, previously the *means* rather than the *ends* of social economy activity, have succumbed to the power of a 'business' discourse and become *ends* in themselves (Dart, 2004). The Social Enterprise Mark contains few of the 'ends' that appeared in the statement of social enterprise advanced by the Social Enterprise Partnership in 1994, or by Social Enterprise London in its 1997 **Memorandum and Articles of Association**. SELs articles specified support for 'participative democracy', 'equal opportunity', 'social justice' and 'co-operative economic development' as objects. The Co-operative Marque retains these commitments, but such language appears only in the Social Enterprise Gold Mark, and not the standard Social Enterprise Mark.

Conclusions

In this chapter, it is worth noting that the relationships between stakeholders, and their interdependencies, present strategic choices to board members and managers of social enterprises. In making choices, they also respond to external and internal accountability 'pulls' (see Figure 9.3).

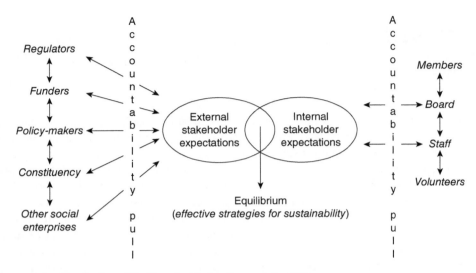

Figure 9.3   Developing effective strategies for sustainability

Source: based on Coule (2008: 256), with permission from the author

We have highlighted that accountability relationships are multiple, diverse, conflicting and fluid. They are also central to organisational sustainability, as many stakeholders have the potential to affect survival. This challenges the idea that 'control' emanates from the top of an organisation. The core theoretical issue is that when different stakeholders' expectations are aligned, there are fewer difficulties. However, when they are not, organisational members must decide whose expectations should be prioritised (or live with their differences). Despite the acknowledgement by many that board and staff members within social enterprises are stakeholders in terms of accountability, there is little research that explicitly considers the way in which accountability pressures can influence the interpretation of governance and staff roles, and the implication this has for board–staff interactions. Our research suggests that a central issue here is the way in which organisational members apply (often implicit and taken-for-granted) social values and theories about the nature of people and organisations to the governance and management of their social enterprises.

   To study, govern and manage social enterprise involves thinking about economics, philosophy, politics and ethics. Accepting the argument presented above – that effective strategies for sustainability involve devising a system of relations that can manage competing stakeholder expectations – consideration must be given to who says what the job is and how it should be done, and how people are affected by doing it one way rather than another (Grey, 2005). Two cases presented a challenge to the commonly held view that management structures in 'for-purpose' organisations, by virtue of a strong sense of altruism, are more democratic than their private and public sector counterparts (Markham et al., 2001; Alatrista and Arrowsmith, 2004). Ultimately, management ideology is more likely to be a result of the social values held by those involved in governance and management than of the sector in which it resides (Green, 2014), or the legal form it takes. It cannot be taken for granted that a social enterprise will attract people who are committed to participatory governance and management styles. It may (to fulfil its mission) employ people who are in need of a job and who (at least at the time of joining) do not subscribe to the political goals of the founders or governing body (Amin, 2009). We exit these debates by raising an important question for the chapters that follow: how can social enterprises be institutionalised in a way that ensures each stakeholder group is accountable to others?

Summary of learning

In this chapter, we have developed the arguments that:

The rationale for managing people is rooted in the ideology of management that emerges from the inter-play of personal values, the ecology within which the enterprise operates, and the discourses that shape management education in a given cultural setting.

Three 'discourses' on managing people (unitary, pluralist and radical) are linked to three norms in industrial relations based on the rights of investor-owners, managing agents and employees/members.

Practices derived from personal and organisational learning tend to override (and can conflict with) the dictates of legal form.

Accountability is complex, and accountability 'pulls' influence the attention given to framing the role of staff and governing body members.

Questions and possible essay assignments

1. What are the benefits and limitations of a 'radical' ideology in the management of social enterprises? (Frame your answer for more than one type of social enterprise.)
2. Critically assess the role of the Social Enterprise Mark and Co-operative Marque in normalising different ideologies of management.
3. 'A unitary ideology of management is a product of internal dynamics more than the external regulatory environment.' Using examples, discuss the extent to which you agree with this statement.

Further reading

Changes in management ideology often go to the heart of social enterprise and yet there are few specific texts that discuss it in detail. In terms of providing a detailed *critique* of the ideology of neo-liberalism (social enterprises are generally against it), there are numerous interesting and instructive documentaries including: *The Corporation* (2004, available on YouTube); a series of *Zeitgeist* films (2007, 2008 and 2011, all available via YouTube/Netflix) and *Capitalism: A Love Affair* released by Michael Moore in 2009.

Documentaries that explore alternative ideologies (of social entrepreneurship and member ownership) are now emerging. On social entrepreneurship, Ashoka promotes the film *Who Cares?* about social activists who turn to enterprise to achieve social goals (see www.whocaresthefilm.com/). For a more collective account of activism and its effects, see *The Take* (www.thetake.org/) about the recovered companies in Argentina. For member ownership in Spain and North America, *Shift Change* (http://shiftchange.org/) is a subtle and understated account of the way co-operative ownership affects a person's thinking. However, the account that still digs most deeply into history, and which provides a compelling and comprehensive account of the mechanisms that transformed the town of Mondragon is *The Mondragon Experiment* (www.youtube.com/watch?v=-obHJfTaQvw). Despite its age, it goes more deeply into *how* the impact of the changed ideology concretely affected the workers and residents in the area.

On sustainable development, it is hard to beat *The Story of Stuff* to understand how neo-liberalism contributes to unsustainability, and how sustainable development changes a person's mind-set from linear to holistic (systems) thinking (www.youtube.com/watch?v=9GorqroigqM).

A useful (short) teaching aid (on worker co-operatives) is available at: www.youtube.com/watch?v=qbZ8ojEuN5I – this visualisation deals effectively with the ideology of worker co-operation and its impact on the meaning of 'profit' and 'surplus', as well as the management practices that are followed in deciding how to distribute wealth more fairly.

Good textbooks on general management issues include *Managing and Organizations* (Clegg et al., 2008) – while not specifically about social enterprises, it is inclusive of alternative models of organising and the range of theory is helpful. To support SRBs, the textbook *Principles of Responsible Management* (Laasch and Conway, 2015) includes extensive discussion of sustainability and 'value-adding' enterprises. For the advanced student (studying for a doctorate), there are books on research practice – e.g. Johnson and Duberly's *Understanding Management Research: An Introduction to Epistemology* (2000) – that unpick the connections between philosophy and different approaches to management and management research.

Coule and Patmore's (2013) paper (recommended for Chapter 3) is a useful read in the context of this chapter as well. In addition, we have also selected four further papers to support student learning. Firstly, in the paper by Ridley-Duff (2007), communitarian and liberal philosophies are discussed in relation to unitarism and pluralism to identify different ways in which the logic of social enterprise differs from private enterprise. Secondly, we recommend the article on critical pedagogy for management education by Dehler et al. (2001), which considers how learning unfolds after a shift in management ideology. Next, we recommend Reedy and Leamonth (2009) who critique management education based on the principle of profit-maximisation, and open up a space to consider alternative ideologies of management. Lastly, we recommend Doherty et al. (2013), which examines the creation of the doctrines that underpinned the fair trade movement, and how these have changed as the ideology of multinational corporations has secured greater influence over time.

Further reading material is available on the companion website at: www.sagepub.co.uk/ridleyduff.

Useful resources

The Corporation: www.thecorporation.com/

FairShares Diagnostics: www.fairshares.coop/wordpress/diagnostics

The Mondragon Experiment: www.youtube.com/watch?v=-obHJfTaQvw

Shift Change: http://shiftchange.org/

The Story of Stuff: http://storyofstuff.org/movies/story-of-stuff/

The Take: www.thetake.org/

Who Cares?: www.whocaresthefilm.com/

Zeitgeist Channel (YouTube): www.zeitgeistmovie.com/

Notes

1 In the UK, charity law permits employee representatives at board meetings only with the consent of the Charity Commission, and this itself is contingent on the charity's articles permitting staff attendance at board meetings.
2 While it might be thought that this practice would be limited to small co-operatives, there is evidence it can scale up to a point. At Suma Wholefoods, where there are

nearly 100 members, all are invited to monthly general meetings, and votes are taken on resolutions prepared in advance. At Mondragon, where membership runs to hundreds in each business unit, general meetings of all members are held quarterly and elected governors meet monthly or fortnightly with appointed managers. With the advent of Loomio, participation in decision-making is straightforward even if a person cannot be present (they can vote using a smart phone, or by email).

3 Members of SoftContact talked of rejecting 'sacred cows' (i.e. culturally embedded ways of thinking) following decisions at their annual review. This was viewed as a product of their democratic decision-making and co-operative management practice.

Leadership, Social and Eco-entrepreneurship

10

Rory Ridley-Duff, Pam Seanor and Mike Bull

Learning objectives

In this chapter, we consider leaders and the concept of leadership, and social entrepreneurs and the concept of social entrepreneurship. By the end of this chapter you will be able to:

- describe and evaluate different theories of leadership
- distinguish between leaders and leadership
- apply leadership theory to social entrepreneurs, social entrepreneurship and eco-entrepreneurship
- compare and contrast individual and collective approaches to socio-ecological entrepreneurship
- critically discuss the drivers and barriers to the practice of different kinds of entrepreneurship.

The key arguments that will be developed in this chapter are:

- Leader-centric and follower-centric theories of leadership emphasise individual and collective processes that produce recognised leaders.

(Continued)

(Continued)

- Leadership can be centralised, co-produced or distributed among a group of people.
- Entrepreneurship theory focuses on a person's or group's capacity to spot opportunities, innovate, assess risk and attract resources.
- Social and eco-entrepreneurship focus on the application of entrepreneurial skills to create social value and enhance the natural environment.
- Different theories of social and eco-entrepreneurship are related to different theories of leadership.

Introduction

In the previous chapters on strategic management and management ideologies, we have emphasised how the different values and assumptions that people bring to the process of social enterprise development leads to many diverse practices. These assumptions also impact on leadership style and the choice of leader. They may even lead to questioning whether leaders (in the formal appointed sense) are needed at all. It is, therefore, helpful to understand theories of leadership to make informed choices about an organisation's context and approach to leadership.

Moreover, the assumptions we make about leadership will, in turn, influence the level of support we give to different approaches to social entrepreneurship. Social entrepreneurs are seen as people committed to radically changing their society, and who benefit their communities. As Bill Drayton, the founder of Ashoka, comments:

> Social entrepreneurs are not content just to give a fish, or teach how to fish. They will not rest until they have revolutionised the fishing industry. (http://philippines.ashoka.org/node/3829, accessed 21 May 2010)

What approaches to leadership and entrepreneurship make socially enterprising activities sustainable? Might the style of leadership vary in different ventures?

So, this chapter explores and discusses both leaders and leadership. As Hosking and Morley (1991) ask: Who are they? What do they do? With whom do they do it? The chapter starts by looking at these questions through the lens of leadership theory, and then moves on to consider the effect that this has on both the theory and practice of social entrepreneurship.

Why leadership matters

Hosking and Morley (1991: 240) describe leadership as 'a more or less skilful process of organizing, achieved through negotiation, to achieve acceptable influence over the description and handling of issues within and between groups'. The systematic study of leadership offers the prospect of being able to develop an understanding of two things. Firstly, it helps to understand the character attributes and skills that leaders acquire, and which both they and others believe are necessary to improve the quality of leadership in an organisation. This is helpful not only to those responsible for leadership, but also to those who have to recruit leaders (and entrepreneurs) or who want to know how to work effectively with them. Secondly, it helps to understand the contexts in which different approaches to leadership are effective. Social enterprises are varied: small, large, rural, urban, in highly regulated and unregulated industries, growing rapidly, or not at all. Add to these variables the many histories that have shaped their development (Spear et al., 2007) and the need for a theoretical understanding becomes more urgent.

In the case of social enterprise, how can users of a service lead its development? How can managers, staff and volunteers combine their efforts in projects to tackle entrenched problems in their communities? One common assumption is that stakeholders in a social enterprise share a common goal or vision that enables them to work together effectively (Pearce, 2003). Making this assumption leads to an emphasis on 'unitary' control, with leadership controlled by a board and/or social entrepreneur. What if the assumption about shared values is mistaken (Willmott, 1993)? Or what if shared values are 'manufactured' to promote passivity and compliance among the organisation's shareholders, membership and workforce (*Manufacturing Consent*, 1992; Alvesson and Deetz, 2000)? How is this type of leadership theorised, and what entrepreneurial approaches might prevent it occurring?

Class exercise: Which social enterprise values lead you?

In Chapter 2, there was an exercise examining the prevalence of different social enterprise values within the wider social economy, which also invite you to state which are most important to you. These questions can also be used to assess leadership in a social enterprise by examining which value commitments are practiced rarely, occasionally, frequently and routinely. Use this diagnostic tool to explore which social enterprise commitments are important to an organisation you are working with (or for).

- Ask students to bring a smart phone, tablet or laptop to class.
- Get each student (and tutor) to fill out the diagnostic survey: www.quicksurveys. com/s/d6RWx3.
- Explore results from this (and previous) surveys at: http://tolu.na/1ChWSml.
- Which characteristics are most fully operationalised in your social enterprise?

(Continued)

(Continued)

- Which characteristics are most important to your organisation?
- Using Table 2.2 (see Chapter 2), assess which approach(es) to social enterprise you are developing.

You can find further supporting materials on the companion website at: www.sagepub. co.uk/ridleyduff.

A key challenge for those working in and with social enterprises is how to help others to be aware of the diverse range of abilities and cultural assumptions that influence the leadership process. All those working in organisations (not just leaders themselves) can benefit from understanding how leadership processes affect their organisation. For this reason, this chapter is aimed not just at 'leaders', but also at 'followers', and considers not only the question of how people lead, but also how leaders are guided and controlled by their followers.

Lastly, those who acquire leadership roles are charged with developing, controlling and excluding people, with nurturing an environment where conversations can take place as well as curtailing conversations that put organisational or institutional survival at risk. They are variously expected to be inspiring, to prioritise, to decide on and give meaning to situations, and to direct the organisation towards its (social) objectives (Smircich and Morgan, 1982).

Theories of leadership

The dominant approach to studying and writing about leadership is to focus on the leader. Prior to the 1940s, most leadership studies explored the qualities of the leader and their leadership style, and assessed their effectiveness by researching the views of their followers. A good example of this is the study by Lewin et al. (1939) who created environments and trained leaders to apply 'authoritarian', 'democratic' and **'laissez-faire'** principles, then studied the behaviours and feelings of those they led. Authoritarian leaders gave instructions and did not permit any challenge to their authority. Democratic leaders adopted a participative style of management, while laissez-faire leaders encouraged group members to make decisions for themselves.[1] The experiments were repeated many times (White and Lippett, 1960) and findings from them suggested that:

- Laissez-faire climates are not the same as democracy:
  - less work is done and it is of poorer quality
  - there is more play in 'laissez-faire' groups
  - 95 per cent of group members prefer a 'democratic leader' to a 'laissez-faire' leader.

- Democracy can be efficient:

  o although the quantity of work can be greater under an autocracy …
  o … work motivation is stronger, particularly when the leader is not present
  o originality is greater in democracy.

- Autocracy leads to:

  o hostility, aggression and submissive behaviour
  o rebellion or people dropping out of the group
  o more discontent than in democracy
  o loss of individuality.

Some substantive criticism can be made of these studies. Firstly, 'democratic' leaders were not elected (and could not be sacked by group members), so issues of legitimacy and trust created by a democratic process are not reproduced in the design of the research. Secondly, questions can be raised over the training of the leaders charged with 'laissez-faire' leadership. Their approach to encouraging collective decision-making and individual participation (Pateman, 1970) was not informed by the knowledge underpinning the high-performing companies and institutions of today (Whyte and Whyte, 1991; Cooperrider et al., 2014). Lastly, no comparison was made with self-managing groups. As a result, the studies do not compare the performance of groups with emergent leadership to those who have appointed leaders. They only compare leadership styles within a paradigm that accepts the dominance of leader-centric theories.[2] Nevertheless, the findings are consistent with the research of Coch and French (1948) who found that change projects were more successful if command and control approaches were replaced by participative approaches.

More recently, writers studying leadership in the private and third sectors (Hubbard, 2005; Jackson and Parry, 2008) have been more sensitive to the distinction between leaders (as people) and leadership (as a process). Part of this shift is a backlash against leader-centric approaches, fuelled by an improved understanding of corporate scandals in the 1980s and 1990s. As Guthey and Jackson (2005) argue, there is now greater receptivity towards alternative theories of leadership (as a process) that may be 'co-produced' (shared by two people), 'distributed' (shared by more than two people) or 'collective' (driven by a 'grassroots' action). Table 10.1 summarises the broadening of leadership studies and the implications of alternative perspectives.

In this consideration of (social and eco-) entrepreneurship, it is worth pausing to evaluate the implications of different perspectives on leadership. The contrast between leader- and follower-centric views of leadership rests on the relative importance attached to the internal qualities of the leader (and their leadership behaviours) and the group processes that shape (and limit the effects of) their leadership. Leader-centric approaches have tended to emphasise the characteristics, traits and competencies of the entrepreneur (London and Morfopoulos, 2010). Within this tradition, there is a drift towards organisation charts and hierarchies of power as a way of

Table 10.1   Theories of leadership

Theory type	Key assumption	Research approaches and implications	Grounded in
Leader-centred theories	Leadership is a product of personal qualities and character traits	We can understand leadership by focusing on who the leader is (leader identity) and what they do (leader behaviour). If we understand their character traits and behaviours, we can screen for people with particular personalities and provide training to mould their behaviour	Liberal philosophy, rationalism
Higher-purpose theories of leadership	Leadership is the product of pursuing a higher purpose, such as support for the intellectual and moral transformation of followers	We can better understand leadership if we investigate the moral frameworks that underpin leaders' actions, and how this influences the actions of followers. If we can do this, we can discover the transformative power of leadership, and increase our capacity for ethically informed leadership behaviour	Virtue ethics, servant leadership
Follower-centred theories	Leadership is a product of followers socialising their leaders, and constructing stories about their leadership	We can understand leadership by focusing on the way followers value particular qualities, create stories, and exercise political control over leaders in their community. If we can understand this, we can interpret which processes and support will enhance a person's leadership potential within a particular community	Communitarian philosophy, interpretivism
Cultural perspectives on leadership	Leadership is a product of culturally defined activities, norms and rituals that reproduce the legitimacy of leaders and the leadership function	We can understand leadership by focusing on the ways leaders socialise (and are socialised) through rituals and stories in order to legitimise the institution of leadership. If we can understand this, we can evaluate the process by which people become leaders, and the ways in which they reproduce the institution of leadership	Institutional theory
Critical perspectives on leadership	Shared forms of leadership that are co-authored, distributed and collective in character have been mystified and obscured by leader-centric theory	We can better understand leadership by deconstructing dominant leadership discourses and re-evaluating how they reflect political interests and power. In doing so, we can re-evaluate 'lost' or 'hidden' discourses, and consider the evidence for co-leadership, distributed leadership and leadership through collective action	Critical theory

Source: an interpretation of Jackson and Parry (2008)

understanding how entrepreneurs practise leadership: the top of the organisational chart shows the entrepreneur, then senior managers, then middle managers, and then the staff they supervise (Hosking and Morley, 1991). From this perspective, organisations are designed to support an authority-driven model of leadership, whereby leaders instruct 'subordinates' on the achievement of organisational goals. This model propagates control downward through the organisation based on an assumption that 'superiors' are equipped to lead their 'subordinates'.

During the 1940s, leader-centric theories underwent a period of intense research. Prior to 1948, it was assumed that character traits differentiated leaders from followers (Stogdill, 1974). Despite popular assumptions about the qualities of 'great' people, systematic study revealed no consistent correlation between character traits and success as a leader. Jackson and Parry (2008) regard these research programmes as historically important for discrediting trait theories of leadership. However, the surge of interest in (social and eco-) entrepreneurship has reignited interest in trait theories, often under the guise of competencies. For example, in one of the most recent additions to the social entrepreneurship literature, London and Morfopoulos instruct us to:

> Be grateful for social entrepreneurs. They are driven by an overarching desire to improve society … They are movers and shakers – people who are not satisfied with the status quo and are always trying to make things better. They care, and they are action-oriented. (2010: 2)

This characterisation of the social entrepreneur as a visionary leader is propagated by umbrella organisations (Ashoka, Skoll Foundation, UnLtd). For example, heroic social entrepreneurs are described by Jeff Skoll, who funded the Skoll Centre for Social Entrepreneurship at Oxford University, as people who:

> have a vision of the future and will stop at nothing to see that future come true. It is up to us to help them succeed in order to ensure that the failures of the past do not become the failures of the future, and to build a world where all people, regardless of geography, background, or economic status, enjoy and employ the full range of their talents and abilities. (Nicholls, 2006: vi)

The policy implications of these beliefs are that agencies should assist dynamic individuals who are catalysts for social change (Martin and Osberg, 2007) and pay less attention to established sociological knowledge about community organising, group processes and organisation development. Leaders who see themselves as 'visionary' and who are lauded through award systems may even come to believe that the design of institutions and the forms they take do not matter (Black and Nicholls, 2004) because social entrepreneurs will check out 'the market' in legal forms and choose the one that suits their needs.

Chell (2007) points out that the popular image of 'economic entrepreneurs' differs from that of 'social entrepreneurs' only in respect of the mission or goal they pursue. The above description acts to reinforce the stereotype that entrepreneurs (of whatever type) are energetic and 'driven' people. Such an image is problematic not only because empirical research does not support such a simplistic statement, but also because it may be an effect of followership rather than a reflection on the leader. Moreover, Paton (1989) reports that half of all entrepreneurial activity is a response to personal or community hardship, and that people become entrepreneurial because it is their best survival option in a given context (Case 10.1). This gives a new meaning to the notion of a 'driven' entrepreneur: they are driven by circumstances as well as innate character traits (*The Take*, 2004).

The view that leadership and entrepreneurship is all about character ignores the knowledge that such entrepreneurs develop over time, and the crafting of the institutions they initiate by hundreds, thousands or even tens of thousands of people. The modesty in the writing of Lewis (1954) is striking. Even after 40 years of sustained growth at the John Lewis Partnership, he argued that it cannot call itself a 'success' unless the institutional arrangements survive both himself and his successor's successor. In short, Lewis argued for entrepreneurship that focused on the integrity and sustainability of institutional relationships that share wealth, power and information, and which rely on the commitment of thousands of people – not a single leader – for their durability (Erdal, 2000, 2011; Cathcart, 2009). Similarly, at Mondragon, despite attempts by his followers to modernise his lifestyle, Fr Arizmendi remained committed to cycling (not driving) around the region, living modestly rather than extravagantly (Whyte and Whyte, 1991).[3]

Despite this, the resurgence of interest in trait theories of leadership has continued to grow. It takes an interesting turn in *Good to Great* (Collins, 2001, 2006). Despite personal scepticism, Collins explains at some length how his research team insisted that there were personal qualities that contributed to long-term sustainability in the enterprises they studied. The research team eventually differentiated between 'level 4 leadership' based on a 'visionary' approach, extrovert personality and individual leadership, and 'level 5 leadership' that was rooted in 'humility' combined with a 'professional will' dedicated to participative leadership.

Case 10.1

Leading a social start-up: a regeneration agency view

I mean if you think about the people that have started business up, if you think about the Denzils of this world, if you think about the Pats of this world, if you expand that out to, you know ... Dave ... they are all charismatic, dogged. I mean you talked about a dog-eared business plan, they are dogged people. But it does take that individual to drive it, and I can't think of [pause] ... a successful social enterprise that I've come across that hasn't been driven by somebody who hasn't got a little bit more, there's a spark, there's something about them, there's a doggedness, there's a determination to succeed, there's a determination not to let the bureaucrats of this world stand in their way. (Regeneration agency manager).

It is worth, at this point, highlighting the difference between 'leader-centric' and 'higher-purpose' leadership, and the way this rests on an assumption that ethical values can be promoted through entrepreneurial action (see also Chapter 7). Collins argues that level 4 leaders make a difference while they are in post, but also that performance deteriorates rapidly after their departure. Level 5 leaders, on the other hand, focus on the 'higher purpose' of developing leadership capabilities throughout their organisation (or social network) and performance does not decline after their departure. Similar findings are reported in the non-profit sector (Hubbard, 2005; Crutchfield and McLeod-Grant, 2007). Hubbard found that qualities of calmness and emotional security among non-profit leaders are more strongly correlated with sustainability than extroversion and charisma.

Case 10.2

The soft side of leadership

Individuals are important and leaders or leadership is important. The trouble is I think it's just more complicated than that ... leadership can be that, you know, thrusting, setting the direction and you know punching the air ahead of the staff following you, and all that sort of thing. That is sometimes appropriate, but so is the sort of peer support, putting yourself in the position of supporting your managers as their peer; so, a kind of equal relationship and a supportive relationship. (Social enterprise manager)

The concept of level 5 leadership – crucially – places emphasis on the quality of the interactions between leaders and followers, and the behaviours that influence these interactions (Case 10.2). They can be studied not just from a leader-centric perspective, but also by considering their effects on followers (follower-centric theory) or the impact of culture and discourse on their legitimacy (a cultural and critical perspective). In follower-centric studies (Meindl, 1993, 1995), five aspects of the leader–follower relationship are highlighted (Table 10.2).

As Smircich and Morgan (1982) also argue, leaders have an impact on followers not only in terms of devising strategies for action, and issuing instructions, but also through the meanings that they ascribe to events that are taking place in their organisation(s). Leadership, more than any other role, is based on 'attempting to frame and define the reality of others' (1982: 258). For example, the cultural and critical perspectives explored in the previous two chapters (approaches to strategic management, the deployment of a management style) are all attempts to create a 'shared reality' and shape the organisational choices open to different stakeholders.

Table 10.2   Follower-centric theories of leadership

Leader–follower dynamic	Interpretation
Followers accept leadership influence	Leaders can only be leaders if accepted by followers. Leadership is legitimised when it is acted upon by followers, leadership is 'in the eye of the 'follower' rather than the leader
Followers moderate leadership impact	Followers have to interpret the desires of leaders, and can moderate the impact of the leader when they operationalise their instructions
Followers can find substitutes for leaders	If followers lose confidence in a leader, they can avoid them and seek advice from leader substitutes (i.e. other followers). High performance may be a product of leader substitutes, rather than the leader
Followers construct leaders and leadership	Leaders are 'constructed' through the stories of their followers, based more in myth than fact, and they sustain these constructions for their own well-being by reproducing particular outcomes, then attributing them to the leader
Followers are leaders	There is no justifiable distinction between leaders and followers: leadership is a 'shared' process that is distributed throughout a group of people. All stakeholder groups affect organisation sustainability, not just formally appointed leaders

Class exercise: Individual and collective models of leadership

Bill Drayton established Ashoka to advance social entrepreneurship. It now operates internationally and involves young people in creating change.
   Watch the following video:

   www.youtube.com/watch?v=DttTSJEO47g&feature=channel

Now critically analyse:

1 The theory or theories of leadership that inform Ashoka's approach.
2 The theory or theories of leadership that Ashoka fellows apply in their enterprises.

Now compare your analysis of Ashoka fellows to leadership in the Venezuelan co-operatives. Watch the following video:

   www.youtube.com/watch?v=yu5DhOHLJ-s

Now consider the following questions:

1 How does leadership function in the Venezuelan co-operatives?
2 What theory or theories of leadership best explain their approach?

Critical perspectives on leadership

A focus on followers, culture and discourse is the starting point for developing a critical perspective on leadership. The question arises, 'What kind of leadership skills should be developed?' Hubbard (2005) argues that leadership in the private sector offers little insight into the development needs of the social enterprise sector. She makes this claim on the basis that leadership development in the private sector is based on the needs of (and findings from) multinational corporations seeking to maximise profit.

Grenier (2006: 137) finds that 'it appears that social entrepreneurship is seeking its learning and legitimacy from business, as well as seeking to make connection into the business world where civil society organisations have generally struggled and often failed'. She continues by suggesting that 'some care therefore needs to be taken as to what extent social entrepreneurship offers an alternative to existing forms of social change, or to what extent it is simply the extension and intrusion of "business" into the "social" and political arenas' (Grenier, 2006: 138). Amin et al. (2002: 125) make the point that in social enterprise 'the key move is to … challenge the dominant conception of the mainstream, rather than to cast the social economy in the image of the mainstream and in the interstices that the mainstream has abandoned'. Amin's argument, therefore, is that the notion of social enterprise leadership should emanate from practices that are effective in the social economy, rather than through the adoption of private or public sector models. With this in mind, we turn our attention to whether social and eco-entrepreneurship are products of group processes, rather than the enactment of an individual's vision.

Perspectives on entrepreneurship

Whereas the study of leadership has developed to focus on understanding the relationships and interactions between leaders and followers, entrepreneurship has a different focus (Table 10.3). Chell (2007) charts three separate strands in entrepreneurship studies. Firstly, there is entrepreneurship as a field of study that focuses on different forms of entrepreneurial behaviour. In this sense, it is a professional discipline that seeks to define and apply knowledge that supports the endeavours of enterprising individuals. Secondly, she draws an analogy between the musician and their musicianship (a term which refers to increased skill levels that are acquired through their practical applications) and the entrepreneur and entrepreneurship. In this sense, entrepreneurship refers to the way entrepreneurs hone and craft their skills and apply their knowledge to practice. Interestingly, Outsios (2013) found that this had been clarified by the House of Lords (2003) which declared that entrepreneurship is 'the mind-set and process by which an individual or group successfully identifies and exploits a new idea or opportunity'. The notions of 'mind-set' and 'process' were useful to Outsios's study of the mind-set of eco-entrepreneurship, and the processes that eco-entrepreneurs establish to support their (social) entrepreneurial ventures.

There is also a third focus, around which Chell (2007) argues that the symbiotic relationship between opportunity recognition and innovation provides a basis for a 'convergent theory' of entrepreneurship based on common ground between the 'economic entrepreneur' (focused on wealth creation) and the 'social entrepreneur' (who seeks a social/environmental outcome). Both seek out opportunities. Both innovate. By extension, social entrepreneurs also take risks and have skills in attracting resources, meaning that social entrepreneurs can be studied through established frameworks in entrepreneurship research.

Table 10.3   Social entrepreneurship research that draws on established entrepreneurship concepts

Aspect of entrepreneurship	Key contributions
Risk assessment	Peredo and McLean (2006); Meyskens, Carsrud and Cardozo (2010)
Innovation	Sullivan Mort, Weerawardena and Carnegie (2003); Alvord, Brown and Letts (2004); Austin, Stevenson and Wei-Skillern (2006); Martin and Osberg (2007); Tapsell and Woods (2010); Perrini, Vuro and Costanzo (2010)
Resource management	Mair and Marti (2006); Tracey and Jarvis (2007); Seelos and Mair (2009); Perrini, Vuro and Costanzo (2010)
Opportunity recognition	Robinson (2006); Tracey and Jarvis (2007); Zahra, Gedajlovic, Neubaum and Shulman (2009); Perrini, Vuro and Costanzo (2010)

One of the more widely quoted definitions of social entrepreneurship – one that focuses on an additional capacity (while also identifying opportunities, attracting resources and forging social systems) – is advanced by Martin and Osberg:

> We define social entrepreneurship as having the following three components: (1) identifying a stable but inherently unjust equilibrium that causes the exclusion, marginalization, or suffering of a segment of humanity that lacks the financial means or political clout to achieve any transformative benefit on its own; (2) identifying an opportunity in this unjust equilibrium, developing a social value proposition, and bringing to bear inspiration, creativity, direct action, courage, and fortitude, thereby challenging the stable state's hegemony; and (3) forging a new, stable equilibrium that releases trapped potential and alleviates the suffering of the targeted group, and through imitation and the creation of a stable ecosystem around the new equilibrium ensuring a better future for the targeted group and even society at large. (2007: 35)

Through a focus on the capacity to identify an 'unjust equilibrium', ethics features centrally in the study of social entrepreneurship (see Chapter 7). Conventional entrepreneurship theory tends to be neutral about the morality of entrepreneurial action by focusing on the commercial exploitation of opportunities that benefit an investment community. Martin and Osberg's definition refocuses attention on the capacity to spot 'unjust equilibria' in society and take action to redistribute wealth and power. Looked at another way, Martin and Osberg identify an important conceptual difference between entrepreneurship that privatises and entrepreneurship that socialises wealth and power (Table 10.4). Ridley-Duff (2012) goes further by suggesting examples of institutions and processes that create unjust equilibria (by privatising rights to control different types of capital), and comparing them to institutions and organisations that have been created by social entrepreneurs to (re-)socialise the control of capital.

Table 10.4   Entrepreneurship, privatisation and socialisation of assets

	Privatisation (creating 'unjust' equilibria)	Socialisation (create 'just' equilibria)
Key characteristic	The acquisition of public/social rights by private individuals/corporations to bring capital** under private (management) control	The sharing of public/social rights among groups representing primary stakeholders* so they can jointly control an enterprise's capital
Human capital	Traditional Copyright Law, Encyclopaedia Britannica, Patents	Creative Commons, Wikipedia, Open Source Software
Intellectual property management	Acquisition of rights to fully formed ideas and designs created by producers/employees so they can be commercially exploited or removed from the market	Distribution and/or sharing of fully formed ideas so that producers can freely use, share and exchange them in new creative works, and prevent their removal from the market
Social capital	Marks & Spencer (Europe), IBM (US), Foxconn (China)	John Lewis (Europe), MindValley (Asia), SEMCO (South America)
Governance and control	Exclusion of primary stakeholders from governance/audit (except as information providers); accountability of stakeholders to executive management/private owners	Equal participation of primary stakeholders in governance and audit; accountability of executives to primary stakeholders through elected governing bodies or statutory requirements
Natural capital	Private control of natural resources (e.g. British Gas, Bechtel Corporation)	Co-operative and community energy projects (e.g. Denmark, Germany, Africa)
Resource management	Individual/corporate control of natural capital by corporate managers; commercial exploitation of 'common pool resources' (water, air, minerals, etc.)	Co-operative/mutual group control of natural resources by stewards and users; micro producer-consumer enterprises (e.g. home owners producing and consuming their own electricity)
Financial capital	Arsenal FC, Holland & Barrett, Enron	Barcelona FC, Suma Wholefoods, SEMCO
Ownership	Individual or corporate control over membership; shares issued in exchange for financial capital	Open membership/capital rights for primary stakeholders; shares issued in exchange for labour/consumer participation

* Primary stakeholders = workforce members, producers, customers and/or service users

** Capital = human, social, natural and financial

Source: based on Ridley-Duff (2012)

- For examples of socialisation see: www.worldblu.com/awardee-profiles/2014.php
- For examples of privatisation see: www.wsws.org/en/articles/2012/05/foxn-m12.html

This work by Ridley-Duff (2012) helps to distinguish the processes of commercial and social entrepreneurship, and critically questions whether acts that privatise ownership, intellectual property, governance and management rights can contribute to the creation of a social economy.[4] So, another way to make the distinction between commercial and social entrepreneurs is on the basis of the 'means' and 'ends' of the entrepreneurial process.

Economic entrepreneurship and 'purpose-driven' enterprises treat labour instrumentally by maintaining that the product of entrepreneurship is the utility value of the goods and services produced (or the financial capital realised). So, 'economic entrepreneurship' tends to adopt a theory X view of both labour and the consumer (McGregor, 1960), to treat them as costs to be minimised or income streams to be maximised. The workforce and customer base (consumers) are not developed as human beings unless such development makes them 'better' labourers or consumers. Economic entrepreneurship regards the workforce and customers as 'means', and entrepreneurial outputs (goods, services and money) as 'ends'. In short, people have an instrumental role in this paradigm of entrepreneurial thought.

If we adopt a relational view of enterprise and the goods they produce (Restakis, 2010), the nature of the entrepreneurial process changes. Now the workforce and customers (who are regarded as instrumental in 'economic entrepreneurship') become ends. Social entrepreneurship, therefore, can be defined as a 'socially rational' form of entrepreneurship (Ridley-Duff, 2008b), in which the 'capital' developed is 'social' (in the form of cohesive and vibrant social networks), 'human' (in the form of intellectual/physical development), 'natural' (in the form of green technologies that facilitate sustainable development) and 'ethical' (in the form of behaviour informed by moral reasoning). Moreover, social, human, natural and ethical capital are developed for their own sake, not as an instrument for the generation of more financial capital (Bull et al., 2010).

Of course, financial capital is still required (and produced) by social and eco-entrepreneurship. Indeed, there are both polemicists and scholars who craft arguments that financial capital can be created more effectively by social entrepreneurship under the right conditions (Forcadell, 2005; Harding and Cowling, 2006; Restakis, 2010; Erdal, 2011).[5] This, however, is to miss the point that the two forms of entrepreneurship switch the priority of – and therefore the value placed upon – the inputs and outputs that shape the entrepreneurial process. People and the environment can be the 'ends' as well as the 'means' of production (see Case 10.3). Moreover, the emerging field of 'integrated' accounting systems seek to develop new ways to report increases in human, natural and social capital alongside financial capital to provide a holistic account of 'wealth' (Eccles and Krzus, 2010).

Case 10.3

The community company model

In 1989, Peter Beeby – helped by his former teacher – invested £5,000 in the creation of Sportasia Ltd. Fifteen years later, Peter stood before the workforce and shareholders of School Trends Ltd (one of the companies created by Sportasia Ltd) and asked the question, 'Who rightly owns this company?' The round of applause told its own story. Two months later, the shareholders (on a one share, one vote basis) and the workforce (on a one person, one vote basis) voted to convert their company to an employee-owned business.

Read the remainder of Case 10.3 (on the companion website at: www.sagepub.co.uk/ridleyduff) and then consider the following questions:

1 Using Table 10.1, analyse the forms of leadership that are practised during this case.
2 To what extent is the organisation led by Peter Beeby?
3 To what extent is the organisation led by the staff?
4 Is Peter Beeby an economic or a social entrepreneur?

Alternative perspectives on social entrepreneurship, therefore, are based on developing individuals in ways that enable them to contribute to the creation and distribution of 'relational goods' (Restakis, 2010). Leadership is viewed as the outcome of many people organising for mutually beneficial purposes, using a social enterprise as the means of achieving this. Visions and decisions are based upon the values of the members who comprise a social network, underpinned by a 'democratic ethos' (Spear, 2006). This view of leadership can be extended to those working in organisations governed by a voluntary or elected board of directors, or to the 'partners' of a firm that comprise the workforce (e.g. the John Lewis Partnership).

This can have a dramatic impact on the notion of entrepreneurship itself, even to the extent that structural and mechanical metaphors are replaced with biological analogies. One of these is offered by Ellerman (1982) who described Mondragon's example as the 'socialisation of entrepreneurship'. Over the years, Ellerman has updated the metaphor and now portrays social entrepreneurship as a process that produces organisational 'offspring'.

> The workers in each part of a company have their own standing as members of the company. This does not mean that the workers in cooperatives are automatically oriented to taking entrepreneurial risks with spinoff cooperatives. The most common attitude in most businesses, cooperative or conventional, is to try to stabilize, improve, and perpetuate one's position with the company. The point is that with a cooperative, there is no structural constraint against … the biological principle of plenitude, growth through offspring. (Ellerman, 2006: 13)

Turnbull (2002) also uses the ecological metaphor of 'DNA' to explain how the banking system that supports the Mondragon co-operative network reproduces social entrepreneurship by institutionalising network governance. A 'contract of association' with the bank sets out the role of governing bodies in reproducing a culture of participatory democracy, embedding entrepreneurial DNA in the 'offspring' enterprises. Both Ellerman and Turnbull argue that this is fundamentally different from the private sector (and, by implication, economic entrepreneurship). It discourages growth through predatory and competitive behaviour (acquisitions, takeovers, capital accumulation and the creation of wholly owned subsidiaries). Instead there is an incubation period, after which a co-operative enterprise is born and treated as a living organism (and composed of living people) entitled to a life of its own.[6] It is not to be regarded as a machine (or 'project') to be switched on and off as needed, or property to be bought and sold at the whim of its owner(s).

This approach has been characterised as 'co-operative entrepreneurship' by Morrison (1991). Its claim to be 'social' is based on two arguments. Firstly, enterprises co-operate, rather than compete, to create new enterprises. Secondly, the result is an enterprise that conforms to social economy norms regarding democratic control of capital, and key decisions based on one member, one vote (see Chapters 1 and 2). Spear (2006), therefore, advances a straightforward proposition. Social entrepreneurship is the process of creating social enterprises within a social economy. There is no need to bolt it onto, or to adapt, 'mainstream' definitions in order to describe it. Indeed, doing so can be highly misleading (not to mention subversive). Its paradigmatic assumptions, particularly regarding the nature and purposes of enterprise, are different. It cannot be adequately explained using public administration or private sector concepts because these concepts reproduce public and private sector notions of enterprise.

While Spear develops a theory of social entrepreneurship that is compatible with CMEs, he stops short of integrating sustainable development/responsible management concepts (Laasch and Conway, 2015). In the work of Scott-Cato et al. (2008), the integration of social and eco-entrepreneur comes together in a study of renewable energy initiatives. Scott-Cato takes a similar view to Spear on the impact and dominance of the US discourse on social entrepreneurship that recognises the entrepreneurship needed for charitable trading activities (CTAs) and socially responsible businesses (SRBs), but marginalises the entrepreneurial processes that occur in co-operative and mutual enterprises (CMEs). While social economy organisations do engage in social entrepreneurship that meet the US definition (entrepreneurship for a social purpose), they can undertake it in a fundamentally different way.

Scott-Cato et al. (2008) use the term 'associative entrepreneurship' to describe entrepreneurship that is driven by collective action and democratic accountability. This distinction can be helpful for distinguishing Anglo-American constructions of the social entrepreneur who is believed to be driven by a personal vision, from a more European perspective on social *coopérateurs* (and *coopérateur*ship) who are driven by a desire – or need – to collaborate in the pursuit of social goals (Green, 2014). The latter term, rarely used in English, comes from the French word for the member-owners of a co-operative enterprise, the body of people that Smith and Teasdale (2012) claim will provide the basis of the 'associative democracy' needed for a social economy.

Eco-entrepreneurship

A specific focus on eco-entrepreneurship – entrepreneurial activity that is oriented towards the protection and enhancement of the natural environment – is a new sub-topic in the entrepreneurship literature. Outsios's (2013) study examined the origins of eco-entrepreneurship among both economic and social entrepreneurs through life-histories and in-depth interviews. He found that personal involvement in environmental projects, living with family members who had made commitments to sustainable living and/or social justice, and cultural experiences (such as visiting areas devastated by acid rain, deforestation and flooding) all had a profound influence on the creation of an 'environmental mind-set'.

Where the above influences coincided with conditions conducive to entrepreneur-ship (e.g. living among family members who are also entrepreneurs, or possessing the specialist engineering skills for green technology), an 'environmental entrepreneurial habitus' (Bourdieu, 1977) could develop and produce a motivation to engage in eco-entrepreneurship. Interestingly, social eco-entrepreneurs valued networking, skill-sharing and IP-sharing more highly than private eco-entrepreneurs. They also experienced fewer barriers in securing start-up capital (nine of ten social entrepre-neurs were able to obtain seed capital from an institution, whereas no economic entrepreneurs were able to do so). However, as these SRBs develop, similar challenges are faced by both social and economic entrepreneurs.

Institutional support for eco-entrepreneurship is now firmly established in bodies supporting CTAs, SRBs and CMEs. The government supported the EAC (Every Action Counts) initiative from 2006 to 2009, and as far back as 2008 the UK's charity regulator published a report on 'Going Green' (Charity Commission, 2008). However, Gilligan's (2014) research found that engagement with environmental management issues was low outside organisations specifically committed to it, that it is hampered by capacity issues, bureaucracy and the perceived constraints of Charity Law. Trustees believed that there would be barriers to investing in projects that are not aligned with their stated charitable objects, and that investments could only be made if they concurrently contributed to a charity's primary purpose. However, the Charity Commission's report clarified (in Appendix B) that justifications could be made on the basis that it would enhance a charity's reputation with funders and donors and could be justified after balanced discussion by governors of the broader costs and benefits.

In the broader social economy, the Social Enterprise Mark is a testament to the zeitgeist influencing SRBs. To obtain the SEM, applicants have to sign a statement that they will 'strive to maximise social impact and minimise environmental damage' (SEM Qualification Criterion F, July 2012). Similarly, the global support body for CMEs (International Co-operative Alliance) has made a decade-long commitment to prioritising sustainability (Blueprint for a Co-operative Decade, Principle 2, January 2013). From 2015 onwards, it will report progress through the World Co-operative Monitor (Euricse, 2013; Ridley-Duff and Hurst, 2014a, 2014b). As a show of further support, educators and researchers have produced a volume that informs efforts to create a socio-ecological (rather than socio-economic) paradigm of co-operative business (Novkovic and Webb, 2014).

Entrepreneurship for the creation of human, social and natural capital

Arguably, all efforts at eco-entrepreneurship draw – at least in part – on concepts and commitments to social entrepreneurship. Protection of the environment depends on more than the creation of technologies – it depends on changing human behaviour so that the technologies are adopted and used in the production and consumption of goods and services (Abrahamsson, 2007). Given this, all eco-entrepreneurship depends for its success on the concurrent adoption of a social entrepreneurial outlook. In short, it depends on achieving a triple bottom line impact: improvements in economic, social and environmental outcomes.

Austin et al. (2006) argue that this will depend on networking activity so that social value spreads outward from one enterprise to other enterprises and wider society:

> Networking across organizational boundaries to create social value is a powerful strategy for social entrepreneurs because the objective of creating social value does not require that value be captured within organizational boundaries. (2006: 16)

This fits with Ridley-Duff's (2008b) argument that social entrepreneurial actions have a 'distributive' logic that reorganises social relations and wealth distribution both internally and externally. Similarly, Crutchfield and McLeod-Grant (2007) use the metaphor of the starfish to illustrate the importance of 'decentralised' network structures in achieving wider social impact. They state that starfish, like successful social enterprises, are:

> highly decentralised, relying on peer-to-peer relationships, widely distributed leadership and collaborative communities united by shared values … with a headless starfish, if you cut off an arm, the old starfish will simply regenerate a new arm, and the other arm will grow into a new starfish. (2007: 125)

So, social enterprises enhance their chances of survival through the adoption of a 'network mind-set', working collaboratively with allies, engaging in partnership and joining enterprise-owned CMEs that achieve wider social impact (Case 10.4).

Case 10.4

Transforming the social entrepreneur

Graham Duncan, the manager at St Mary's Church, assisted by two colleagues (Aroose and Saffeina), undertook an action research project in 2007 (Duncan, 2009b).

They set out to establish an employee-owned social enterprise called the Food Factory involving Pakistani women in the Sharrow region of Sheffield. His first encounter with writers on social entrepreneurship offered encouragement:

> I was attracted to this discourse and loved the promise of certainty and control implied by the objective language and economic terminology – it offered the clarity which I yearned for – in contrast to the muddle and confusion of my everyday working life.

He found that the work of Alibeth Somers, Alex Nicholls and Jim Collins talked 'confidently of value propositions, social impact metrics, robust mechanisms, double bottom lines and social capital'. Six months later, he and his colleagues were on the point of giving up their project. It had not worked out as expected. All blamed the women's attitude and believed that 'they do not want to change'. To achieve the social change they desired, they had to switch to a collaborative networking mind-set through the use of appreciative inquiry (Duncan and Ridley-Duff, 2014).

Read the rest of Case 10.4 on the companion website at: www.sagepub.co.uk/ridleyduff and consider the following questions:

1 What theory of leadership informed Graham's approach to social entrepreneurship at the outset of the project? Have you ever presumed that this approach to leadership is most effective?
2 Assess the extent to which follower-centric views of leadership provide an explanation for Graham's changing view of social entrepreneurship. What insights do follower-centric views provide into your own experiences?
3 In what circumstances might leader-centric theories maintain their applicability?

Conclusions

Table 10.5 summarises the discussions in this chapter and the implications for practice. The treatment of different approaches to leadership is not intended to obscure that leader-centric theories may still be applicable to situations where:

- followers are familiar with the discourse used by their leaders
- followers understand the stories and cultural references used by the leader to develop and explain their plans
- followers are prepared to accept (or conform to) the discursive and behavioural norms of a leader.

Table 10.5   Applying leadership theory to social entrepreneurship

Leadership theory	Social entrepreneurial assumptions	Implications for practice
Leader-centred theories	Social entrepreneurship occurs when individually 'driven' people pursue a social mission or purpose	Support for social entrepreneurship can be provided by selecting and developing individuals with the greatest ability to catalyse change
Higher-purpose theories of leadership	Social entrepreneurship is a morally driven variant of traditional entrepreneurship, rooted in the pursuit and propagation of a religious, charitable or transformational lifestyle	Support for social entrepreneurship depends on the capacity of moral leaders to steer organisational members towards 'higher' ethical behaviours, social aims and transformative outcomes
Follower-centred theories	Social entrepreneurship is a socially constructed concept that arises out of the collective actions of followers who benefit from sustaining particular views of the leadership process	Support for social entrepreneurship will be achieved when a sufficient number of followers 'tell a better story' or 'support a more compelling vision' and start to propagate a new (social) entrepreneurial discourse
Cultural perspectives on leadership	Social entrepreneurship is a culturally defined variant of (or antithesis to) economic entrepreneurship	Support for social entrepreneurship depends on the value propositions of social entrepreneurs and the extent to which they are accepted and adopted in a given cultural setting
Critical perspectives on leadership	Social entrepreneurship is a *social* (collective) not individual phenomenon: it describes collective processes that lead to the creation of social enterprises	Support for social entrepreneurship depends on developing institutions capable of supporting collective action, and maintaining discursive democratic debate about the use of economic, social and human capital

However, if one or more of the above does not hold, other theories of leadership provide insights into alternative leadership strategies. For example, in the case of the Food Factory (Case 10.4), follower-centric theory provides an insight into how effective leadership was re-established. If 'support for social entrepreneurship will be achieved when a sufficient number of followers "tell a better story" or "support a more compelling vision"', then the role of the leader might need to change to one that helps followers establish and propagate a story, a vision and a discourse that inspire them to follow a new course of action. Viewed another way, the leader has to (temporarily) become the follower until sufficiently knowledgeable to perform the leadership function effectively.

In concluding this chapter, we highlight that US dominance of the definition of social entrepreneurship has replicated philanthropic assumptions that solutions are brought to impoverished people by social entrepreneurs (Martin and Osberg, 2007). Such definitions fit well with Yunus's (2007) 'first type' of social business and provide a useful framework for teaching entrepreneurship to leaders of CTAs and SRBs.

However, CMEs benefit from a different definition of social entrepreneurship because of their emphasis on self-help and self-responsibility. The definition below emerged from Ridley-Duff's tour of Indonesian universities in 2012 and 2013 to advance the British Council's 'skills for social entrepreneurship' programme. The definition was adapted to accommodate the mind-set of mutuality (rather than philanthropy) and the logic of equitable distribution (rather than asset-locked control). It is consistent with Yunus's (2007) 'second type' of social business (see Chapter 2).

For CMEs, social entrepreneurship is:

> the mind-set of identifying ideas followed by the process of generating socio-economic benefits consistent with a social purpose. It is achieved through sustainable wealth creation in member-owned businesses that deploy participatory management and/or democratic governance to ensure that most of the wealth created is available to members for the development of their community. (British Council Skills for Social Entrepreneurship Programme, visits to universities in Jakarta and Yogyakarta by Rory Ridley-Duff, Indonesia, 10–13 April 2012 and 7–11 September 2013)

Social transformation occurs when large populations of people accept and institutionalise new norms of behaviour (i.e. rooted in changed ethical values). Leader and follower-centric theories alert us to the dual nature of this transformation. It will be achieved not only by the social entrepreneurs changing others and encouraging them to accept their vision, but also by social and eco-entrepreneurs adopting a reflexive stance when member-led enterprises challenge the (false) logic that a social economy can thrive if common pool resources are privatised rather than socialised (Ostrom et al., 1999).

Summary of learning

In this chapter, we have argued that:

Leadership theory was initially leader centric, and focused on the traits, qualities and behaviours of individual leaders.

As the field has matured, leadership theory has taken more account of follower, culture and critical approaches that emphasise the social processes that legitimise different approaches to leadership.

Social entrepreneurship (and entrepreneurship studies generally) has generated renewed interest in leader-centric views of organisation.

Collective forms of social entrepreneurship have been characterised as 'co-operative entrepreneurship' and 'associative entrepreneurship' to reflect their focus on collective action.

Social and economic entrepreneurship can be regarded as 'convergent' in their shared interest in risk-taking, innovation, opportunity recognition and resource management, but 'divergent' on the 'means' and 'ends' of entrepreneurship.

Economic entrepreneurship adopts an instrumental view of strategic stakeholders (workforce, customers, suppliers, community institutions) and treats them as a 'means' of accumulating financial capital and producing goods and services that have utility value.

Social entrepreneurship can adopt a relational view of strategic stakeholders and regards them as the 'ends' of entrepreneurship (i.e. as the recipients or beneficiaries of the financial, social, natural, human and ethical capital that the enterprise creates).

Questions and possible essay assignments

1. 'Leadership [is] thrusting, setting the direction and ... punching the air ahead of the staff following you.' Critically assess the limitations of this statement with specific reference to follower-centric theories of leadership.
2. 'Social entrepreneurship is a process of encouraging collective action and community solidarity.' With reference to US theories of social entrepreneurship, critically assess this statement and consider the impact of Ashoka on the development of the field.
3. 'We need to study *coopérateurs* as well as entrepreneurs.' Explain the term *coopérateur* and critically assess the link between co-operative entrepreneurship and sustainable development.

Further reading

An excellent text to consider perspectives on leadership (and how they might inform leadership education in social enterprise) is *A Very Short, Fairly Interesting and Reasonably Cheap Book about Studying Leadership* (Jackson and Parry, 2008). Do not be fooled by its title. This is an accessible, well-researched introduction to perspectives on leadership that fit well with social enterprise practitioners' needs. While not discussed directly in this chapter, we also recommend a close reading of Clutterbuck and Megginson's *Creating a Coaching Culture* (2005) and Garvey et al.'s (2009) contribution to *Coaching and Mentoring*. These describe leadership development programmes based on cultivating sensitivity to the needs of peer group members through coaching techniques, rather than through attempts by leaders to be 'inspirational'.

Introductory books on social entrepreneurship tend to address one or other strand of thought set out in this chapter, but rarely all of them. A well-established text is Alex Nicholls's edited book, *Social Entrepreneurship: New Models of Sustainable Social Change* (2006). This brings together the views of a number of leading social entrepreneurs.

For a tightly argued paper on how social entrepreneurship can be defined in relation to the broader field of enterprise and entrepreneurship studies, see Chell's (2007) paper on the companion website. She moves towards, but stops slightly short of, the critical perspective in Curtis's (2008) paper, 'Finding that grit makes a pearl'. Other papers that focus on social entrepreneurship from an individualistic perspective include Martin and Osberg (2007) and Mair and Marti (2006), who examine the mind-set of 'changemakers'.

For more on social entrepreneurship as a collective approach, Spear's (2006) paper argues for a straightforward relationship between social entrepreneurship, social enterprise and the social economy. Scott-Cato et al.'s (2008) study of the renewal energy sector in Wales makes a similar argument to advance a theory of 'associative entrepreneurship' in the context of eco-entrepreneurial commitments.

Further reading material is available on the companion website at: www.sagepub. co.uk/ ridleyduff.

Useful resources

Ashoka (Global Reach): www.ashoka.org/regions

Community Action Network (CAN) (UK): http://can-online.org.uk/

Co-operative College (Global Reach): www.co-op.ac.uk/co-operative-learning/

East Africa Social Enterprise Network (EASEN): http://easenetwork.net/

Global Social Economy Forum (GSEF) (Asia): http://gsef2014.org/

International Summit of Cooperatives (Global Reach): www.intlsummit.coop/

School for Social Entrepreneurs (UK): www.the-sse.org/

Skoll World Forum (Global): http://skollworldforum.org/

Social Entrepreneurship Resource Hub (US): http://sehub.stanford.edu/

UnLtd (Indonesia): http://unltd-indonesia.org/

UnLtd (South Africa): www.unltdsouthafrica.org/

UnLtd (UK): www.unltd.org.uk/

Notes

1 Establishing participatory techniques include action learning, appreciative inquiry and Open Space Technology. The last includes the 'law of two feet' that encourage minimum management control to ensure each person self-regulates the groups they join to maximise learning opportunities.

2   In fairness to the researchers, they undertook much of their research on after-school clubs and these had to be supervised because the participants were not adults.

3   This was verified in person by Rory Ridley-Duff during a field visit to Mondragon in 2003. Locals who knew Fr Arizmendi recounted an occasion when they bought him a motorbike, but he abandoned it insisting that his pedal bike was sufficient.

4   For example, one of this book's authors has read court statements/papers in a case brought by a regional social enterprise agency against Social Enterprise UK because it promoted 'social franchising' (i.e. privatisation) instead of 'social licensing' (i.e. socialisation). The regional agency won the case.

5   A powerful argument can be made on the basis that areas of Europe with the highest density of co-operatives, mutuals and social businesses (and which were previously devastated by World War II or civil war, such as Northern Italy/the Spanish Basque Region) are now among the richest in Europe.

6   Charities such as NCVO have a history of incubating new organisations before proactively spinning them off. For example, the Directory of Social Change was previously a project within NCVO.

Identities and Legalities

11

In this chapter we consider how legal forms can be selected and designed to meet the needs of social enterprises. By the end of this chapter you will be able to:

- critically evaluate how the legal membership of an organisation is established
- articulate how issues of social identity affect the choice of legal form and management practice
- compare and contrast **model rules** for social enterprises
- develop and critique the concept of a democratic multi-stakeholder social enterprise.

The key arguments that will be developed in this chapter are:

- Social identity and business purpose influence the choice of legal form.
- Different legal forms influence the power and benefits allocated to each stakeholder.
- Social enterprises are developing legal forms that enfranchise more than one stakeholder.

(Continued)

(Continued)

- In the last 15 years, new models for democratising business have been established.
- Multi-stakeholder social enterprise can be regarded as a 'paradigmatic' shift in the constitutional underpinning of business, or a naïve form of liberalism.

Introduction

In previous chapters, we have considered a number of debates that affect the choices made in the management of social enterprises. In this chapter, we turn our attention to one of the critical tasks facing a person or group that wishes to create a social enterprise: the identity that they will adopt and how to express this through a legal form. We will argue that the decision to choose a particular legal form is often an afterthought, or something decided by business advisers on the basis of the forms they are familiar supporting (or which benefit themselves more than the business they are advising). Alternatively, the legal form may be imposed by a funder to protect their own investment.

As Davies (2002: 17) points out:

> It is the initial shareholders of a company who bring it into existence … and who become the first members of the organization thus created. Subsequent shareholders also become members of the company. The point is of theoretical, even ideological, significance, because the train of thought which makes the shareholders the members of the company leads naturally to making the shareholders' interests predominant within company law.

Davies questions why appointed directors, employees and creditors are not recognised as legal members of the company and why they have no voting rights in general meetings that decide future policy and strategy. The question is not an idle one because virtually all forms of social enterprise seek to constrain or reverse the legal arrangement that reproduces the hegemony of financial investors.

In the first part of the chapter, we consider the issue of social identity and the way this can influence the choice of legal form. We explore how different legal forms are designed to privilege one or other stakeholder and ensure they can acquire or retain control over intellectual property, **physical assets**, trading surpluses and decision-making bodies. To illustrate these points, we examine how legal forms for establishing charitable trading activities (CTAs), co-operative and mutual enterprises (CMEs) and socially responsible businesses (SRBs) distribute rights within the organisation. In the second half of the chapter, we consider the emergence of model rules for social enterprises rooted in the values of the social and solidarity economy that seek to reconcile divergent interests by enfranchising stakeholders excluded from membership in private or state enterprises to create a new business paradigm (see Figure 11.1). By way of an example, we examine antecedents to the FairShares Model – a development pathway for solidarity enterprises – to learn about the emergence of multi-stakeholder legal forms (Birchall, 2012; Ridley-Duff and Bull, 2013).

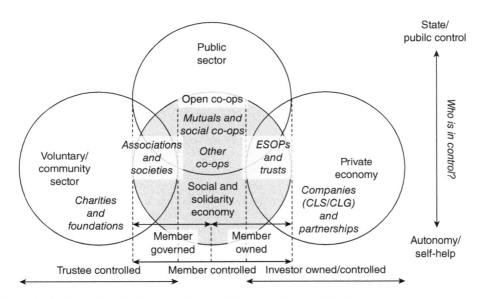

Figure 11.1   Variations in the legal forms of the social and solidarity economy

By comparing these examples, and considering the history of their development, we can observe two things: firstly, social enterprises develop legal forms that seek to reconcile divergent economic and social interests; and secondly, these interests still influence the way power is distributed to different stakeholders. In the conclusions, we review whether the attempt to enfranchise groups typically excluded from membership represents a paradigm shift in business thinking (Kuhn, 1970), or a form of naïve liberalism that continues to privilege an elite.

Values, identities and social practices

Many writers on the left of the political spectrum have alluded to the tendency of people in a society to become imbued with particular ways of thinking, and for the ideas of a dominant class to become pervasive in educational, governmental and economic institutions. In Marxian thought, it is argued there has been a transition from primitive to **feudal society**, then feudal to **capitalist society** (Cornforth, 1995). The question that preoccupied later generations became the manner in which capitalism would give way to socialism, and then how socialism would give way to communism. Marx wrote little about the next stage of transition: how the *relations of production* would have to be changed to produce both socialism and communism. He was, however, explicit that revolutions occur when a class of people in society who were subordinated under the previous socio-economic system establish a way to become dominant. For example, in the case of feudal society, Marx tracked how a class of privately financed merchants increased their control of economic and political thought until their way of thinking became dominant in government (Gray, 1998). Kalmi (2007) highlights how this dominant mode of thought gradually colonised educational texts and excluded alternatives.

In the case of capitalism, Marx and Engels are uncompromising in their criticisms of the changes that took place:

> The bourgeoisie, wherever it has got the upper hand, has put an end to all feudal, patriarchal, idyllic relations. It has pitilessly torn asunder the motley feudal ties that bound man to his 'natural superiors', and has left remaining no other nexus between man and man than naked self-interest, than callous 'cash payment'. It has drowned the most heavenly ecstasies of religious fervour, of chivalrous enthusiasm, of philistine sentimentalism, in the icy water of egotistical calculation. It has resolved personal worth into exchange value ... veiled by religious and political illusions, it has substituted naked, shameless, direct, brutal exploitation. (1998 [1848]: 37–8)

A number of more contemporary analyses reach similar conclusions. The documentary *The Corporation* draws attention to the way financial capital is continually moved out of organisations where workplace democracy and trade union organisation are effective, and reinvested in regional economies where those movements are either unsupported by the state or actively suppressed (Achbar et al., 2004). As Klein (2007) and Gray (2009) would later argue, corporations did not stop at the level of the nation, but sought to dominate policy and practice in the IMF and World Bank. The effect has been that the top 10 per cent (and particularly the top 1 per cent) have become enormously rich at everyone else's expense (Leonard, 2007; Hardoon, 2015). With successive banking crises in 1997 (Far East), 2001 (South America) and 2008 (US and Europe), sustained investigation and criticism of the effects of inequality have begun to change perceptions about the organising principles of the economy, and become more open to restructuring business organisations for societal benefit (Wilkinson and Pickett, 2010; Piketty, 2014).

Class exercise: Visualising wealth inequalities in America

Watch the following video based on data presented in an academic study at Harvard University about wealth inequality (Norton and Ariely, 2011):

www.youtube.com/watch?v=QPKKQnijnsM

In small groups, read 'New co-operativism and the FairShares Model' (http://shura. shu.ac.uk/8856/) (also available on the companion website at www.sagepub. co.uk/ridleyduff) then discuss the following two questions:

1 How does the constitution of an enterprise control the distribution of wealth created by its workforce?
2 What rules can be added to a constitution to ensure that a different 'ideal' distribution is achieved?

There is another perspective, however. Liberal democracies based on the assumptions of the Magna Carta, however imperfectly they succeed in their goals, have successfully advanced the principle of equality before the law, equality of voice in political deliberations and decision-making, and equality of opportunity to participate fully in work and society, and the right of all people to own property (Friedman, 1962; Rawls, 1999). Friedman argues in *Capitalism and Freedom* that distributing political power is much harder to achieve than the distribution of economic power. For this reason, he argues for the widest possible distribution of economic power in order to provide a counter to the political power of governmental institutions. Rawls goes even further in outlining his *Theory of Justice* by arguing that social rights are needed to limit the powers of both the state and powerful non-state interests. Taken together, economic and social liberalism still provide intellectual bedrocks from which spring arguments for a strong civil society, employee ownership and for treating employees as corporate citizens with voice *rights* rather than chattels to be treated as slaves or servants (Ellerman, 2005).

As Norton and Ariely's (2011) study demonstrated, it is not that people with communitarian and liberal sentiments have wildly different views on the ideal distribution of wealth (support for Swedish norms of wealth distribution were supported equally by democrats and republicans irrespective of personal income), it is that they differ in their understanding of institutional arrangements capable of delivering such an equitable outcome. With this in mind, it is worth comparing the outcomes and dynamics that arise when private and social ownership systems are deployed. Consider Table 11.1 and ask yourself whether you would prefer to be like Barcelona FC (socially owned) or Arsenal FC (privately owned)?

Table 11.1   The Camp Nou Way

	Barcelona	**Arsenal**
Shareholders	In 2006, there were 142,000 members ('socios') (Conn, 2006)	In 2006, four major shareholders owned 87% of voting shares[*]
	By 2014, this had risen to more than 160,000, with 91% living locally (Source: www.fcbarcelona.com/)	By 2011, two major shareholders (in the form of three overseas businessmen) acquired 96% of voting shares eventually leading to the closure of the 'Fanshare' scheme (See: www.arsenalfanshare.com)
	One member, one vote	One share, one vote
Leadership	The president is elected by members for a four-year term (maximum two terms)	No meaningful elections
	All board members need 5,000 member signatures before they can stand for election	Chair of the board, and board members are decided by the major (overseas) shareholders
Cheapest adult season ticket	2006 – £69	2006 – £885
	2013[**] – £172 (+103)	2013 – £985 (+100)
Most expensive adult season ticket	2006 – £579	2006 – £1825
	2013 – £634 (+55)	2013 – £1955 (+130)

[*]Wikipedia, on 8 December 2009, stated that 86.9 per cent of shares were held by four shareholders: Stan Kroenke (29.9 per cent), Danny Fiszman (16.1 per cent), Nina Bracewell-Smith (15.9 per cent) and Red & White Securities (25 per cent). Red & White Securities is a company owned by Russian billionaire Alisher Usmanov and financier Farhad Moshiri who lives in Monaco. Stan Kroenke is the US owner of Kroenke Sports Enterprises. On 15 August 2014, Wikipedia stated that in 2011 Kroenke took a 66.82 per cent holding, and Red & White Securities acquired a 29.35 per cent stake.

[**]2013 prices provided by the Guardian News DataBlog (Sedghi and Chalbi, 2013).

The key issue is how the legal form contributes to social and economic outcomes. The scale of the differences should not be underestimated, as the following examples will illustrate. The first example (Table 11.1) involves a comparison between Barcelona and Arsenal football clubs based on an article about football supporter trusts (Conn, 2006). The body of law under which Barcelona is constituted is similar to the Mondragon co-operatives (Exemplar Case, Part 1 – Introduction). There are three things to note here. Firstly, Barcelona is spreading local ownership (91 per cent of owners live in Catalonia). Arsenal is concentrating ownership, and putting it into the hands of overseas investors. By 2011, 96 per cent of shares are owned by people who do not live in London. Today, Arsenal fans are the third largest shareholder, but own just 116 shares compared to 60,291 by the two main shareholders – a 0.002 per cent holding – and the scheme that enabled this is closing (www.arsenalfanshare.com). Secondly, in 2013 the *most expensive* season ticket at Barcelona still cost less than the *cheapest* season ticket at Arsenal. Lastly, the president at Barcelona needs to get 5,000 signed up supporters to stand for election and is elected by a vote of the whole membership. At Arsenal, the chair can be decided by one person.

The outcomes are a product of the ownership structure at Barcelona where the dominant group is consumers (football fans). At Barcelona, fans can bring pressure to ensure prices are set at a reasonable level, even if disparities in the pay of the workforce remain wide: undoubtedly the wage of an administrator will still be a tiny fraction of a footballer's wage. However, the primary stakeholder matters a lot. The Mondragon industrial enterprises are owned by the workforce rather than consumers and this affects the price of labour. They set a ratio (the average is 5:1) between the *highest* and *lowest* paid members in the Mondragon companies, establish a base salary with local trade unions, and only change the ratio after a vote of all members (Ridley-Duff, 2012). By way of contrast, the gap between CEO pay and the *average* manual worker in US corporations increased from 85:1 to 419:1 throughout the 1990s (Aslam, 1999). This is possible because the private sector model is designed to benefit founding entrepreneurs, major shareholders and senior managers. As they decide the remuneration systems *for* employees (but not *with* employees), it is unsurprising that they design it to favour their own interests. Where an economy is based on championing support for entrepreneurs, managers and shareholders who maximise financial profits, huge income inequalities are bound to occur. Stanford University's 'State of the Union' report on poverty and inequality shows that incomes for the top 20 per cent have steadily risen since 1957, but have fallen for everyone else (Stanford Center for Poverty and Equality, 2014).

So, to understand how income inequalities occurs, we need look no further than who has legal rights: (a) to use the assets of an organisation; (b) to set prices for its goods and services; and (c) to set the levels of pay for different jobs. The easiest way to change outcomes, is to change who acquires these legal rights. Where these have been changed, vastly different *long-term* outcomes occur because the constitutions (Articles of Association) adopted distribute these rights differently. It is possible to extend ownership across a community, dramatically reduce the cost of goods to members, and ensure that leadership is representative of the collective interests.

Coule (2008: 2) summarises a key point about identity and membership when she states:

> Resources have the potential to steer organisations and how they raise the resources they need has a strong influence on what an organisation is and what it can be. From a sustainability perspective, reducing resource vulnerability through the diversification of funding sources is recognised as an important task … [Organisations] are vulnerable in another way as well. Strategic choices in terms of resources have implications beyond their reliability, they affect what the organisation stands for.

It is important, therefore, to understand the intersection between legal form and social control. It would, for example, be easy to compare the wages of the footballers at Barcelona and Arsenal and conclude that the clubs are not so different. This would miss the social and economic outcomes for the 'consumers' of football rather than those who work to produce it. Similarly, we could compare the prices charged by the Mondragon co-operatives for the domestic appliances they manufacture and conclude that they are not so different from the prices charged by Anglo-American corporations. This would ignore the social and economic outcomes for the 'producers' of these domestic appliances, and how these differ from other producers.

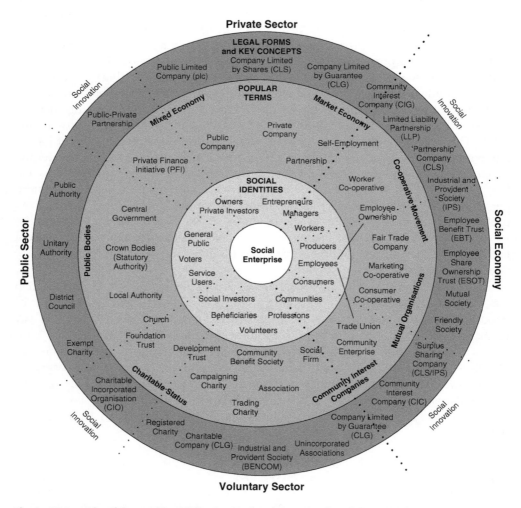

Figure 11.2   Identities and legalities in the development of social enterprise

Put simply, legal forms evolve to suit the needs of key stakeholder groups. They are retained to the extent that they are successful (i.e. produce the outcomes that are sought) and can develop and protect the educational, political and economic environments needed to sustain them. In the context of a discussion about social enterprise, the question is whether legal forms that privilege a particular group over others are a barrier to, or an enabler of, social enterprise itself. Figure 11.2 summarises the different stakeholders (social identities) that are associated with particular legal forms. Some of these are well established (such as a company limited by shares and a company limited by guarantee) while others are less well known, even though they have been popular (or dominant) during other historical periods (e.g. charitable companies, friendly and mutual societies, and co-operatives).

It is beyond the scope of this chapter to discuss each legal form (see 'Useful Resources' at the end of the chapter for more on this). It is, however, relevant to ask how previously dominant models for CTAs, SRBs and CMEs compare to new forms of organisation that have emerged in the last two decades. With the growth of social enterprise as a concept, there has been a conscious attempt to recognise the need for management education in *multi*-stakeholder governance and the legal forms that support their enfranchisement (Moreau and Mertens, 2013).

In Figure 11.2, the perspective outlined towards the end of Chapter 2 is echoed. Social enterprise is framed as a way of brokering and balancing the interests of stakeholders by including them in the membership of the enterprise (legally and/or culturally). In Figure 11.2, the 'third system' identified by Pearce (2003) is elaborated to identify legal forms and concepts of the voluntary sector and social economy, and the porous boundaries between these sectors and the public and private sectors where key innovations in the constitution of organisations is taking place. Underpinning their differences is a consideration of who the legal forms operate *for* (for the benefit of the public, for the community, for private individuals or a large membership group).

Class exercise: Linking economic and social interests to legal forms

Using Figure 11.2, make a list of the legal forms you have encountered in your studies and working life, then sort them into the following six groups. Based on what you know about each organisation's criteria for *legal membership*, enquire which legal forms are:

1 designed to benefit the *economic* interests of those who invest money
2 designed to benefit the *economic* interests of those who buy/sell particular goods and services

(Continued)

(Continued)

3 designed to benefit the *economic* interests of those who supply labour
4 designed to benefit the *social* interests of those who invest money
5 designed to benefit the *social* interests of those who use particular goods and services
6 designed to benefit the *social* interests of those who supply labour.

Materials to support this exercise can be found on the companion website at: www.sagepub.co.uk/ridleyduff.

Old legal identities and hegemonic power

To develop a sense of the issues facing those starting up or developing social enterprises, it is worth highlighting how forms of organisation (see Table 11.2) are designed (consciously or unconsciously) to produce **hegemonic power** (Lukes, 1974). Hegemonic power occurs where staff members and supporters have been 'schooled' in a particular discourse (i.e. to use particular language, concepts and ideas) and find it difficult to conceptualise alternative ways of thinking and talking. The language may have a 'unitary' feel to it, claiming that all parties to an enterprise have 'shared interests', that all parties should have 'shared values' or that all parties are 'equal before the law'.

Since the first edition of this book, we have both had opportunities to travel internationally to learn more about the different ways in which nations create legislative frameworks for social enterprise. As we argued in Chapter 2 (Defining Social Enterprise), these can be grouped broadly into:

- co-operative and mutual enterprises, which draw on co-operative, society and association legislation to create member-owned businesses (CMEs)
- socially responsible businesses, which adapt legislation for private companies to build in 'socialised' ownership, governance or management or which embed 'social purposes' to ensure they are run more in the interests of wider society (SRBs)
- charitable trading activities, which draw heavily on legislative support for philanthropy (charities, trusts, foundations) to channel funds raised towards explicit 'social purposes' (CTAs).

In Table 11.2, we show examples of how the application of this framework is expressed in different countries.

Table 11.2   Popular legal forms for social enterprise

Category	UK	USA & Canada	Croatia	Indonesia	Japan
Charity/Trust or Foundation (CTAs)	Charity	Foundation	Foundation	Foundation	Foundation
	Charitable company	Non-profit corporation	Association	Association	Certified non-profit association
	Charitable incorporated foundation or association (CIO)	Public benefit corporation			Specified non-profit association
	Foundation trust				
Co-operative/Mutual (CMEs)	Min. 3 members	Min. (n) members (varies by state)	Min. 7 members	Min. 20 members	Min. (n) (varies by form)
	Co-operative society	Co-operative society	Association that trades for a social purpose	Producer co-op	Producer co-op
	Community benefit society (BENCOM)	Credit union	Solidarity co-op	Consumer co-op	Consumer co-op
	Credit union	Solidarity co-op	Credit union	Saving and lending co-op	Social co-op
				Service co-op	Worker co-op (pending)
Socially Responsible Businesses (SRBs)	Community interest company (CIC) (min. 1 member)	Benefit corporation (B-Corp)	Small company with social objects (min. 1, max. 3)	Private company (CLS or CLG) with social objects	Social welfare corporation
	Private company (CLG or CLS) with social objects (Min 1 member)	Private company (C3) with non-profit trading activities	Private company (CLS) with social objects		Private company (CLS) with social objects
	Employee-owned business	Low Profit Corporation (L3C)			
		Employee-owned business			

In private companies, the norm is for membership to be extended to shareholders in accordance with their financial investment (Davies, 2002). People employed by an unaltered private company are required by law to act in the (financial) interests of their employer (i.e. the private company) with directors required by law to practice 'enlightened' governance by considering the interests of other stakeholders. In charities, membership may be extended differently, but the expectation is that everyone will prioritise the charitable objects set by the board of trustees. Trustees themselves, and those employed by trustees, are assessed (in law) against the pursuit and achievement of charitable objectives (Charity Commission, 2012). Similarly, in worker co-operatives, membership is extended to the workforce, and those employed by them are obliged to act in their interests. In consumer co-operatives, the obligation is to act in consumer interests.

The act of including or excluding particular groups from membership (and thereby limiting their voice in making decisions about the future of the organisation) is one of the processes affecting the distribution of both power and wealth. In different bodies of academic theory, the behaviour of 'other' stakeholders is framed as problematic. For example, in private companies, the behaviour of directors and managers is framed as the 'problem' of corporate governance by shareholders (Joerg et al., 2004; Slapnicar et al., 2004). In both management and economic theory, the 'problem' of staff motivation is the focus of attention (Herzberg, 1985; Watson, 1996). In co-operative theory, the behaviour of *external* investors is framed as a 'problem', so much so that there is a history of excluding them from legal membership (Oakeshott, 1990).

In all these unadapted forms of organisation, the rights of the dominant group are regarded as paramount and taken for granted, leading to unitary forms of governance in the interests of a single stakeholder group. Legal and governance theory, in relation to each form, develops to address the perceived 'problems' created by the exclusion of other groups, often enacted in other statutes (e.g. employment law, health and safety laws, human rights laws) to curb the owners' unfettered right to acquire power and wealth.

For example, the concept of **hard HRM** in traditional management theory regards labour as a cost to be minimised by paying a fixed wage that is the minimum the labour market will bear (Truss, 1999). This may apply equally in private companies (to maximise investor returns) and charities (who are obliged to maximise the funds available for charitable projects). As Kalmi (2007) argues, the same logic can also apply in consumer co-operatives (to maximise dividends for consumer members). Theories about how to treat 'labour' may vary, but they are all taken within a paradigm of thought leading to the exclusion of labour from membership (and therefore governance) of the organisation. Alternatively, they are accepted into membership only if they abandon or lessen their commitment to institutions designed to protect labour interests (e.g. trade unions) (Lewis, 1954; Cathcart, 2013).[1]

Similar injunctions exist in charity and co-operative practice with regard to financial investors. In this case, external investors are not permitted to buy equity in the charity or co-operative (although such rights are preserved when the charity or co-operative wishes to buy equity in other enterprises). If external investment is permitted, the rights of investors are reduced either by barring them from membership, or by adjusting their membership rights so that they do not acquire decision-making rights accorded to full members (Ridley-Duff, 2007).

As we will see below, however, successive iterations of social enterprise model rules as well as frameworks for management education (Moreau and Mertens, 2013) now openly challenge these assumptions by recognising multiple interest groups and forms of relationship in their constitutions. These seek to institute democratic forums to manage the competition and conflicts that arise to create solidarity among stakeholders. It is worth recalling the comment of Michels (1961: 36) that:

Democracy in large measure rests on the fact that no one group is able to secure a basis of power and command over the majority so that it can effectively suppress or deny the claims of the groups it opposes.

While some neo-liberal theorists – most notably Friedman and his followers – abhor attempts to advance social democracy in a business context, the views of Pateman (1970), Ellerman (1982, 1984) and Turnbull (1994) put democracy at the core of social-ised enterprises (CMEs) by attaching decision-making rights to corporate citizenship rather than property. Attempts to institutionalise arrangements in business so that 'no one group is able to secure a basis of power and command over the majority so that it can effectively suppress or deny the claims of the groups it opposes' represent an evolution in business norms (just as it previously reshaped norms in the world of politics).

Arguments about management education move beyond 'single-loop' arguments that social enterprises can be more efficient (within the same paradigm). They progress to 'double-loop' arguments that social enterprises can redesign systems of trade, owner-ship and governance to place social objectives and new ethical norms at the centre of responsible business practice (Laasch and Conway, 2015). As Smith (2001) comments:

Single-loop learning seems to be present when goals, values, frameworks and, to a sig-nificant extent, strategies are taken for granted. The emphasis is on 'techniques and making techniques more efficient'… Any reflection is directed toward making the strategy more effective. Double-loop learning, in contrast, 'involves questioning the role of the framing and learning systems which underlie actual goals and strategies'.

Table 11.3   Model 1 and Model 2 enterprise design

Model 1 – Unitary Norms	Model 2 – Pluralist Alternatives
Governing values	
• Achieve the purpose as the actor defines it • Win, do not lose • Suppress negative feelings • Emphasise rationality	• Valid information • Free and informed choice • Internal commitment
Primary strategies	
• Control environment and task unilaterally • Protect self and others unilaterally	• Share control • Participate in the design and implementation of choices
Usually operationalised by	
• Un-illustrated attributions and evaluations • Advocating courses of action that discourage inquiry • Treating one's own views as obviously correct • Making covert attributions and evaluations • Face-saving moves that leave potentially embarrassing facts unstated	• Attribution and evaluation illustrated with observable examples • Surfacing conflicting views • Encouraging public testing of evaluations • Acknowledging sources of thought

(Continued)

Table 11.3   Continued

Model 1 – Unitary Norms	Model 2 – Pluralist Alternatives
Consequences include	
• Defensive relationships	• Minimally defensive/intimate relationships
• Low freedom of choice	• High freedom of choice
• Reduced production of valid information	• Increasing likelihood of double-loop learning
• Little public testing of ideas	

Argyris et al. (1985) summarised the characteristics and management strategies of Model 1 and Model 2 organisations (see Table 11.3). In as much as interest groups seek to perfect the use of existing legal forms (e.g. the private company, the charity, the co-operative, etc.), they represent examples of single-loop learning within a framework of Model 1 behaviours. Where groups are collaborating to reformulate the norms and objectives of business, embracing both *value* commitments and links to evidence-based reasoning, seeking to integrate and synthesise knowledge from diverse sources, they are orienting themselves towards Model 2 thinking, opening up the possibility of double-loop learning.

Social enterprise, in its *emergent* legal forms, and social networks, within the social and solidarity economy (Gold, 2004; Lund, 2011), can be viewed as attempts to address business problems using Model 2 thinking in the *constitution* of business, and not just through the supply of goods and services to disenfranchised sections of the population, or through sophisticated HRM practices to induce 'high commitment' (Benson and Brown, 2007). To explore this further, we discuss five sets of social enterprise model rules identified as antecedents of a FairShares Model of social enterprise. Later we will critique these forms and discuss their possible limitations.

New legal identities and social power

Each of the following sets of model rules illustrates how social entrepreneurs have attempted to recognise and legitimise the interests of multiple stakeholders. We will firstly explore the key characteristics of each set of rules by discussing how they change the relative balance of power (Table 11.4). Subsequently, we will explore the extent to which different rules *still* privilege one group over others and shape their levels of involvement in decision-making. The sets of rules are illustrative, and have been selected for their educational value and influence on the FairShares Model.

Table 11.4   Multi-stakeholder model rules for social enterprises: Cases 11.1–11.5

Stakeholder Model Ltd (Case 11.1)

With a heritage stretching back to fair trade food co-operatives in the 1980s, the rules were designed by Geof Cox Associates, a specialist in the development and support of social firms, and were published by the Common Cause Foundation.

Underpinned by a company limited by shares, the model rules define the power of an active board, elected by each shareholder group. Three share types are defined:

- stewardship shares; partnership/customer shares; investment shares

Co-operative CIC Model (Case 11.2)

Designed and published by Co-operatives UK in response to the introduction of community interest company legislation (in 2005). Underpinned by a company limited by guarantee (or shares), the model rules are framed to encourage active service user and workforce membership on the basis of one person, one vote, with a commitment to consult:

- employees; funders; suppliers; customers; community representatives

NewCo Model (Case 11.3)

With thinking rooted in studies of Polanyi (in the 1990s), these rules were designed by Morgan Killick and Bill Barker in 2002, with support from the Sheffield Community Economic Development Unit. Underpinned by a company limited by shares, a 2004 version gave control and decision-making power to three classes of shareholder, and investment rights to a fourth:

- class A shares (for social entrepreneurs); class B shares (for charities and social enterprises); class C shares (for employees); class D shares (for supporting organisations)

Surplus Sharing Model (Case 11.4)

With a heritage stretching back to the work of Guy Major and Gavin Body in the mid-1990s, the surplus sharing rules developed by Rory Ridley-Duff at Computercraft Ltd, then Sheffield Business School, embrace co-operative principles across the labour/capital divide. The rules provide for active membership control on the basis of one person, one vote, with special provisions for issuing:

- founder shares; labour shares; investor shares

Somerset Model Rules (Case 11.5)

Part of the new 'open co-operative' movement (Davies-Coates, 2014), Somerset Model Rules were devised by Somerset Co-operative Services in 2009 to permit founders of a co-operative venture to create up to four stakeholder groups. The rules were among the first in the UK to advocate multi-stakeholder design principles under co-operative law.

The full case studies are on the companion website at: www.sagepub.co.uk/ridleyduff.

At first glance, each set of model rules enfranchises both internal and external stakeholders. *Stakeholder Model Ltd* (Case 11.1) offers shares to three groups: *stewardship shares* provide for a role similar to trustees in a charity who safeguard the objectives and values of the organisation; *partnership shares* are provided for staff, customers and suppliers who have long-term contracts with the enterprise; *investment shares* influence the distribution of profits and are offered to both staff and external funders. Each group controls one-third of the votes in general meetings.

The *Co-operative CIC Model* (Case 11.2) provides membership options for both service users (consumers) and workers (employees), but has no specific provision for external investors. The decision to use either a company limited by guarantee or shares is a product of CIC legislation. Membership confers voting rights typical of a co-operative, but limited rights to profits and assets. As a CIC, the rules include an asset lock: a clause naming a registered charity or other asset-locked social enterprise to which residual assets will be transferred upon dissolution.

The *NewCo Model* (Case 11.3) has superficial similarities to Stakeholder Model Ltd. It provides for three groups to receive ordinary shares: founding social entrepreneur(s) and investors; social enterprises and charities; and employees. Unlike Stakeholder Model Ltd, however, the balance between the shareholdings in the three groups is not fixed. Furthermore, in addition to ordinary shares, additional 'social equity' preference shares enable supporting organisations to invest in the enterprise and receive a fixed dividend.

The *Surplus Sharing Model* (Case 11.4) provides for shares to be held by founders (*founder shares*), suppliers of labour (*labour shares*), and suppliers of financial capital (*investor shares*). Labour shares entitle holders to a share of surpluses (typically split 50/50 with investor shareholders). As in the case of Stakeholder Model Ltd, founder shares recognise the value of a trustee role oriented towards protecting the democratic ethos and social objectives of the enterprise.

Somerset Rules (Case 11.5), available from Somerset Co-operative Services (SCS) (www.somerset.coop), enables enterprise founders to apply multi-stakeholder principles under Co-operative and Community Benefit Society Law. It re-interprets the notion of a *common bond* derived from a single characteristic (e.g. customer, saver, worker, sports fan), and assumes that the common bond can be rooted in solidarity between stakeholders (particularly consumers and producers) to share wealth within a community (Lund, 2011). First approved in 2009 (updated between 2012 and 2014) versions are now available under Company Law (for CICs) and Co-operative and Community Benefit Society Law (Somerset Co-operative Services, 2014).

What is striking about all these models is that they seek to change the nature of company membership so that both internal and external stakeholders have voting rights, and – in four of the five models – rights to share in profits *and assets*. Of the five, only the guarantee version of the Co-operative CIC Model (Case 11.2) fully observes the traditional interpretation of common ownership (i.e. that monies invested are locked into commonly owned (indivisible) assets that are held in trust for the benefit of members and the community). Are the other models, therefore, a degradation or reformulation of the idea of social ownership?

Consideration of this question is assisted by a review of the histories of the various models. The Co-operative CIC Model (Case 11.2) is rooted in a historical connection to the industrial common ownership movement (ICOM). It was developed in response to enquiries requesting a co-operative model that integrated the provisions of the CIC regulations. Part of this demand was created by the removal of a statutory commitment to stakeholder governance during the government consultation on CICs in 2003. The Co-operative CIC Model filled this gap in provision.

The other models all have a more mixed heritage. Stakeholder Model Ltd (Case 11.1) was developed in response to the needs of whole-food companies that depended on both a workforce and a loyal customer base, and to advances in the concept of a social firm.[2] Ideological sympathy with principles of co-operative management are combined with charitable objects and **equity investment instruments**. In place of a charity and a wholly owned subsidiary is a single enterprise that accommodates multiple stakeholders. The Surplus Sharing Model (Case 11.4) was initially a product of a co-operative encountering problems raising finance from *both* members and external parties. The first iteration of the rules was developed when it was found that government funding for co-operatives could not be accessed without the ability to convert loan finance into equity (Ridley-Duff, 2002). The rules were then developed after collaborations with employers seeking to extend employee ownership, with the goal of facilitating trust and community ownership alongside co-operative management. Of interest here is a mechanism for value-added sharing that enables a gradual succession in ownership (to the workforce and community) that does not involve a trade sale or private floatation.

The NewCo Model (Case 11.3), on the other hand, was conceived during an attempt to establish an information and communications technology organisation servicing social economy clients. The model aimed not only to provide services, but also to share profits with recipients of the services provided. Interestingly, this allows customers to share the costs of establishing the enterprise, and shape the way that services are provided to meet their needs. Help was provided by a Community Enterprise Development Unit which recognised the need to provide rewards for founding entrepreneurs and investors as well as employees and customers. Over time, the stake of the workforce increased and its shares were redefined to gain recognition as a multi-stakeholder co-operative. The CIC model was rejected so that those taking entrepreneurial risks could achieve higher capital gains through the issue of shares that accrue in value. Under the CIC model, directors (and others) can financially benefit from dividend payments, but these are capped at 35 per cent (BIS, 2014).

Somerset rules were a product of growing awareness of solidarity co-operatives in the US and Canada, particularly in the field of community energy and food production (Lund, 2011). Its relevance to the FairShares Model (first published in 2013) is the idea of applying solidarity co-operative principles across more than one body of law. When Somerset rules were first written (according to SCS), Co-operatives UK did not offer any model rules for solidarity co-operatives. However, under these rules, hegemonic control can still be achieved by one stakeholder where voting power is unbalanced (e.g. 60 per cent producers and 40 per cent consumers, or vice versa). Stakeholder (Case 11.1), NewCo (Case 11.3) and the later FairShares Model all seek to prevent stakeholder hegemony to preserve the incentive for a collaborative rather than a competitive governance system. Furthermore, under Somerset rules, a member can only belong to one member class. In the FairShares Model, members belong to any class where they satisfy the 'qualifying contribution' (Ridley-Duff and Southcombe, 2014).

In each of the models, various rights are allocated to different classes of shareholder. Gates (1998) describes the rights that can be defined in Articles of Association in Appendix B of *The Ownership Solution*. These are summarised, with reference to social enterprise practice, in Table 11.5.

Table 11.5   Analysis of rights in the case studies

Liquidation Rights

Liquidation rights enable shareholders or creditors to force a company into liquidation if it becomes apparent that it is insolvent, or likely to go insolvent. As Jensen (2006) argues, liquidation rights give investors the ability to force a profitable company into liquidation (either to remove competition or cash in the value of its assets). In all sets of model rules, multiple shareholder classes make it harder to liquidate a profitable enterprise. In the FairShares Model, a majority of voters in all classes must agree before liquidation can occur (if outside the provisions of insolvency law).

Appreciation Rights

Appreciation rights define how the value of an organisation is reflected in its share price. An entity that does not issue shares cannot grant appreciation rights. Case 11.2 does not issue shares in its CLG form, and in Case 11.5 shares cannot appreciate in value, but in Cases 11.1, 11.3 and 11.4 at least one share type can vary in value to reflect an (internal) market for shares in the enterprise. In one example of Case 11.3, Class C shareholder rights were re-written to prevent appreciation rights. In Cases 11.1 and 11.4 appreciation rights are not granted to those in a 'trustee' role, although they can acquire these rights if they qualify for additional types of membership (by contributing labour/finance capital). Evidence from employee ownership research suggests that granting appreciation rights may help substantially with the recruitment and retention of members (Erdal, 2011; McDonnell and MacKnight, 2012). In the FairShares Model, labour, users and investors share appreciation rights through their respective rights to receive investor shares commensurate with their labour, trading and capital contributions.

Transfer Rights

Transfer rights permit the sale of assets and shares to other legal and natural persons. Shares may not be transferable to prevent their acquisition by interests unsympathetic to the goals of the social enterprise, or to ensure that voting and incomes rights are retained by active members. Case 11.2 issues no share capital, but permits the transfer of other assets at market value. Case 11.3 issues share capital, but does not permit the sales of shares by one shareholder class to another. Case 11.4 does not permit the transfer of labour shares, but does allow the trading of investor shares among members. In the FairShares Model only one share type (investor shares) can be transferred, and trading rights are permitted among members and with social enterprises constituted for employee, community or public benefit.

Income Rights

Income rights define how earnings can be derived from member ownership (via loan interest and/or dividend payments). In co-operatives, there needs to be a cap on loan interest and/or dividend payments to satisfy Rochdale Principles. Case 11.2 has no share capital and – as a CIC – is subject to statutory caps on payments to members. Case 11.3 allows shareholders in Classes A, B and C to receive dividends on shareholdings. Case 11.4 includes rules that ensure surpluses are distributed 50/50 between labour and investor shareholders, and that a percentage of surpluses is issued as investor shares to labour shareholders. In the FairShares Model, labour, users and investors share the income rights.

Voting Rights

Voting rights influence who can participate in key decisions (such as mergers, acquisitions, dissolution, rule changes, and the election of a governing body and/or company officers). Cases 11.2, 11.4 and 11.5 establish one person, one vote principles. Case 11.3 allows voting based on shareholdings, but is structured so that two stakeholder groups must be in agreement before a resolution can be passed. A new implementation includes a block of class C shares with co-operative characteristics – one person, one vote principles apply when workers' cast their votes, but may not apply among a group of entrepreneurs. In Case 11.4 (and the FairShares Model) there must be a one person, one vote majority in each class, plus 75 per cent in favour overall, to pass a special resolution (required for mergers, dissolutions and rule changes).

Information Rights

Information rights define who can access information held by company officers and staff, and what information is covered. Rights may be extended only to the governing body, or to all members. In all cases except 11.1, information rights are granted to all members during normal working hours.

Public Rights

Public rights can include a 'golden share' to protect the public interest, or social objects that are approved by a regulator. Case 11.2 is subject to public rights and regulation by the CIC regulator, and Case 11.5 grants public rights to satisfy the norms of the co-operative movement. Other cases are not under a statutory duty to grant public rights.

Shareholdings influence voting rights at general meetings, and define what can take place inside and outside different types of meeting. They can also be used to distribute rights to a proportion of annual trading surpluses or profits (however this is expressed) and a proportion of the organisation's assets. Charitable associations, and CLGs, typically declare that they have 'no share capital'. Even if this is the case, the Articles of Association can still define who is a member, the rights and responsibilities that members acquire, the powers that members have to elect and control their executive, and the powers they have to distribute surplus income and assets.

The Stakeholder Model Ltd and NewCo Model allocate most rights to either founders or directors. The board, in both cases, is free to exercise its powers largely unchecked by the wider membership who are cast mainly as beneficiaries. The Co-operative CIC Model, Surplus Sharing Model and Somerset Rules build in greater powers for the wider membership. They contain clauses on the operation of general meetings as well as board meetings. Importantly, both sets of rules require executives to maintain open management systems accessible to all members during normal working hours.[3] In the Stakeholder Model Ltd, only board members have unrestricted access to management information.

The implications for practice should be noted in each case. Of the five examples, only the Co-operative CIC Model – constituted as a CLG – is likely to be a good vehicle for philanthropic fundraising. While this is not the priority of social enterprises trading in commercial markets, it is a concern for social enterprises contracting with public authorities and local government bodies, particularly where contracts do not meet the full cost of providing a particular service. These social enterprises benefit from an asset lock to secure further public and charitable funding on which they may depend for survival. The choice, however, is not always voluntary. It can be the case that public and charitable funders instruct recipients of grants (or contracts) that their enterprises need to be constituted in a particular way to be eligible for funding (or contracts).

Despite its popularity in the UK as the majority organisational type, the CLG is not a good vehicle for raising money from staff, suppliers, customers and other investors as it fails to provide security or a return commensurate with the risks associated with an unsecured investment (see Chapter 6). Faced with investing in one's own business or an established savings scheme, a social enterprise has to compete with other saving schemes. In the cases reviewed, the enterprises are structured to increase voice and control (governance), and/or to increase participation in the rewards of trading (i.e. through surplus or profit sharing). The underlying philosophy of the legal forms, therefore, is to spread the risks and benefits across multiple internal and external stakeholders.

A new project by North East Social Enterprise Partnership (NESEP), Geof Cox Associates and Social Enterprise Europe Ltd has created a theoretical framework that informs the choice of legal model (www.socentstructures.org.uk/find-my-structure). In this project, two dimensions are considered: firstly, there is the desired level of participation in governance; secondly there is the intended income generation strategy (see Chapter 5). Where participatory governance is combined with a trading/private investment strategy, the recommendations lean towards co-operative/company forms with share issuing capabilities. Where participatory governance is not desired, and the enterprise will be funded by fundraising or contracting, a guarantee company or CIO foundation is recommended. There are many shades of practice in between these extremes, and the framework links through to more (UK) sets of model rules prepared by Geof Cox Associates and the FairShares Association to cater to different requirements.

The relevance of the FairShares Model

The relevance of the FairShares Model is less related to its direct impact on practice (which is too early to judge) and more related to evidence that networks of educators, consultants and scholars within the social and solidarity economy are converging on new norms for member ownership in solidarity enterprises (see Table 11.6). However, take up is likely to be sensitive to discourses operating at sectoral, regional and national levels. For example, the Social Enterprise Mark (in the UK) only recognises stakeholder *governance* (let alone ownership) and even then it is part of their 'gold' award. This sharply contrasts with European countries who write it into their legislation as a basic requirement (see Denmark and Croatia). At Social Enterprise Europe meetings (attended by Rory) board members have discussed a fall in interest in solidarity models in the UK, but increasing interest elsewhere.[4] It remains the norm in Mondragon's banking, education and retailing (Spain), for food and care projects in Quebec (Canada), and in Bologna's social care and work integration sector (Italy) (Lund, 2011; Davies-Coates, 2014; Defourny et al., 2014).

Table 11.6   Convergence on solidarity enterprise models at the FairShares Association

Approach in Antecedent Models	Approach in FairShares Model
• Stewardship/Class A/Founder	• Founder shares
• Partnership/Class B shares	• User shares
• Partnership/Class C shares/Labour	• Labour shares
• Investor/Class A shares	• Investor shares
• Co-ownership (individual/organisational members)	• Founder, user and labour shareholders acquire investor shares based on active participation
• At least two (and in other cases three) classes of member at incorporation.	• One class at incorporation (founders), with constitutional provisions to create the other classes when production, trading and surplus generation occurs
• Preference for unitary boards elected from each class of shareholder	• Main/sub boards elected by shareholder classes (elections triggered by a member threshold fixed at incorporation)
• All stakeholders have a route to membership • Limited protection of minorities	• All stakeholders have a route to membership, plus explicit protection of minority interests (special resolutions) and mediation to resolve member conflicts

Approach in Antecedent Models	Approach in FairShares Model
• Electoral college in general meetings (Stakeholder) • Employees hold the balance of power (NewCo) • Shareholder classes with the same rights in general meetings (Surplus Sharing)	• One member, one vote for ordinary and special resolutions; electoral college when a poll is called; one class, one vote for special resolutions • For a special resolution to pass, there must be majority support in *every* class of shareholder

On closer examination, the UK situation looks mixed. Papers on fair trade have revealed pioneering work to adopt solidarity models throughout the supply chain (Lacey, 2009; Davies et al., 2010). Local food projects are starting to copy examples from Canada (Somerset Co-operative Services, 2014) and the multi-stakeholder model for governing schools developed by the Co-operative College continues to be out-standingly popular (Birch, 2012; Wilson, 2014). In manufacturing and engineering, the bias is towards a single stakeholder employee ownership model in which solidarity between senior managers and staff members is the goal (e.g. Scott-Bader, Arup, and John Lewis). However, hybrid models involving employee trusts and financial institutions can also be seen as experiments that test whether city institutions can adapt to the norms advanced by solidarity enterprises (e.g. Eaga plc, Circle Partnership plc).

Conclusions

Close examination of each multi-stakeholder model reveals that they are not free of potential conflicts between stakeholders, and that the relative power of one stakeholder over others still remains an issue. As such, they are vulnerable to the criticism that they constitute a naïve form of liberalism that ignores or glosses over disparities in power, and fail – on their own – to address the capacity and confidence of those socialised to accept subordination in decision-making (Heaney, 1995). The *recognition* of 'other' stakeholders does not necessarily mean they participate equally, nor does it guarantee that collaboration will occur.

Nevertheless, the model rules discussed reopen the question raised by Davies (2002) regarding who can be a company member, the rights they can acquire through membership, and the potential of member-owned (rather than investor-owned) enterprises (Birchall, 2009). Each acts as a template in reframing business norms so that corporate citizenship either limits or replaces property rights as the basis for membership, voting power and wealth distribution. How this is operationalised becomes a matter of management practice. Devising a set of rules does not guarantee that the rules are followed; this rests on the understandings, ability and commitment of those currently involved in an enterprise, and their capacity and willingness to devise appropriate management systems (Ridley-Duff, 2009). Each emergent model – and the consolidated approach represented by *FairShares* – challenges business norms in a different way (informed by the social contexts in which they developed). Each shifts business thinking towards participatory democratic models envisaged by Pateman (1970) by operationalising multi-stakeholder governance and ownership (Turnbull, 1994, 2002).

The model rules discussed in this chapter provided the antecedents for the development of the FairShares Model – a philosophy, brand and set of design protocols for multi-stakeholder, member-owned enterprises (Ridley-Duff and Bull, 2013; Ridley-Duff and Southcombe, 2014). Importantly, the goal is not achieved by super-imposing employee and stakeholder consultation on top of existing charity or company structures. Instead, there is an attempt to rewrite the legal principles and social norms on which business activity is based from the ground up. Consequently, they represent early attempts at Argyris's Model 2 thinking regarding the nature of (and possibilities inherent in) business itself. New models for enterprise membership allocate rights in different ways, and lead to organisations with social identities more aligned to the complexities of the societies in which they are embedded.

Class exercise: Building a solidarity enterprise model

Materials to support this exercise can be found on the companion website at: www.sagepub.co.uk/ridleyduff.

Watch this video (*Shift Change*) to get a feel for how solidarity principles work:

http://vimeo.com/38342677

Imagine that you are planning to establish a new solidarity enterprise that will source fair trade goods and then supply them to cafés, universities, housing groups, public authorities, schools and private companies in your city/region. You have been tasked with designing an enterprise that will incorporate FairShares Model principles. Information about antecedent models to FairShares have been circulated to your team.

- Divide the class into groups of five students. Allocate each group member one antecedent case to study (from Cases 11.1, 11.2, 11.3, 11.4 and 11.5 – see Table 11.4). (If undertaking as a module project, you can issue copies of model rules as well.)
- Ask team members to study one antecedent model each to establish its contribution to the FairShares Model.
- Ask team members to share their findings on the merits (or not) of each antecedent model.
- Establish your own FairShares Model adapted to serve the needs of your new enterprise.
- Ask each team to present the *guiding principles* that they have agreed, which will be applied to the new social enterprise.
- The following FairShares Model Enterprise on Loomio is a study aid for students: www.loomio.org/g/ugICXanW/fairshares-model-enterprise-an-example.

- As a group project, why not get each student group to implement their guiding principles as a new Loomio Group, invite other students to join it so they can examine and critique it? You can set an assignment task in which students compare different implementations.

Summary of learning

In this chapter, we have argued the following:

An organisation's rules influence how members are selected and included in decision-making.

Unlike private enterprises, social enterprise rules aim to balance the needs and rights of members to ensure they match or exceed the rights granted to private (financial) investors.

The long-term impacts of a constitution are evident only after many years/decades of trading.

Model 1 (single-loop learning) seeks to *improve upon existing models*.

Model 2 (double-loop learning) seeks to reformulate the norms of enterprise activity.

Emerging norms, such as the *Somerset Rules* and the *FairShares Model*, provide models for solidarity enterprises in which multiple stakeholders share the ownership, governance and management responsibility of their social enterprise.

Questions and possible essay assignments

1. Critically compare the ownership, governance and management of a privately and socially owned sports clubs of your choice. Identify similarities and difference in their identities and legal structures. *Suggestion*: you could compare Manchester United (www.manutd.com) and FC United of Manchester (www.fc-utd.co.uk/).
2. Using examples, critically assess the claim that a social enterprise can constitute itself so that 'no one group is able to secure a basis of power and command over the majority so that it can effectively suppress or deny the claims of the groups it opposes'.
3. 'Social identity is a matter of management practice, not company rules.' Using examples, critically assess the role of legal rules in shaping social identity and management practices.

Further reading

In the UK, a number of practitioner guides are available. One widely publicised guide is *Keeping It Legal*, available from the Social Enterprise Coalition and co-authored with Bates, Wells and Braithwaite (SEC, 2005). One weakness of this publication is the relatively poor coverage on co-operative and employee ownership structures. Stronger guidance on this is available in *Simply Legal*, updated in 2009 with support from the Big Lottery (downloadable from Co-operatives UK: www.uk.coop/simplylegal). Information on the use of trusts and share incentive schemes can be obtained from the Employee Ownership Association (UK) and the National Center for Employee Ownership (US) (see links in the 'Useful resources' section). Charity-specific information on the link between governance and the Charities Act 2006 has been commissioned by NCVO.

Academic discussion of the link between social identity and legal forms is relatively rare. Nevertheless, a readable introduction to general issues in company law that considers both historical and theoretical issues can be found in Davies's *Introduction to Company Law* (2002). A highly watchable (and critical analysis) of the impact of legal structures of the modern corporation is *The Corporation*, available on both DVD and YouTube.

Comprehensive books arguing for new structures are developed in Ellerman's *The Democratic Worker-owned Firm* (1990), Gates's *The Ownership Solution* (1998) and Erdal's *Beyond the Corporation* (2011). A critical response to Ellerman has been published by Zundel (2002) in the *Journal of Business Ethics*.

Further reading material is available on the companion website at: www.sagepub.co.uk/ ridleyduff.

Useful resources

Places to start

- Global

   Social enterprise: http://skollworldforum.org/, www.ashoka.org/
   Social economy: http://gsef2014.org/
   Co-operatives: http://ica.coop/
   Employee (worker) ownership: http://www.cicopa.coop/
   Philanthropy: http://philanthropyforum.org/

- Africa

   Social enterprise: www.ontheup.org.uk/
   Co-operatives: http://ica.coop/en/alliance-africa
   Philanthropy: http://
   philanthropyforum.org/apf/

- Asia

   Social enterprise: www.socialenterpriseeurope.co.uk/
   Social economy: http://gsef2014.org/

Co-operatives: www.ica-ap.coop/
Philanthropy: www.avpn.asia/en/

- Europe

  Social enterprise: www.socialenterpriseeurope.co.uk/
  Social economy: www.socialeconomy.eu.org/
  Co-operatives: https://coopseurope.coop/
  Employee ownership: www.efesonline.org/
  Philanthropy: http://evpa.eu.com/

- Latin America

  Social economy: www.eesc.europa.eu/?i=portal.en.rex-opinions.21732
  Co-operatives: www.aciamericas.coop/?lang=en
  Philanthropy: www.hiponline.org/

- Australia

  Social enterprise: www.socialtraders.com.au/
  Co-operatives: www.australia.coop/ca/
  Employee ownership: www.employeeownership.com.au/
  Philanthropy: www.philanthropy.org.au/

- China

  Social enterprise: www.youcheng.org/
  Co-operatives: www.chinacoop.coop/
  English/Philanthropy: http://cszh.mca.gov.cn/article/english/

- Indonesia

  Social enterprise: http://unltd-indonesia.org/
  Social economy (Asia-led): http://gsef2014.org/
  Co-operatives: http://induk-kud.com/
  Philanthropy: http://filantropi.or.id/

- New Zealand

  Social enterprise: www.nzsef.org.nz/
  Co-operatives: http://nz.coop/
  Employee ownership: www.employeeownership.com.au/
  Philanthropy: www.charities.govt.nz/

- Philippines

  Social enterprise: http://philsocialenterprisenetwork.com/
  Social economy (Asia-led): http://gsef2014.org/
  Co-operatives: www.ica-ap.coop/
  Philanthropy: www.afonline.org/

- UK

  Social enterprise/social economy: www.socialenterprise.org.uk
  Co-operatives: www.coop.co.uk
  Employee ownership: www.employeeownership.co.uk
  Philanthropy: www.ncvo.org.uk/

- US

  Social enterprise: www.se-alliance.org/
  Social economy: www.socialeconomynetwork.org/
  Co-operatives: www.ncba.coop/, www.aciamericas.coop/?lang=en
  Employee ownership: www.nceo.org/, www.usworker.coop/
  Philanthropy: www.usa.gov/Business/Nonprofit.shtml

Models rules (UK)

- Charity Commission Model Rules: www.charitycommission.gov.uk/detailed-guidance/registering-a-charity/model-governing-documents/
- Community Interest Companies: www.companylawclub.co.uk/topics/model_articles.shtml
- Co-operatives UK Model Rules: www.uk.coop/advise/modelrules
- FairShares Association: www.fairshares.coop
- NESEP/SEE – Social Enterprise Structures: www.socentstructures.org.uk
- Somerset Model Rules: www.somerset.coop

Notes

1 An interesting aspect of the John Lewis Partnership constitution is an explicit recognition that loyalty to a trade union and the partnership will create conflict. The constitution asks partners to consider their loyalties (to JLP and their union) in the event of internal conflict. Union membership is low in the JLP, but the right to belong to a trade union is protected.
2 Social firm in the UK equates to a subset of the social economy that focuses on people who are disadvantaged in the labour market. In the US, Europe and particularly in Oceania, we find that people use the term to describe something closer to a social business (as advanced in this textbook).
3 This is also true of a NewCo implementation developed in 2004.
4 This was specifically communicated by Geof Cox based on comments about the level of interest in his Stakeholder Model. However, this may be more a function of the sectors in which Cox is working (or which are being channelled to him) than a reflection of the wider UK situation.

Governance and Human Relations

12

Rory Ridley-Duff, Tracey Coule and
Mike Bull

Learning objectives

In this chapter, we bring together the discussions of strategic management, ideology, leadership and legal identities to consider the challenges of governance and human relationships. By the end of this chapter you will be able to:

- outline system and relational views of governance
- explain the nature, logic and impact of the employment relationship on human relations
- critically evaluate the impact of your management ideology on your governance practices and employment relations policies
- critically assess the viability of alternatives to employment based on member ownership and supported self-employment.

The key arguments that will be developed in this chapter are:

- The concept of 'best practice' changes depending on the stakeholder perspective adopted.
- Multiple bodies of knowledge compete to shape thinking on governance and human relationship development.

(Continued)

(Continued)

- The employment relationship is a legal mechanism that enables the employer to acquire/re-acquire all the property created by employees.
- Social enterprises that operate through social networks and employment co-operatives offer a new way to organise production in which producers maintain rights to their produce.

Introduction

In this chapter, attention is focused on management practices that seek to control and develop people. As we discussed in Chapter 9, the development and control of people at work is generally studied as 'human resource development' when the focus is on learning, and 'human resource management' when the focus is on social control and employment. In this chapter, we resist the temptation to use the language of human *resources* to emphasise a perspective based on human *relationship* development consistent with the values of sustainable development, co-operation and mutuality. Control is a complex issue, and it does not always emanate from the 'top' of organisations. Moreover, new forms of solidarity enterprise usurp the traditional employer–employee relationship and replace it with organization–member relations (Gold, 2004; Baudhardt, 2014). Nor is it the case that organization–member relations are confined to service delivery. The OpenSource and Creative Commons movements (see Chapter 2) show that *production* and *consumption* of goods – particularly digital goods – can forge new norms of interaction.

To illustrate the issue, consider the tools created by the Enspiral network that we introduced in Chapter 9. Firstly, Enspiral developed Loomio as an online collaborative decision-making tool (www.loomio.org). This enabled dialogue (both in real-time online, or asynchronously off-line) among people anywhere in the world. The connection of these engineers to the Occupy Movement meant that the design goal was to enable every member to participate, make comments, upload documents, initiate proposals, vote for their own and others' proposals and share results with their community. Their design goal is to limit hierarchy development except where it arises out of respect for others' contributions and knowhow, or might arise out of protocols linked to the acceptance of new group members.

Enspiral's work on Loomio only covers decision-making in a governance context. They have now embarked on a second web-based application called Co-budget which allows each organisation member to control how their capital contributions are allocated. Each member can decide how to allocate a small amount of capital (instead of an executive group collectively controlling a larger amount). Furthermore, each member can propose projects. They run or do not run based on the support given by other members. In short, technology developed to support crowdfunding techniques (Chapter 6) is now being reworked to support new approaches to *internal* budgeting within organisations. Whereas crowdfunding is an interface with *external* 'supporters', Co-budget changes the relationships *internally* and this has the potential to change the structures of power across all domains of interaction, with substantial ramifications for both governance and human relations management.

Class exercise: Collaborative decision-making and human relations

Watch this video: www.youtube.com/watch?v=iR9ivaUg9wo
In groups of three to four people, consider the following questions:

1 If you set up Loomio and Co-budget in a social enterprise to give every workforce member access, what impact would you expect it to have on:

- The decision-making powers of governing bodies, managers, workers and other stakeholders?
- The budgeting power of boards, managers, work teams and individual workers?

Now watch this short video on participatory budgeting: www.youtube.com/watch?v=S7JwPekH5U0

1 How is the logic of participatory budgeting linked to the logic of Co-budget?
2 How much of your organisation's (community's) budget could be allocated using participatory budgeting?

For a more detailed look at participatory budgeting, read this article about Brazil (Touchton and Wampler, 2013) on the companion website.

Coule (2008) identifies a number of inter-related organisational and environmental systems that trigger the production of operating rules and norms within an organisation to promote its sustainability (Figure 12.1). These include:

- a governance system
- a funding system
- an HR system
- an explanatory system
- an internal accountability system.

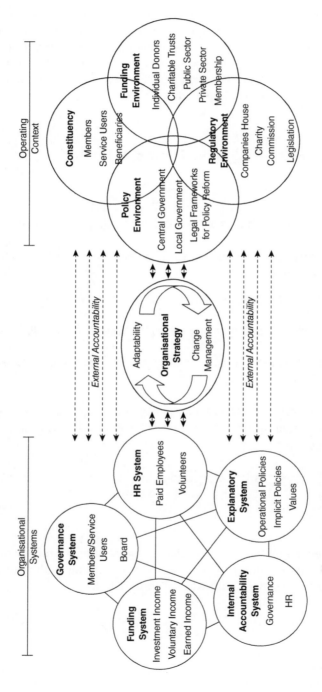

Figure 12.1 Organisational systems and operating contexts

Source: Coule (2008), with permission from the author

This chapter is focused on the development of *governance systems* and *employee relations* – implicit cultural norms communicated through written artefacts and social practices. Public administration had traditionally made the assumption that an elected or nominated executive is capable of discovering, defining and then enforcing the general will of a population (Younkins, 2005; Coule and Patmore, 2013). This managerialist mind-set obscures how frequently governing bodies, management groups and individuals establish structures and practices that minimise the power of other organisational stakeholders (Alvesson and Willmott, 2003; Dart, 2004; Johnson, 2006). As a result, an alternative perspective on governance is to address asymmetries in the relationships between different stakeholder groups, and to establish 'new public governance' that fosters collaborative working through networks and new institutional logics (Osborne, 2006; Coule and Patmore, 2013).

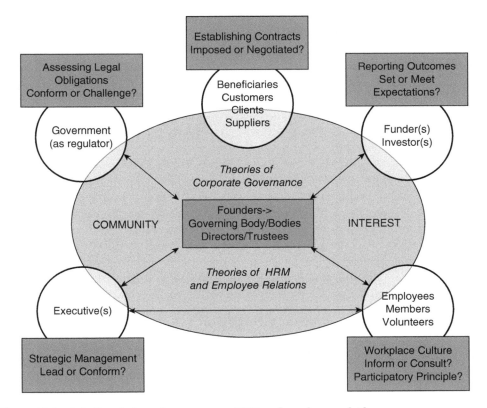

Figure 12.2   Relational view of governance, HRM and employee relations

Source: adapted from Ridley-Duff (2008a)

As suggested in Figure 12.2, there are different bodies of theory depending on your perspective of the organisation. Firstly, *governance* theory focuses on relationships between regulators, external stakeholders, funders and governing bodies (and the systems that sustain them). Secondly, there is *human resource management* that studies the relationships and interactions between executives and the productive workforce. While *HRM theory* generally adopts a management perspective, there is a third body of theory (**employee relations**) that studies the role of trade unions and employees in negotiating and resisting changes to HRM practice. This third body of theory is much more open to the possibility that organisations can be controlled 'from below' by collective action on the part of the workforce, or by networks of producers who operate outside the confines of a legal entity.

All bodies of theory have an interest in the processes by which the 'rules' of organisational life are decided, and the way governments, employers and employees react to their introduction (Salamon, 2000). This three-pronged theoretical approach encourages a more holistic view of organisational life, and provides a framework for rethinking human relations policies (Martin, 2002). It does not, however, go far enough because it omits the issue of how to involve customers and suppliers in governance. To achieve this, we have to turn to the concept of network governance that has advanced understanding of successful co-operatives and employee-owned enterprises (Turnbull, 1994, 2001). This holistic view not only makes visible the way strategic stakeholders (employees, customers, suppliers and community institutions) influence each other, but also makes visible the *bodies of knowledge* that compete to influence our understanding of human interaction.

There are any number of books and resources that can advise on employment law in different countries (Dundon and Rollinson, 2011; Bamber et al., 2011), so it is not the goal of this chapter to cover this. We do, however, consider at length the principles on which employment is based: the master–servant relationship that evolved into an employer–employee relationship, and which (still) underpins the conceptualisation of 'employment' outside the social and solidarity economy. So, unlike a standard HRM chapter that focuses on human 'resource' management, we devote attention to problematising the employment relationship in order to develop a conversation about human *relationship* management fit for the social and solidarity economy.

We start by examining the discourses of governance, HRM and employee relations and set out some useful concepts: soft/hard management practices; written and psychological contracts. Then, we discuss diagnostics that can build governance capacity by revealing the underlying logics of different approaches to governance and employee relations. In doing so, we make the argument that while employment improves on unemployment, member ownership improves on the employment relationship because it ends the 'money trick' by which employers capture all the residual value created by employees. In the conclusions, we advance an argument that creating a social economy involves two phases in the development of governance and employment relations. The first phase involves charitable trading activities (CTAs) and socially responsible businesses (SRBs) that create *employment*. The second phase, involving co-operative and mutual enterprises (CMEs) advances member ownership and/or supported self-employment. Both phases are by-products of social entrepreneurship, the first reconfigures social relations to secure gainful (or improved) employment relations for beneficiaries. The second reorganises employers to transform master–servant relations into mutual relations.

Discourses on managing people

In both mainstream and voluntary sector literatures, HRM and governance are portrayed as benign management 'functions' capable of selecting and implementing 'best practice'. This is fuelled by a concern to comply with legislation, or government attempts to use legislation to promote 'best practice' (Cornforth and Edwards, 1998; Monks and Minow, 2004; NCVO, 2005). The idea of 'best practice', however, *narrows* the choices presented to practising managers, and draws 'theory' mainly from untested prescriptions devised by consultants, regulators, organisation founders, board members and senior managers (Storey, 2001).

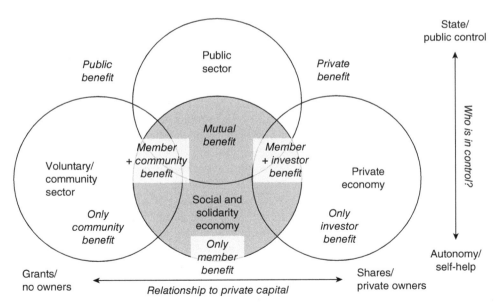

Figure 12.3   Governance orientations and intended beneficiaries

In the social and solidarity economy the norms governing interaction between the wider community, workforce and executive managers can be fundamentally different due to variations in member-benefit orientation (see Figure 12.3). Governance needs to be more broadly defined because conventional advice on the separation of governance and management collapses when either there is a 'closed-loop' form of control, as happens when a workforce elects its own management (see Chapter 3), or multiple (compound) boards replace a single (unitary) board (Turnbull, 2001). Compound boards, because they are dispersed, are more accepting of network governance where stakeholder relationships occur both within and across governing bodies. They are also of interest because they invite study of the way (staff) members can control executive groups through elections and **participatory democracy** (Cornforth, 2004).

While the ideological perspectives of **corporate governance theory** and employee relations theory tend to mirror each other, the advent of social enterprise encourages study of the common ground between them where both study the effects of employee directors, employee and community ownership, and forms of 'voice' that allow multiple stakeholders a more direct role in defining strategic goals (Dundon et al., 2004; Jensen, 2011; Cathcart, 2013; Moreau and Mertens, 2013). The governance focus of some SRBs and all CMEs necessarily includes employees (staff) and consumers, and not just funders, donors and clients who support CTAs. In CTAs, democratic participation is generally more oriented to *external* stakeholders because charity and non-profit law frames employee-governors as having a conflict of interest. Any 'democratic' claims, therefore, are limited to the representation and involvement of community stakeholders (NCVO, 2005; Low, 2006; Ridley-Duff, 2007). The logic of charity/non-profit laws reinforces the view that employees are subordinate to board authority, and are confined to the 'servant' role in the master–servant relationship.

As a result, there is a danger of giving too much consideration to external stakeholders, and not enough to internal ones. For example, Doherty et al.'s (2009) consideration of governance has extensive discussion of the role and purpose of trustees (responsible to donors/funders), but limited (if any) discussion of the value of beneficiaries, producers and employees in governing bodies. By considering governance norms in contexts where there is a challenge to unitary employment relations through member ownership, a full complement of responsible management practices can be developed (Birchall, 2009; McDonnell and MacKnight, 2012; Laasch and Conway, 2015).

As set out in Chapters 1, 2, 3, 8 and 11, we value the enfranchisement of both internal and external stakeholders through more balanced ownership and governance practices (Bull, 2006, 2007) and more equitable systems of ownership and control (Brown, 2006; Ridley-Duff, 2007) and view these as important alternatives to public, corporate and (traditional) charity sector governance practices.

Class exercise: Discovering your governance orientation

Additional materials (including a paper-based version) of this Governance Diagnostic Survey are available from the companion website at www.sagepub. co.uk/ridleyduff.

In 2014, the FairShares Association created an online version of a Governance Diagnostic Questionnaire included in the first edition of this book. For this edition, the questions were revised to cover principles of responsible management such as sustainability, ethics and stakeholder representation. Aside this, the diagnostic retains the same underlying meta-theoretical assumptions (Ridley-Duff, 2007; Coule, 2013). Governance systems are seen as something that emerges dynamically from the responses of stakeholders who have power and which takes on an individual/collective unitarist and/or individual/collective pluralist orientation towards 'other' stakeholders. The diagnostics enable scrutiny (and reflection) on which orientations are dominant in an organisation, industrial sector or organisation type.

The diagnostics are designed primarily for people who interact with governing bodies (elected members, executives, secretariats, directors). It can also be used as a capacity building tool for future governors.

Take the survey here: www.quicksurveys.com/s/a7D9EoZ

Review the results here: http://tolu.na/15TW9Mr

As an assignment, or a class discussion, debate the following questions:

1 Which *stakeholders* are recognised in this meta-theory of governance?
2 What are the key issues raised in relation to each stakeholder group?
3 Can you determine any patterns in the responses you have given (or studied) (i.e. preferences for individual or collective decision-making, or preferences for unitary or pluralist systems of control)?

Theories of governance spotlight the processes of selection, development, retention and replacement of board members, as well as the decision-making processes that affect the relationship between regulators, investors (funders), creditors, executives and governing bodies. In law, governance activities are encouraged and regulated through the laws covering the operations of the legal form (see Table 11.2). In the UK, the Co-operatives and Community Benefit Society Act (2014), **Community Interest Company Amendment Regulations** (2012) and the **Charities Act** (2011) provide the governance frameworks for CMEs, SRBs and CTAs respectively.

The nature of the employment relationship

HRM theory, on the other hand, has been developed by management researchers to clarify the selection, retention, development, reward and control of productive staff. These activities are regulated by employment relations law (such as the Employment Relations Act 2004 and Equality Act 2010). In an excellent overview, Clegg et al. (2008) point out that the language of HRM shows its managerialist origins. Firstly, it is applied to productive staff, not board or company members. Secondly, humans are constructed as 'resources' that appear as 'costs' on the profit and loss account, and 'liabilities' on a balance sheet. This frames working people as work objects contributing *labour* instrumentally alongside other 'inputs' such as finance, equipment and technology, with only the *outputs* of work considered assets. Ellerman (1990) discusses how people are dehumanised by the way their labour is represented in economics and argues for new thinking in which people are constituted as the *only* party that *adds* value in the production process. He argues that the application of the labour theory of property, based on Locke's assertion that only producers add value, is the basis of their inalienable right to the products of their labour. In short, capital creates nothing, labour creates everything, so the value created by production processes should accrue to the providers of labour, not the providers of capital.

But this is not what happens in practice for the majority of people (except for the relatively few entrepreneurs, artisans and artists who retain all rights to their works). Employment law frames employees as 'servants', and employers as 'masters' in the employment relationship (Gardiner, 2009). Put simply, employees rent out their capacity for labour, and then hand over what they produce to their employer. The products of work belong to the owners of capital (employers), and not the providers for labour (employees). As a UK's Business Link blog commented:

> The good news is that rights to IP created by employees generally belong to the employer. Showing that a member of staff has an employment contract is usually enough to prove that you own all IP rights. But it's a good idea to state the position explicitly in separate clauses of employees' contracts. This prevents any confusion arising – perhaps over work created outside office hours or as a by-product of specified work. (Business Link, 2012)

Employment law presumes, therefore, that all creative works – even those produced outside working hours, belong to a person's employer. Traditional copyright law assigns rights to the 'creator'. However, under employment law, employees are *non-people*. Within a private economy, it is the legal personality of the employer – the company, co-operative, association or partnership – that acquires the legal right to IP created by the people employed by it. This is equally true of CTAs, SRBs and CMEs *unless* Articles of Association and/or Contracts of Employment are rewritten to maintain the rights of producers over their produce, or are rewritten to assign rights to a 'commons' that enables all members (or the public) to access to it.

In terms of human relations, these issues could hardly be more important because it places every 'employee' and 'worker' (as defined by employment law) in the role of 'servant' with an entitlement to retain only their *skills and abilities* when they leave a job, and not the intellectual or physical property they have created. It is for this reason that Erdal devotes a whole chapter in *Beyond the Corporation* to the origins and purposes of the employment contract, and how it is 'perpetuating a legal system that does not acknowledge the humanity of […] employees, or their right to share in the wealth they create' (2011: 124).

He explains, following Ellerman (1990), how the employment contract is the document in which employees sign away their share of wealth in exchange for (highly limited) employment protection. For Erdal, employment rights are inadequate compensation for a lifetime's loss of the *fundamental* right to own everything you produce and to participate in decisions about *what and how* to produce. However, even Erdal's proposed solution (employee ownership) cannot fully stem the loss of equity in the products of work. Under employee ownership, a person is still – in law – an employee and will lose access to the assets they have helped to create. The best they can hope for is greater compensation for that loss.

The employment contract, and the HRM policies that arise to protect it, are rooted in this centuries old system that permits organisations as legal entities to acquire all the surplus value created by producers. Moreover, it is this interest in acquiring surplus value that incentivises employers to reduce wages, close factories and adopt other HRM policies that increase labour productivity without equitably sharing the wealth produced by current or former employees

Class exercise: 'The Great Money Trick' (Robert Tressell)

Watch this video: www.youtube.com/watch?v=j_f_FdOqbgk

In this video, a famous passage from *The Ragged Trousered Philanthropists* – 'The Great Money Trick' (Chapter 21) – is reproduced to celebrate the novel's 100th anniversary. Watch the video and consider how human relations at work are affected by the nature of the employment relationship. Carefully consider the relative power of labour and capital in the relationship described and critically assess its relevance today.

(Continued)

(Continued)

1 Does this tale capture the nature of the employment relationship?
2 How can a social enterprise design its ownership, governance and human relations systems to ensure the Great Money Trick does not occur (by accident or by design)?
3 While employment is preferable to unemployment, is member ownership preferable to employment?

Employment law applies only when particular relations of power and control are satisfied in law: a multiple test is needed in tribunals to determine whether a person is an employee or not. These tests seek to establish whether a person is controlling, or is controlled by, the enterprise to which they belong (Dundon and Rollinson, 2011). Only where a relationship of power and control over the labour process is established do courts recognise a person as an employee (and grant them the rights they are due under employment law).

In the field of social enterprise, there are three pinch points: the first is the boundary between self-employment (or worker ownership) and employment; the second is the blurred line between being an employee and a 'worker' (within the EU); the third is between being a paid worker and a volunteer. The boundaries vary in different countries. For example, under Spanish law, the worker-owners of CMEs are *not* employees while in the UK worker-owners are usually treated as employees under employment law. In the UK (and Anglo-American cultures), there are a number of proxy indicators that indicate an employment relationship: working under a contract; having to ask to take time off; having taxes deducted by your employers at source; being supervised by (or accountable to) a line manager; having appraisals; receiving regular pay (i.e. not invoicing for services). These are the basis of the multiple control test that establishes employment status.

In Morris (1999), the ease with which volunteers can become employees within CTAs is discussed through a number of legal cases. Switching from paying expenses after claims to a regular expense payment, and introducing volunteer agreements that include a management right to control volunteers' hours of work, or to discipline 'bad' behaviour, or which restricts volunteers' freedom to work on days of their choosing, can all contribute to the creation of an employment relationship. At the other end of the social enterprise spectrum, CMEs also have to maintain 'voluntary association' but this time it is among paid workers. Cannell's (2012) thoughtful contribution on the differences between co-operative governance (hierarchical, unitary) and co-operative culture (egalitarian, pluralist) draw strongly on the argument that mutuality depends on mastering skills in *relationship management under conditions of complexity* (Stacey, 2007). He rejects the idea that traditional 'control' mechanisms can contribute to either democratic working or a co-operative culture.

Hard and soft HRM

Clegg et al. (2008) summarise the concepts of hard and soft HRM (Table 12.1). They trace 'hard' approaches to the Michigan school and contrast these with 'soft' approaches advocated at Harvard. In recent years, soft HRM has become the orthodoxy in Anglo-American and Japanese corporations. Doherty et al. (2009) argue that soft HRM, with its focus on a suite of 'high-commitment' HRM practices, provides a model for social enterprises. This argument is based on empirical studies showing that soft HRM benefits both employees and employers, and that it is linked to good performance outcomes (Huselid, 1995; Purcell, 1999). Soft HRM – on the surface – appears to be well suited to workplace cultures seeking to actively develop shared missions and social goals.

Table 12.1 Hard (theory X) and soft (theory Y) HRM

	Hard	Soft
Assumptions about people	Staff will work to rule if not managed correctly. Emphasis is on individualising management and maximising control. People are regarded as a 'resource', and should be managed as such. Emphasis is on matching people with particular traits to defined tasks	Staff are looking for self-fulfilment and meaning, or social relationships at work. Emphasis is on teamwork, collaboration and participation. Managers should focus on creating fulfilling work that supports autonomous decision-making and self-management. People are assets
Selection	Is focused on finding the best person for the job	Is focused on finding the best person for the organisation, with regard to knowledge and expertise beyond immediate job tasks
Retention	Is less important than maintaining productivity and efficiency. Low-level jobs are relatively easy to fill so staff turnover is not regarded as a problem	Is important so that social networks can develop and encourage affiliation and a sense of commitment to the organisation
Learning and development	Is tailored to specific jobs, and used to develop task-specific skills that improve efficiency. The best training should be provided to the best people	Is geared towards personal and organisational development, to harness the full intellectual potential of each individual. If people are not right for the task, redesign the tasks, or find the right job for the individual
Performance	Is set by managers, measured at an individual level against job-specific outcomes. Poor performance is rationalised as a product of poor management control	Is set within teams; is assessed against task requirements and also in terms of a person's contribution to team effectiveness. Performance is measured in a holistic way, taking account of non-job-specific skills and contributions (e.g. community work)
Motivation	Grounded in a theory X orientation (McGregor, 1960), based on extrinsic rewards such as money, benefits and performing well against targets	Grounded in a theory Y orientation (McGregor, 1960), where intrinsic rewards such as promotion, recognition, autonomy and social opportunities are prioritised
HR model	Michigan	Harvard

Source: adapted from Clegg et al. (2008: 175–6)

Legge (2001), however, offers a powerful critique of 'high-commitment' practices and the research assumptions that underpin them. She points out the paucity and inconsistency of the evidence on which claims are based, and the management bias built into measures of performance. Moreover, high-commitment HRM practices are often selectively employed to benefit 'core' staff (i.e. those already favoured within the organisation) rather than the larger ranks of low-paid, temporary, voluntary or contract staff. As such, the practices not only exacerbate social exclusion, they actually tighten rather than loosen managerial control over the thoughts and choices of core staff, increasing the frequency of 'burnout' after periods of work intensification (see Kunda, 1992; Willmott, 1993).

The hegemony of employment law

Because employment law is so pervasive in OECD countries, social enterprise managers need to develop a response to it (either to embrace and mitigate its effects, or avoid and develop alternatives to it). As the range of rights extended to those who are regarded as employees has grown considerably (particularly within the Europe Union), it is worth quickly setting out a range of laws that capture where employee rights limit the rights of the employer. After the adoption of the 'social chapter' (1992 Maastricht Treaty) employee rights have been extended to the following:

- freedom to travel and work anywhere within the EU (Directive 2004/38/EC)
- equitable remuneration (National Minimum Wage Act)
- maximum working hours each week (Directive 93/104/EC)
- freedom to associate in trade unions (Human Rights Act)
- rights to collective bargaining (Employment Relations Act)
- training and development
- freedom from various forms of discrimination (Single Equality Act)
- minimum health and safety provisions (Health and Safety at Work Act)
- employer–employee consultation and participation forums (ICE Regulations)
- minimum working age of 16
- minimum pension rights.

Outside the EU, the International Labour Organisation (www.ilo.org) monitors the adoption of 12 conventions (eight 'fundamental' conventions and four related to 'governance' shown in Table 12.2) and the SA8000 auditing standard (based on ILO guidelines) is used by multinational corporations for auditing their progress on employment relations. However, even here conventions simply *mitigate* the inherent asymmetries in the employment relationship and do not seek to replace it with more equitable shared ownership arrangements that distribute shares of the wealth among social equals.

Table 12.2   ILO conventions on employment relations with UK ratification dates

Convention	UK Ratification Date
C087 – Freedom of Association and Protection of the Right to Organise	1949
C098 – Principles of the Right to Organise and to Bargain Collectively	1950
C029 – Forced or Compulsory Labour	1931
C105 – Abolition of Forced Labour	1957
C100 – Equal Remuneration Convention	1971
C111 – Discrimination in Respect of Employment and Occupation	1999
C138 – Minimum Age for Admission to Employment	2000
C182 – Prohibition/Elimination of the Worst Forms of Child Labour	2000
C081 – Labour Inspection in Industry and Commerce	1949
C122 – Employment Policy (right to work, freedom of employment choice)	1966
C129 – Labour Inspection in Agriculture	Not ratified
C144 – Tripartite Consultations to Promote the Implementation of International Labour Standards (Social Dialogue)	1977

While social enterprises may seek to advance principles, a great many accept labour markets, employment law, management hierarchy as a taken for granted assumption, or as an 'inevitable' constraint. The more such assumptions are accepted, the more assumptions of Master and Servant Acts dating back to 1823 are tacitly accepted. Employment relations law, however, now provides numerous ways for employees (both individually and collectively) to mitigate their employers' power. The Employment Relations Acts 1999, 2000 and 2004 (in the UK) all supported co-determination on terms and conditions at work, and require consultations when changes in the social and economic environment affect the future prospects of a workforce. In the past, such 'rights' were only won through concerted industrial action. Since the introduction of the Companies Act 2006 in the UK, a board must *consider the interests* of employees, customers, suppliers and the community, but does *not* have to be bound by their interests or include their representatives in governing bodies.

Despite this, the fiduciary duty of directors to put the company before the interests of stakeholders has been removed from UK company law and has been replaced by a series of directors' duties (Wainwright, 2009). In future, directors' duties rather than fiduciary duties will be used as the benchmark for standards without involving them directly in service development, strategic management and governance. When considered alongside the creation of incorporated forms where profit-maximisation is no longer a priority (e.g. CICs in the UK, B-Corps and Low-Profit Corporations in the US, Social Welfare Corporations in Japan), there is an emerging body of law that erodes the dominance of the 'Master' who provided financial capital.

Looking across all bodies of law, there are various documents in which unitary (rule-making) control is established, and various relationships in which it is possible to pluralise and 'soften' the hardness of rule enforcement (by providing greater scope for rule-*interpreting*). The value of distinguishing the rule-making and rule-interpreting forums is to make visible the points within a culture where written and psychological contracts are negotiated (Rousseau, 1995; Guest, 1998). The concept of a psychological contract – based on the unstated and unwritten expectations that organisation stakeholders have of each other – has become useful for understanding the volatile and evolving nature of contractual relationships. In Table 12.3, we suggest sources of written and psychological contracts. Taken together, they offer strategic choices for managing people in social enterprises, and 'spaces' that can be created for the integration of internal and external stakeholders.

Table 12.3   The foundations of written and psychological contracts

Written contracts embedded in:	Psychological contracts embedded in:
Governance perspective	
• Articles of association (members) • Governing document (trustees) • Shareholder agreements (investors) • Board minutes (directors/trustees) • Trading contracts (suppliers of goods) • Service-level agreements • Member agreements (co-operatives/mutuals) • Company law (company regulator) • Charity law (charity/associations regulator) • Co-operative law (co-operatives/societies regulator)	• Previous personal and working relationships • Family/friendship commitments • Experiences during recruitment to the board/executive • Social interaction in tender processes • Social interaction in contract negotiations • Social interaction in board meetings • Knowledge of interpersonal/corporate goals and aspirations
Human resource management perspective	
• Offer letters (to new staff) • Contracts of employment (and company policies referred therein) • Disciplinary and grievance procedures • Contract for services (self-employed staff) • Employment law • Appraisal recommendations and outcomes (non-binding)	• Experience of recruitment, selection, induction, development and promotion • Impact of HRM policy and practice on work friends, colleagues and family members • Attitudes observed in appraisal and disciplinary meetings • Willingness to mediate/negotiate resolution to disputes • Interpretation of organisational goals and policies
Employee relations perspective	
• Union recognition agreements • Collective bargaining agreements • Employment relations law • ACAS codes of conduct (non-binding) • Employment tribunal procedures • Articles of association (worker-owned enterprises)	• The scope and quality of participation in managerial decision-making • Evaluations of the integrity of staff consultation exercises • Interpretation of collective bargaining processes • Experience of employment tribunal proceedings

As Cornforth (2004) outlines, different theories of governance each emphasise a different aspect of contractual relations (biased towards the perspective of one or other set of interests). Taken together, however, they serve to emphasise the multifaceted nature and paradoxical experience of governing an enterprise. When we consider the multitude of written and psychological contracts (Table 12.3) and how these can be framed and interpreted from unitary, pluralist and radical perspectives, the ambiguity of managing people becomes more understandable (and bearable).

Social innovations that subvert master–servant employment relations

In neo-liberal discourse, employment is framed as preferable to unemployment (Friedman, 1962; Borzaga and Defourny, 2001). But within social economy discourse, member ownership is framed as preferable to employment (Ellerman, 1990; Erdal, 2011; Smith and Teasdale, 2012). The discourse advanced is that the power of the employment contract can be weakened in favour of regulation through mutual relations and institutional processes that promote democracy, solidarity and co-operation. But how is this achieved, and what dangers might it expose people to? In this final section, we highlight a number of lawful approaches that have sparked our interest, and which have generated interest among our peers.

Firstly, we return to the role of IP management. In the Free Software, OpenSource and Creative Commons movements, the relationship between producers, their products and consumers of their work are fundamentally transformed. Norms in this movement are more informal with dozens (or even hundreds) of individuals and/or micro-businesses operating as loose co-operative associations or informal social networks that create common pool resources (Ostrom, 1990). In the field of technology, the 'commons' has a different quality because there is no practical limit to the replication of digital media.

Class exercise: Private property vs the commons

Watch this video: www.youtube.com/watch?v=Ag1AKll_2GM
  In groups of three to four people, consider the following questions:

1 What is the impact of the four freedoms described in this video on relations between producers:

  - freedom to use something (i.e. run a program)
  - freedom to study the underlying designs (e.g. source code)
  - freedom to redistribute (or sell) exact copies
  - freedom to amend, revise and distribute (individually and/or collectively).

(Continued)

(Continued)

> To understand these freedoms more fully, examine the licences available from www.creativecommons.org by watching this video: www.youtube.com/watch? v=8YkbeycRa2A.
>
> 2 What would be the impact on the employment relationship if the outputs of work were automatically licensed to employers using Creative Commons instead of your employer taking ownership and copyright?
> 3 Could you devise arrangements for members of a social enterprise to collectively give each other access to (and use of) intellectual property while continuing to trade, and without compromising all the social rights acquired through the EU Social Charter?
>
> Further materials to support this exercise are available on the companion website at: www.sagepub.co.uk/ridleyduff.

The theoretical significance of Creative Commons is that each member acts as a self-regulating agent, committing what time and resources they can, and deriving revenues based on their own need for commercial income. As a video presentation by Dan Pink clarifies, this production activity may take place alongside traditional employment and is not always a full alternative to traditional employment (Pink, 2013). The relevance to the argument in this chapter is the change in the relationship of producers to their produce. OpenSource products like Wordpress have established a new principle that producers can develop 'add-ons' to an OpenSource product/brand and derive value from it. This effectively changes the nature of work from wage-labour to income generating self-employment.

Other creative industries are beginning to use internet technologies to create similar supported self-employment networks that offer a full alternative to traditional employment (see www.cdbaby.com/about and http://booktrope.com/our_story). At CDBABY, independent musicians can manufacture CDs and get digital content into iTunes, Amazon, derive income from YouTube and music libraries through royalties, and even obtain support for direct sales and music events. Booktrope, on the other hand, enables authors to assemble teams of publishing professionals (based anywhere in the world with an internet connection) and work collaboratively to bring books to market. Within these enterprise networks, each producer receives income *directly* from the sales of their finished products, and not indirectly through wages.

The above examples are SRBs that deploy the logic of a CME. However, it can apply also to CTAs that provide support for marginalised groups (Pagán, 2009). Below we offer information on the rise of employment co-operatives in France, and then discuss two UK examples (miEnterprise and Regather). On economic rights, producers retain rights to the works they create, and input directly into decisions on how their products are sold in markets. On the social side, producers can get training, support, access to facilities and social support (Hagner and Davies, 2002).

The quote below is a verbatim note from an event in Paris on the social economy. Noemie du Grenier describes the rising influence of 'multi-activity employment co-operatives' throughout France (Grenier, 2012):

> Each worker has their own business – we have 550 activities – organized into groups of people. We have landscape designers, tapestry, plumbers … this is our model. Each person is autonomous, in charge of their business, with turnover. But they also have a strong cooperative structure, a partner as well within the cooperative … This is a large movement to change the nature of employment at work. Mass unemployment has increased, and many people created their own business. Some may want that autonomy, but others find that there is a lack of meaning … Once I have a business idea, I can become a cooperative member. I can test the feasibility of my idea and then leave the cooperative, or stay in the cooperative and become a partner. Previously, you had colleagues. Now you have clients [other cooperative members and the public]. With over 500 people, we can reinforce each other's position. There are groups of entrepreneurs … expanding markets by working together.
>
> A full transcript of this interview is available on the companion website at: www.sagepub.co.uk/ridleyduff.

Grenier goes on to comment that hierarchy is unnecessary because the model works on the basis of tenders and offers between members. Also, the number of members is higher than the number of partners (80 are now partners out of 550 members). Only when a member makes a decision on how to advance their business do they choose between partnership and self-employment, and Grenier sees advantages to increasing the number of partners.

However, experience from Colombia – where 4,000 such co-operatives were formed in the 1990s and early 2000s (employing 500,000 workers) – suggests they can be abused by employers who corrupt their original intentions. They take advantage of tax breaks given to micro-entrepreneurs by forcing workers to form an employment co-operative, and then rehiring them through a contract with the co-operative rather than each individual. This reduces bureaucracy, ends the employer's responsibility for employee insurance, and eliminates claims for unfair dismissal under employment law (Eslava et al., 2013).

In the UK, there are a limited number of interesting examples of supported self-employment for people who find it hard to do a 9–5 job (see www.miEnterprise.org.uk). There are others designed for those who want a lifestyle change based on co-operative working. A good description of the norms that have emerged from one grassroots co-operative of traders is available at: www.regather.net/trade-regather.

In each case, the co-operative provides back office support, accounting, premises, shared branding, training and support. Members pay a monthly subscription and a management fee based on the value of work invoiced. At Regather, everything is project-based and within each project, members are variously:

- Volunteer – a volunteer (un-paid) of Regather Co-Op
- Worker – a casual employee (paid) of Regather Co-Op
- Staff – a permanent employee (paid) of Regather Co-Op
- Associate – an individual or organisation operating independently of Regather Co-Op.

Members can have a different status in different projects, but only one status within each project. The governance and human relations outcomes of this way of working are succinctly described, together with sober warnings about the tendency of self-employed workers to self-exploit, overwork, take greater financial and legal risks, experience isolation and receive less feedback about the quality of their work. The co-operative structure exists to address these tendencies.

> Regather Trade has been developed over 3 years with the involvement of people who are actively engaged in 'portfolio working' or what we call more simply 'trading' – which is making a living and meeting your day to day needs through a combination of activities – buy, sell, work, volunteer, exchange, share, lend and borrow. Typically it's the people with co-operative values who do some or all of these things … We call these people traders … Traders are essentially co-operative entrepreneurs … Importantly traders can choose the terms on which they make their skills, ideas, time and resources available to the co-op, other traders and the open market. They can choose how much, when and how to trade these things. This gives them an important degree of control over their productive life.
>
> *Source*: www.regather.net/trade-regather

How can the IP management we described earlier be integrated into these new types of co-operative venture? The clause below is drawn from the model Articles of Association of the FairShares Association (www.fairshares.coop). They outline a collective commitment to protecting members' rights to their produce (using Creative Commons licences) but also to sharing (and protecting) their co-operative's need to engage in commerce. For enterprises like Regather and miEnterprise, the tricky issue is whether IP created by members is part of a 'commons' or the property of each member. Critically review whether the following clause can both protect and grant the necessary rights to each party at the same time.

Clause 53 – Intellectual Property (IP), Model Articles of Association V2.0a, FairShares Association

The Company [Co-operative or Association] shall record which members have created and contributed intellectual property (IP) to further company objects, and ensure that ownership of all IP remains vested in its creator(s). For the avoidance of doubt, the Company shall not own IP created by members before, during or after their period of membership unless ownership is freely and voluntarily transferred by those members to the Company.

a. All IP created by members while working for the Company will be vested in them individually and/or collectively.

b. As a condition of membership and/or employment, all IP created by members during their work for the Company shall be licensed to the Company under a Creative Commons Licence for both non-commercial and commercial trading, with permission to adapt, share and re-use the IP in product and service development. Any product or service offered will use the same Creative Commons licence unless a variation of this is negotiated with the creator(s) of the IP.

   i. Where a member creates (or members create) IP for the Company during their period of membership, the Company shall have an exclusive right to use and commercialise the IP while they remain a member. If the member leaves the Company, upon termination of their membership, the Company shall retain a non-exclusive right to continue using and adapting their IP in both non-commercial and commercial ventures.

   ii. Members who leave the Company retain a non-exclusive right to use IP they created for the Company in both non-commercial and commercial ventures.

c. IP transferred to the Company by members, and IP bought by the Company from third parties, shall be owned collectively by all members and made freely available to them for non-commercial use and private study.

d. The Company shall use its best endeavours to manage IP as if it were an 'intellectual commons' for the benefit of Company members.

Source: www.fairshares.coop/wiki/index.php?title=FairShares_Articles_of_Association

This clause – if added to the Articles of Association of a social enterprise – could be used by a member (or employee) to overturn any attempt to remove their rights to their produce, but not to remove their enterprise's right to derive commercial benefit from their work. In short, the rights of labour and capital to IP become shared: each acquires some rights, necessary for their own survival. The master–servant norm is changed because the master (employer) no longer acquires all the produce of its servants (employees) to do with as she or he wishes. Instead, there is a shared right that perpetuates collaboration and the autonomy of both parties.

If the advice from Business Link (to private enterprises) is that adding clauses to employment contracts removes any doubt about the employer's right to *privatise* knowledge (restrict access to it), it follows that the opposite advice can be given to social enterprises. In this case, contracts of employment can add clauses that reinforce the employer's and employee's rights to *socialise* their knowledge (i.e. provide open access). Such advice would be a radical departure from the norms of the neo-liberal economy which thrives by privatising rights to use, distribute and sell IP, goods and services. By socialising the knowledge base, the *capacity* to generate assets and profits is also socialised. Furthermore, the quality of human relations would likely change where an enterprise no longer has exclusive ownership of the products created by its workforce. It would necessarily have to make more effort to satisfy its workforce if it wished to retain exclusive commercial exploitation rights.

Conclusions

In this chapter, we have offered a radical alternative to texts that describe the legal obligations employers have to their employees under employment law. We have done this to start a new conversation about the role of social enterprises in transforming the purposes, nature and impact of employment within a social economy. Nothing we say here is intended to dispute that employment is preferable to unemployment. However, we do question whether employment is preferable to member ownership and supported self-employment (Hagner and Davies, 2002; Pagán, 2009; Borzaga and Depedri, 2014). In making that argument, we devoted the first half of the chapter to problematising the governance and human relations that arise from the logic of the employment contract.

In the second half of the chapter, we advanced the argument that member ownership, particularly when combined with supported self-employment, offers a viable alternative for managing human relations that transforms both governance and HRM practices. These legal arrangements enable producers to reconnect with their produce, producing mutual relations with mutual benefits, and not employer–employee relations that permit (often without the knowledge of the worker) the acquisition of their property rights (Ellerman, 1990; Erdal, 2011). The relationships that spring from member ownership and/or partnership working are more aligned with the ethics of voluntary association than employment relations. They encourage democracy, solidarity and co-operation instead of master–servant principles.

The successful implementation of member ownership systems provides an important rebuff to 'The Great Money Trick' still practised today (Achbar et al., 2004; Positive Money, 2012; Piketty, 2014). In our conclusions, therefore, we ask for two types of recognition. Firstly, we recognise that many social entrepreneurs are primarily concerned with moving people from unemployment to employment using CTAs and SRBs. In doing so, they have a strong need to understand the rights denied to the unemployed, and which can be acquired through employment. This is the *first* step.

However, we ask for recognition that there are other social entrepreneurs – co-operative entrepreneurs – concerned to move beyond the first step to a *second* step. It is only with this second step that a social, rather than a private, economy is created. Employment rights improve the situation for people at work compared to situations in which owner-managers exercise unfettered power. But it is the second step, combined with new approaches to IP management, which reconnects producers to the full fruits of their labour, and puts an end to 'The Great Money Trick'.

The fruits of labour are many: dignity, self-respect, income, companionship and personal development to name a few. We hope this chapter (and book) acts to (re)stimulate debates that raged among the Rochdale Pioneers in 1844, and which were advanced by John Spedan Lewis in the 1940s and 1950s. Their achievements show that governance systems can change (for the better) and replace human *resource* management with human *relationship* management. This is the HRM that social enterprises can aspire to. In developing this approach, HRM looks beyond material incentives, and rights to share fairly in the financial 'gains' of enterprise (or share its assets collectively). It also involves enfranchising producers, consumers and the wider community in such a way that they fairly share access to information and knowledge that sustains and protects the wealth needed by the next generation (Smith and Teasdale, 2012; Ridley-Duff and Southcombe, 2014) through innovative approaches to IP management.

Summary of learning

In this chapter, we have developed arguments that:

The rationale for managing people need not be grounded in theories of HRM.

Three 'discourses' on managing people derive from bodies of knowledge developed for owners, managers and employees.

Theories of *corporate governance*, *HRM* and *employee relations* compete to provide explanations of the best way to develop the 'rules' governing organisational life.

Contrasting perspectives on the nature and needs of human beings are expressed in theories of 'hard' and 'soft' HRM, as well as written and psychological contracts.

Employment relationships can be transformed by reconnecting producers to their products, and protecting their right to socialise their IP.

The goals of human relationship management in social enterprises can be two-fold: 1) to move people from unemployment to employment; 2) to move people from employment into member ownership and/or supported self-employment.

Questions and possible essay assignments

1. Using examples, critically assess whether a 'radical' approach to governance and human relationship management changes the power of written and psychological contracts?

2. Can a 'systems' view of governance ever fully meet the governance needs of a social enterprise? Using examples, outline the benefits and limitations of a 'systems' view of governance.

3. 'Supported self-employment replaces master–servant relations with mutual relations.' Explain the concepts of master–servant relations and mutual relations, then critically evaluate the potential of employment co-operatives (like miEnterprise and Regather) to transform HRM practices.

Further reading

A vital read for students is the NEF pocket book *A New Way to Govern* (Turnbull, 2002) which describes the concept of network governance, and how *strategic stakeholders* (employees, customers, suppliers, community representatives) can be incorporated into company management. We also recommend Chapter 4 of *Managing and Organizations* (Clegg et al., 2008). This readable text covers both HRM and employee relations, asking key questions about the nature and purpose of HRM.

For more detailed coverage, there is a thoughtful textbook called *Corporate Governance* by Monks and Minow (2004). This has a useful and surprisingly detailed section on governance practices in the Mondragon co-operatives. For social enterprise-specific discussions, see Low (2006) for an overview of the tensions arising out of non-profit and for-profit orientations, and Cornforth (2004), Ridley-Duff (2007) and Coule (2013) for recent developments in theories of non-profit and co-operative governance. Doherty et al. (2009) provide useful guidance for social enterprises relying on trustee governance within CTAs, while Ridley-Duff's (2010) ethnographic study highlights key differences in the practices of established and emerging CMEs.

For critical coverage of HRM, David Storey's edited volume *Human Resource Management: A Critical Text* (2001) provides insightful coverage of the tension between managerial and non-managerial interests. Social enterprise-specific discussions are rare, but useful insights have been contributed by Royce and Doherty in relation to volunteering and soft HRM (Doherty et al., 2009). For an overview of co-operative self-management, it is still hard to improve on the study by Rothschild and Allen-Whitt (1986) and the ILO textbook by Peter Davis (2004).

Finally, in writing the second edition of this book, we re-read sections of *The Ragged Trousered Philanthropists*. A generation ago, when the welfare state was stronger, this novel looked anachronistic. However, in light of the events taking place in Argentina (2001–5), in Spain, Portugal, Italy and particularly Greece in Europe (from 2010–15), and with the ongoing problems of labour conditions in South East Asia and Latin America (Achbar et al., 2004), it is time for the contemporary relevance of this novel to be re-evaluated. It provides a thorough understanding of what happens to the minds of workers, supervisors, managers, owners and politicians when human relations are shaped by uncontrolled market forces.

Further reading material is available on the companion website at: www.sagepub.co.uk/ ridleyduff.

Useful resources

Chartered Institution of Personnel and Development: www.cipd.co.uk/

Open Space Technology: www.openspaceworld.org

Governance Hub: www.governancehub.org.uk/

International Labour Organisation: www.ilo.org/global/lang--en/index.htm

International Trade Union Confederation: www.ituc-csi.org/

KnowHow NonProfit: http://knowhownonprofit.org/leadership/governance

Mediation: www.bls.gov/ooh/legal/arbitrators-mediators-and-conciliators.htm

Workforce Hub: www.ukworkforcehub.org.uk/

Glossary

actors – a term used in some types of academic research to refer to the people being studied.

AI – appreciative inquiry.

Articles of Association – see Memorandum and Articles of Association.

Ashoka – a global association of social entrepreneurs established by Bill Drayton in the USA.

asset lock – a term used to refer to the permanent retention of assets which can only be used for the purposes set out in an organisation's constitution, and which must be transferred to another asset-locked organisation with similar objectives if it is wound up.

authoritarian – the directive, dominant characteristic of an absolute ruler.

BENCOM – see community benefit society.

Big Society – see Chapter 1. The term has been strongly linked to the rhetoric and policies of David Cameron and the Conservative Party in the United Kingdom.

blended value – the pursuit of both economic and social value simultaneously, sometimes used interchangeably with the term 'double bottom line'.

British Empire – colonies established for the purposes of trade by the British government between the late sixteenth century and mid-twentieth century.

BSC – Balanced Scorecard: a measurement-based strategic management analysis tool.

capitalist society – a society in which the economic system is based on the principle of capital accumulation, and the private ownership of capital, land and the 'means of production' is considered preferable to co-operative and state ownership.

CDFIs – community development finance initiatives. The UK Social Investment Forum describes CDFIs as 'financial service providers whose mission specifically requires them to achieve social objectives'.

CECOP – the European Confederation of Workers' Co-operatives, Social Co-operatives and Social and Participative Enterprises.

Charities Act – an Act of parliament passed by the UK government to update the regulation of charities in England and Wales.

charity – a type of organisation that pursues public interest objectives defined in the Charities Act 2006. Historically, charities have prioritised the advancement of (religious) education, provided poverty relief, and sought to improve the lives of disadvantaged social groups.

Charity Commission – a statutory organisation operating in England and Wales that provides a range of services and guidance to charities, and with whom all charities must register and report their annual results.

Chicago School – school of economic thought associated with academics in the 1970s who had anti-state sentiments and an ideological commitment to free market monetarist economics.

CIC – community interest company: a new company form intended as a brand for social enterprise in the UK. Can be registered as a CLG or CLS, has limited profit distribution, board-level decision-making power and an asset lock. They cannot register as charities.

CIO – charitable incorporated organisation: introduced in the Charities Act 2006 as a legal structure that was designed to alleviate the problems charities face in reporting to two governing bodies under the structure of a company (Companies House) and a registered charity (Charity Commission).

CIPD – Chartered Institute of Personnel and Development: the United Kingdom's leading professional body for those involved in the management and development of people.

civil society – forms of organisation that are not part of the public or private sectors that promote freedom of association and public debate about a 'good society'.

CLG – company limited by guarantee: an alternative private form of incorporation that limits liability to members upon insolvency (usually to £1). CLGs have no share capital or shareholders. Members act as guarantors. This has been a popular company form for both charitable companies, non-profit and not-for-profit social enterprises.

CLS – company limited by shares: a private form of incorporation that allows for shareholders. It limits the liability of shareholders upon insolvency to the sum of money invested. It is usually set up to allow people to buy share capital, but this cannot be offered to the general public without a due diligence report. This has been a popular company form for private businesses, more-than-profit and for-profit social enterprises.

CME – co-operative and mutual enterprise (owned by members who collectively finance industrial and agricultural production, or who create financial and insurance products that protect members in times of need). CMEs are 'defined by their commitment to (or innovative systems for advancing) democratic/inclusive ownership and governance' (see Chapter 2).

commissioning – an organised process through which a group of people scope the deliverables (products and services) into a contract for services, then seek a supplier to provide them on their behalf.

commons – a term applied to 'common pool resources' on which all people in a community draw. In Ostrom's (1990) work, land, air, seas are common pool resources. More recently, the internet and Cloud-based computing has been framed as a new common pool resource. While some types of commons are depleted by overuse (i.e. physical commons), others are believe not to be depleted (because digital resources can be replicated rather than used).

communitarianism – a philosophy that emphasises how individuality evolves as a person reacts to developments in their community relationships and assimilates socio-cultural assumptions. It is often contrasted with liberalism, a philosophy that emphasises the autonomy of the individual and their capacity to make their own reasoned judgements.

community benefit society – a co-operative organisation, registered under the Industrial and Provident Society Act, that acts as a society for the benefit of the community. Unlike other co-operatives, profit distributions are limited and may be ring-fenced for the benefit of the community. On dissolution, assets must pass to a similar organisation, or community organisation, rather than members.

Community Interest Company Regulations – regulatory rules laid down by the UK's Community Interest Companies Regulator based in Companies House.

community of practice – a group of people who share a set of cultural assumptions and engage in taken-for-granted social practices.

constructivist – a theory of knowledge (epistemology) that people generate knowledge and meaning by applying their learning from previous experiences to new situations. As no two people have the same previous experience, the learning processes developed by people are believed to be infinitely variable.

consumer co-operative – a co-operative business owned by its customers for their mutual benefit. Examples include the Co-operative Group (retailing), housing co-operatives, mutual insurers and credit unions.

corporate governance theory – a body of theory about the ways in which corporations can be controlled by different interest groups. Most theory focuses on the roles of directors within corporate boards and their relationships with government bodies, industry associations, shareholders and executive managers.

cost–benefit analysis – an analysis of a project proposal or enterprise that seeks to identify and report its anticipated costs and benefits.

credit unions – a society form devoted to providing credit to members once they have established a track record of regular saving. Credit unions have a long history of providing credit to people in poorer communities.

critical management school – a school of management thought that draws inspiration from the works of writers who have been influenced by critical theory. Critical theorists argue that organisations become exploitative and oppressive if they allow management control to be institutionalised. Critical management scholars are interested in organisation development techniques that limit management power in order to advance social and economic democracy.

crowdfunding/investing – a new name given to the practice of raising philanthropic/co-operative/private capital from a large 'crowd' of people rather than institutional investors. The institutional norm of crowdfunding/investment sites is to allow social entrepreneurs to pitch directly to investors through an intermediate (often internet-based) institution that lists their projects. Investors contribute capital directly to the projects they want to support on a case by case basis.

CSR – corporate social responsibility. This concept relates to commercial businesses engaging proactively with: (1) ecological responsibility (i.e. considering the external impact of business operations on the environment); (2) social responsibility (proactively complying with employment law, safeguarding and acknowledging workers' rights and showing consideration for local communities by respecting their human rights); (3) demonstrating ethical responsibility (becoming more thoughtful about how business is done, about the impact of their supply chains, and the health of all their stakeholders).

CTAs – charitable trading activities (i.e. primary purpose trading that fulfils the charitable objects of the enterprise). CTAs are 'defined by their commitment to specified social purposes that positively impact on human or environmental well-being' (see Chapter 2).

debt finance – loans and other forms of finance that appear as 'debts' in company accounts and which must eventually be repaid by the company. Debt finance differs from equity finance as the latter appears as an asset in company accounts.

democratic – a system of governance in which people who govern are accountable to the people who are affected by their decisions.

development trusts – organisations that are community owned and led, and which pursue economic, social and environmental regeneration activities in a given area or region.

directors – a legal and popular term for the people appointed by the members of an organisation to run their affairs.

discourse – a set of inter-related, mutually supporting concepts, theories and stories that lead to a particular 'thought-style' or 'paradigm' of thought.

discursive reasoning – knowledge development that depends on reasoned argument in dialogue with other people. It is often contrasted with decision-making based on intuition.

dividends – payments made to the shareholders of an incorporated company, or the members of a co-operative, after a period of profitable trading.

DTI – Department of Trade and Industry: a department in the UK government from 1970–2007 responsible for trade, energy and other business related issues.

EBT – employee benefit trust. A legal entity created to manage shares in an employee owned business on behalf of employees. The income from shareholdings are invested by the trustees in projects that increase employees well-being.

ecological perspective – a perspective based on the deployment of metaphors and arguments drawn from the study of animals in their natural environments.

economic rationality – is defined in the first edition of this textbook as 'skills in getting and giving assistance in order to complete tasks'. It can be contrasted with the logic of social rationality which is focused on relationships, rather than tasks.

EFQM – European Foundation for Quality Management.

EMES – a network comprising 11 research centres in different European universities who specialise in social economy research.

employee-owned – organisations, businesses, etc. that are wholly or majority owned by employees who work in them.

employee relations – a field of study focused on examining the development of rules that govern the relationship between employers (the buyers of labour) and employees (the sellers of labour). Employee relations theory focuses on the social and economic impact of inequalities in the employment relationship.

enfranchising – increasing opportunities for individual and group representation in a given social setting, such as granting them full citizenship, or providing social recognition by granting them voting and participation rights.

equity capital – risk capital provided by the members of an organisation to support its development and to which are attached rights to information, speaking and voting during meetings, and a share of the wealth created by the organisation.

equity investment instruments – legal and social norms that an organisation can adopt to enable existing and new members to purchase equity capital.

ESF – European Social Fund.

ESOC – Employee Share Ownership Centre: an organisation established in the UK in 1989 to promote US-style employee ownership.

ESOP – Employee Share Ownership Plan.

ethnography – a type of research based on anthropological techniques in which the researcher lives or works among the research participants in order to gain first-hand experience of their thoughts, feelings and cultural norms.

EU – European Union.

fair trade – a system of (international) trade that seeks to advance sustainable development through guaranteed minimum prices to producers and premiums for social investments under the control of democratically run community organisations.

feudal society – an agrarian society based on land-ownership and agricultural production. Legal and economic power is vested in a lord of the manor (or local elite) who derive their wealth from artisans and a peasant population who provide labour, or who give a proportion of their produce for the right to live and work on the land. Feudal societies are (have been) replaced by money-based market economies and/or state-owned industry after industrialisation.

Foucault, Michel – French philosopher best known for his studies of institutions and writings on power, knowledge, sexuality and discourse. His concept of discourse has been taken up by feminist, critical and postmodern writers to explain the power of language to shape (and limit) the way in which things can be known.

full cost recovery – an approach to costing that takes into account indirect costs and overheads when bidding for contracts.

functionalist – a term used in the work of Burrell and Morgan (1979) to describe research activity and management thought that regards people as if they are part of a machine with discrete parts, and who combine their labour to achieve organisational objectives. They compare functionalist thought with other perspectives emphasising the way humans assign meaning to objects and events, and can 'reframe' these meanings through learning and reflection to emancipate themselves from cultural and social constraints imposed by functionalist thought.

gearing – the ratio of debt to equity finance in a company. Accounting theory hypotheses that risks are lowest when the ratio of debt and equity finance is 1:1 (i.e. that risks are shared equally by suppliers of equity capital and debt finance).

governance – the institutional arrangements, powers and processes that enable individuals and groups working together in an organisation, and/or living together, to regulate their relationships.

governing body – a legal term for the group of people who have been assigned responsibility to govern a particular organisation or community.

hard HRM – an approach to human resource management that tends to treat labour as a cost rather than an asset and which should be managed as a resource that can be replaced if needed. It emphasises technical rather than social considerations in the management of people.

hegemonic power – power based on the ability to shape others' thoughts and feelings by acquiring control over education curricula, the mass media and political institutions.

hegemony – a pervasive form of social control based on hegemonic power.

heuristic – something that provides a learning experience which accelerates the discovery of useful knowledge.

HRM – human resource management.

hub – a term derived from a metaphor of a wheel, spokes and hub. The hub exists to support and maintain relationships between different parts of a wheel for it to function to its full potential. In organisation studies it is helpful for describing organisations that emphasise the primacy of front-line production and marketing activities, but retain a 'hub' for the co-ordination of activities.

ICA – International Co-operative Alliance.

ILM – Intermediate Labour Market: an organisation, or group of organisations, that work together to help people acquire the skills they need to obtain permanent employment. Organisations in an ILM employ people for relatively short periods to help them acquire technical, personal and 'employability' skills.

IMF – International Monetary Fund.

Industrial and Provident Societies Act – a body of UK law that supports the formation and development of industrial and welfare organisations using one-member, one-vote systems of governance.

IP – intellectual property.

IPS – an organisation registered under the Industrial and Provident Societies Act.

kitemark – an award, usually accompanied by a logo and brand that promotes the public profile of an industry (or industry standard practice).

KPI – key performance indicators.

laissez-faire – an approach to trade where transactions between people are not regulated by a higher authority. In economics, laissez-faire refers to the doctrine of free markets that minimise state intervention and regulation. In management, it refers to a culture in which figures of authority are not accorded unlimited rights to impose their will and where formal systems of management are not accorded high social status.

legal compliance – compliance with statutory laws and industry regulations.

legitimacy (organisational) – a term used in institutional theory to describe the ways in which legitimacy is accorded to organisations and affects their chances of survival.

liberalism – a philosophy that emphasises individuality, and the human capacity for personal reflection and autonomous decision-making. In economics, liberalism is associated with freedom from state controls, private property rights and trade based on contracts between 'free' persons.

local socialism – a description applied to local authorities where politicians commit themselves to the development of a social economy based on community ownership and democratic control of capital.

managerialism – a body of thought that proceeds from the assumption that all organisations are essentially similar. Based on this assumption, management is regarded as a neutral technical activity capable of improving organisational efficiency through the application of generic management techniques. In critical writing, managerialism is regarded as a 'thought-style' that emphasises and prioritises management perspectives, or an organisational culture in which managers (and the staff they manage) have succumbed to a hegemonic discourse emphasising the right of managers to manage.

Marxian – a body of political, sociological and economic thought derived from the writings of Karl Marx and his followers. Marx argued that political and economic thought changes in different historical periods based on the arrangements that prevail in the sphere of paid work (the 'relations of production'). New epochs begin when the relationships between people at work are transformed by technological, cultural and political changes.

MBO – management by objective: a performance management system based on the agreement and monitoring of objectives set by staff and managers during individual appraisals.

MCC – the Mondragon Co-operative Corporation: a network of co-operatives in the Basque region of Spain in which there are now approximately 100,000 worker-owners.

Memorandum and Articles of Association – documents that set out the purposes, powers and governance arrangements of an organisation. The UK Companies Act 2006 removed the need for a separate Memorandum.

micro-finance – a financial system where small producers own their own banking institutions, or a social enterprise lends philanthropic capital in small amounts to build home- or community-based businesses. The Grameen Bank developed a credit union-based model that limited ownership to people on low incomes and invested only in production activities.

mission drift – the tendency of an organisation to deviate from their stated social objectives when they face political or economic obstacles to their fulfilment.

mixed receipts – an approach to income generation based on a mixture of market trading, traditional fundraising and investment activity.

MNC – multinational corporation

model rules – a set of rules that provide a starting point for developing Articles of Association. The availability of model rules can speed up the process of incorporating a new company.

Mondragon – a town in the Basque region of Spain.

mutuality – bi-directional or network relationship in which parties help, support and supervise each other. The reciprocity and interdependence implicit in mutuality clearly distinguishes it from charity in which there is no mutual support. Also, mutuality should not be confused with 'mutual obligations' in the employment relationship which are based on a division of powers and responsibilities rather than an assumption of equal care and support.

National Lottery – a lottery franchise created and supported by the UK government under a licence requiring 28p in every £1 to be allocated to good causes.

NCVO – National Council for Voluntary Organisations.

nef – New Economics Foundation.

neo-liberalism – a label given to the economic doctrines (and underlying ideology) developed within the Chicago school of economists. This prioritised 'free' markets and consumer choice over the rights of producers and organised labour. The term is frequently linked to the works and arguments of Milton Friedman.

network governance – a term used extensively by Shann Turnbull to describe approaches to corporate governance that do not depend on the dominance of a unitary board of directors (or trustees), or centralised control over decision-making.

New Economics Foundation (nef) – an organisation founded in 1986 that describes itself as a 'think-and-do tank' promoting economics research and accounting practices that support human well-being.

New Labour – a term applied to the Labour Party in the UK to mark its break with old-style socialist politics, and the adoption of a 'social justice' agenda that appealed to a broader coalition of interests. New Labour won three consecutive victories between 1997–2010 before it was replaced by a coalition government of the Conservative and Liberal Democrat parties.

New Right – a term applied to the emergence of new political thinking in the 1970s and 1980s that emphasised an economy based on private property, free markets and reductions in state welfare provision.

NGO – non-governmental organisation.

NPG – new public governance: a shift in attitudes to public service design that emphasises co-construction of services with users by dense networks of provider organisations. NPG is often contrasted to 'management control' that characterises NPM.

NPM – new public management: a series of doctrines defined by Christopher Hood (1995) to describe the shift from holistic, collaborative service design by professionals in the civil service to one based on smaller corporate units more directly accountable to managers using private sector techniques.

OECD – Organisation for Economic Co-operation and Development: an international organisation that brings together representatives of governments committed to liberal democracy to share knowledge and experience of market economics.

paradigm – a term used in philosophy to describe the relationship between a particular world view and the methods of inquiry that sustain and support it. Thomas Kuhn (1970) argued that scientific inquiry does not describe the world in which we live, but *sustains* particular world views through acceptance of underlying philosophical premises. He argued that 'paradigm shifts' occur when new methods of inquiring into the world, or a new theoretical perspective, provides a more plausible explanation for observed phenomena. Accepting a new theoretical perspective and the methods of inquiry that support them leads to a new world view.

participatory democracy – a form of democracy that seeks to increase direct participation in the formation and development of opinion, as well as final decision-making. It is often contrasted with representative democracy based on the election of political/business elites from a small group of approved candidates.

patient capital – equity or loan finance that is repaid over long periods, usually at lower rates of return. It is called 'patient' because of the length of time it takes to generate a return on investment.

patronage refund – a payment made to a member of a CME based on their level of patronage (as a worker or consumer). For compliance with modern accounting norms, the patronage refund may be called a dividend (on share capital) or profit-share/bonus (if added to wages).

philanthropy – a way of life, or form of social action, based on systematic charitable giving and social investment.

physical assets – buildings and other property that are tangible (i.e. can be seen and touched). It can be contrasted with 'intangible' assets such as goodwill and reputation.

pluralist – a view of organisations that accepts the likelihood that individuals and groups use their agency to formulate and pursue different interests.

positivism – a branch of philosophy derived from the writings of Auguste Comte that valid knowledge is based on systematic analysis of 'positively given' evidence collected through a scientific process.

pragmatism – a branch of philosophy and decision-making theory that considers the consequences of accepting a proposition as true. Pragmatists argue that the true content of a proposition is not discovered until it is applied to practice. We accept as true any proposition that is practically adequate for a given purpose or task.

property rights – legal rights attached to the ownership of property. Property rights are defined in Articles of Association and statutory laws that apply after incorporation.

radical (employment relations) – a Marxist view of workplace relations in which the employment contract is superseded by one based on mutuality, reciprocity combined with joint (co-operative) or common (mutual) ownership by the workforce. It is useful as a counter to unitary and pluralist views of industrial relations because the former are seen as uncritically accepting the legitimacy of the employment contract.

rationalism – a branch of philosophy that explores decision-making based on the application of reason and abstract reflection. It is often contrasted with empiricism, a branch of philosophy that emphasises the need to test theoretical claims after systematic collection and analysis of empirical evidence.

reciprocity – positive or negative inkind responses associated with the development of an equitable relationship (sometimes framed as 'give and take' within a relationship).

recovered company movement – a movement in South America which involves workers taking over the management and/or ownership of abandoned factories to bring them back into productive use.

restricted funds – funds donated under trust law which must be used for the purpose designated by the trustor.

SAA – social accounting and auditing.

SEC – Social Enterprise Coalition.

secular associations – voluntary associations that are not affiliated to a religious tradition, are not influenced by religious authorities, or maintain neutrality in religious matters.

social accounting and auditing (SAA) – an approach to establishing, verifying and reporting the social value created by an organisation. Social capital – see Chapter 4.

Social Enterprise Coalition (SEC) – the UK's national body that lobbies on behalf of social enterprises and which provides an infrastructure of regional and national networks to support development of the social economy.

Social Enterprise Mark (SEM) – a trade mark created by RISE, a social enterprise agency in south-west England, and later endorsed by the Social Enterprise Coalition. The mark is based on conformance to six criteria believed by RISE/SEC to define the characteristics of a social enterprise.

social firm – a type of social enterprise that actively seeks to employ people who are disadvantaged in the labour market and to provide them with career and personal development opportunities.

social inclusion – attempts to enfranchise a greater number of people through radical management practices and social investment initiatives.

social innovation – a sub-field of social entrepreneurship concerned with the reconfiguration of organisations and institutions to address social problems and increase social value creation.

social investment – a form of investment in which investors track both social and economic value creation to maximise their learning about the impact of investment activities.

social rationality – a term applied to 'skills in getting and giving attention in order to form, develop, maintain and end relationships'. From a socially rational perspective, decision-making is guided by the projected impact on human relationships, rather than the likelihood of completing a task or mission.

social value – a term applied to the value created by social enterprises. In this text, we highlight four types of value creation: social innovations that create a more inclusive and just society; the capacity of social entrepreneurs to define and pursue social goals; increasing the ability and capacity of people to act collectively; the creation of wealth sharing arrangements that distribute wealth and power to an ever larger (not ever smaller) number of people.

soft HRM – an approach to human resource management that treats labour as an asset, supported by personal development initiatives and opportunities to socialise at work. It emphasises social rather than technical considerations in the management of people.

solidarity – intense loyalty between members of a community, social movement, workplace or trade union that inclines them to act together and protect each other's interests.

SORP regulations – SORPs are 'statements of recommended practice' for organisations operating in a particular sector or industry. In the UK, SORP regulations were introduced in 1993 to improve the management (and reporting) of charitable funds. The regulations were updated in 2005.

special resolution – a type of resolution in the General Meeting of a charity, society, co-operative or company that requires more than a simple majority. In UK Company Law, 75 per cent of votes cast are needed to pass a special resolution.

SRB – socially responsible business: which establishes operations for social and/or environmental benefit. SRBs are 'defined by their commitment to (or innovative technologies for) ethical trading and sustainable development' (see Chapter 2).

SROI – social return on investment: a methodology pioneered at the Roberts Enterprise Development Fund in the US and adapted by the UK's New Economics Foundation (nef) to capture the non-market value created by investment activity.

SSE – social and solidarity economy.

supply chain – the chain of suppliers that support a particular productive activity. The supply chain extends to all the people and organisations who extract and add value to materials in the course of producing a particular good or service.

surplus – the net value assigned to all value-adding activities undertaken by an organisation in an accounting period minus all costs. Unlike profit, which usually refers to productive trading activities, surplus may include rents, investment interest and other gains in income or asset revaluations derived from non-productive activities.

technocratic – a culture in which management is regarded as a technical activity to be undertaken by qualified professionals who provide impartial expert advice. It can be contrasted with a critical management perspective that emphasises how political and moral commitments are embedded in professional qualifications, undermining all claims to neutrality and impartiality.

totalitarianism – a form of management and governance that seeks to maximise the power of a ruler (or ruling elite) to control the physical and psychological environments of those they govern.

TQM – total quality management: a management philosophy based on the writings of Edward Deming that reconceptualises staff as 'customers' and 'suppliers' of each other's skills and expertise, and which advocates continuous improvements in control systems to reduce (or eliminate) production errors.

trading arm – a subsidiary organisation, usually created by a non-profit or charitable company to make profits that can be gifted back to its parent company under trust law.

triple bottom line – a system of accounting that seeks to measure the economic, social and environmental impact of trading activities.

trustees – the people to whom monies have been transferred under trust law and who manage the money in accordance with the wishes of the trustor. Charities are run by a board of trustees (to whom charitable funds have been given to pursue the objects of the charity).

trust law – a body of law that covers the rights and obligations attached to gifts and donations intended to support a particular purpose, beneficiary or activity.

TSO – third sector organisation.

unincorporated – an organisation that has not registered Articles of Association in accordance with a body of law that regulates the formation of organisations. In an unincorporated organisation, individuals remain personally liable for any debts they incur.

unitary – a view of organisations that emphasises the logic and benefits of a single loyalty structure and chain of command and which subsequently regards as illegitimate any organisation or outside interest that competes for the loyalty of its members.

unrestricted funds – funds that are not subject to trust law that can be used for any purpose.

VAT – value added tax.

venture philanthropy – a form of investment that emphasises social rather than financial returns and which provides a board or organisational role for a philanthropist to monitor the social and economic return on their investment.

voluntary sector – a subsector of the third sector that depends on volunteer staff and/or trustees to help run organisations and provide services.

whole economy – an approach to income generation based wholly on trading in commercial markets, without reliance on grants or fundraising activity.

worker (or producer) co-operative – generally regarded as a trading organisation that provides goods and services to a market where a majority of the workforce own shares, and the majority of shares are owned by the workforce. In IPS law, there is a definition of a *bona fide* worker co-operative wholly owned by those who work for it and governed using a system of one-person, one-vote.

World Bank – an international organisation that aims to bring about 'inclusive and sustainable globalisation' through two complementary institutions: the International Bank for Reconstruction and Development and the International Development Association. The bank offers loans and advice to around 100 developing countries.

Bibliography

Abrahamsson, A. (2007) 'Researching sustainopreneurship – conditions, concepts, approaches, areanas and questions' [Online]. Available at: http://andersabrahamsson.typepad.com/blog/files/researchingsustainopreneurship-abrahamsson.pdf (accessed 3 March 2015).

Achbar, M., Abbott, J. and Bakan, J. (2004) 'The corporation' [Online]. Available at: www.thecorporation.com/media/Transcript_finalpt1%20copy.pdf (accessed 8 December 2009).

Adler, P., Forbes, L. and Willmott, H. (2007) 'Critical management studies', *The Academy of Management Annals*. London: Routledge, pp. 119–79.

Adler, P. and Kwon, S. (2002) 'Social capital: prospects for a new concept', *Academy of Management Review*, 27(1): 17–40.

Alatrista, J. and Arrowsmith, J. (2004) 'Managing employee commitments in the not-for-profit sector', *Personnel Review*, 33(5): 536–48.

Albert, M. (2003) *ParEcon: Life After Capitalism*. New York: Verso.

Alter, K. (2007) *Social Enterprise Typology* (Version 1.5), Virtue Ventures: www.virtueventures.com/typology.

Alternative Commission on Social Investment (2015) 'After the Gold Rush', March [Online]. Available at: http://socinvalternativecommission.org.uk/home/ (accessed 18 May (2015).

Alvesson, M. and Deetz, S. (2000) *Doing Critical Management Research*. London: Sage.

Alvesson, M. and Willmott, H. (1996) *Making Sense of Management: A Critical Introduction*. London: Sage.

Alvesson, M. and Willmott, H. (2003) *Studying Management Critically*. London: Sage.

Alvord, S., Brown, L. and Letts, C. (2004) 'Social entrepreneurship and societal transformation: an exploratory study', *Journal of Applied Behavioral Science*, 40: 260–82.

Amin, A. (2009) 'Extraordinarily ordinary: working in the social economy', *Social Enterprise Journal*, 5(1): 30–49.

Amin, A., Cameron, A. and Hudson, R. (1999) 'Welfare as work? The potential of the UK social economy', *Environment and Planning*, 31: 2033–51.

Amin, A., Cameron, A. and Hudson, R. (2002) *Placing the Social Economy*. London: Routledge.

Anheier, H. (2000) 'Managing non-profit organisations: towards a new approach' (Civil Society Working Paper 1) [Online]. Available at: www.lse.ac.uk/collections/CCS/pdf/cswp1.pdf (accessed 27 May 2010).

Argyris, C., Putnam, R. and McLain-Smith, D. (1985) *Action Science: Concepts, Methods, and Skills for Research and Intervention*. San Francisco: Jossey-Bass.

Arizmendiarrieta, J.M. (n.d.) 'Historic background, Mondragon Corporation' [Online]. Available at: www.mondragon-corporation.com/ENG/Co-operativism/Co-operative-Experience/Historic-Background.aspx (accessed 7 November 2012).

Aronson, E. (2003) *The Social Animal* (9th edn). New York: Worth.

Arthur, L., Scott-Cato, M., Keenoy, T. and Smith, R. (2003) 'Developing an operational definition of the social economy', *Journal of Co-operative Studies*, 36(3): 163–89.

Aslam, A. (1999) 'U.S. wage gap widens', Global Policy Forum [Online]. Available at: www.globalpolicy.org/component/content/article/218-injustice-and-inequality/46639.html (accessed 14 December 2009).

Austin, J., Stevenson, H. and Wei-Skillern, J. (2006) 'Social and commercial entrepreneurship: same, different, or both?', *Entrepreneurship Theory and Practice*, 30(1): 1–22.

Avila, R.C. and Campos, R.J.M. (2006) *The Social Economy in the European Union*. The European Economic and Social Committee: CIRIEC no. CESE/COMM/05/2005.

Ball, J. and Rodgers, S. (2011) 'Coalition cuts for £10 billion in public sector savings', *The Guardian*, 26 October.

Bamber, G., Lansbury, R. and Wailes, N. (2011) *International and Comparative Employment Relations* (5th edn). London: Sage.

Banks, J. (1972) *The Sociology of Social Movements*. London: Macmillan.

Barbier, E. (1987) 'The concept of sustainable development', *Environmental Conservation*, 14(2): 101–10.

Baudhardt, C. (2014) 'Solutions to the crisis? The green new deal, degrowth and the solidarity economy: alternatives to capitalist growth economy from an eco-feminist perspective', *Ecological Economics*, 102: 60–8.

BBC (1980) *The Mondragon Experiment – Corporate Cooperativism*. London: BBC.

BBC (2015) 'Hinchingbrooke Hospital: circle to withdraw from contact' [Online]. Available at: www.bbc.co.uk/news/uk-england-cambridgeshire-30740956 (accessed 5 February 2015).

Beer, S. (1966) *Decision and Control: The Meaning of Operational Research Management Cybernetics*. London: Wiley.

Beer, S. (1972) *Brain of the Firm: Managerial Cybernetics of Organization*. London: Wiley.

Beinhocker, E. (2007) *The Origin of Wealth*. London: Random House.

Bennett, M., Rikhardsson, P. and Schaltegger, S. (2003) *Environmental Management Accounting: Purpose and Progress*. Dordrecht: Kluwer.

Benson, J. and Brown, M. (2007) 'Knowledge workers: what keeps them committed; what turns them away', *Work, Employment and Society*, 21(1): 121–41.

Berle, A. and Means, G. (1932) *The Modern Corporation and Private Property*. New York: Commerce Clearing House Inc.

Berry, A., Broadbent, J. and Otley, D. (2005) *Management Control: Theories, Issues and Practices* (2nd edn). Basingstoke: Palgrave.

Berry, L. (1983) *Relationship Marketing*. Chicago: American Marketing Association.

Big Society Capital (2014) *Social Investment: From Ambition to Action*. London: Big Society Capital.

Billis, D. (1993) *Organizing Public and Voluntary Agencies*. London: Routledge.

Birch, K. and Whittam, G. (2008) 'The third sector and the regional development of social capital', *Regional Studies*, 43(3): 437–50.

Birch, S. (2012) 'Co-op schools: is the future of education co-operation?', *The Guardian*, 26 July.

Birchall, J. (2009) *People Centred Businesses: Co-operatives, Mutuals and Idea of Membership*. Basingstoke: Palgrave.

Birchall, J. (2012) 'A member-owned business approach to the classification of co-operatives and mutuals', in D. McDonnell and E. Macknight (eds), *The Co-operative Model in Practice*. Glasgow: Co-operative Education Trust Scotland, pp. 67–82.

BIS (2014) 'Chapter 6: The asset lock' [Online]. Available at: www.gov.uk/government/uploads/system/uploads/attachment_data/file/357361/CIC-14-1089-community-interest-companies-chapter-6-the-asset-lock.pdf (accessed 3 March 2015).

Black, L. and Nicholls, J. (2004) *There's No Business Like Social Business*. Liverpool: The Cat's Pyjamas.

Blitzer, J. (2014) 'In Spain, politics via Reddit' (*The New Yorker*) [Online]. Available at: www.newyorker.com/tech/elements/spain-politics-via-reddit (accessed 21 January 2015).

Block, F. (2001) 'Introduction', in K. Polanyi, *The Great Transformation: The Political and Economic Origins of Our Time*. Boston: Beacon, pp. xviii–xxxviii.

Bock, W. (2005) 'Supervisory leadership: lessons from Semco on structure, growth and change' [Online]. Available at: www.agreatsupervisor.com/articles/lessons.htm (accessed 20 August 2014).

Bornstein, D. (1996) *The Price of a Dream: The Story of the Grameen Bank and the Idea That Is Helping the Poor to Change their Lives*. New York: Simon & Schuster.

Borzaga, C. and Defourny, J. (2001) *The Emergence of Social Enterprise*. London: Routledge.

Borzaga, C. and Depedri, S. (2014) 'When social enterprises do it better: efficiency and efficacy of work integration in Italian social co-operatives', in S. Denny and F. Seddon (eds), *Social Enterprise: Accountability and Evaluation Around the World*. London: Routledge, pp. 85–101.

Bounds, A. (2014) 'Co-operative Group agrees to reform', *Financial Times*, 17 May.

Bourdieu, P. (1977) *Outline of a Theory of Practice*. Cambridge: Cambridge University Press.

Bourdieu, P. (1986) 'The forms of capital', in J Richardson (ed.), *Handbook of Theory and Research for the Sociology of Education*. New York: Greenwood, pp. 241–58.

Bradley, K. and Gelb, A. (1980) 'Motivation and control in the Mondragon experiment', *British Journal of Industrial Relations*, 19(2): 211–31.

Bradley, K. and Gelb, A.H. (1983) *Cooperation at Work: The Mondragon Experience*. London: Heinemann Educational.

Bridge, S., Murtagh, B. and O'Neill, K. (2009) *Understanding the Social Economy and the Third Sector*. Basingstoke: Palgrave.

Brinckerhoff, P. (1994) *Mission-based Management*. Illinois: Alpine Guild.

Brinckerhoff, P. (2000) *Mission-based Management* (2nd edn). New York: Wiley and Sons.

Brouard, F. and Larivet, S. (2010) 'Essay of clarifications and definitions of the related concepts of social enterprise, social entrepreneur and social entrepreneurship', in *Handbook of Research on Social Entrepreneurship*. Cheltenham: Edward Elgar, pp. 29–56.

Brown, A. and Swersky, A. (2012) *The First Billion: A Forecast of Social Investment Demand*. London: Big Society Capital/Boston Consulting Group.

Brown, J. (2004) *Cooperative Capital: A New Approach to Investment in Cooperatives and Other Forms of Social Enterprise*. Manchester: Cooperative Action.

Brown, J. (2006) 'Designing equity finance for social enterprises', *Social Enterprise Journal*, 2(1): 73–81.

Brown, J. (2007) *Tools for Loans and Other Forms of Finance*. London: NCVO

Bruntland, G. (1987) *Our Common Future*. Oxford: Oxford University Press.

Buchanan, R. and Gilles, C. (1990) 'Value managed relationships: the key to customer retention and profitability', *European Management Journal*, 8(4): 523–6.

Bull, M. (2006) *Balance: Unlocking Performance in Social Enterprises*. Manchester: Centre for Enterprise, Manchester Metropolitan University.

Bull, M. (2007) 'Balance: the development of a social enterprise business performance analysis tool', *Social Enterprise Journal*, 3(1): 49–66.

Bull, M. (2008) 'Challenging tensions: critical, theoretical and empirical perspectives on social enterprise', *International Journal of Entrepreneurial Behaviour and Research*, 14(5): 268–75.

Bull, M. and Crompton, H. (2005) *Business Practices in Social Enterprises* (ESF Project Report). Manchester: Manchester Metropolitan University.

Bull, M. and Crompton, H. (2006) 'Business practices in social enterprises', *Social Enterprise Journal*, 2(1): 42–60.

Bull, M., Ridley-Duff, R., Foster, D. and Seanor, P. (2010) 'Conceptualising ethical capital in social enterprises', *Social Enterprise Journal*, 6(3): 250–64.

Burrell, G. and Morgan, G. (1979) *Sociological Paradigms and Organisation Analysis*. Farnham: Ashgate.

Business Link (2012) 'Intellectual property and your work' [Online]. Available at: www.business-link.gov.uk/bdotg/action/detail?itemId=1074300742&type=RESOURCES (accessed 8 January 2012).

Cabinet Office (2007) *Social Capital: A Discussion Paper*. London: Performance and Innovation Unit, HM Treasury.

Cabinet Office (2013) 'Social enterprise: market trends' [Online]. Available at: www.gov.uk/government/publications/social-enterprise-market-trends (accessed 12 August 2014).

Cameron, D. (2009) 'David Cameron: The Big Society', *ResPublica*, 10 November [Online]. Available at: www.respublica.org.uk/item/ResPublica-mentioned-in-Camerons-speech-ggtc (accessed 14 May 2015).

Campbell, K. (1998) 'When even your accountant betrays you', *CAUT Bulletin*, ACPPU, 45(9): 28.

Cannell, B. (2012) 'The problem with co-ops – no boss' [Online]. Available at: http://bobcannell.blogspot.co.uk/2012/01/problem-with-co-ops-no-boss.html (accessed 28 January 2015).

Capitalism: A Love Story (2009) [Film] Directed by M. Moore.

Carver, J. (1990) *Boards That Make a Difference*. San Francisco: Jossey-Bass.

CASC (2011) 'Clubs – charity and CASC status' [Online]. Available at: www.cascinfo.co.uk/Resources/CASC/Documents/PDF/Clubs%20CASC%20v%20charity.pdf (accessed 26 February 2015).

Cathcart, A. (2009) 'Directing democracy: the case of the John Lewis Partnership', unpublished PhD thesis, Leicester: University of Leicester.

Cathcart, A. (2013) 'Paradoxes of participation: non-union workforce participation at the John Lewis Partnership', *International Journal of Human Resource Management*, 25(6): 762–80.

CECOP-CICOPA Europe (2015) 'Together: how cooperatives show resilience to the crisis' [Online]. Available at: www.together-thedocumentary.coop/ (accessed 4 February 2015).

Chadwick-Coule, T. (2011) 'Social dynamics and the strategy process: bridging or creating a divide between trustees and staff?', *Nonprofit and Voluntary Sector Quarterly*, 40(1): 33–56.

Chandler, J. (2008) *Explaining Local Government: Local Government in Britain Since 1800*. Manchester: Manchester University Press.

Charity Commission (2005) 'Accounting and reporting by charities: statement of recommended practice' [Online]. Available at: www.charity-commission.gov.uk/Library/guidance/sorp05t-extcolour.pdf (accessed 11 May 2010).

Charity Commission (2008) *Going Green*. London: Charity Commission.

Charity Commission (2012) 'The essential trustee: what you need to know' [Online]. Available at: www.gov.uk/government/publications/the-essential-trustee-what-you-need-to-know-cc3 (accessed 16 August 2014).

Charity Commission (2014) 'Recent charity register statistics: Charity Commission' [Online]. Available at: www.gov.uk/government/publications/charity-register-statistics/recent-charity-register-statistics-charity-commission (accessed 18 May 2015).

Chell, E. (2007) 'Social enterprise and entrepreneurship: towards a convergent theory of the entrepreneurial process', *International Small Business Journal*, 25(1): 5–26.

Chomsky, N. and Herman, E. (1988) *Manufacturing Consent: The Political Economy of the Mass Media*. New York: Pantheon Books.

CIM (2009) 'Marketing and the 7Ps: a brief summary of marketing and how it works' [Online]. Available at: www.cim.co.uk/files/7ps.pdf (accessed 27 April 2015).

Clawson, J. (1996) 'Mentoring in the information age', *Leadership and Organisation*, 17(3): 6–15.

Clegg, S., Kornberger, M. and Pitsis, T. (2008) *Managing and Organizations*. London: Sage.

Clutterbuck, D. and Megginson, D. (2005) *Making Coaching Work: Creating a Coaching Culture*. London: CIPD.

Coch, L. and French, L. (1948) 'Overcoming resistance to change', *Human Relations*, 1: 512–32.

Cohen, D. and Prusak, L. (2001) *In Good Company: How Social Capital Makes Organizations Work*. Boston: Harvard Business School Press.

Coleman, J. (1988) 'Social capital in the creation of human capital', *American Journal of Sociology*, 94: 95–120.

Collins, J. (2001) *Good to Great*. London: Random House.

Collins, J. (2006) *Good to Great and the Social Sectors*. London: Random House.

Collins, J. and Porras, J. (2000) *Built to Last: Successful Habits of Visionary Companies*. London: Random House.

Conn, D. (2006) 'Barcelona's model of integrity show right is might', *The Guardian*, 17 May.

Connelly, S. (2007) 'Mapping sustainable development as a contested concept', *Local Environment*, 12(3): 259–78.

Conway, C. (2008) 'Business planning training for social enterprise', *Social Enterprise Journal*, 4(1): 57–73.

Cook, J., Deakin, S. and Hughes, A. (2002) 'Mutuality and corporate governance: the evolution of building societies following deregulation', *Journal of Corporate Law*, 2(1): 110–38.

Co-operatives UK (2014) *The Co-operative Economy 2014: Untold Resilience*. Manchester: Co-operatives UK.

Cooperrider, D. (1999) 'Positive image, positive action: the affirmative basis of organizing', in S. Srivastra and D. Cooperrider (eds), *Appreciative Management and Leadership*. San Francisco: Jossey-Bass, pp. 91–125.

Cooperrider, D. and Srivastva, S. (1987) 'Appreciative inquiry in organizational life', in R.W. Woodman and W.A. Pasmore (eds), *Research in Organizational Change and Development*, Vol. 1. Stamford, CT: JAI Press, pp. 129–69.

Cooperrider, D. and Whitney, D. (2005) *Appreciative Inquiry: A Positive Revolution in Change*. San Francisco: Berrett-Koelher .

Cooperrider, D., Whitney, D. and Stavros, J. (2008) *Appreciative Inquiry Handbook* (2nd edn). Brunswick: Crown Custom Publishing.

Cooperrider, D., Zandee, D.P., Godwin, L., Avital, M. and Boland, B. (2014) *Organizational Generativity: The Appreciative Inquiry Summit and a Scholarship of Transformation (Vol. 4, Advances in Appreciative Inquiry)*. Bingley: Emerald Group Publishing Limited.

Coote, A. (2010) 'Ten big questions about the Big Society' [Online]. Available at: www.neweco nomics.org/publications/entry/ten-big-questions-about-the-big-society (accessed 12 March 2015)

Cope, J., Jack, S. and Rose, M. (2007) 'Social capital and entrepreneurialism: an introduction', *International Small Business Journal*, 25(3): 213–19.

Corbett, S. and Walker, A. (2012) 'Big Society: back to the future', *Political Quarterly*, 83(3): 487–93.

Cornforth, C. (1995) 'Patterns of cooperative management', *Economic and Industrial Democracy*, 16: 487–523.

Cornforth, C. (2004) 'The governance of cooperatives and mutual associations: a paradox perspective', *Annals of Public and Cooperative Economics*, 16: 487–523.

Cornforth, C. and Edwards, C. (1998) *Good Governance: Developing Effective Board-Management Relations in Public and Voluntary Organisations*. London: CIMA.

Cornforth, C., Thomas, A., Spear, R. and Lewis, J. (1988) *Developing Successful Worker Co-ops*. London: Sage.

Coule, T. (2007) 'Developing strategies for sustainability: implications for governance and accountability', paper presented at the NCVO/BSSN Researching the Voluntary Sector Conference. University of Warwick, NCVO/VSSN, 5–6 September.

Coule, T. (2008) 'Sustainability in voluntary organisations: exploring the dynamics of organisational strategy', unpublished PhD thesis, Sheffield: Sheffield Hallam University.

Coule, T. (2013) 'Nonprofit governance and accountability: broadening the theoretical perspective', *Nonprofit and Voluntary Sector Quarterly*, 44(1): 75–97.

Coule, T. and Patmore, B. (2013) 'Institutional logics, institutional work, and public service innovation in non-profits', *Public Administration*, 91(4): 980–97.

Coulson, N. (2009) *ILM Level 5 Award in Understanding Social Enterprise* (Course Materials, Segment 3). Barnsley: Northern College and the Academy for Community Leadership.

Crawford, J. (2011) 'How can systems thinking help as members of the National Council for Voluntary Organisations?' [Online]. Available at: www.touchpointchange.co.uk/documents/NCVO%20Handouts%20James%20Crawford%20Touchpoint%20Change%20-%20Feb%202011.pdf (accessed 11 February 2015).

Creative Commons Foundation (2014) 'State of the Commons' [Online]. Available at: https://stateof.creativecommons.org/report/ (accessed 9 January 2015).

Crutchfield, L. and McLeod-Grant, H. (2007) *Forces for Good: The Six Practices of High Impact Nonprofits*. San Francisco: Jossey-Bass.

Curtis, T. (2008) 'Finding that grit makes a pearl: a critical re-reading of research into social enterprise', *International Journal of Entrepreneurial Behaviour and Research*, 14(5): 276–90.

Curtis, T. (2014) 'Intensive community engagement: Locally Identified Solutions and Practices (LISP)' [Online]. Available at: www.slideshare.net/curtistim/police-and-intensive-community-engagement-lisp-toolkit-powerpoin-t6 (accessed 17 January 2015).

Curtis, T. and Bowkett, A. (2014) *Locally Identified Solutions and Practices: A Guide to Intensive Community Engagement*. Northampton: University of Northampton and Northampton Police.

Dahlgren, J.J. (2007) 'Do co-operatives destroy or create value?', in *The Law of Co-operatives*. Minneapolis: Stoel Rives Agribusiness and Coops Team, Chapter 2 [Online]. Available at: web.missouri.edu/~cookml/AE4972/lawofcooperatives.pdf (accessed 25 April 2015).

Dandridge, T. (1979) 'Small business needs its own organization theory', *Journal of Small Business Management*, 17(2): 53–7.

Dart, R. (2004) 'The legitimacy of social enterprise', *Non-Profit Management and Leadership*, 4(4): 411–24.

Darwin, J., Johnson, P. and McAuley, J. (2002) *Developing Strategies for Change*. London: Prentice Hall.

Davies, I., Doherty, B. and Knox, S. (2010) 'The rise and fall of a fair trade pioneer: The CafeDirect story', *Journal of Business Ethics*, 92: 127–47.

Davies, P. (2002) *An Introduction to Company Law*. Oxford: Oxford University Press.

Davies-Coates, J. (2014) 'Open co-ops: inspirations, legal structure and tools' [Online]. Available at: http://uniteddiversity.coop/2014/08/14/open-co-ops-inspirations-legal-structure-and-tools/ (accessed 18 August 2014).

Davis, P. (2004) *Human Resource Management in Co-operatives: Theory, Process and Practice.* Geneva: Co-operative Branch, International Labour Office.

Decanay, M. (2011) *Measuring Social Enterprises.* Quezon City: Institute for Social Entrepreneurship in Asia.

Dees, G. (1998) 'Enterprising non-profits: what do you do when traditional sources of funding fall short?', *Harvard Business Review*, January–February: 54–67.

Defourny, J. (2001) 'Introduction: from third sector to social enterprise', in C. Borzaga and J. Defourny (eds), *The Emergence of Social Enterprise.* London: Routledge, pp. 3–26.

Defourny, J. (2010) 'Concepts and realities of social enterprise: a European perspective', in A. Fayolle and H. Matlay (eds), *Handbook of Research on Social Entrepreneurship.* Northampton, MA: Edward Elgar, pp. 57–87.

Defourny, J., Hulgård, L. and Pestoff, V. (2014) *Social Enterprise and the Third Sector: Changing European Landscapes in a Comparative Perspective.* London: Routledge.

Defourny, J. and Nyssens, M. (2006) 'Defining social enterprise', in M. Nyssens (ed.), *Social Enterprise at the Crossroads of Market, Public and Civil Society.* London: Routledge, pp. 3–26.

Dehler, G., Welsh, A. and Lewis, M. (2001) 'Critical pedagogy in the "new paradigm"', *Management Learning*, 32(4): 493–511.

Della Paolera, G. and Taylor, A. (2004) *A New Economic History of Argentina.* New York: Cambridge University Press.

Dewar, J. (2007) 'How can we be free? The meaning of Karl Marx's struggle with Mikhail Bukunin' [Online]. Available at: www.fifthinternational.org/content/how-can-we-be-free-meaning-karl-marx%E2%80%99s-struggle-mikhail-bakunin (accessed 05 September 2014).

Dey, P. and Steyaert, C. (2012) 'Social entrepreneurship: critique and the radical enactment of the social', *Social Enterprise Journal*, 8(2): 90–107.

Dey, P. and Teasdale, S. (2013) 'Social enterprise and dis/identification', *Administrative Theory and Praxis*, 35(2): 248–70.

Dholakia, N. and Dholakia, R. (1975) 'Marketing planning in a social enterprise: a conceptual approach', *European Journal of Marketing*, 9(3): 250–8.

Dickson, N. (1999) 'What is the Third Way?', *BBC News*, 27 September.

DiMaggio, P. and Powell, W. (1983) 'The iron cage revisited: institutional isomorphism and collective rationality in organizational fields', *American Sociological Review*, 48: 147–60.

Dobson, S., Sukumar, A., Ridley-Duff, R., Roast, C., Abell, B. (2015) 'Reciprocity and resilience: teaching and learning sustainable social enterprise through gaming', *Journal of Organisational Transformation and Social Change*, forthcoming.

Doherty, B. (2011) 'Resource advantage theory and fair trade social enterprises', *Journal of Strategic Marketing*, 19(4): 357–80.

Doherty, B., Davies, I. and Tranchell, S. (2013) 'Where now for Fair Trade?', *Business History*, 55(2): 161–89.

Doherty, B., Foster, G., Mason, C., Meehan, J., Meehan, K., Rotheroe, N. and Royce, M. (2009) *Management for Social Enterprise.* London: Sage.

Doherty, B., Haugh, H. and Lyon, F. (2014) 'Social enterprises and hybrid organizations: a review and research agenda', *International Journal of Management Reviews*, 16(9): 417–36.

Domenico, M., Tracey, P. and Haugh, H. (2009) 'The dialectic of social exchange: theorizing corporate-social enterprise collaboration', *Organization Studies*, 30(8): 887–907.

Douglas, H. and Grant, S. (2014) *Social Entrepreneurship and Enterprise: Concepts in Context.* Prahan: Tilde Publishing.

Dowla, A. (2006) 'In credit we trust: building social capital by the Grameen Bank in Bangladesh', *Journal of Socio-Economics*, 35(1): 202–22.

Drayton, B. (2005) 'Where the real power lies', *Alliance*, 10(1): 29–30.

DTI (2002) *Social Enterprise: A Strategy for Success*. London: HM Treasury.

DTI (2003) *Enterprise for Communities: Report on the Public Consultation and the Government's Intentions*. London: HM Treasury.

Duncan, G. (2009a) 'British slump will be worst in the developed world, says IMF', *The Times*, 29 January.

Duncan, G. (2009b) 'How the use of springboard stories helps Pakistani women to develop a social enterprise', unpublished MSc thesis, Sheffield: Sheffield Hallam University.

Duncan, G. and Ridley-Duff, R. (2014) 'Appreciative inquiry as a method of transforming identity and power in Pakistani women', *Action Research*, 12(2): 117–35.

Dundon, T. and Rollinson, D. (2011) *Understanding Employment Relations* (2nd edn). Maidenhead: McGraw-Hill.

Dundon, T., Wilkinson, A., Marchington, M. and Ackers, P. (2004) 'The meaning and purpose of employee voice', *The International Journal of Human Resource Management*, 15(6): 1149–70.

Dunning, R., Gregory, D., Boyle, D., Butler, J., Monaghan, P., Harrington, C., Brown, B. and Hebditch, R. (2015) *The Right to Invest*. London: Social Economy Alliance.

Eccles, R. and Krzus, M. (2010) *One Report: Integrated Reporting for a Sustainable Strategy*. New York: John Wiley & Sons.

Edwards, E. (2004) *Civil Society*. Cambridge: Polity.

Ehnert, I., Harry, W. and Zink, K. (2013) *Sustainability and Human Resource Management: Developing Sustainable Business Organisations*. Berlin: Springer-Verlag.

Elkington, J. (2004) 'Enter the triple bottom line', in A. Henriques and J. Richardson (eds), *The Triple Bottom Line: Does It All Add Up?* Abingdon: Earthscan, pp. 1–16.

Ellerman, D. (1982) *The Empresarial Division of the Caja Laboral Popular*. Somerville: Industrial Co-operative Association.

Ellerman, D. (1984) 'Entrepreneurship in the Mondragon Cooperatives', *Review of Social Economy*, 42(3): 272–94.

Ellerman, D. (1990) *The Democratic Worker-owned Firm: A New Model for East and West*. Boston: Unwin.

Ellerman, D. (1997) *The Democratic Firm*. Xingua Publishing House, Beijing. Available at: www.ellerman.org/the-democratic-worker-owned-firm/ (accessed 14 May 2015).

Ellerman, D. (2005) *Helping People Help Themselves: From World Bank to an Alternative Philosophy of Development Assistance*. Ann Arbor, MI: University of Michigan Press.

Ellerman, D. (2006) 'Three themes about democratic enterprises: capital structure, education and spin-offs', paper presented at the IAFEP Conference, Mondragon, 13–15 July.

Emerson, J. (2000) 'The nature of returns: a social capital markets inquiry into elements of investment and the blended value proposition', working paper, Harvard Business School.

EOA (2013) *Employee Ownership Impact Report*. London: Employee Ownership Association.

Erdal, D. (2000) 'The psychology of sharing: an evolutionary approach', unpublished PhD thesis, St Andrews: University of St Andrews.

Erdal, D. (2011) *Beyond the Corporation: Humanity Working*. London: The Bodley Head.

Erdal, D. (2014) 'Employee ownership and health: an initial study', in S. Novkovic and T. Webb (eds), *Co-operatives in a Post-Growth Era: Creating Co-operative Economics*. New York: Zed Books, pp. 210–20.

Eslava, M., Haltiwanger, J., Kugler, A. and Kulger, M. (2013) 'The effects of regulation on business cycles on temporary contracts, the organization of firms and productivity' [Online]. Available at: www.webmeets.com/files/papers/lacea-lames/2013/430/tempworkers_EHKK_31May2013.pdf (accessed 30 January 2015).

ESOC (2014) 'Employee share ownership: an introduction' [Online]. Available at: www.esopcentre. com/about-the-esop-centre/ (accessed 10 January 2014].

Etherington, S. (2008) 'Does a strong and independent third sector mean a strong and independent civil society?' [Online]. Available at: www.shu.ac.uk/_assets/pdf/cvsr-10thAnnivLectureStuartEth erington.pdf (accessed 23 October 2008].

Etzioni, A. (1973) 'The third sector and domestic missions', *Public Administration Review*, 33: 314–23.

Euricse (2013) *World Co-operative Monitor: Exploring the Co-operative Economy*. Geneva: International Co-operative Alliance.

Evans, K. (2011) '"Big Society" in the UK: a policy review', *Children and Society*, 25(2): 164–71.

Evers, A. (2001) 'The significance of social capital in the multiple goal and resource structures of social enterprises', in C. Borzaga and J. Defourny (eds), *The Emergence of Social Enterprise*. London: Routledge, pp. 298–311.

Evers, M. and Syrett, S. (2007) 'Generating social capital? The social economy and local economic development', *European Urban and Regional Studies*, 1: 14.

FairShares Association (2014) 'FairShares membership 2014–15' [Online]. Available at: www. dropbox.com/s/t9dv6ufdx0ir4od/V2-0-FairSharesMembership%20-%202014-15.pdf?dl=0 (accessed 26 February 2015).

Fayol, H. (1916) 'Administration industrielle et generale', *Bulletin de la Societe de l'Industrie Minerale*, 10(3): 5–162.

Fenton, N., Passey, A. and Hems, L. (1999) 'Trust, the voluntary sector and civil society', *International Journal of Sociology and Social Policy*, 19(7/8): 21–42.

Finlay, L. (2011) 'The Social Enterprise Mark research agenda: a response', paper presented at the International Social Innovation Research Conference. London, ISIRC, 11–12 September.

Flockhart, A. (2005) 'Raising the profile of social enterprises: the use of social return on investment (SROI) and investment ready tools (IRT) to bridge the financial credibility gap', *Social Enterprise Journal*, 1(1): 29–42.

Floyd, D. (2011) 'Lack of co-operation' [Online]. Available at: http://beanbagsandbullsh1t. com/2011/09/15/lack-of-co-operation/ (accessed 26 August 2014).

Fonterra (n.d.) 'Constitution of Fonterra Co-operative Group Ltd', Clause 3.4 [Online]. Available at: www.fonterra.com/wps/wcm/connect/8cc45d4f-6ff6-436d-98dd-f8c89aec07c4/Fonterra+C onstitution+2012-12-17.pdf?MOD=AJPERES (accessed 18 May 2015).

Forcadell, F. (2005) 'Democracy, cooperation and business success: the case of Mondragon Corporacion Cooperativa', *Journal of Business Ethics*, 56(3): 225–74.

Forrester, J. (1989) *Planning in the Face of Power*. Berkeley, CA: University of California Press.

Foucault, M. (1970) 'The archaeology of knowledge', *Social Science Information*, 9(1): 175–85.

Fox, A. (1966) *Industrial Sociology and Industrial Relations* (Research Paper 3). London, HMSO: Royal Commission of Trade Unions and Employers Associations.

Fox, A. (1974) *Man Mismanagement*. London: Hutchinson.

Frail, C. and Pedwell, C. (2003) *Keeping it Legal: Forms for Social Enterprises*. London: Social Enterprise London.

Freire, P. (1970) *Pedagogy of the Oppressed*, trans. Myra Bergman Ramos. New York: Continuum.

Friedman, M. (1962) *Capitalism and Freedom*. Chicago: University of Chicago.

Friedman, M. (1968) 'The role of monetary policy', *American Economic Review*, 58: 1–17.

Friedman, M. (2003) 'Social responsibility: a waste of money' [Interview].

Friedman, V. and Desivilya, H. (2010) 'Integrating social entrepreneurship and conflict engagement for regional development in divided societies', *Entrepreneurship and Regional Development*, 22(6): 495–514.

Fujitsu, N. (2010) *Beyond Logframe: Using Systems Concepts in Evaluation*. Tokyo: Foundation for Advanced Studies of International Development.

Fukuyama, F. (1995) *The Social Virtues and the Creation of Prosperity*. London: Penguin.

Fukuyama, F. (2001) 'Social capital, civil society and development', *Third World Quarterly*, 22(1): 7–20.

Fulda, J.S. (1999) 'In defense of charity and philanthropy', *Business and Society Review*, 104: 179–89.

Gallup (2014) 'Confidence in institutions' [Online]. Available at: www.gallup.com/poll/1597/confidence-institutions.aspx (accessed 13 January 2015).

Gardiner, M. (2009) 'His master's voice: work choices as a return to master and servant concepts', *Sydney Law Review*, 31: 53–64.

Garvey, R., Stokes, P. and Megginson, D. (2009) *Coaching and Mentoring: Theory and Practice*. London: Sage.

Garvey, R. and Williamson, B. (2002) *Beyond Knowledge Management: Dialogue, Creativity and the Corporate Curriculum*. Essex: Prentice Hall.

Gates, J. (1998) *The Ownership Solution*. London: Penguin.

Giddens, A. (1998) *The Third Way*. Cambridge: Polity.

Giddings, B., Hopwood, B. and O'Brien, G. (2002) 'Environment, economy and society: fitting them together into sustainable development', *Sustainable Development*, 10: 187–96.

Gilbert, E., Marwaha, S., Milton, A., Johnson, S., Morant, N., Parsons, N., Fisher, A., Singh, S. and Cunliffe, D. (2013) 'Social firms as a means of vocational recovery for people with mental illness: a UK survey', *BMC Health Services Research*, 13: 270–9.

Gilligan, C. (2014) 'Understanding sustainable development in the voluntary sector: a complex problem', paper presented at the Sustainable and Responsible Business Seminar. Sheffield, Sheffield Hallam University, December.

Glasby, J. (1999) *Poverty and Opportunity: 100 Years of the Birmingham Settlement*. Studley: Brewin.

GlobalScan (2011) 'Shopping choices can make a positive difference to farmers and workers in developing countries: global poll' [Online]. Available at: www.globescan.com/news-and-analysis/press-releases/press-releases-2011/94-press-releases-2011/145-high-trust-and-global-recognition-makes-fairtrade-an-enabler-of-ethical-consumer-choice.html (accessed 5 February 2015).

Goerke, J. (2003) 'Taking the quantum leap: nonprofits are now in business. An Australian perspective', *International Journal of Nonprofit and Voluntary Sector Marketing*, 8(4): 317–27.

Gold, L. (2004) *The Sharing Economy: Solidarity Networks Transforming Globalisation*. Aldershot: Ashgate Publishing Ltd.

Goldstein, J., Hazy, J. and Sibberstang, J. (2008) 'Complexity and social entrepreneurship: a fortuitous meeting', *Emergence, Complexity and Organization*, 10(3): 9–24.

Gordon, M. (2009) 'Accounting for making a difference', *Social Enterprise Magazine*, 25 November.

Gordy, V., Hawkins, N., Josephs, M., Merten, W., Miller, R., Rodrick, S., Rosen, C. and Solimine, J. (2013) *Leveraged ESOPs and Employee Buyouts* (6th edn). Oakland, CA: National Center for Employee Ownership.

Gosling, P. (2008) 'Has ECT failed the social enterprise sector?', *Cooperative News*, 18 July. Available at: www.thenews.coop/35558/news/business/has-ect-failed-social-enterprise-sector/ (accessed 25 April 2015).

Grameen Research Inc. (2012) 'History of Grameen Bank' [Online]. Available at: http://grameen-research.org/history-of-grameen-bank/ (accessed 1 January 2014).

Granitz, N. and Loewy, D. (2007) 'Applying ethical theories: interpreting and responding to student plagiarism', *Journal of Business Ethics*, 72(3): 293–306.

Granovetter, M. (1973) 'The strength of weak ties', *American Journal of Sociology*, 78(6):1360–80.

Granovetter, M. (1983) 'The strength of weak ties: a network theory revisited', *Sociological Theory*, 1(1): 201–33.

Grant, S. (2006) 'A paradox in action? A critical analysis of an appreciative inquiry', PhD Thesis. Waikato: University of Waikato.

Gray, J. (1998) *False Dawn: The Delusions of Global Capitalism* (1st edn). London: Granta.

Gray, J. (2009) *False Dawn: The Delusions of Global Capitalism* (revised edn). London: Granta.

Green, E. (2014) 'The importance of personal values in creating prosocial enterprises: a search for the localist social *coopérateur*', unpublished MSc thesis, Sheffield: Sheffield Hallam University.

Grenier, N. (2012) 'CJDES, Universite de Printemps' (Innovation Panel) [Interview] (5 April).

Grenier, P. (2002) 'The function of social entrepreneurship in the UK', draft paper presented at the ISTR Conference, Cape Town, July. Available at: www.istr.org/?WP_Capetown (accessed 27 April 2015).

Grenier, P. (2006) 'Social entrepreneurship: agency in a globalizing world', in A. Nicholls (ed.), *Social Entrepreneurship: New Models of Sustainable Social Change*. Oxford: Oxford University Press, pp. 119–43.

Grey, C. (2005) *A Very Short, Fairly Interesting and Reasonably Cheap Book about Studying Organizations* (2nd edn). London: Sage.

The Guardian (2014a) 'Banking will be transformed by technology, not politics' (Observer Editorial) [Online]. Available at: www.theguardian.com/commentisfree/2014/jan/19/online-banking-high-street-labour-reforms (accessed 24 February 2015).

The Guardian (2014b) 'Coop members vote to back radical changes', *The Guardian*, 30 August.

Guest, D. (1998) 'Is the psychological contract worth taking seriously?', *Journal of Organizational Behavior*, 19: 649–64.

Gupta, A., Sinha, R., Koradin, D. and Patel, R. (2003) 'Mobilizing grassroots' technological innovations and traditional knowledge, values and institutions: articulating social and ethical capital', *Futures*, 35(9): 975–87.

Guthey, E. and Jackson, B. (2005) 'CEO portraits and the authenticity paradox', *Journal of Management Studies*, 42(5): 1057–82.

Hagner, D. and Davies, T. (2002) 'Doing my own thing: supported self-employment for individuals with cognitive disabilities', *Journal of Vocational Rehabilitation*, 17(2): 65–74.

Hardin, G. (1968) 'The tragedy of the commons', *Science*, 162: 1243–8.

Harding, R. and Cowling, M. (2006) *Social Entrepreneurship Monitor*. London: London Business School.

Hardoon, D. (2015) *Wealth: Having It All and Wanting More* (Oxfam Edition Briefing), Oxford: Oxfam.

Harris, J. and Harvey, F. (2012) '"Fair fishing" manifesto calls for greater quota share for small boats', *The Guardian*, 8 August.

Harrison, J. (1969) *Robert Owen and the Owenites in Britain and America*. London: Routledge and Kegan Paul.

Harrison, R. (2005) *Learning and Development*. London: CIPD.

Hart, K. (2013) 'The limits of Karl Polanyi's anti-market approach in the struggle for economic democracy' [Online]. Available at: http://thememorybank.co.uk/2013/01/16/the-limits-of-polanyis-anti-market-approach-in-the-struggle-for-economic-democracy/ (accessed 31 January 2015).

Harvey, D. (2010) 'RSA animate – the crises of capitalism' [Online]. Available at: www.youtube.com/watch?v=qOP2V_np2c0.

Haugh, H. and Kitson, M. (2007) 'The Third Way and the third sector: New Labour's economic policy and the social economy', *Cambridge Journal of Economics*, 31(6): 973–94.

Hawken, P. (2010) *The Ecology of Commerce: A Declaration of Sustainability*. New York: Harper Paperbacks.

Hazenburg, R. (2014) 'Public service spin outs: needs and wants' [Online]. Available at: www.collaboratei.com/media/9488/public_service_spin-outs.pdf (accessed 5 February 2015).

Heaney, T. (1995) 'Issues in Freirean pedagogy' [Online]. Available at: www.paulofreire.ufpb.br/paulofreire/Files/outros/Issues_in_Freirean_Pedagogy.pdf (accessed 4 January 2010).

Hebson, G., Grimshaw, D. and Marchington, M. (2003) 'PPPs and the changing public sector ethos: case-study evidence from the health and local authority sectors', *Work, Employment and Society*, 17(3): 481–500.

Herzberg, F. (1985) 'One more time: how do you motivate employees?', *Harvard Business Review*, 65(5): 109–20.

Hirst, P. (1994) *Associative Democracy: New Forms of Economics and Social Governance*. Cambridge: Polity Press.

Hirtz, N. and Giacone, M. (2013) 'The recovered companies workers' struggle in Argentina: between autonomy and new forms of control', *Latin American Perspectives*, 40(4): 88–100.

HMRC (2014) 'Tax incentives for Employee Ownership Trust (Finance Bill 2014)' [Online]. Available at: www.gov.uk/government/uploads/system/uploads/attachment_data/file/264598/7._Employee_ownership.pdf (accessed 26 February 2015).

HMRC (n.d.) 'Mutual insurance: what is mutuality?' [Online]. Available at: www.hmrc.gov.uk/manuals/gimanual/gim9010.htm (accessed 12 August 2014).

HM Treasury (1999) *Enterprise and Social Exclusion*. London: HM Treasury National Strategy for Neighbourhood Renewal Policy Action Team 3.

Holmes, C. (2014) 'Introduction: a post-Polanyian political economy for our times', *Economy and Society*, 43(4): 525–40.

Hood, C. (1995) 'The new public management in the 1980s: variations on a theme', *Accounting, Organisation and Society*, 20(2/3): 93–109.

Hosking, D. and Morley, I. (1991) *Social Psychology of Organizing: People, Processes and Contexts*. London: Harvester Wheatsheaf.

House of Lords (2003) *The Commission's Green Paper: Entrepreneurship in Europe* (Evidence/Select Committee). London: UK Parliament.

Howarth, M. (2007) *Worker Co-operatives and the Phenomenon of Empresas Recuperadas in Argentina: An Analysis of Their Potential for Replication*. Manchester: Co-operative College.

Hubbard, B. (2005) *Investing in Leadership, Volume 1: A Grantmaker's Framework for Understanding Nonprofit Leadership Development*. Washington, DC: Grantmakers for Effective Organizations.

Huckfield, L. (2015) '2015 – a year for killing social enterprise, coops and mutuals' [Online]. Available at: www.huckfield.com/blog/2015-a-year-for-killing-social-enterprise-coops-and-mutuals/ (accessed 22 February 2015).

Hudson, M. (2002) *Managing Without Profit* (2nd edn). London: Penguin.

Hunt, J. (1981) *Managing People at Work: A Manager's Guide to Behaviour In Organizations*. London: Pan.

Hunt, T. (2004) 'Robert Tressell: the man and his times', in *The Ragged Trousered Philanthropists*. London: Penguin.

Huselid, M. (1995) 'The impact of human resource management practice on turnover, productivity, and corporate financial performance', *Academy of Management Journal*, 38(3): 635–72.

ICA (2005) 'World Declaration on worker cooperatives' [Online]. Available at: www.cecop.coop/World-standards-on-cooperatives-in (accessed 23 April 2015).

Jackson, B. and Parry, K. (2008) *A Very Short, Fairly Interesting and Reasonably Cheap Book about Studying Leadership*. London: Sage.

Jain, P. (1996) 'Managing credit for the rural poor: lessons from the Grameen Bank', *World Development*, 24(1): 79–89.

James, A. (2009) 'Academies of the apocalypse?', *The Guardian*, 7 April.

Jennings, P. and Beaver, G. (1997) 'The performance and competitive advantage of small firms: a management perspective', *Small Business Journal*, 15(2): 63–75.

Jensen, A. (2006) *Insolvency, Employee Rights and Employee Buyouts: A Strategy for Restructuring*. Almouth: Common Cause Foundation (Parliamentary Report).

Jensen, A. (2011) 'Insolvency, employee rights and employee buyouts: a strategy for restructuring', unpublished PhD thesis, Syndey: Department of Work and Organization Studies, University of Sydney.

Jenson, I. (n.d.) 'Loomio: a new tool to maximize people power' (Occupy Wall Street) [Online]. Available at: www.occupywallstreet.net/story/loomio-new-tool-maximize-people-power (accessed 21 January 2015).

JLP (2013) *The Constitution of the John Lewis Partnership*. London: JLP.

Joerg, P., Loderer, C. and Roth, L. (2004) 'Shareholder value maximization: what managers say and what they do', paper presented at the BSI Camma Foundation Corporate Governance Conference, London, 4 June.

Johnson, P. (2003) 'Towards an epistemology for radical accounting: beyond objectivism and relativism', *Critical Perspectives on Accounting*, 6: 485–509.

Johnson, P. (2006) 'Whence democracy? A review and critique of the conceptual dimensions and implications of the business case for organizational democracy', *Organization*, 13(2): 245–74.

Johnson, P. and Duberly, J. (2000) *Understanding Management Research: An Introduction to Epistemology*. London: Sage Publications.

Jones, D. (2000) 'A cultural development strategy for sustainability', *Greener Management International*, 31: 71–85.

Kalmi, P. (2007) 'The disappearance of cooperatives from economics textbooks', *Cambridge Journal of Economics*, 31(4): 625–47.

Kant, I. (1998 [1788]) *Critique of Pure Reason*, trans. M. Gregor. Cambridge: Cambridge University Press.

Kaplan, R. and Norton, D. (1992) 'The Balanced Scorecard: measures that drive performance', *Harvard Business Review*, January–February: 71–9.

Kasmir, S. (1996) *The Myth of Mondragon*. New York: State University of New York Press.

Kelly, S., Morgan, G.G. and Coule, T. (2014) 'Celebrity altruism: the good, the bad and the ugly in relationships with fundraising charities', *Nonprofit and Voluntary Sector Marketing*, 19(2): 57–75.

Kerlin, J. (2006) 'Social enterprise in the United States and Europe: understanding and learning from the differences', *Voluntas*, 17(3): 246–62.

Kerlin, J. (2010) *Social Enterprise: An International Comparison*. Medford: Tuffs University Press.

Keynes, J. (2008 [1936]) *The General Theory of Employment, Interest and Money*. New Delhi: Atlantic Publishers Ltd.

Klein, N. (2007) *The Shock Doctrine: The Rise of Disaster Capitalism*. New York: Metropolitan Books.

Knell, J. (2008) *Share Value: How Employee Ownership Is Changing the Face of Business*. London: All Party Parliamentary Group on Employee Ownership.

Kollewe, J. (2009) 'Recession Britain: it's official', *The Guardian*, 23 January.

Kolter, P. and Zaltman, G. (1971) 'Social marketing: an approach to planned, social change', *Journal of Marketing*, 35: 3–12.

Krueger, N., Kickul, J., Gundry, L.K., Verman, R. and Wilson, F. (2009) 'Discrete choices, trade-offs and advantages: modelling social venture opportunities and intentions', in J. Robinson, J. Mair and K. Hockerts (eds), *International Perspectives on Social Entrepreneurship*. Basingstoke: Palgrave, pp. 117–44.

Kuhn, T. (1970) *The Structure of Scientific Revolutions*. Chicago: University of Chicago.

Kunda, G. (1992) *Engineering Culture: Control and Commitment in a High-Tech Corporation*. Philadelphia: Temple University Press.

Laasch, O. and Conway, R. (2015) *Principles of Responsible Management*. New York: Cengage Learning.

Lacey, S. (2009) *Beyond a Fair Price: The Cooperative Movement and Fair Trade*. Manchester: Co-operative College.

Laratta, R., Nakagawa, S. and Sakurai, M. (2011) 'Japanese social enterprises: major contemporary issues and challenges', *Social Enterprise Journal*, 7(1): 50–68.

Latour, B. (2005) *Reassembling the Social: An Introduction to Actor-Network Theory*. Oxford: Oxford University Press.

Laville, J. and Nyssens, M. (2001) 'Towards a theoretical socio-economic approach', in C. Borzaga and J. Defourny (eds), *The Emergence of Social Enterprise*. London: Routledge, pp. 312–32.

Law, A. and Mooney, G. (2006) 'The maladies of social capital II: resisting neo-liberal confirms', *Critique*, 34(3): 253–68.

Leadbeater, C. (1997) *The Rise of the Social Entrepreneur*. London: Demos.

Lehner, O. (2013) 'Crowdfunding social ventures: a model and research agenda', *Venture Capital: An International Journal of Entrepreneurial Finance*, 15(4): 289–311.

Leonard, A. (2007) '*The Story of Stuff*, referenced and annotated script' [Online]. Available at: http://storyofstuff.org/wp-content/uploads/movies/scripts/Story%20of%20Stuff.pdf (accessed 21 August 2014).

Lewin, K., Lippitt, R. and White, R. (1939) 'Patterns of aggressive behavior in experimentally created social climates', *Journal of Social Psychology*, 10: 271–301.

Lewis, J. (1948) *Partnership for All: A Third Four Year Old Experiment in Industrial Democracy*. London: Kerr-Cross Publishing.

Lewis, J. (1954) *Fairer Shares: A Possible Advance in Civilisation and Perhaps the Only Alternative to Communism*. London: Staples Press Ltd.

Lezamiz, M. (2014) International Co-operative Summit, interview, 5 October.

Light, P. (2008) *The Search for Social Entrepreneurship*. Washington: Brookings Institution Press.

Lindsay, G. and Hems, L. (2004) 'Sociétés coopératives d'intérêt collectif: the arrival of social enterprises within the French social economy', *Voluntas*, 15(3): 265–86.

Lloyd, S. and Faure Walker, A. (2009) *Charities, Trading and the Law* (2nd edn). Bristol: Jordon Publishing.

London, M. and Morfopoulos, R. (2010) *Social Entrepreneurship*. New York: Routledge.

Long Island University (2000) 'Spanish town without poverty' [Online]. Available at: www.news wise.com/articles/view/17012 (accessed 2 September 2015).

Low, C. (2006) 'A framework for governance of social enterprise', *International Journal of Social Economics*, 33(5/6): 376–85.

Lukes, S. (1974) *Power: A Radical View*. Basingstoke: Macmillan.

Lund, M. (2011) *Solidarity as a Business Model: A Multi-stakeholder Co-operative's Manual*. Kent, OH: Kent State University.

Luxton, P. (2001) *The Law of Charities*. Oxford: Open University Press.

Lyon, F. and Sepulveda, L. (2009) 'Mapping social enterprises; past approaches, challenges and future directions', *Social Enterprise Journal*, 5(1): 83–94.

MacDonald, M. (2008) 'Social enterprise experiments in England: 1660–1908', paper presented at the Social Enterprise Research Conference (SERC), London Southbank University, 26–27 June.

MacFayden, L., Stead, M. and Hastings, G. (1999) 'A synopsis of social marketing' [Online]. Available at: www.evidenceintopractice.scot.nhs.uk/media/135280/social_marketing_synopsis.pdf (accessed 27 April 2015).

MacGillivray, A., Conaty, P. and Wadhams, C. (2001) *Low Flying Heroes: Micro-Social Enterprise Below the Radar*. London: New Economics Foundation.

Mair, J. and Marti, I. (2006) 'Social entrepreneurship research: a source of explanation, prediction and delight', *Journal of World Business*, 41(1): 36–44.

Maitland, I. (1997) 'Virtuous markets', *Business Ethics Quarterly*, 7(1): 17–31.

Major, G. (1996) 'Solving the under-investment and degeneration problems of worker's co-ops', *Annals of Public and Co-operative Economics*, 67: 545–601.

Major, G. (1998) 'The need for NOVARS (non-voting value added sharing renewable shares)', *Journal of Co-operative Studies*, 31(2): 57–72.

Mann, N. (1989) *Keys to Excellence: The Story of the Deming Philosophy* (3rd edn). Los Angeles: Prestwick Books.

Manufacturing Consent (1992) [Film] Directed by N. Chomsky. Montreal, Quebec: National Film Board of Canada.

MAPA Group (2013) 'Lagun-Aro EPSV's General Assembly agrees to improve early retirement benefits and the employment aid fund' [Online]. Available at: www.mapagroup.net/2013/12/lagun-aro-epsvs-general-assembly/ (accessed 23 April 2015).

Markham, W., Walters, J. and Bonjean, C. (2001) 'Leadership in voluntary associations: the case of the International Association of Women', Voluntas, 12(2): 103–30.

Martin, J. (2002) *Organization Culture: Mapping the Terrain*. Thousand Islands, CA: Sage.

Martin, R. and Osberg, S. (2007) 'Social entrepreneurship: the case for definition', *Stanford Social Innovation Review*, Spring: 29–39.

Marx, K. (1887) *Capital, Volume 1*. Moscow: Progress Publishers.

Marx, K. and Engels, F. (1998 [1848]) *The Communist Manifesto: A Modern Edition*. London: Verso.

Mason, R. (2011) 'Eaga takeover jolted as staff attack loss of cash pay-out', *The Telegraph*, 28 February.

Mawson, A. (2008) *The Social Entrepreneur*. Bodmin: MPG.

Mayer, N. (2012) '100% biogas-fuelled public transport in Linköping, Sweden' [Online]. Sustainability Writer, 27 July. Available at: https://sustainabilitywriter.wordpress.com/2012/07/27/100-biogas-fuelled-public-transport-in-linkoping-sweden/ (accessed 23 April 2015).

McBurney, M. (2014) 'Social reporting within a housing context', unpublished MSc dissertation, Sheffield: Sheffield Hallam University.

MCC (2014) '2013 Annual Report' [Online]. Available at: www.mondragon-corporation.com/eng/about-us/economic-and-financial-indicators/annual-report/#datos-basicos (accessed 23 April 2015).

McCulloch, M. (2013) 'The problems accounting for capital in collaborative organisations', unpublished Doctoral essay, Sheffield: Sheffield Hallam University.

McDonnell, D. and MacKnight, E. (2012) *Democratic Enterprise: Ethical Business for the 21st Century*. Glasgow: Cooperative Education Trust/University of Aberdeen.

McGoey, L. (2014) 'The philanthropic state: market-state hybrids in the philanthrocapitalist turn', *Third World Quarterly*, 35(1): 109–25.

McGregor, D. (1960) *The Human Side of Enterprise*. New York: McGraw-Hill.

McKenzie-Mohr, D., Lee, N., Schultz, P. and Kotler, P. (2012) *Social Marketing to Protect the Environment*. Thousand Oaks, CA: Sage.

Meindl, J. (1993) 'Reinventing leadership: a radical social psychological approach', in J. Murningham (ed.), *Social Psychology in Organizations*. Englewood Cliffs, NJ: Prentice Hall, pp. 89–118.

Meindl, J. (1995) 'The romance of leadership as a follower-centric theory: a social constructionist approach', *Leadership Quarterly*, 6(3): 329–41.

Melman, S. (2001) *After Capitalism: From Managerialism to Workplace Democracy*. New York: Knopf.

Melton, S. (2015) 'A statement of Hinchingbrooke' [Online]. Available at: www.circlepartnership.co.uk/about-circle/media/a-statement-on-hinchingbrooke (accessed 5 February 2015).

Mertens, S. (1999) 'Nonprofit organisations and social economy: two ways of understanding the third sector', *Annals of Public and Cooperative Economics*, 70(3): 501–20.

Meyer, D. (2013) 'Exploring the duality of structure and agency: the changing dependency paradigms of tourism development on the Swahili coast on Kenya and Zanzibar', *Current Issues In Tourism*, 16(7–8): 773–91.

Meyskens, M., Carsrud, A. and Cardozo, R. (2010) 'The symbiosis of entities in the social engagement network: the role of social ventures', *Entrepreneurship & Regional Development*, 22(5): 425–55.

Michels, R. (1961) *Political Parties: A Sociological Study of the Oligarchical Tendencies of Modern Democracy*. New York: Free Press .

Miller, E. and Rice, A. (1967) *Systems of Organization*. London: Tavistock.

Mintzberg, H., Ahlstrand, B. and Lampel, J. (1998) *Strategy Safari: A Guided Tour through the Wilds of Strategic Management*. New York: Free Press.

Monks, R. and Minow, N. (2004) *Corporate Governance* (3rd edn). Malden, MA: Blackwell.

Monzon, J. and Chaves, R. (2008) 'The European social economy: concept and dimensions of the third sector', *Annals of Public and Cooperative Economics*, 79(3/4): 549–77.

Mook, L., Quarter, J. and Richmond, B. (2007) *What Counts: Social Accounting for Nonprofits and Cooperatives* (2nd edn). London: Siegel.

Moreau, C. and Mertens, S. (2013) 'Managers' competences in social enterprises: which specificities?', *Social Enterprise Journal*, 9(2): 164–83.

Morgan, G. (1986) *Images of Organization*. Thousand Oaks, CA: Sage.

Morgan, G.G. (2008) 'The Spirit of Charity' (professorial lecture), Sheffield Hallam University, Sheffield.

Morgan, G. and Smircich, L. (1980) 'The case for qualitative research', *The Academy of Management Review*, 5(4): 491–500.

Morris, D. (1999) 'Volunteering: the long arm of the law', *International Journal of Nonprofit and Voluntary Sector Marketing*, 4(4): 320–6.

Morrison, R. (1991) *We Build the Road as We Travel*. Gabriola Island, BC: New Society.

Murdock, A. (2005) 'Social entrepreneurial ventures and the value of social networks', paper presented at the Social Enterprise Research Conference (SERC), Milton Keynes, 1–2 July.

Murdock, A. (2007) 'No man's land or promised land? The lure of local public service delivery contracts for social enterprise', paper presented at the Social Enterprise Research Conference (SERC), Southbank University, London, 3–6 July.

Murray, R. (2010) *Co-operation in the Age of Google*. Manchester: Co-operatives UK.

Mutuo (2012) *Mutuals Yearbook: The Definitive Guide to the Mutuals Sector*. Oxford: Kellogg College, Oxford University.

Naess, A. (1983) 'The shallow and the deep, long-range ecology movement: a summary', *Inquiry*, 16(1): 95–100.

NCEO (2014) 'A brief overview of employee ownership in the U.S.' [Online]. Available at: www.nceo.org/articles/employee-ownership-esop-united-states (accessed 10 January 2015).

NCEO (2015) 'How an employee stock plan works (major tax advantages)' [Online]. Available at: www.nceo.org/articles/esop-employee-stock-ownership-plan (accessed 26 February 2015).

NCVO (2005) *Good Governance: A Code for the Voluntary Sector*. London: NCVO.

NCVO (2014) 'The UK Civil Society Almanac' [Online]. Available at: http://data.ncvo.org.uk/ (accessed 23 April 2015).

nef (2006) *Prove and Improve: A Quality and Impact Toolkit*. London: New Economics Foundation.

nfpSynergy (2014) *Trust Levels in Charities and Other Institutions: Charity Awareness Monitor*. London: nfpSynergy.

NHS (2008) *Social Enterprise – Making a Difference: A Guide to the Right to Request*. London: Department of Health.

Nicholls, A. (2006) *Social Entrepreneurship: New Models of Sustainable Social Change*. Oxford: Oxford University Press.

Nicholls, A. (2009a) 'Capturing the performance of the socially entrepreneurial organization: an organizational legitimacy approach', in J. Robinson, J. Mair and K. Hockerts (eds), *International Perspectives on Social Entrepreneurship*. Basingstoke: Palgrave, pp. 27–74.

Nicholls, A. (2009b) 'We do good things, don't we?', *Accounting, Organization and Society*, 34: 755–67.

Nicholls, A. (2010) 'The institutionalization of social investment: the interplay of investment logics and investor rationalities', *Journal of Social Entrepreneurship*, 1(1): 70–100.

Nicholls, A. and Opal, C. (2004) *Fair Trade*. London: Sage.

Norton, M. and Ariely, D. (2011) 'Building a better America: one wealth quintile at a time', *Perspectives on Psychological Science*, 6(1): 9–12.

Nove, A. (1983) *The Economics of Feasible Socialism*. London, George Allen and Unwin.

Novkovic, S. and Webb, T. (2014) *Co-operatives in a Post-Growth Era: Creating Co-operative Economics*. London: Zed Books.

Nyssens, M. (2006) *Social Enterprise at the Crossroads of Market, Public and Civil Society*. London: Routledge.

Oakeshott, R. (1990) *The Case for Worker Co-ops* (2nd edn). Basingstoke: Macmillan.

Osborne, S. (2006) 'The new public governance', *Public Management Review*, 8(3): 377–87.

Ostrom, E. (1990) *Governing the Commons: The Evolution of Institutions for Collective Action*. Cambridge: Cambridge University Press.

Ostrom, E., Burger, J., Field, C.B., Norgaard, R.B. and Policansky, D. (1999) 'Revisiting the commons: local lessons, global challenges', *Science*, 284: 278–82.

Outsios, G. (2013) 'The emergence of UK environmental entrepreneurs: a practice theory view on mindsets and constraints', unpublished PhD thesis, Stirling: University of Stirling.

Owen, R. (1849) *The Revolution in the Mind and the Practice of the Human Race*. London: Wilson.

Owen, R. (2014 [1816]) *A New View of Society* (Kindle edn: Gold Books).

Pagán, R. (2009) 'Self-employment among people with disabilities: evidence for Europe', *Disability & Society*, 24(2): 217–29.

Parkinson, C. and Howarth, C. (2008) 'The language of social entrepreneurs', *Entrepreneurship and Regional Development*, 20(3): 285–309.

Pateman, C. (1970) *Participation and Democratic Theory*. Cambridge: Cambridge University Press.

Paton, R. (1989) *Reluctant Entrepreneurs*. Milton Keynes: Open University Press.

Paton, R. (2003) *Managing and Measuring Social Enterprise*. London: Sage Publications.

Pearce, J. (2003) *Social Enterprise in Anytown*. London: Calouste Gulbenkian Foundation.

Pearce, J. (2009) 'Social economy: engaging as a third system', in A. Amin (ed.), *The Social Economy: International Perspectives on Economic Solidarity*. London: Zed Books, pp. 3–21.

Pearce, J. and Kay, A. (2008) *Really Telling Accounts: Report of a Social Accounting and Audit Research Project*. Exeter: Social Audit Network.

Pearl, D. and Philips, M. (2001) 'Grameen Bank, which pioneered loans for the poor, has hit a repayment snag' [Online]. Available at: http://online.wsj.com/public/resources/documents/pearl112701.htm (accessed 18 January 2010).

Peattie, K. and Morley, A. (2008) *Social Enterprises: Diversity and Dynamics, Contexts and Contributions*. Cardiff: ESRC/Brass Research Centre.

Peredo, A. and McClean, M. (2006) 'Social entrepreneurship: a critical review of the concept', *Journal of World Business*, 41(1): 56–65.

Perotin, V. and Robinson, A. (2004) *Employee Participation, Firm Performance and Survival: Advanced in the Economic Analysis of Participatory and Labor-managed Firms*, Volume 8. Oxford: Elsevier.

Perrini, F. (2006) *The New Social Entrepreneurship: What Awaits Social Entrepreneurial Ventures?*. Northampton, MA: Elgar.

Perrini, F., Vurro, C. and Costanzo, L. (2010) 'A process based view of social entrepreneurship: from opportunity identification to scaling-up social change in the case of San Patrignano', *Entrepreneurship and Regional Development*, 22(6): 515–34.

Peters, T. (1989) *Thriving on Chaos*. New York: Perennial.

PEX (2013) *Creating Winning Businesses: Deming's System of Profound Knowledge*. London: Process Excellence Network.

Pharoah, C., Scott, D. and Fisher, A. (2004) *Social Enterprise in the Balance: Challenges for the Voluntary Sector*. West Malling: Charities Aid Foundation.

Piketty, T. (2014) *Capital in the Twenty-first Century* (Kindle edn). Cambridge, MA: Harvard University Press.

Pink, D. (2013) 'Drive – our motivations are unbelievably interesting' [Online]. Available at: www.youtube.com/watch?v=avnHUxSVfVM (accessed 30 January 2015).

Polanyi, K. (2001 [1944]) *The Great Transformation: The Political and Economic Origins of Our Time*. Boston: Beacon.

Positive Money (2012) '97% owned – positive money cut' [Online]. Available at: www.positive-money.org/videos/97-owned-monetary-reform-documentary/ (accessed 9 January 2015).

Powell, W. and DiMaggio, P. (1991) *The New Institutionalism in Organizational Analysis*. Chicago: University of Chicago Press.

Pratchett, L. and Wingfield, M. (1996) 'Petty bureaucracy and woolly minded liberalism? The changing ethos of local government officers', *Public Administration*, 74: 639–56.

Preuss, L. (2004) 'Aristotle in your garage: enlarging social capital with an ethics test', in L. Spence, A. Habisch and R. Schmidpeter (eds), *Responsibility and Social Capital: The World of SMEs*. Basingstoke: Palgrave, pp. 154–64.

Price, M. (2008) *Social Enterprise: What it is and Why it Matters*. Dinas Powys: Fflan.

Prieg, L. (2012) 'Banks are still too big to fail', New Economics Foundation. Available at: www.neweconomics.org/blog/entry/banks-are-still-too-big-to-fail (accessed 14 May 2015).

Prochaska, F. (1990) 'Philanthropy', in F. Thompson (ed.), *The Cambridge Social History of England, 1750–1950*. Cambridge: Cambridge University Press, pp. 357–94.

Purcell, J. (1987) 'Mapping management style in employee relations', *Journal of Management Studies*, 24(5): 533–48.

Purcell, J. (1999) 'Best practice and best fit: chimera or cul-de-sac', *Human Resource Management Journal*, 9(3): 311–31.

Putnam, R. (1994) *Making Democracy Work: Civic Traditions in Modern Italy*. Princeton, NJ: Princeton University Press.

Putnam, R. (2001) *Bowling Alone: The Collapse and Revival of American Community*. New York: Simon and Schuster.

Ranis, P. (2005) 'Argentina's worker-occupied factories and enterprises', *Socialism and Democracy*, 19(3): 93–115.

Rathzell, N., Uzzell, D. and Jackson, T. (2012) *Trade Unions in the Green Economy: Working for the Environment*. London: Routledge.

Rawls, J. (1999) *The Theory of Justice* (revised edn). Oxford: Oxford University Press.

Reedy, P. and Learmonth, M. (2009) 'Other possibilities? The contribution to management education of alternative organizations', *Management Learning*, 40(3): 241–58.

Reeves, R. (2007) *CoCo Companies: Work, Happiness and Employee Ownership*. London: Employee Ownership Association.

Restakis, J. (2010) *Humanizing the Economy: Cooperatives in the Age of Capital*. Gabroila Island, BC: New Society Publishers.

Ridley-Duff, R. (2002) *Silent Revolution: Creating and Managing Social Enterprises*. Sheffield: First Contact Software Ltd.

Ridley-Duff, R. (2005) 'Communitarian perspectives on corporate governance', unpublished PhD thesis, Sheffield: Sheffield Hallam University.

Ridley-Duff, R. (2007) 'Communitarian perspectives on social enterprise', *Corporate Governance: An International Review*, 15(2): 382–92.

Ridley-Duff, R. (2008a) 'Interpreting results: Governance Diagnostic Questionnaire', paper presented at 'Bridging the Divide: Governance and Decision-Making in the Third Sector', Sheffield: Sheffield Hallam University, 9–10 July.

Ridley-Duff, R. (2008b) 'Social enterprise as a socially rational business', *International Journal of Entrepreneurial Behaviour and Research*, 14(5): 291–312.

Ridley-Duff, R. (2009) 'Co-operative social enterprises: company rules, access to finance and management practice', *Social Enterprise Journal*, 5(1): 50–68.

Ridley-Duff, R. (2010) 'Communitarian governance in social enterprises: case evidence from the Mondragon Cooperative Corporation and School Trends Ltd', *Social Enterprise Journal*, 6(2): 125–45.

Ridley-Duff, R. (2011) 'Social enterprise: how is it making its mark?', *The Guardian*, 1 September.

Ridley-Duff, R. (2012) 'New frontiers in democratic self-management', in *The Co-operative Model in Practice: International Perspectives*. Glasgow: Co-operative Education Trust Scotland, pp. 99–117.

Ridley-Duff, R. (2014) *The Dragons' Apprentice: A Social Enterprise Novel*. Charleston: CreateSpace Independent Publishing Platform.

Ridley-Duff, R. and Bennett, A. (2011) 'Towards mediation: developing a theoretical framework to understand alternative dispute resolution', *Industrial Relations Journal*, 42(2): 106–23.

Ridley-Duff, R. and Bull, M. (2011) *Understanding Social Enterprise: Theory and Practice*. London: Sage Publications.

Ridley-Duff, R. and Bull, M. (2013) 'The FairShares Model: a communitarian pluralist approach to constituting social enterprises?', paper presented at the Institute of Small Business and Entrepreneurship, Cardiff, 4–6 November.

Ridley-Duff, R. and Bull, M. (2014) 'Solidarity co-operatives: an embedded historical communitarian pluralist approach to social enterprise development?' paper presented at the RMIT Social Innovation and Entrepreneurship Colloquium, Sydney, 26–28 November.

Ridley-Duff, R. and Bull, M. (2015) 'Entrepreneurship: value-added ventures', in O. R. Conway (eds), *Principles of Responsible Management*. New York: Cengage pp. 186–219.

Ridley-Duff, R. and Duncan, G. (2015) 'What is critical appreciation? Insights from critical turn in an appreciative inquiry', *Human Relations*, forthcoming. A doi:10.1177/0018726714561698.

Ridley-Duff, R. and Hurst, J. (2014a) 'International Cooperative Summit: a video report by members of the FairShares Association' [Online]. Available at: www.youtube.com/watch?v=uErStUtgFSo (accessed 16 January 2015).

Ridley-Duff, R. and Hurst, J. (2014b) 'Responsible management in the Cooperative Movement: a report by Sheffield Business School' [Online]. Available at: www.youtube.com/watch?v=wjnSYv5KlzI (accessed 9 January 2015).

Ridley-Duff, R. and Ponton, A. (2013) 'Workforce participation: developing a theoretical framework for longitudinal research', *Journal of Cooperative Studies*, 46(3): 5–23.

Ridley-Duff, R. and Southcombe, C. (2012) 'The Social Enterprise Mark: a critical review of its conceptual dimensions', *Social Enterprise Journal*, 8(3): 178–200.

Ridley-Duff, R. and Southcombe, C. (2014) *FairShares Model V2.0: A New Model for Self-Governing Social Enterprises Operating Under Association, Company and Co-operative Law*. Sheffield: FairShares Association.

Robinson, J. (2006) 'Navigating social and institutional barriers to markets: how social entrepreneurs identify and evaluate opportunities', in J. Mair, J. Robinson and K. Hockerts (eds), *Social Entrepreneurship*. London: Palgrave, pp. 95–120.

Roelants, B., Hyungsik, E. and Terassi, E. (2014) *Cooperatives and Employment: A Global Report*. Quebec: CICOPA/Desjardin.

Roodman, D. (2009) 'Kiva is not quite what it seems' [Online]. Available at: www.cgdev.org/blog/kiva-not-quite-what-it-seems (accessed 24 February 2015).

Rothschild, J. and Allen-Whitt, J. (1986) *The Cooperative Workplace*. New York: Cambridge University Press.

Rousseau, D. (1995) *Psychological Contracts in Organizations: Understanding Written and Unwritten Agreements*. Thousand Oaks, CA: Sage.

Rowson, J., Broome, S. and Jones, A. (2010) *Connected Communities: How Social Networks Power and Sustain the Big Society*. London: RSA.

Sahakian, M. and Dunand, C. (2014) 'The social and solidarity economy towards greater "sustainability": learning across contexts and cultures, from Geneva to Manilla', *Community Development Journal* [Online]. Available at: http://cdj.oxfordjournals.org/content/early/2014/11/12/cdj.bsu054.abstract (accessed 14 May 2015).

Salamon, M. (2000) *Industrial Relations: Theory and Practice* (4th edn). Englewood Cliffs, NJ: Prentice Hall.

Savio, M. and Righetti, A. (1993) 'Cooperatives as a social enterprise: a place for social integration and rehabilitation', *Psychiatrica Scandanavica*, 88(4): 238–42.

Scase, R. and Goffee, R. (1980) *The Real World of the Small Business Owner*. London: Croom Helm.

Schumacher, E. (1993) *Small is Beautiful: A Study of Economics as if People Mattered*. London: Vintage.

Schwabenland, C. (2006) *Stories, Visions and Values in Voluntary Organisations*. Hampshire: Ashgate.

Schwartz, R. (2008) 'The sale of ECT Recycling: a cause for celebration of a cause for concern?' [Online]. Available at: www.clearlyso.com/sbblog/?p=62#comment-3001 (accessed 12 May 2010).

Scofield, R. (2011) *The Social Entrepreneur's Handbook*. New York: McGraw-Hill.

Scott-Cato, M., Arthur, L., Keenoy, T. and Smith, J. (2008) 'Entrepreneurial energy: associative entrepreneurship in the renewable energy sector', *International Journal of Entrepreneurial Behaviour and Research*, 14(5): 313–29.

Bibliography

Seanor, P., Bull, M., Baines, S. and Ridley-Duff, R. (2013) 'Narratives of transition from social to enterprise: you can't get there from here!', *International Journal of Entrepreneurial Behaviour and Research*, 19(3): 324–43.

Seanor, P., Bull, M. and Ridley-Duff, R. (2007) 'Contradictions in social enterprises: do they draw in straight lines or circles?', paper presented at the 31st Institute of Small Business and Entrepreneurship, Glasgow, ISBE, 5–7 November, http://shura.shu.ac.uk/732/ (accessed 23 April 2015).

Seanor, P. and Meaton, J. (2008) 'Learning from failure: ambiguity and trust in social enterprise', *Social Enterprise Journal*, 4(1): 24–40.

SEC (2005) *Keeping It Legal: A Guide to Legal Forms for Social Enterprises*. London: Social Enterprise Coalition.

SEC (2013) *State of Social Enterprise Survey*. London: Social Enterprise Coalition.

SEC (n.d.) 'Margaret Elliott – Sunderland Care Home Associates' [Online]. Available at: www.socialenterprise.org.uk/pages/margaret-elliott-sunderland-care-home-associates.html (accessed 30 March 2010).

Sedghi, A. and Chalbi, M. (2013) 'How do ticket prices for the Premier League compare with Europe?', *The Guardian*, 17 January.

Seelos, C. and Mair, J. (2009) 'Hope for sustainable development: how social entrepreneurs make it happen', in R. Ziegler (ed.), *An Introduction to Social Entrepreneurship: Voices, Preconditions, Contexts*. Cheltenham: Elgar, pp. 228–46.

Semler, R. (1993) *Maverick: The Story Behind the World's Most Unusual Workplace*. New York: Warner Books Inc..

Sen, A. (2000) *Social Exclusion: Concept, Application and Scrutiny*. Manila: Asian Development Bank.

Sepulveda, L. (2014) 'Social enterprise – a new phenomenon in the field of economic and social welfare?', *Social Policy and Administration* [Online]. Available at: http://onlinelibrary.wiley.com/doi/10.1111/spol.12106/abstract (accessed 14 may 2015).

Simon, G. and Mayo, E. (2010) *Good Business? Public Perceptions of Co-operatives*. Manchester: Co-operatives UK.

Slapnicar, S., Gregoric, A. and Rejc, A. (2004) 'Managerial entrenchment and senior executives compensation', paper presented at the 6th International MCA Conference, Edinburgh, 12–14 July.

Sloman, J. and Sutcliffe, M. (2001) *Economics for Business*. London: Prentice Hall.

Smallbone, D. and Lyon, F. (2005) 'Social enterprise development in the UK: some contemporary policy issues' [Online]. Available at: www.sbaer.uca.edu/research/icsb/2005/177.pdf (accessed 15 October 2008).

Smircich, L. and Morgan, G. (1982) 'Leadership: the management of meaning', *Journal of Applied Behavioural Studies*, 18: 257–73.

Smit, T. (2007) *The Monkey Business*. London: innerpreneur.com.

Smith, G. and Teasdale, S. (2012) 'Associative democracy and the social economy: exploring the regulatory challenge', *Economy and Society*, 41(2): 151–76.

Smith, M.K. (2001) 'Chris Argyris: theories of action, double-loop learning and organizational learning' [Online]. Available at: www.infed.org/thinkers/argyris.htm (accessed 5 January 2010).

Smith, S. and Kulynych, J. (2002) 'It may be social, but why is it capital?', *Politics and Society*, 30(1): 149–86.

Social Economy Alliance (2015) *The Best Ideas from the Left and the Right: Manifesto General Election 2015*. London: Social Economy Alliance.

Somers, A. (2005) 'Shaping the Balanced Scorecard for use in UK social enterprise', *Social Enterprise Journal*, 1(1): 1–12.

Somers, A. (2013) 'The emergence of social enterprise policy in New Labour's second term' [Online]. Available at: http://research.gold.ac.uk/8051/1/POL_thesis_Somers_2013.pdf (accessed 8 January 2015).

Somerset Co-operative Services (2014) 'Somerset Model rules' [Online]. Available at: www.som erset.coop/somersetrules (accessed 16 August 2014).

Southcombe, C. (2014) 'Planka Nu Interview' [Interview] (5 January 2014).

Southcombe, C. (2015) *The Relevance of Social Enterprise (Workbook)*. Robin Hoods Bay, Whitby: Social Enterprise Europe Ltd.

Spear, R. (1999) 'Employee-owned UK bus companies', *Economic and Industrial Democracy*, 20: 253–68.

Spear, R. (2006) 'Social entrepreneurship: a different model?', *International Journal of Social Economics*, 33(5/6): 399–410.

Spear, R. (2008) 'Personal communication: discussion at the Social Entrepreneurial Mindset', University of East London [Interview] (9 October 2008).

Spear, R., Cornforth, C. and Aitken, M. (2007) *For Love and Money: Governance and Social Enterprise*. Milton Keynes: Open University Press.

Sport Matters (n.d.) 'Why sport matters' [Online]. Available at: www.sportmatters.org.au/docs/ sports%20matters%20flyer-email%20version.pdf (accessed 26 February 2015).

Spreckbacher, G. (2003) 'The economics of performance management in non-profit organisations', *Nonprofit Management and Leadership*, 13(3): 267–81.

Spreckley, F. (1981) *Social Audit: A Management Tool for Co-operative Working*. Leeds: Beechwood College.

Spreckley, F. (2008) *The Social Audit Toolkit* (4th edn). Herefordshire: Local Livelihood.

SROI Network (2012) *A Guide to Social Return on Investment* [Online]. Available at: www.thes roinetwork.org/sroi-analysis/the-sroi-guide (accessed 14 May 2015).

Stacey, R. (2007) *Strategic Management and Organisational Dynamics: The Challenge of Complexity* (5th edn). Harlow: Pearson Education.

Stanford Center for Poverty and Equality (2014) *State of the Union: The Poverty and Inequality Report 2014*. Stanford, CA: Stanford University.

Steen, M., Manschot, M. and De Koning, N. (2011) 'Benefits of co-design in service design projects', *International Journal of Design*, 5(2): 53–60.

Stern, P. (2000) 'Toward a coherent theory of environmentally significant behavior', *Journal of Social Issues*, 56(3): 407–24.

Stewart, R. (1983) 'Managerial behaviour: how research has changed the traditional picture', in M. Earl (ed.), *Perspectives in Management*. Oxford: Oxford University Press, pp. 82–98.

Stogdill, R. (1974) *Handbook of Leadership: A Survey of the Literature*. New York: Free.

Storey, D. (1994) *Understanding the Small Business Sector*. London: Routledge.

Storey, J. (2001) *Human Resource Management: A Critical Text*. London: Thompson.

Subramanian, J. (1998) *Rural Women's Right to Property: A Bangladesh Case Study*. Madison, WI: Land Tenure Center, University of Wisconsin.

Sullivan Mort, G., Weerawardena, J. and Carnegie, K. (2003) 'Social entrepreneurship: towards conceptualisation', *International Journal of Nonprofit and Voluntary Sector Marketing*, 8(1): 76–88.

Swan, A. and Pidcock, D. (2009) *The Crash of 2008: A History of the Abuse of Money from Plato to Nato and Beyond*. Winscombe: Universal Empire UK Ltd/Pentagon Press.

Sydow, J. (1998) 'Understanding the constitutions of interorganizational trust', in C. Lane and R. Bachmann (eds), *Trust within and between Organisations: Conceptual Issues and Empirical Applications*. Oxford: Oxford University Press, pp. 31–63.

Tan, W., Williams, J. and Tan, T. (2005) 'Defining the social in social entrepreneurship: altruism and entrepreneurship', *International Entrepreneurship and Management Journal*, 1: 353–65.

Tapsell, P. and Woods, C. (2010) 'Social entrepreneurship and innovation: self-organization in an indigenous context', *Entrepreneurship and Regional Development*, 22(6): 535–56.

Taylor, F. (1917) *Principles of Scientific Management*. New York: Harper and Brothers.

Teasdale, S. (2012) 'What's in a name? Making sense of social enterprise discourses', *Public Policy and Administration*, 27(2): 99–119.

Teasdale, S., Lyon, F. and Baldock, R. (2013) 'Playing with numbers: a methodological critique of the social enterprise growth myth', *Journal of Social Entrepreneurship*, 4(2): 113–31.

The Take (2004) [Film] Directed by A. Lewis and N. Klein. Canada: Barna-Alpa Productions and the National Film Board of Canada.

Thomas, H. and Logan, C. (1982) *Mondragon: An Economic Analysis*. New York: Harper Collins.

Thomas, P. (2004) 'Performance measurement, reporting and accountability: recent trends and future directions' (Public Policy Paper 23). Saskatoon, SK: The Saskatchewan Institute of Public Policy.

Tighe, C. (2011) 'Eaga agrees to give employees pay-out', *The Times*, 16 March.

Tighe, C. (2012) 'Partnership status brings start-up funding for ex-staff', *The Times*, 24 February.

Touchton, M. and Wampler, B. (2013) 'Improving social well-being through new democratic institutions', *Comparative Political Studies*, 47(10): 1442–69.

Tracey, P. and Jarvis, O. (2007) 'Toward a theory of social venture franchising', *Entrepreneurship, Theory and Practice*, 31: 667–85.

Tressell, R. (2004 [1914]) *The Ragged Trousered Philanthropists*. London: Penguin.

Trigona, M. (2006) 'Recuperated factories in Argentina: reversing the logic of capitalism' [Online]. Available at: http://americas.irc-online.org/pdf/series/19.recoupent.pdf (accessed 9 April 2010).

Trigona, M. (2009) 'Argentine factory wins legal battle: FASINPAT Zanon belongs to the people' [Online]. Available at: http://upsidedownworld.org/main/content/view/2052/1/ (accessed 9 April 2010).

Truss, C. (1999) 'Soft and hard models of human resource management', in L. Graton, V. Hailey, P. Stiles and C. Truss (eds), *Strategic Human Resource Management: Corporate Rhetoric and Human Reality*. Oxford: Oxford University Press, pp. 40–58.

Turnbull, S. (1994) 'Stakeholder democracy: redesigning the governance of firms and bureaucracies', *Journal of Socio-Economics*, 23(3): 321–60.

Turnbull, S. (2001) 'The science of corporate governance', *Corporate Governance: An International Review*, 10(4): 261–77.

Turnbull, S. (2002) *A New Way to Govern*. London: New Economics Foundation.

Tuttle, B. (2014) 'Walmart's worst nightmare is expanding massively' [Online]. Available at: http://time.com/4701/walmarts-worst-nightmare/ (accessed 27 February 2015).

UK Coalition Government (2010) *Big Society Programme*. London: Cabinet Office.

UK Government (2015) 'Small Business Survey reports', Department for Business, Innovation and Skills [Online]. Available at: www.gov.uk/government/collections/small-business-survey-reports (accessed 20 May 2015).

UN (n.d.) 'Why sport?' [Online]. Available at: www.un.org/wcm/content/site/sport/home/sport (accessed 26 February 2015).

UN Global Compact (2007) *The Principles for Responsible Management Education*. New York: United Nations Global Compact Office.

United Nations (2005) *2005 World Summit Outcome: Resolution Adopted by the General Assembly*. New York: United Nations.

University of Massachusetts (n.d.) 'Sustainable products – info sheet' [Online]. Available at: www.sustainableproduction.org/downloads/SustainableProductsFramework.pdf (accessed 26 February 2015).

van der Haar, D. and Hosking, D. (2004) 'Evaluating appreciative inquiry: a relational constructionist perspective', *Human Relations*, 57(8): 1017–36.

Vieta, M. (2010) 'The new co-operativism', *Affinities*, 4(1). Available at: http://affinitiesjournal.org/index.php/affinities/article/view/47/147 (accessed 23 April 2015).

Wagner-Tsukamoto, S. (2007) 'Moral agency, profits and the firm: economics revisions to the Friedman theorem', *Journal of Business Ethics*, 70: 209–20.

Wainwright, T. (2009) *The Companies Act 2006 for Cooperatives*. Manchester: Cobbetts Solicitors.

Wallace, B. (2005) 'Exploring the meaning(s) of sustainability for community-based social entrepreneurs', *Social Enterprise Journal*, 1(1): 78–89.

Ward, E. (2015) 'Social investment: friend or foe? It's complicated ...', *Pioneers Post*, 16 January. Available at: www.pioneerspost.com/news-views/20150116/social-investment-friend-or-foe-its-complicated (accessed 23 April 2015).

Watkins, J. and Mohr, B. (2001) *Appreciative Inquiry: Change at the Speed of Imagination*. San Francisco: Jossey-Bass.

Watson, T. (1994) *In Search of Management*. London: Routledge.

Watson, T. (1996) 'Motivation: that's Maslow isn't it?', *Management Learning*, 27(4): 447–64.

Weber, M. (1978) *Economy and Society*. California: University of California Press.

Weick, K. (2001) *Making Sense of the Organization*. Malden, MA: Blackwell.

Weinbren, D. (2007) 'Supporting self-help: charity, mutuality and reciprocity in nineteenth-century Britain', in P. Bridgen and B. Harris (eds), *Charity and Mutual Aid in Europe and North America Since 1800*, Routledge Studies in Modern History. London: Routledge, pp. 67–88.

Weinbren, D. and James, B. (2005) 'Getting a grip: the role of friendly societies in Australia and Britain reappraised', *Labour History*, 88, pp. 95–6.

Wei-Skillern, J., Austin, J., Leonard, H. and Stevenson, H. (2007) *Entrepreneurship in the Social Sector*. Thousand Oaks, CA: Sage.

Wenger, E. (1998) *Communities of Practice: Learning, Meaning and Identity*. Cambridge: Cambridge University Press.

Westall, A. (2001) *Value-led, Market-driven: Social Enterprise Solutions to Public Policy Goals*. London: IPPR.

Westall, A. and Chalkley, D. (2007) *Social Enterprise Futures*. London: The Smith Institute.

White, L. (2002) 'Connection matters: exploring the implication of social capital and social networks for social policy', *Systems Research and Behavioural Science*, 19: 255–69.

White, R. and Lippett, R. (1960) *Autocracy and Democracy: An Experimental Inquiry*. New York: Harper.

Whyte, W. and Whyte, K. (1991) *Making Mondragon*. Ithaca, NY: Cornell University Press/ILR Press.

Wikimedia Foundation (2014) 'Ten years of sharing and learning' [Online]. Available at: http://upload.wikimedia.org/wikipedia/commons/c/ce/Wmf_AR12_v11_SHIP_2pp_hyper_14jan14.pdf (accessed 9 January 2015).

Wilkinson, R. and Pickett, K. (2010) *The Spirit Level: Why Equality Is Better for Everyone*. London: Penguin.

Williams, C. (2007) 'De-linking enterprise culture from capitalism and its public policy implications', *Public Policy and Administration*, 22(4): 461–74.

Willmott, H. (1993) 'Strength is ignorance; slavery is freedom; managing culture in modern organisations', *Journal of Management Studies*, 30(4): 515–52.

Wilson, D. and Bull, M. (2013) 'SROI in practice: the Wooden Boat Canal Society', *Social Enterprise Journal*, 9(3): 315–25.

Wilson, M. (2014) 'Learning together: perspectives in cooperative education' (keynote address), Manchester: Co-operative College, 9 December.

Woodin, T. (2007) *A Good Way to Do Business: Supporting Social Enterprises in Greater Manchester*. Manchester: Co-operative College.

Wynarczyk, P., Watson, R., Storey, D., Short, H. and Keasey, K. (1993) *Managerial Labour Markets in SMEs*. London: Routledge.

Younkins, E. (2005) 'Rousseau's general will and the well-ordered society' [Online]. Available at: www.quebecoislibre.org/05/050715-16.htm (accessed 27 January 2015).

Yunus, M. (2007) *Creating A World Without Poverty: Social Business and the Future of Capitalism* (Kindle edn). New York: Public Affairs.

Zahra, S., Gedajlovic, E., Neubaum, D. and Shulman, J. (2009) 'A typology of social entrepreneurs: motives, search processes and ethical challenges', *Journal of Business Venturing*, 24: 519–32.

Zundel, A.F. (2002) 'Ordinary jurisprudence and the democratic firm: a response to David Ellerman', *Journal of Business Ethics*, 35(1): 51–6.

Index